# EXPORT MANAGEMENT



**T.A.S. BALAGOPAL**

*(Former Export Director of Tata Motors (TELCO) and Chairman, Engineering Export Promotion council of India)*

***Foreword by***

**Bharat Ratna Dr. A.P.J. Abdul Kalam**

Himalaya Publishing House

ISO 9001:2015 CERTIFIED

| | | | | | |
|---|---|---|---|---|---|
| First Edition | : | 1977 | Fourteenth Edition | : | 1999 |
| Second Edition | : | 1979 | Fifteenth Edition | : | 2000 |
| Third Edition | : | 1981 | Sixteenth Edition | : | 2001 |
| Fourth Edition | : | 1984 | Seventeenth Edition | : | 2002 |
| Fifth Edition | : | 1986 | Eighteenth Edition | : | 2006 |
| Sixth Edition | : | 1989 | Nineteenth Edition | : | 2009 |
| Seventh Edition | : | 1992 | Twentieth Edition | : | 2010 |
| Eighth Edition | : | 1992 | Twenty-first Edition | : | 2011 |
| Ninth Edition | : | 1993 | Twenty-second Edition | : | 2014 |
| Tenth Edition | : | 1995 | Edition | : | 2016 |
| Eleventh Edition | : | 1996 | Edition | : | 2020 |
| Twelfth Edition | : | 1997 | Edition | : | 2023 |
| Thirteenth Edition | : | 1998 | Edition | : | 2025 |
| | | | Edition | : | 2026 |

**Published by** : Mrs. Meena Pandey
for **Himalaya Publishing House Pvt. Ltd.,**
Vishal Industrial Estate, 1st Floor, Office No. 63/64,
Bhandup Village Road, Subhash Nagar (Opp. CEAT Tyres),
Nahur (W), Mumbai - 400 078. Phone: 022-35131464/65/66/67
E-mail: himpub@bharatmail.co.in; Website: www.himpub.com

**Branch Offices :**

**New Delhi** : "Pooja Apartments", 4-B, Murari Lal Street, Ansari Road, Darya Ganj, New Delhi - 110 002.
Phone: 011-23270392, 23278631; Fax: 011-23256286

**Nagpur** : Kundanlal Chandak Industrial Estate, Ghat Road, Nagpur - 440 018. Mobile: 09325409992, 09325908881

**Bengaluru** : Plot No. 91-33, 2nd Main Road, Seshadripuram, Behind Nataraja Theatre, Bengaluru - 560 020.
Phone: 080-41138821; Mobile: 09379847017, 09379847005

**Hyderabad** : No. 3-4-184, Lingampally, Besides Raghavendra Swamy Matham, Kachiguda, Hyderabad - 500 027.
Phone: 040-27560041, 27550139

**Chennai** : No. 34/44, Motilal Street, T. Nagar, Chennai - 600 017.
Mobile: 09380460419

**Pune** : "Laksha" Apartment, First Floor, No. 527, Mehunpura, Shaniwarpeth (Near Prabhat Theatre), Pune - 411 030.
Phone: 020-24496323, 24496333; Mobile: 09370579333

**Cuttack** : Plot No 5F-755/4, Sector-9, CDA Markat Nagar, Cuttack - 753 014, Odisha. Mobile: 09338746007

**Kolkata** : 3, S.M. Bose Road, Near Gate No. 5, Agarpara Railway Station, North 24 Parganas, West Bengal - 700109.
Mobile: 09674536325

**DTP by** : Rajani Tambe

**Printed at** : Geetanjali Press Pvt. Ltd., Nagpur. On behalf of HPH (P).

# FOREWORD

by Dr. A.P.J. Abdul Kalam

(This is to be exactly the same as in the 2004 edition)

# PREFACE

As this new edition is going to the press, Global Financial Crisis is sweeping the world, severely straining the economy and exports of all countries. A separate chapter on the origin and background of the crisis and how it can affect our economy and exports has been added as chapter IV in the book. The full impact of this crisis will be known only in the year ahead.

In the course of the last decade, the export scene in India has undergone a tremendous change. The changes have been unprecedented. The liberalization initiated by the Government, the keen competition in the marketplace, and the rapid increases in export of services, have all combined to change the picture completely.

This has thrown up several challenges, and the chief among them is the need of a trained professional cadre which has a total comprehension of international trade and economics. There is a tendency in our country to equate Export Management with a vast array of policy and procedural details. Though knowledge of these is extremely important in India, it is only the development of professional export management skills in the areas of conceptual planning, and marketing skills, that will enable us to compete with the best in the world.

A chapter on 'India's Export Potential' is included, giving clearly the present trends and the future efforts needed to attain an export target befitting a developed country by 2020. This is based on the brilliant exposition by Dr.A.P.J.Abdul Kalam and Mr.Y.S.Rajan in their book 'INDIA 2020 - A vision for the New Millennium'

In the chapter on 'Globalisation' an effort has been made to show the limited extent to which India has travelled on this road, and its importance to exports and economy. The purpose of this is to provoke the students to think, debate and understand these developments and to draw their own conclusions.

The most important lesson one should learn in Export Management is never to have any preconceived notions. One should always be pragmatic, and have an open mind. It would be more beneficial to be realistic rather than be consistent per se.

I am greatly indebted to the TATA organization, which has provided inspirational leadership and encouragement in my career and endeavours in the field of international trade.

I am extremely grateful to Bharat Ratna Dr.A.P.J. Abdul Kalam, who is crusading to convert India into a 'developed country by 2020' by using technology and hard work, for providing a Foreword to this book.

I request the academic and exporting professional communities to send in their suggestions for making this book more useful.

November 2008

**T.A.S. BALAGOPAL**

Email: tasbalagopal@airtelmail.in

# CONTENTS

**Note:**

1 US Dollar = 48.30 Rupees (November 2008)
One Lakh = 100,000
One Crore = 10,000,000

# 1

# INTERNATIONAL TRADE, ECONOMY AND EXPORTS

This chapter indicates the situation as of August 2008. How the global financial crisis will affect international trade, economy and exports will only unravel in the year ahead.

International Trade has emerged as a separate and important branch of management education and training in International Business Schools the world over. There has been a rapid increase in the growth, and the complex nature of problems posed by international trade. Today it has transcended the traditional exports of goods to various types of commercial services, capital deployment, investment, transfer of technologies, intellectual property rights, movement of personnel, computer software development and exports, e-commerce, - and the list is growing. These in turn give rise to new and unique problems to be solved by the management. This is further complicated by the policies adopted by the various governments to further its trade efforts.

Hence the subject requires considerable study and thought, to enable countries and organisations to devise strategies to be adopted to further their own objectives. Every year, why, even every day brings its own new set of problems to be resolved, and hence it is a dynamic subject challenging the best of brains. It will be an extremely important subject of study in the new millennium and in the years to come.

## International Trade

When one studies the macro picture of international trade, one has to look at the world as a whole, and understand the economic trends. The countries in the world today are so interdependent that any significant development in one part of the world will have its repercussions in other countries in a small or big measure. Hence a constant and continuous study of the economic developments in various parts of the world and the twists and turns of world trade becomes essential.

Students of International Trade will have to study World Trade in general, its growth, the sectors in which it is growing, the countries or regions in which it is growing or dwindling, and the nature of growth both in merchandise trade as well as trade in services, to know the trends and the benchmarks against which they can evaluate a country's exports.

When we study these trends we should also bear in mind certain factors:

1. The effect of any fluctuations of world trade due to sudden developments in the market place will be evident only after a lapse of a certain period. The change could be because of competition, government policies, or wide fluctuations in financial sectors such as exchange rates, or steep increase in energy costs, all of which will have a serious impact. An example is the 'East Asian crisis', as it is called, resulting in sudden and huge devaluation of currencies of the East Asian Nations in 1997. But the extent to which it affected the countries became apparent only in 1998, and thereafter.

   Similarly the steep increase in the price of crude oil going up to $145 per barrel in the middle of 2008 affected many economies, and if the price of oil remains high, the effect on the economic growth and exports will be discernible only in the latter half of 2008-09.

2. The trends one can discern in world trade can only be based on the actual trade figures, and these are available only after a considerable period of time. For example in early 2008, one has only got the detailed trade figures for 2006.

3. India's international trade (consisting of both its Imports & Exports) has grown from US $ 42.2 billion in 1990-91 to about US $316 billion in 2006-07, and as the country has to plan on substantial increases in the years to come, it is essential to look at world trade and the trends therein, as these have a direct impact on the export performance of any country.

## Global Economy

It is interesting to note that in spite of the turmoil in world capital markets, global economy and trade have expanded at a very steady pace till 2007. The annual average growth of world economy as measured by the GDP was 2.6% between 1990 and 2000, and increased to 3% between 2000 and 2006. During this period there was a surge in foreign direct investment (FDI), and the Net Foreign Direct Investment increased from $24 billion in 1990 to $280 billion in 2006. Out of this, the chief beneficiaries in 2006 were China to the extent of $69 billion and India to the extent of $17 billion, which indicates the interdependence of the economies of various countries. This also led to the phenomenon that disturbances in one country or region could have an impact elsewhere, as for example global financial crisis which suddenly erupted in Sep 2008 would seriously affect economies of all the countries of the world. These developments emphasize the need for careful and well directed policies based on adequate international cooperation.

The strong global GDP growth in 1990-2000 was largely attributable to the economic performance of America together with the recovery in Europe. These developments offset weaker growth in those regions which had fallen back from the above-average growth performance in 1996, namely in certain countries in Asia, Africa and the Middle East. One indicator of the broad based economic expansion is the large number of countries which recorded positive per capita income growth. Out of a sample of 153 countries taken up by WTO, 126 recorded an increase in the per-capita income levels.

The contraction of economic activity in Asia, sparked by the financial crisis in a number of South East Asian countries in 1997 and largely unanticipated recession in Japan in 1997-98 had created a somber business climate worldwide. Reverse Capital flows from emerging markets had led to downward pressure on interest rates in the United States and Western Europe and had contributed to a booming stock market in these countries. The perceptions of the prospects in Asia, the economic crisis in Russia, and the fear of contagion in other emerging markets, have raised the spectra of more generalised contractions in demand and economic downturn worldwide.

The year 2001 witnessed an unexpectedly sharp downturn in the expansion of global output and a decline in world trade. The world GDP increased by 1.5% and world trade decreased by 1.5%. For the first time since 1982 the world trade growth was negative.

However, the recessionary trends were reversed by the year 2001. In 2002, USA had a GDP growth of 2.3%, China 8%, S.Korea 6%, Thailand 5%, South Africa 2.7%, and India 4.5%, whereas the growth in Japan and Europe was negligible. There have been good signs of further improvement, and in 2007 USA recorded a growth of 2.5% Japan and European Union 2.3%, India 7.4%, and China 9.8%.

But one troubling factor is the trade deficit in the Trade Balance of USA. The trade balance deficit has increased steadily and stood at -$758 billion in 2006. In other words the imports of goods and services into USA was higher compared to the exports in 2006, to the extent of $759 billion. A main consequence has been the weakening of the US Dollar compared to Sterling, Euro and other currencies.

Another serious development in 2008 is the enormous increase in the price of crude oil. In India we produce about 24% of our petroleum requirements, and the balance has to be imported. Our consumption is of the order of 120 million tonnes. Hence the amount needed to import crude oil at a price of $140 per barrel will be almost $90 billion. Our average imports of all other goods excluding oil, would be around $115 billion. Hence the total foreign exchange needed for all our imports including oil in a year, would be around $200 billion, if crude oil rules at $140 per barrel. With national foreign exchange reserves of $308.5 billion as of July 8, 2008, one can easily imagine how long it will be possible to import all our requirements, if the price of oil continues at this high level.

It has become imperative for government to (a) carry out a serious campaign to reduce oil consumption (many western countries have done this and succeeded) and (b) to devise strategies, very seriously for alternate energy sources, with a time-bound programme, and investment.

Figure 1.1 below gives the pattern of world merchandise exports in this decade.

**Table 1.1**

**WORLD MERCHANDISE TRADE - $ BILLION**

| *Year* | *Merchandise Trade* |
|---|---|
| 2001 | 6163 |
| 2005 | 10431 |
| 2006 | 12083 |

The above is only a broad indication of the growth of world trade. This Table depicts only merchandise trade. Of late, the trade in commercial services have also increased and in the year 2006, it was estimated to be around $ 2755 billion. Commercial services are tending to reach 20% of overall export trade. And it reflects a broad picture of the trends in the world.

We have given a broad summary of the developments in the economy of the world in the past. But what message does it give to one involved in the export trade in India? The simple answer to that is that global economy and trade are interrelated. The export trade of an organisation or a country in the new millennium will be greatly influenced by the economies in other countries as well.

Having said this, we should also bear in mind that India's merchandise export is hardly 1% of world trade and our exports in commercial services trade is hardly 2.7%. With such a small percentage, the areas or sectors in which we are planning fast growth may affect the trade only in that particular area and sector marginally, and should not normally create any serious dislocation of world trade, except perhaps in the field of Software Exports and Business Process Outsourcing where some countries feel that it takes away jobs from their country affecting their employment potential.

Hence, India's exports, even if they are good by our standards, will not make any appreciable impact on world trade.

In India, throughout the decades of the seventies and eighties, we evolved a system where the industry and the government concentrated on the specific problems of the export trade of our country, and devised certain specific measures to address them alone. This might have helped the country at that point in time, when our exports were much smaller, but not any more. Unless the industry and government look at the problems holistically and devise means to meet the challenges, be it of technology, production, competition, infrastructure, finance or any other impediment, we will never achieve our full export potential.

A very good yardstick that we have in measuring the World Economy is the Gross Domestic Product (GDP) of countries. A simple definition of GDP is the sum total of the value of all domestic goods and services produced in the country. This is invariably expressed in terms of US Dollars for convenience and comparison. Each country assesses its GDP in its own currency - the fluctuations in the exchange rate also have an important bearing on the final figure.

The total Global Economy was estimated at a GDP of US Dollars 48,245 billion in 2006. The GDP of the first ten countries in 2006 were as follows:

**Table 1.2**

| *Country* | *GDP ($ Billion)* |
|---|---|
| 1. U.S.A | 13,202 |
| 2. Japan | 4340 |
| 3. Germany | 2907 |
| 4. China | 2668 |
| 5. France | 2231 |
| 6. Italy | 1845 |
| 7. Brazil | 1068 |
| 8. India | 906 |
| 9. South Korea | 888 |
| 10. Australia | 768 |

Global economy has become unpredictable due to various developments, the most important being the Iraq war, the diminishing value of the US dollar till the middle of 2008, and the enormous fluctuations in the price of oil.

In any evaluation of world economy and its effect on the other countries and international trade, USA occupies a prominent place. It is mainly because the GDP of USA alone is $ 13202 billion out of a world GDP of $ 48245 billion (in the year 2006). USA constitutes practically 27% of the total GDP of the world. Almost 20% of the goods and services exported by the world goes into US economy. In other words, the state of US economy has a great bearing on international trade, and on the export trade of most of the countries. From India, 20% of the goods exported and 60% of services exported goes to the USA.

This is the very reason that in policy planning, discussions and debates in India and elsewhere, so much importance is attached to the trade with USA It is understandable that the government and industry always try to stabilise this trade, for a big decline in our exports to USA can never be compensated by any other country. This fact stares in our face after the global financial crisis.

Japan whose GDP is $4340 billion amounted to 8.9%, Germany whose GDP is $2907 billion amounted to almost 6%, and China whose GDP is $2668 billion amounted to 5.5% of the global economy, in 2006.

The first ten countries in the world's leading GDP list above, account for two thirds of the world's economic activity. Hence a country's external trade and exports is greatly affected one way or other based on what exports it is able to achieve with these leading countries.

## Foreign Trade

Let us look at the total foreign trade transacted by all the countries in the world economy as a whole. It is estimated that the total foreign trade in goods and services in 2006 amounted to US $ 29901 billion amounting to 62% of the total world economy. This has grown steadily over the years. Foreign Trade was hardly one third of the world economy in 1990, and this perhaps more than any thing else, shows that the world is becoming more and more interdependent. We in India have to face this situation and prepare ourselves in the quickest possible time to meet the challenges posed by this interdependence, which is sometimes loosely called 'Globalisation.'

Foreign trade is of paramount importance for all the countries for their economic growth, and also for providing a better quality of life to its citizens. The world in the new millennium is going to be quite different from the one we had at our independence in 1947.

After the ravages of the second world war, India was industrialising and the establishment of basic industries and self-sufficiency in the country's needs were the main objectives in the early fifties. The cost of materials and machinery as well as wages were very much lower, and the cost of production did not matter that much. Producing everything indigenously was the policy. Further, a strict import control regime in India prevented the free trade of goods. Services industry was not in existence then.

Today commercial services are one of the fastest growing sectors, and can no longer be neglected.

The trade dialogue under GATT earlier, and now under WTO, has reduced the tariff barriers considerably.

All the above have had a tremendous impact on the export trade. The sum total of all these developments has resulted in the following:

*(a)* Most of the goods or merchandise produced in the country have to be of international quality and price, especially if it is to be exported.

*(b)* The services sector has grown considerably and is 20% of the total world trade. This is bound to increase, and India has tremendous potential in this area. It is predicted that before 2020, Services trade may even exceed Goods trade.

*(c)* Such of those goods that can be produced in the country but are not economically viable at international prices, may always be imported.

*(d)* Due to the explosion in the visual and written media, and the exposure to international products, the people have started demanding products of high quality and convenience, and will not accept poor substitutes.

*(e)* The information technology industry which has touched life at all points and at all levels, has certainly affected manufacture, production and commercial services in the country. It has given a chance for many industries, business and even government to leap-frog into the new millennium by many innovations and clever use of the new technologies. It makes possible to bring tremendous improvements in areas where we never thought we could, and is an irreversible process.

## Indian Economy

The state of the economy of a country has a direct bearing on its exports and international trade. The growth in international trade in turn fuels the domestic economy not only for growth, but also sets in motion modernisation, competitive production, and effective marketing etc., so that we can compete in the international market place successfully.

The changes in the economy of the country since 1991 have been profound and fundamental. Any student of economy or export management should not only know the significant changes which have been brought about but also their implications for international trade. The changes have not only opened a vista of great opportunities but also thrown tremendous challenges to the economy and exports of the country. The country is standing up to these challenges in the field of exports, and recasting the export efforts in productive channels resulting in the exports having increased from $ 18 billion in 1990-91 to $ 126 billion in 2006-07.

The important changes brought about since 1990-91 are:

(1) The process of dismantling the system of industrial licensing which enabled entrepreneurs to decide on the new productive ventures that they would undertake.

(2) Allowing foreign investment, and in many cases without setting any upper limit.

(3) Allowing Foreign Direct Investment (FDI), and Institutional Investment in industries and in the primary and secondary markets.

(4) Free flow of technology for modernising and upgrading industries and hiring foreign technical and managerial personnel.

(5) Import restrictions gradually decreasing, as also the tariff barriers, in line with the global trend.

(6) The Rupee being made completely convertible on the trade account and current account transactions, and delegating power to scheduled banks for practically all foreign exchange transactions.

(7) Allowing the retention of the foreign exchange earnings by exporters for all their legitimate expenses.

(8) Allowing new private ventures, Indian and foreign in the field of banking, civil aviation, telecom and automobile industries and gradually in other industries.

(9) Opening up of the private sector for investment in the field of Oil Exploration, Refining, and also in other infrastructure fields such as Telecom, Roads, Power Projects etc.

These and various other measures introduced in the economy have had a healthy impact and have brought about attitudinal changes.

From the earlier day slogans of self-sufficiency and import substitution, we are today talking of production of world class products;

and there are more instances of making India a source for worldwide needs of many products and services. We are gearing up to be an active and meaningful member of the global economy. We have made a good beginning, but have a long way to go.

Of course, there are veiled criticisms that the country has gone too far, and the opening up of our economy for foreign investment will edge the Indian entrepreneurs out of the business, and the lot of the poor in India has not been bettered. But on the other hand GDP has increased from Rs.132520 crores in 1990-91 to Rs.37900630 crores in 2006-07 and exports increased from Rs.32,553 crores in 1990-91 to Rs.5,71,779 crores by 2006-07. The per capita income which was $ 460 in 2000-01 increased to $ 960 in 2006. Indian Industry and entrepreneurs are going strong and expanding their horizons, and buying industries abroad. The typical examples of these are the TATA Group in India buying CORUS Steel in UK., TATA buying Jaguar and Land Rover from Ford Motor Co., and the Sterling Group endeavouring to buy ASARCO, a huge metal mining and refining co. in the US, and the Kalyani Group buying foundries in Germany and United Kingdom.

What prompted the government to embark on this phase of economic reforms in 1991?

First, one should recapitulate the conditions in the country in 1991, when this reform process was set in motion. The country's foreign exchange reserves were at their lowest level, and we were about to default on foreign debt repayment for the first time after independence, and had to pledge gold into the vaults of the Bank of England to tide over the crisis.

Second, the whole world including the erstwhile communist countries were moving towards an open market system and there was no way in which India could have ignored the pressures, and continued in its own old ways.

Third, the resources at the disposal of the government were absolutely inadequate for the vast investments needed in the various core sectors to build up a robust economy, as well as for the developmental needs of the country.

Fourth, the massive investment in the public sector, which was made in the hope that it would reach 'commanding heights' of the economy did not materialise. The government, for the vast investment and protection given to the public sector units over the years was not getting adequate returns from most of them, and a large number were becoming sick.

Under these circumstances, the policy measures taken were inevitable ones, as we are seeing today the results which brought the country out of a serious crisis into a state where it has foreign exchange reserves which can be called adequate. This has not happened in India before.

But having achieved this, the basic problems of raising the living standards, and bringing more of the population above the poverty line have to be addressed seriously by the state and central governments. If these have been not done adequately or in a cost-effective way in the past, one cannot fault the economic reforms for them.

Conversely, if the economic reforms had not been taken up in 1991, we would have been in a much worse situation than we are in today to help the underprivileged of our country.

## Exports

It was stated earlier that the total merchandise exports of India in 2001-02 was $ 43 billion, and it has increased to $126 billion in 2006-07. It is instructive to see what the exports of some of the advanced countries are, and where we stand in comparison to them. Table 1.3 below gives the exports of some of these countries.

**Table 1.3**

**MERCHANDISE EXPORTS BY COUNTRIES**

| *Country* | *US $ Billion* | | |
|---|---|---|---|
| | *1990* | *2001* | *2006* |
| U.S.A | 394 | 730.8 | 1038 |
| Germany | 421 | 570.8 | 1112 |
| Japan | 285 | 403.5 | 650 |
| France | 216 | 321.8 | 490 |
| U.K. | 184 | 273.1 | 448 |
| China | NA | 266.2 | 969 |
| Italy | 170 | 241.1 | 410 |
| Canada | 132 | 259.9 | 390 |
| Netherlands | 136 | 229.5 | 462 |
| Belgium | 118 | 179.7 | 369 |
| India | 18 | 43.0 | 126 |

The above table shows the exports of ten countries of the world in 2001. We have also given the exports of these countries in 1990, to give an idea of their increases. The export of India is also given in the last line, which gives an idea of how far we have to go before we can be considered by the world community as a country worth reckoning with in the field of exports. Another indicator is that the export of U.S.A., the largest exporter in the world, is 9% of the total exports of the world, whereas India's exports amount to hardly 0.9%.

Another aspect of exports which is of great importance, is the nature of exports. For example, roughly one-third of the exports in goods are raw materials, such as oil, minerals as well as agricultural products. This proportion is likely to fall over a period of time. Already the exports in manufactured goods are rising fast. Further, each country in its own way is trying to become less dependent on imports. Typical examples of such efforts are developing alternates such as synthetic textiles in place of cotton, or prospecting for oil in their own countries to reduce imports of mineral oil etc. But these efforts can help only to a certain extent as the growth and demand increase rapidly.

India's merchandise export was of the order of $ 18 billion in 1991-92, and has risen to $43 billion in 2001-02, and $126 billion in 2006-07. It would appear that India's export compared to other countries is not growing fast. But the more important aspect of our export is the strong linkages it is forging with the world economy. Both the turn of events in the last few years and the latest government policies are linking India's export to the global economy, and provide an excellent opportunity for a fast growth rate.

Among the various developments in the past, one would identify the following factors which are mostly responsible for the level of exports being what it is today.

The liberalisation of constraints on foreign investment, and relaxation of controls on industrial licensing:

Government has enunciated a policy for automatic approval for technical collaboration and foreign equity participation of up to 51% or even more in Indian companies. They have also allowed 51% foreign equity participation in Indian Trading Companies primarily engaged in export activities. Further, Indian Companies are permitted to raise capital abroad through issue of bonds/shares. This has already led to very many new collaborations/investment proposals by international companies in India for production of goods meant for the international market.

(a) The rupee which was made partially convertible in 1992, was improved upon in 1994 for all current account convertibility purposes, as per Article VIII of the IMF, under which, India is committed to forsake the use of exchange restrictions on current international transactions as an instrument in managing the balance of payments.

(b) Exporters who earn foreign exchange are allowed to retain their export earnings in foreign exchange and use it for all their legitimate expenses, without any need to take Reserve Bank permission, which used to be the case a few years ago.

(c) The new Export-Import Policies are now announced for five years, and they allow free import and export of goods barring a few items included in the negative list. This has not only given substantial freedom for import of all essential requirements for the industry and trade, but has also helped the import of essential goods, such as sugar, edible oil etc. to prevent abnormal price increases in the market.

Another area of growth is in Services. By this we mean the increase in the trade in services, such as consultancy services, financial services, information services such as computer software services, travel services etc., which are growing at a very fast rate.

By these developments, the basic direction of India's new economic policies is helping the country to face a robust, competitive market economy of the world. The opening of the economy gradually to foreign investment, encouraging the private sector to expand, with the world market in view, and allowing Indian companies to buy outright foreign companies germane to their international trade, etc, have not come a day too soon, as all other countries around us had started on this path much earlier. These developments will help in integrating the Indian economy with the global economy.

## INTERDEPENDENCE OF COUNTRIES

The developments in the world in the last couple of decades have not only changed the face of the world as we know and understand it, but have forcefully brought to our attention how interdependent the various countries of the world are. The economy of each and every country, however big or small it may be, clearly proves this.

The usual reasons we give for interdependence of the countries are well known, such as:

(a) No country can be completely self-reliant, as natural resources are dispersed unevenly all over the world, and the countries have to depend on each other for their requirements. A typical example is petroleum products, which every country needs badly, but are found only in a few countries in abundance.

(b) Industrial advances have proved that it is not economical to produce certain products within the country, and it is always economical to import them from the countries where they are produced efficiently and cheaply.

(c) The technological development in the world is not uniform - in some countries it is extremely advanced and consequently they are able to produce certain categories of products and services which are very economical, and as they are indispensable, they have to be imported by the others.

Typical examples of these are life-saving drugs in the pharmaceutical industry, and certain computerised modern machine tools which increase production substantially.

(d) The dynamics of progress brings in its own wake rapid changes in what a country produces. These changes result in some countries importing goods which they were once producing themselves and exporting to other countries.

A classic example of this is the textile industry. The countries, who were in the early part of last century buying cotton from developing countries and selling fabrics and finished products back to them, have in the closing years of the last century, became the biggest importers of fabrics and garments from the very countries to whom they were exporting these before.

Apart from these known factors, certain developments in recent times, have brought other compelling reasons to the fore in the interdependence of countries.

(1) A developing country like India has to maintain rapid economic growth so as to meet the demands of the growing population, to generate more employment and raise the standard of living. In the present day world, the rapid growth of agricultural and industrial production has become more capital-intensive than ever before.

Hence, the paramount need today is capital for development and growth. For getting this capital one has to go across the national borders and depend on other countries who can invest. In the four decades after independence, it was assumed in India though incorrectly, that the savings generated in the country, as well as loans and aids of international financial institutions such as World Bank, International Monetary Fund, Asian Development Bank and loans and aids we were getting from other countries, would be sufficient for all our development and growth. This is no longer true. It is now clear to one and all that we have to solicit and woo private investments from abroad for rapid growth, especially in infrastructure, as well as in industry.

(2) The fact that the world was divided into two power blocks - communist and non-communist, and the ideologies thereof, strongly influenced other countries in their economic planning for well over four decades after the war. A sudden change was brought about by the collapse of communist regimes and the radical conversion of all those countries to free market economies. They are fiercely soliciting foreign aid and investment for their development. This not only shows how interdependent countries have become, but also the intense competition among them, to attract foreign investment for their economic growth and development.

All these lead us to the conclusion that in today's world, interdependence of countries has grown to such an extent that any serious disturbance in the economy of a large country will affect all the others.

## INDIA'S COMMITMENTS

### Debt Servicing

India has been taking loans on concessional terms from the World Bank and its associates. It is also borrowing from abroad, a sizable amount on a commercial basis. It has short term as well long term debt commitments. The effect of all this has been a steady increase in external debt. It was of the order of US $ 83.8 billion in 1991 and has increased to US $ 138.1 billion by 2006. The external debt to GDP is of the order of 15% and is quite high.

This repayment as agreed to of the various debts is a must, and in the international financial world no country can afford to default on its external debt. The moment this happens, a country's credibility suffers badly and it cannot attract any foreign loan or investment. India came perilously close to this in 1991, and the Reserve Bank of India had to pledge the gold from its reserves to the Bank of England, to fulfil its debt commitments.

Due to the drastic changes in the economic policies and liberalisation measures adopted by the country, it was taken out of this dire situation.

The foreign exchange reserves which were US $ 2.26 million in March 1991, and hardly enough to cover even one month's import requirements has gradually risen (after meeting all debt service requirements) to US $ 305.5 billion in July 2008. This places us in a comfortable position.

## Oil Imports

The uninterrupted supply of petroleum products are of great importance in the economy of any nation. It is essential for agricultural, transport, industry, and energy needs of the nation.

The consumption of petroleum products in India which was of the order of 30 million tons in 1980-81, increased to 55 million tons in 1990-91 and is at present 120 million tons. Out of the total consumption of 120 million tons, the country produces both in its offshore and onshore fields only 33 million tons. The balance has to imported. The domestic production of Crude Oil is hovering around 32 million tons for the past few years, and no new worthwhile find of oil has materialized. (However the recent findings of gas and oil by Reliance in the Krishna-Godavari region of the Bay of Bengal is welcome). However, at present we have to import more than 70% of our needs, or approximately 88 million tons. In today's price of oil (with an average price of $130 per barrel in July 2008) this amounts to about $74 billion. This is equivalent to about 50% of the total value of our merchandise exports today. But it is well known that oil prices are always subjected to great fluctuations, and the oil bill may increase, if it follows an upward trend, or vice versa.

Of course there are other important needs of the country requiring foreign exchange for imports. Just two factors have been highlighted, i.e., debt servicing and the petroleum bill to bring home the absolute need for a steady and substantial increase in exports from our country in order to meet the higher import demands. The demand for more exports is bound to increase further due to the rapid economic development envisaged in the liberalisation of our policies and the high foreign investment anticipated.

## Export or Perish

Many writers attribute this slogan to Pandit Jawaharlal Nehru. This author feels, to the best of his knowledge and recollection, that Nehru never made such a statement. In the situation which we were in when the thrust of the 1st, 2nd and 3rd five-year plans were in the direction of import substitution and self-reliance, this slogan would not have been relevant or made.

This slogan was used by many foreign countries, especially countries like Singapore, Hong Kong and even Japan, who did not have any natural resources of their own, and depended solely upon imports. For them, it was evident that they could not survive without exports, and hence this slogan would have been apt.

However, in today's context, one can perhaps apply this slogan to India, since it is facing a free market economy in the outside world, rapid economic development and increasing the standard of living of the vast majority of the people, - all of which will need substantial capital inflows both from domestic savings as well as international investments. This is possible only by a very rapid rise in the exports of the country. Perhaps a more apt slogan today would be "Export to make the country flourish".

## Export of Services

In the distribution of Gross Domestic products in the year 2006, agriculture amounted to 18%, industry 43%, and Services 54%. This is in line with the developed countries where services are predominant. For example, the service component in the GDP in Germany, Japan and France were respectively 68%, 66% and 71%. In the USA also it was over 70%.

This is an area where India has forged ahead already. In the year 2006-07 there was a growth of 32% and it reached US $76.2 billion, which consisted of software and IT enabled services, tourism and travel, financial services, consultancy services and a variety of other services. The pride of place in Service Exports goes to software, information technology and IT enabled services, which amounted to $ 40 billion. This comprises two important elements – one being the software and IT, and the other being BPO (Business Process Outsourcing) The software and IT sector exports are increasing at the rate of 25% - 30% annually whereas the BPO sector is increasing at a much higher rate. However there is opposition to BPO efforts by India especially in the USA as they feel that they are losing 'white collar' jobs due to this outsourcing. Even though it has been proved that outsourcing helps the industry in USA considerably, the cause has been politicized, and became prominent during elections in USA. Nevertheless, BPO endeavour will increase in India in the next few years.

However the global financial crisis which erupted in Sep 2008 has cast a shadow on the future earnings in this sector, the extent of which we will know in the year ahead.

The export earnings in services which are around 35% of our total exports, will increase more rapidly in the future, provided India takes various steps necessary to become the most sought-after nation for such services.

## NEW DEVELOPMENTS

The serious efforts undertaken by Indian enterprises and industry on all fronts over the last few years are bearing fruit, and it looks as if India is on a better wicket now than ever before.

The Indian manufacturing sector has emerged strong and competitive. We are the largest manufacturers of two-wheelers and motorcycles, and also the lowest cost producer of steel, aluminium, cement and CDs. It can be said that India's engineering edge in manufacturing has finally come of age. Five Indian companies have won the Deming Prize for Total Quality Management, and many more are in the waiting list.

What is remarkable is that India is on a fast track in many areas. China which has achieved a significant position in manufacturing, has primarily addressed the manufacturing segment in the USA market which accounts for 15% of the GDP, while India is trying to penetrate the service sector which accounts for 70% of the US GDP.

The areas in which India is concentrating are software development, IT consulting, BPO services, chip design, financial analysis, drug research and manufacturing outsourcing and many others.

It is in Information Technology and IT enabled services that India is well placed with more IT professionals in Bangalore than in Silicon Valley in the US. It is estimated that GE of USA saves $349 million per annum just by performing 700 tasks in India instead of in the USA. It is no surprise that world majors such as IBM, Intel, Oracle, Texas Instruments and Citigroup are all in India setting up their own BPO operations.

The Indian manufacturing industries have become so confident that they are looking at ongoing industrial concerns abroad to purchase, in order to acquire extra production capacities as well as a new range of products to add to their domestic and export demands. Recently Tata Motors acquired the Daewoo Commercial Vehicle Unit in South Korea, to expand their range of products and export possibilities, for a wider market abroad. In the year 2007-08, they increased the production in the acquired unit by 38% and increased its market share from 24.3% to 32.3% in the HCV market, and they became the largest exporter from South Korea in this segment.

Sundaram Fasteners which has been a recognized ancillary supplier to General Motors, has acquired an ongoing industrial unit in the United Kingdom to increase its range and export capability. Bharat Forge has acquired a forging company in Germany which has made it the second largest forging company in the world.

Further, to boost the production and capabilities of Indian enterprises, there have been foreign direct investments, and in 2006-07 it was of the order of $ 19.5 billion as against $7.7 billion in 2005-06. Foreign institutional investments were on an average $ 10 billion per year for the last four years.

These developments do not include areas like the food processing industry where the McKinsey report suggests that India has a potential to produce $ 50 billion worth of products of international standards.

Another area which India has entered into, and has great potential is printing. Outsourcing in printing by leading publishers will eventually come to India. It has just entered the market after buying the latest technology from abroad and is installing the latest machinery. The range at present includes journals, dictionaries, hard cover coffee-table books, and even magazines for circulation in the USA. India is able to compete with Singapore and Hong Kong mainly because of the cost advantage. As the market for books is increasing, this sector, if well nurtured will make a significant contribution to our exports.

We still have to overcome a few impediments for exports to flourish. Some of these are:

(1) There is a dire need to get high quality infrastructure in the quickest possible time, as it cuts cost on production, transport, rapid and reliable delivery.

(2) Labour productivity has to be improved through higher educational standards and training of personnel.

(3) Modern financial markets with a strong base have to be created so as to lower the costs of capital and transactions.

(4) Well enforced, and flexible laws have to be laid down covering land, labour and capital to aid the rapid deployment of these factors of production, whenever needed, to increase productivity and competitiveness for export.

(5) Appropriate judicial mechanisms to resolve disputes fairly and quickly have to be in place.

There should be a serious debate and discussion about all these in the government, various political parties, and the society at large, and we should arrive at a consensus that will help us to cut the Gordian knot, and set us on the road to real progress to make India a strong economic power and a developed country in the years ahead.

❖ ❖ ❖

# 2

# INDIA'S EXPORT TRADE

## HISTORICAL PERSPECTIVE

India has had a glorious export tradition. Indian spices and fine cloth have been exported over centuries to the East as well as to West. But during the colonial era we were forced to export raw materials in abundance, and had to import manufactures as perceived by the colonial power.

Even with the limitations imposed by the circumstances we were in, India's exports amounted to Rs.300 crores in the 1920s. In 1926, India was reported to have been the fifth largest exporting nation in the world. In 1947-48, in the first year of independence and the aftermath of partition, India's exports amounted to Rs.400 crores.

India followed a liberal import policy after independence to overcome the war time shortages of consumer goods and also to help the nascent industrial development. The export effort of India received comparatively little attention in the fifties when the balance of payments was well supported from accumulated sterling balances of the second world war, and the large amount of external aid obtained by the country. It was soon realized that this comfortable position would not last long. The pressures on the foreign exchange reserves soon necessitated a tight control over all imports, to conserve the reserves for essential imports. A serious export effort commenced by the early sixties.

However, the exports averaged Rs.962 crores in the First Five Year Plan between 1951 and 1956, and continued to be in the range of Rs.977 crores in the Second Five Year Plan between 1956 and 1961. While world exports had doubled in the fifties, India's share in it changed from 2.57% in 1948, to 1.27% in 1958. This was partly due to rising domestic demand and also due to world trends like recession in the international market and the changing pattern of international trade in the fifties.

To contain the demand on foreign exchange which was increasing substantially, the government made the import regime more rigorous from July 1957 permitting the import of only essential raw materials and other specific needs for the industrial development of the country.

## TRENDS

A major and significant step to boost the exports was the step taken to devalue the Indian rupee in 1966, so as to make Indian products more competitive. Simultaneously a new Export-Import Policy was brought into being to provide specific measures to help exporters to increase export production. Together with this, other export promotion measures were also taken to provide a firm base to increase exports.

The trend from 1967-68 to 1972-73 shows that the imports fell from Rs.2,008 crores in 1967-68 to Rs.1.861 crores in 1972-73, while exports rose from Rs.1,193 crores in 1967-68 to Rs.1,971 crores in 1972-73, an export increase of 65%.

A spectacular growth in the field of exports was registered between 1972-73 and 1976-77 with an annual average increase of 25%. This perhaps brings into focus an important factor in the evolution of the export trade of the country. As stated earlier, devaluation was effected in 1966 to help exports and specific export promotion measures and programs were brought into being to give a positive drive to increase the exports.

But the actual effect in a substantial manner was seen only between 1972-73 and 1976-77.

Table 2.1 gives India's foreign trade from 1950-51, to 2006-07, indicating the growth in its exports and imports. As stated earlier, there was a significant growth in the field of exports between 1972-73 and 1976-77 with an annual average increase of over 25%, which was mainly due to a series of measures taken by the government to encourage exports, and the response of the exporting community to these measures.

There was a recession in the world market in the seventies. The consequences of the increase in oil price in the early seventies were two fold. On the one hand, the developed countries embarked on a drive to reduce their imports of oil and also on consumption of energy to balance their trade. On the other, many of the developing countries which had to import their entire oil needs had no choice than to curtail their other imports. These developments had their adverse effect on the growth of export trade.

India had embarked also upon a planned effort to increase its non-traditional export products and manufactures. As some of these exports were in direct competition with that of the western countries and Japan, as also with the nearby industrialized countries such as Taiwan, South Korea etc., there was stiff resistance. Further, the exchange rates of various currencies were maintained in such a way by the developed countries that it did not help Indian exports. In spite of all this, as by Indian standards the domestic economy was in good shape, and the government's efforts to encourage exports were well directed, our exports increased.

Exports increased by 25% in 1987-88 to Rs.15,719 crores. In 1988-89, it increased by 28%, and by 17% in 1990-91, when it was Rs.32,553 crores. One should remember that the world trade was growing fast during this period and our export base on which these annual percentage increases were shown was comparatively small.

However, after the radical political changes in East Europe in the early nineties, the exports of our country took in its stride, the loss of the Russian and East European markets by virtue of the changes brought about in their political and economic set-ups. In the year 1990-91, our exports to USSR alone amounted to Rs.5,254 crores out of a total exports of Rs.32,553 crores amounting to 16%. This export dwindled considerably and in the year 1992-93 our exports to entire Eastern Europe including Russia amounted to Rs.2,359 crores out of a total Rs.53350 cores, or a mere 4.4%. There were many who prophesied that the loss of the East European markets would seriously affect our exports. Even though there was an initial set-back, India recovered quickly.

This perhaps illustrates a very important point that the Indian Exports were stabilizing and the exporters were becoming a professional lot, who were able to withstand such reversals and exploit other areas and markets to increase the exports.

**Table 2.1**

**INDIA'S FOREIGN TRADE**

| *Year* | *Imports* | *Exports* | *Exports Imports% (Rs. crores)* |
|---|---|---|---|
| *1950-51* | *1025* | *947* | *92.3* |
| **First Plan** | | | |
| 1951-52 | 1379 | 1106 | 80.2 |
| 1952-53 | 1002 | 873 | 87.1 |
| 1953-54 | 855 | 813 | 95.1 |
| 1954-55 | 988 | 918 | 92.0 |
| 1955-56 | 1224 | 922 | 75.3 |
| **Second Plan** | | | |
| 1956-57 | 1423 | 977 | 68.7 |
| 1957-58 | 1633 | 1001 | 61.3 |
| 1958-59 | 1424 | 903 | 63.4 |
| 1959-60 | 1515 | 1008 | 66.5 |
| 1960-61 | 1768 | 997 | 56.4 |
| **Third Plan** | | | |
| 1961-62 | 1718 | 1033 | 60.1 |
| 1962-63 | 1783 | 1069 | 60.0 |
| 1963-64 | 1927 | 1244 | 64.6 |
| 1964-65 | 2126 | 1282 | 60.3 |
| 1965-66 | 2194 | 1264 | 57.6 |
| **Annual Plan** | | | |
| 1966-67 | 2078 | 1153 | 55.5 |
| 1967-68 | 2008 | 1193 | 59.4 |
| 1968-69 | 1909 | 1354 | 0.9 |
| **Fourth Plan** | | | |
| 1969-70 | 1582 | 1413 | 89.3 |
| 1970-71 | 1634 | 1535 | 93.9 |
| 1971-72 | 1825 | 1608 | 88.1 |

| | | | |
|---|---|---|---|
| 1972-73 | 1867 | 1971 | 105.6 |
| 1973-74 | 2955 | 2523 | 85.4 |
| **Fifth Plan** | | | |
| 1974-75 | 4519 | 3329 | 73.7 |
| 1975-76 | 5275 | 4042 | 76.6 |
| 1976-77 | 5074 | 5143 | 101.5 |
| 1977-78 | 6026 | 5374 | 89.2 |
| 1978-79 | 6811 | 5726 | 84.0 |
| **Annual Plan** | | | |
| 1978-80 | 9143 | 3413 | 37.3 |
| **Sixth Plan** | | | |
| 1980-81 | 12549 | 6711 | 53.5 |
| 1981-82 | 13608 | 7806 | 57.4 |
| 1982-83 | 14356 | 8908 | 62 |
| 1983-84 | 15763 | 9867 | 62.6 |
| 1984-85 | 17134 | 11743 | 68.5 |
| **Seventh Plan** | | | |
| 1985-86 | 19658 | 10895 | 55.4 |
| 1986-87 | 20063 | 12550 | 62.5 |
| 1987-88 | 22343 | 15719 | 70.3 |
| 1988-89 | 27693 | 20281 | 73.2 |
| 1989-90 | 25412 | 27658 | 78.2 |
| **Annual Plan** | | | |
| 1990-91 | 43193 | 32553 | 75.3 |
| 1991-92 | 47850 | 43828 | 91.5 |
| **Eighth Plan** | | | |
| 1992-93 | 68375 | 53350 | 84.18 |
| 1993-94 | 73101 | 69548 | 95.13 |
| 1994-95 | 89971 | 82338 | 94.10 |
| 1995-96 | 122678 | 106353 | 86.69 |
| 1996-97 | 138919 | 118817 | 85.52 |
| **Ninth Plan** | | | |
| 1997-98 | 151554 | 126286 | 83.32 |
| 1998-99 | 178332 | 139752 | 78.36 |

| | | | |
|---|---|---|---|
| 1999-00 | 215236 | 159561 | 74.13 |
| 2000-01 | 230873 | 203571 | 88.17 |
| 2001-02 | 245199 | 209018 | 85.24 |
| **Tenth Plan** | | | |
| 2002-03 | 296597 | 252790 | 85.23 |
| 2003-04 | 359108 | 293367 | 81.7 |
| 2004-05 | 501065 | 375340 | 75 |
| 2005-06 | 660409 | 456418 | 69.1 |
| 2006-07 | 862302 | 571642 | 66.3 |

Since imports outpaced exports, trade deficits began to build up steadily from 1970 onwards. However, due to the solid increase in the exports of services, and also due to foreign investment in India, and the remittances by Non-Resident Indians, and other 'invisible earnings', the trade balance not only became positive, but India also started building sizable foreign exchange reserves which has kept growing and touched US $308 billion by July 2008.

When our foreign exchange reserves were at their lowest in 1991 - not even in a position to cover our imports for a month - the government made certain far-reaching reforms. The most important of these was the devaluation of the rupee by 23% in the first week of July 1991; and removing major incentives for exports.

Since then, the reforms have been extended and the rupee has been made current account convertible, accepting the obligations under Article VII of the IMF, under which India is committed to forsake the use of exchange restrictions on current international transactions as an instrument in managing the balance of payments.

Another fundamental change brought about was a new industrial policy, which changed the very concept of regulated industrial licensing, foreign investment, and ownership criteria of industries. For the first time since independence, an entrepreneur had full freedom to choose what he wanted to produce, where, and what process or technology to adopt, and the manner of investment, without any governmental interference or edict.

The new Export-Import Policy was made for a period of five years and was quite liberal, and also reduced many of the import restrictions. It almost eliminated canalization, and was export and industry oriented.

All these galvanized the Indian eonomy as nothing else had done in the past, and had a positive impact on the export scenario.

Our exports increased in a spectacular fashion from 1991-92 onwards. In the year 1991-92 the export was Rs.47850 crores and in 2001-02, it was of the order of Rs.209,018 crores. In 2006-07 it was Rs.571,642 crores.

Our imports also correspondingly increased. It was Rs.43,828 crores in 1991-92, and increased to Rs.245,199 crores in 2001-02, and Rs.862,302 crores in 2006-07.

In international trade, the difference between the exports and imports is usually referred to as Trade Balance. It is referred to as surplus if exports exceed imports, and is referred to as deficit if import exceeds exports.

Strictly speaking, the foreign exchange balance of the country is arrived at after taking all the inward remittances of foreign exchange due to Foreign Direct Investment, multilateral funding, NRI remittances, 'invisibles', together with exports on the one hand, and all other foreign exchange outgoes such as debt servicing, foreign expense payments the country has to make, and imports on the other hand, and arrive at the figure, which theoretically will give a zero sum, or in the positive. Any surplus thereafter will be kept as such and built upon.

But in all economic debate, the difference between exports and imports is referred to as Trade Balance, because this is what ultimately matters, and if the exports are much lower than the imports continuously, the deficit builds up. In such cases, the economy suffers, and the country has no alternative but to bring down the imports at all costs. In other words, nobody is going to finance us indefinitely, if we spend more foreign exchange than we earn.

On the other hand if our exports and other earnings exceed the imports on a continuous basis, we can accumulate our foreign exchange reserves, and build up a surplus over the years. A judicious use of these reserves can help in industrial development, bring in latest technologies, help to maintain the price line by imports if the domestic prices go up, and can meet a host of other needs.

The trade deficit of Rs.25,000 crores for the year 1997-98 was reckoned to be manageable by the country, taking into account all other inward flows, and thereafter; the foreign exchange reserves was US $ 30 billion.

In 2002-03 export was of the order of $52.2 billion as against an import of $61.3 billion, giving a deficit of $9.1 billion. This was more than offset by Service exports and other invisibles as explained earlier. Similarly in 2006-07, the merchandise export was of the order of $128 billion and import was $191 billion and the deficit of $63 billion was more than offset by service exports which was of the order of $76.2 billion, and the invisible earnings and various inward remittances. Our total foreign exchange earnings has been in the positive for quite a few years, and in July 2008, our reserves touched $308 billion dollars.

Compared to the situation we were in, in 1991, we have come a long way, and the reforms undertaken have vindicated themselves in the foreign trade sector of the economy. We are in a situation where the country can continue to allow greater imports not only to enhance the industrial growth, but also for greater exports. The trade deficits are manageable, and it is indeed a reasonable percentage of the GDP of the country.

It will be interesting for the student of exports to know where we stand in the league of countries holding sizable foreign exchange reserves in Asia. The table below provides the same.

**Table 2.2**

**FOREIGN EXCHANGE RESERVES IN SELECTED COUNTRIES**

*( $ billion )*

| *Country* | *1999* | *2001* | *2005* |
|---|---|---|---|
| China | 157.4 | 217.9 | 818.9 |
| South Korea | 73.8 | 103.8 | 115.3 |
| India | 32.6 | 46.4 | 131 |
| Singapore | 76.7 | 76.2 | 210 |
| Brazil | 34.7 | 36.1 | 50.5 |

As stated earlier the foreign exchange reserves in India were $308.5 billion in July 2008. But at the same time a word of caution is called for. The foreign exchange reserve we talk about in India, has a very large component - deposits of Non-Residents Indians, which can be recalled at any time of their choice, as also the foreign investment in the stocks and shares of the companies in India which is subject to huge fluctuations.

## COMPOSITION OF EXPORTS

The striking feature of India's Export has been the distinct change in its composition.

Exports used to be broadly classified into two categories - traditional products and non-traditional products. India by virtue of being a colonial country was allowed to export mostly our natural resource, which can all be termed as Traditional. But Government, in the steps taken from 1970 onwards, had placed emphasis on non-traditional exports

## Traditional Exports

These are primarily products which India has been exporting over a long period. They include Jute, Tea, Cotton fabrics, Cashew, Spices, Coffee etc. The total exports of these products which used to comprise 72% of exports in 1965-66, have come down to 24% of the total exports in 1997-98. It should be remembered that the scope of exports in these products is limited. Some of these products are produced by other developing countries also which provide us stiff competition, and the share of traditional products has been diminishing in the overall exports of the country.

A typical example is tea, in which competition is provided to us by Sri Lanka and East Africa, and even Vietnam.

We should persist in our efforts to increase our productivity and yield, and reduce the cost of production, so as to be competitive, diversify exports to other countries and improve our share in the market in these exports.

## Non-Traditional Exports

When we seriously tried to increase our exports in the Seventies these were new avenues for exports for India. These are related to the sectoral growth in the economy and the industries of the country, and better exploitation of our natural resources, where India has the potential to expand its export trade substantially. The products in this group consist of Engineering goods, Marine Products, Leather Products, Chemicals, Textile Garments, Gem and Jewellery, Computer Software etc.

The well-planned export promotion measures taken by the government from the late seventies, had an excellent impact on the export of manufactures. This led to the steady growth of non-traditional products in the export basket.

Table 2.3 traces the exports of major non-traditional products over the last two decade, and proves that the steps taken have borne fruit.

The export of major non-traditional products in India's exports was almost 70% in 1997-98.

**Table 2.3**

**MAJOR NON-TRADITIONAL EXPORTS OF INDIA**

*Rs. Crores*

| | 1990—91 | 2001-02 | 2006-07 |
|---|---|---|---|
| Engineering goods | 3,876 | 27,406 | 1,18,337 |
| Readymade garments | 4,012 | 23,877 | 39,342 |
| Leather manufactures | 2,566 | 9110 | 13,272 |
| Marine products | 960 | 5897 | 7890 |
| Gem and jewellery | 5,240 | 34,845 | 70,524 |
| Chemicals and allied products | 2,334 | 25,860 | 80,148 |
| Software and IT allied services | — | 36,500 | 123,063 |

The other significant point in the composition of our exports is the transformation in the individual groups of products which contribute most to our exports.

In 1965/66 the top groups in the export arena were Jute(22.6%), Tea (14.2%). But in 2002-03 the top groups in export were engineering goods (16.1%),

Readymade Garments (10.3%), Gem and Jewellery (16.9%), Software and IT allied services Export (5.3%). Out of these, software and IT related products export was increasing at the rate 30% every year. But in 2006-07 engineering goods was the top export with 20.7% of our merchandising trade, with Textiles and Gem & Jewellery coming a close second at about 14%.

Another new entrant in the export arena was that of petroleum products, which amounted to around 14%. It may surprise many to know that India became an exporter of petroleum products to the extent of 14% of our merchandising exports, earning about $19.8 billion in foreign exchange in 2006-07, when all along we have been saying that India imports almost 75% of its petroleum requirements. This is because the private sector in India has established a refinery for 28 million tons, one of the biggest in the world, in the west coast of India. In the past decade very few new refineries have come up in the world, and there is a shortage of refining capacity. Hence this refinery imports crude, and exports all its refined products. This kind of export will continue as two other big refineries are under construction in India.

## DIRECTION OF EXPORT TRADE

A knowledge of the countries to which we export and the trend of their increase or decrease is important. It would indicate the direction in which our exports are growing and gives clear signals to the planners as well as to individual firms, the potential available for exports, our strengths and weaknesses and also the utilization of the resources we have for maximizing exports.

The table below shows our exports to the various regions of the world. The year 1980-81 has been taken as the base to show the trend over the past decades.

**Table 2.4**

**DIRECTION OF EXPORT TRADE**

*(in crores)*

| *Region* | *1980-81* | *1990-91* | *2006-07* |
|---|---|---|---|
| OECD Countries | 3126 | 17426 | 235,563 |
| OPEC Countries | 745 | 1831 | 93,521 |
| Eastern Europe | 1486 | 5819 | 11377 |
| ASIA & ASEAN | 1286 | 5465 | 229,509 |

OECD countries include EU, USA, Canada, Australia and Japan etc.

OPEC Countries include Iran, Iraq, Kuwait, Saudi Arabia etc.

Eastern Europe included E.Germany till 1989 and thereafter only CIS countries and Russia.

ASIA and ASEAN include East Asia, ASEAN, WANA, NE Asia including China, and South Asia

The obvious inference is that the OECD countries consisting of the major industrial economies, such as USA, Europe, Japan etc., occupied a prominent position in our export trade. It amounted to 60% of our exports in 2000-01. But as we diversified our exports to other regions as well, the exports to OECD countries in 2006-07 amounted to only 45.5% of our exports.

But one has to remember that their capacity to absorb exports are much higher than any other group of countries because of the extremely diversified nature of their economies, and also to a great extent the open nature of their export and import trade. Another factor contributing to this is also the fast development of our economy to supply goods and services required by them. The economic reforms brought about by the government in 1991 have also aided this substantially.

It is interesting to note that our exports to ASIA and ASEAN ( most of them were formerly referred to as developing countries) have increased from Rs.7,965 crores in 1990-91 to Rs.33,059 crores in 1997-1998, and 284535 by 2006-07. This is a fast growing area, since many of the developing countries have come out of the debt burden of the eighties and are fast becoming open market economies and India who is a long standing partner to them can concentrate and increase trade with them, substantially, and also with China, the fastest growing country.

The five countries which always had a lead over all other countries in our exports over the years were USA, Old USSR (now the diminished Russia), Japan, Germany & UK. The pattern of exports of these countries is shown below:

**Table 2.5**

**LEADING COUNTRIES IN INDIA'S EXPORTS**

*Rs. Crores*

| *Country* | *1980-81* | *1990-91* | *2006-07* |
|---|---|---|---|
| USA | 743 | 4,797 | 85,395 |
| UK | 395 | 2,128 | 25,101 |
| Germany | 385 | 2,549 | 18,043 |
| Japan | 596 | 3,039 | 12,728 |
| Russia | 1,226 | 5,255 | 4,110 |

These are conventional countries which are important for our exports. But of late China has become an important avenue for exports as well as for imports. Our exports to China in 2006-07 amounted to Rs. 37514 crores, almost occupying the second place after USA. Export to Hong Kong is Rs.21195 crores. Even though Hong Kong is referred to as the transit destination in that most of the exports go to mainland and other countries, the increase is considerable. We should ensure that our economic and trade cooperation with all these countries are nurtured very carefully.ortscipal Products

India's exports of principal products during this decade is given in Table 2.6 below:

**Table 2.6**

**PRINCIPAL PRODUCTS IN INDIA'S EXPORTS**

*Rs. Crores*

| *Number* | *Product* | *2001-02* | *2006-07* | *% Change* |
|---|---|---|---|---|
| *1* | *2* | *3* | *4* | *5* |
| I. | Plantations | 2814 | 3925.17 | 39.48 |
| | 1. Tea | 1719 | 1956.30 | 13.80 |
| | 2. Coffee | 1095 | 1968.87 | 79.80 |
| II. | Agriculture and allied | 18827 | 38711.16 | 105.61 |
| | 1. Cereal | | | |
| | a. Rice | 3174 | 7036.20 | 121.77 |
| | b. Wheat | 1330 | 36.15 | -97.28 |
| | c. Others | 116 | 591.12 | 409.58 |
| | d. Pulses | 369 | 764.51 | 107.18 |
| | 2. Tobacco | | | |
| | a. un-manufactured | 582 | 1252.26 | 115.16 |
| | b. manufactured | 226 | 429.77 | 90.16 |
| | 3. Spices | 1497 | 3122.88 | 108.60 |
| | 4. Nuts and seeds | 2513 | 4311.61 | 71.57 |
| | a. Cashew incl. CNSL | 1652 | 2506.09 | 51.70 |
| | b. Sesame and niger seed | 610 | 1005.44 | 64.82 |
| | c. groundnut | 251 | 800.08 | 218.75 |
| | 5. Oil Meals | 2263 | 5502.97 | 143.17 |
| | 6. Guargum meal | 403 | 1123.46 | 178.77 |
| | 7. Castor oil | 626 | 1083.92 | 73.15 |
| | 8. Shellac | 73 | 146.75 | 101.02 |
| | 9. Sugar and molasses | 1782 | 3184.73 | 78.71 |
| | 10.Processed Food | 2427 | 5448.60 | 124.49 |
| | a. Fruits and vegetables | 1191 | 2890.37 | 142.68 |
| | b. Misc.Processed Items | 724 | 2442.75 | 237.39 |
| | 11. Meat and Meat Products | 1193 | 3239.73 | 171.56 |

| | | | | |
|---|---|---|---|---|
| | 12. Floriculture Products | 127 | 380.93 | 199.94 |
| | 13. Spirits and beverages | 126 | 258.02 | 109.78 |
| III. | Marine Products | 5897 | 7889.84 | 33.79 |
| IV. | Ores and minerals | 6020 | 31824.59 | 428.64 |
| | 1. Iron ore | 2034 | 17609.59 | 765.76 |
| | 2. Mica | 56 | 76.44 | 36.50 |
| | 3. Processed Minerals | 1675 | 5772.58 | 244.63 |
| | 4. Others Ores & Minerals | 1965 | 8053.25 | 309.83 |
| | 5. Coal | 290 | 312.73 | 7.83 |
| V. | Leather manufactures | 9110 | 13272.10 | 45.68 |
| | 1. Footwear | 3002 | 5635.37 | 87.72 |
| | 2. Leather and manufacs. | 6108 | 7636.73 | 25.02 |
| VI. | Gem and Jewellery | 34845 | 70524.45 | 102.39 |
| VII. | Sports goods | 328 | 569.26 | 73.55 |
| VIII. | Chemicals and allied | 28860 | 80148.73 | 177.71 |
| | 1. Basic chemls, pharma | 17630 | 47266.61 | 168.10 |
| | 2. Plastic and Linoleum | 4709 | 14440.94 | 206.66 |
| | 3. Rubber, glass | 4695 | 15046.95 | 220.48 |
| | 4. Residual chemicals and other products | 1826 | 3394.23 | 85.88 |
| IX. | Engineering goods | 28497 | 118337.17 | 315.26 |
| X. | Electronic Goods | 5586 | 12648.81 | 126.43 |
| XI. | Project goods | 88 | 595.50 | 576.70 |
| XII. | Textiles | 46094 | 72930.45 | 58.22 |
| | 1. Readymad Garments | 23877 | 39342.90 | 64.77 |
| | 2. Cotton yarn, fabrics, made-ups etc. | 14655 | 18717.70 | 27.72 |
| | 3. Manmade textiles, made-ups etc. | 5079 | 10684.16 | 110.35 |
| | 4. Natural silk textiles | 1327 | 1933.52 | 45.70 |
| | 5. Wool & woolen manufactures | 249 | 379.28 | 52.32 |

| | | | | |
|---|---|---|---|---|
| | 6. Coil & Coir manufactureș | 295 | 707.61 | 139.86 |
| | 7. Jute manufactures | 612 | 1165.28 | 90.40 |
| XIII. | Handicrafts | 2618 | 1682.15 | -35.74 |
| XIV. | Carpets | 2433 | 4015.49 | 65.04 |
| | 1. Hand-made(exclud. Silk) | 1788 | 3891.48 | 117.64 |
| | 2. Silk carpet | 172 | 124.01 | 27.90 |
| XV. | Cotton raw including waste | 43 | 6101.84 | 140.90 |
| XVI. | Petroleum products | 10107 | 83946.45 | 730.57 |
| XVII. | Unclassified Items | 6859 | 24518.72 | 257.46 |
| | **Grand Total** | **327139** | **825316.75** | |

**P = Provisional** *** Includes Paints, Enamels & Varnish**

A detailed analysis of our export trade in various products and sectors has been given below till the year 2006-2007, and the future prospects.

However, by the third quarter of 2008, the global financial crisis gave a severe blow to the economy and trade of all countries. How this will affect future trade is too early to predict.

Let us look into some areas of exports and discern the trend.

**1. Tea**

If we look at the export of tea in the last three years for which records are available, the pattern is as follows:

| *Year* | *Value (crores)* |
|---|---|
| 1999-2000 | 1785 |
| 2000-2001 | 1976 |
| 2001-2002 | 1719 |
| 2005-2006 | 1730 |
| 2006-2007 | 1956 |

The exports are practically static.

India is the largest producer as well as consumer of tea in the world. There are distinctly different tea growing areas in India. Assam is the largest tea producer, amounting to 50%, with West Bengal next at 24%, and the southern states, including Tamil Nadu producing 17%.

The total production of tea in India is around 940 million kg, out of which around 200 million kg is exported. The domestic demand is also good for tea and the average per capita consumption is 700 gms a year.

Russia was one of the largest importers of Indian tea of around 40 million kg, followed by UK, UAE, Iran and Iraq. Iraq used to be a good market for Indian tea earlier, absorbing 20% of our exports, but this has suffered due to the disturbing conditions in the country.

Indian exporters have to quickly adapt to the fast changing preferences in the consuming nations, if they have to keep the global profile. For example, in Russia, the increasing prosperity has raised the demand for the more expensive orthodox tea. Realising this, India is planning to produce 120 million kg. of orthodox tea, mostly in South India in the coming year.

On the other hand, tea is allowed to be imported into India, especially from Sri Lanka. Even though initially it was feared that it might dilute and affect the Indian tea industry, it has not done so, as the quantum imported every year from 2001 is around 15 to 20 million kg only.

The tea gardens in many areas suffered due to low yield, in view of the fact that they were old and were in urgent need of re-plantation and rejuvenation. The government has launched a 'Special purpose Tea Fund' to help the plantations to restructure themselves and go in for re-plantation, to increase the yield.

The major tea producing countries met in China in 2008 and agreed on the constitution of 'International Tea Producers Forum' (ITPF). The focus of ITPF will be on the common issues facing these countries - such as development of e-auction system for tea, generic promotion,, R & D, market research, collection of data and sharing of information. The ten countries comprising ITPF include India, Sri Lanka, Kenya, Mauritius, Indonesia, Bangladesh, Nepal, Malawi, Tanzania and Zimbabwe. The Chairman of Tea Board of Kenya will be the Chairman of ITPF. China, although a major producer of tea, has preferred to remain outside the Forum. It is felt that China the only green tea producing country may not have many things in common with the other members of the group, all producing black tea.

We should not forget that the tea industry gives direct employment to a million people, and indirectly to two million people. Employment of three million people is indeed very important, and even the much hyped IT industry does not employ that many people!

### 2. Coffee

The export of coffee in the recent past is given below:

**Table 2.7**

**EXPORT OF COFFEE**

| *Year* | *2001-02* | *2005-06* | *2006-07* |
|---|---|---|---|
| Quantity (Tons) | 176,300 | 177,000 | 213,600 |
| Value in Cr | 1095 | 1599 | 1969 |

Indian coffee has created a niche for itself in the International Market, particularly Indian 'Robusta' which is highly preferred for its good blending quality

India is perhaps the only coffee producing country, whose coffees are fully shade grown, entirely hand-picked, and completely sun dried.

In India, coffee plantations occupy an area of 3,00,000 hectares, providing rural employment, predominantly in Karnataka, Kerala, and Tamil Nadu. These three states contribute 99% of the total coffee produced in the country.

Of the total production of 3,00,000 tons, 33% is 'Arabica' and 66% 'Robusta'. About 75% of the total coffee produced in the country is exported to over 88 countries. The important markets are Russia, Italy, Germany, Belgium and Spain.

In the world market India contributes around 4%. The big exporters are Brazil, which holds 40% of the market, followed by Columbia. One of the recent entrants is Vietnam. The world coffee fraternity feels that Vietnam, which has increased its production substantially for a country of its size, is responsible for the flood of cheaper coffee of lower quality, and has reduced the realization of world coffee growers.

Indian coffee, essential in the international blends, is expected to deliver 'Arabica' around February, and 'Robusta' in April. The international buyers finalise contracts for these supplies in October of the previous year, and if there are any doubts regarding the quality or ability to supply, they can promptly shift to other suppliers.

By monitoring and catering to the taste of the world community, and increasing the production of coffee, we have a good chance of increasing coffee exports substantially.

**3. Textiles**

This is one of the fastest growing sectors and has tremendous significance in the context of India's efforts to substantially increase exports. The total exports have increased in the last decade.

The total exports in the Textile field were Rs. 72930 crores in 2006-07. The fastest growing sectors of Textiles are 'Readymade Garments', and 'Cotton Yarn, fabrics, made-ups etc' Let us see how they have fared:

**Table 2.8**

**EXPORT OF TEXTILE GOODS**

*(Rs. Crores)*

| *Product* | *1995-96* | *2001-02* | *2006-07* |
|---|---|---|---|
| Readymade Garments | 12295 | 23877 | 39343 |
| Cotton yarn, Fabric, Made-ups Etc. | 8619 | 14655 | 18718 |

However, international trade in textiles and clothing has been regulated since 1974 under the aegis of Multi Fibre Arrangement (MFA). An important provision of MFA is the regulation of export through bilateral textile pacts between the exporting and importing countries. These agreements set down the quantitative level of exports of each country every year. These are referred to as 'quotas'. These have restricted our exports considerably in the past.

After the formation of WTO in 1995, one of the benefits has been the decision to dismantle the MFA at the end of a ten year transition phase. This came about in January 2005, and thereafter, our textile exports in these restricted areas have increased substantially.

However the industry has to prepare itself comprehensively. In international trade where each country tries to get the best benefit in such a free trade situation, the industry should prepare for a larger volume of production, especially in the garment sector. With the dismantling of the MFA and the quota system, the rules of doing business in garment export have changed rapidly from the vanishing quotas and other drawbacks, to increased competition from other countries like China.

Garment exports is an area of tremendous potential, where India has proven experience, and has infinite opportunities. As you will see above, exports after 2005 have increased considerably. In 2006-07 our export was Rs. 39343 crores as against Rs.23877 crores in 2001-02.

India prepared reasonably well to increase the exports substantially, but the appreciation of the Indian rupee against the US Dollar in 2007 was a serious setback, as many of the exporters could not absorb the appreciation of the rupee by 14%, as they had to supply goods at the earlier contracted rate. It will take some time to regain the old momentum. By the time the rupee depreciated and the exports revived, the financial crisis abroad and the power cuts in many states is seriously affecting exports.

It is the garment sector which calls for our immediate action. The key to change is the complete revamp of the entire operation by removing all inefficiencies, eliminating the weak areas in the manufacturing process, and enhancing productivity by efficient material management, as also better and close interaction with the buyers, and flexibility in the manufacturing systems. Modernization of the industry, especially the cutting room, with the deployment of full featured CAD system, with automatic cut and spread systems etc. will all go a long way and infuse more confidence in the buyers.

There is always a dearth of trained personnel in the industry. It is worthwhile to note that 15 years ago China enacted a legislation according to which any entrepreneur putting up a garment factory should earmark 5% of the turnover for training which would be tax free. As a result, now they have a wealth of trained manpower, and it is no wonder that China accounts for 20% of world trade in garments, whereas we are way down in the scale.

Apart from these there are external factors such as 'social norms' imposed by western countries. For example, Germany which insists on the supplier paying minimum wages to the labour, elimination of child labour, safety, and clean and healthy working conditions etc. In addition, the usual protectionist measures such as anti-dumping may also be taken by some countries.

Indian exporters who have faced much more restrictions during the quota system prevailing earlier, are capable of planning and overcoming all the obstacles and increasing their exports. It is possible and can be done.

The prospect of increasing the export of garments is very good indeed and as stated earlier, India has the raw material, and necessary manpower and should go all out.

The production capacity in India is low and it has to be increased substantially. Knowing India's potential and capabilities, a large number of western buyers are already approaching India. In the reports published in the press, Wal-Mart and Target, the leading garment importers are already in the field . Apart from that, Russel Corporation, and Sears Roebuck are also in the field for finalizing additional as well as new orders for supply, every year.

Another interesting development is that many of these importers are also planning to have joint ventures with Indian manufacturers. The entire effort of most of them seems to be to generate large quantities of supplies needed by them. For example, it is reported that J C Penny, one of the large importers in USA is in need of $700-$800 million worth of garments on a long-term basis.

These efforts are also reinforced by the fact that these large importers have always had buying offices in India.

Even though China is capable of meeting the demand, it is evident that the American buyers whose needs are very large, do not want to put "all their eggs in one basket" as the saying goes.

The Indian government should form a working group immediately to look into the needs of the garment exporters by way of finance, factories, infrastructure needs, port/air facilities etc. to dispatch large consignments and help the industry to overcome the various drawbacks, at this crucial juncture when new doors have been opened to us. If this is done in an organized manner, the industry will be able to increase its exports fivefold in the shortest possible time.

A road map is given above for the future, but the global financial crisis in late 2008 is a serious setback and we should see how soon the buying countries come out of it and resume their trade.

**4. Cashew**

The export of cashew kernels and cashew nut shell liquid amounted to Rs.2506 crores in the year 2006-07 as against Rs.1,883 crores in 2000-01

One of the important factors in the development of exports of this product is the fact that we have to import the raw nuts from East Africa. Further, those countries have also set up their own processing units.

Based on the needs of the importing countries, Government has a financial assistance scheme for exporters to improve cashew kernel quality and packaging to an internationally accepted certificate scheme. This has helped our exports of cashew. The composition of our exports are 40% to USA, 35% to EU, 16$ to West Asia and 6$ to East Asia.

**5. Tobacco**

The exports of tobacco and tobacco products in the year 2006-07 amounted to Rs.1685 crores, as against Rs.871 crores in the year 2000-01.

In India about 6 million farmers and farm hands are engaged in the cultivation of tobacco and the industry, directly or indirectly. In order to regulate the production of tobacco so as to reduce imbalances of supply and demand and to promote exports of tobacco, government set up the Tobacco Board in 1976. The Board also helps in the curing and marketing of Virginia Tobacco to achieve the objective of ensuring remunerative returns for tobacco growers.

In view of the sustained and successful campaign against smoking, and other forms of tobacco use, on health grounds, one cannot hope for a great future for this product, unless some new and productive uses are found.

**6. Carpets**

This is a very interesting sector of our exports. Indian exports of carpets consist of handmade and hand-knotted, mill made and silk carpets. Handmade carpets contribute 90% of the total carpet exports which amounted to Rs.3891 crores in 2006-07. One of the important reasons for this development is that Iran, the traditional supplier of carpets has not been able to fulfil the world demand.

Most of India's production comes from the Bhadoi-Mirzapur belt in U.P from units situated in an area of 40 sq.km. The industry is unorganized, and most of the looms are operated by artisans in their homes.

By 1983, India emerged as the largest exporter of hand-knotted carpets. With Iran disappearing from the market, India, China, and Turkey have become the main suppliers in the international market. Now is the opportune time to take the necessary steps to organize and strengthen this industry as the demand is continuously on the increase. The profitability of the industry is very high and about 95% of the entire production is exported. Further, this industry is heavily labour-oriented and dispersed in the rural sector.

### 7. Engineering Exports:

Engineering goods export forms an important and major component of our exports. It was of the order of Rs.38,093 crores in 2002-03, and has increased to Rs.118,337 crores in 2006-07., more than trebling in this period.

**Table 2.9**

**ENGINEERING GOODS EXPORTS**

*(Rs.Crores)*

| 2002-03 | 2006-07 | % change |
|---|---|---|
| 38,093 | 1,18,337 | 38.5 |

The author of this book who was the former Chairman of Engineering Export Promotion Council of India , has been of the strong conviction that if we modernize and restructure our manufacturing industries, it will enable us to become competitive, high quality suppliers and the sourcing hub for the world. This would become the engine of our export growth. It has taken almost two decades for us to start our journey in this direction.

In the eighties and nineties USA and Europe declined in the manufacturing sector due to high overheads and labour costs, and many of the industries tried to shift manufacturing to developing countries. China got the lion's share in view of the very low labour costs and good infrastructure provided by the government.

It was felt in India also that with the WTO prodding the government to reduce the tariff, China would flood our country with their products, and Indian manufacturers would not be able to meet the competition. But this view did not reckon with the capabilities of Indian entrepreneurs and industry. Recession and low industrial growth in the late nineties gave a severe jolt to Indian industry, and set them thinking about their future prospects. Their analysis of the industry revealed that in many areas, their capacities were sub-optimal and that they had managed with substandard machinery, due to severe import restrictions. Operating under these circumstances, and still trying to meet domestic demands and exports, they had unconsciously developed a strong and resilient middle management cadre capable of handling the most complex tasks with the existing facilities. They developed a unique mechanical skill pool capable of getting the best out of the existing machinery, and at the same time, were also resourceful enough to use the most modern machinery to produce world class products. It is this class of skilled workforce that is helping the country now in exports.

The industry also realized that with import duties coming down rapidly, they are today manufacturing for a world market and not to a protected Indian market. The result was that from basic industries to sophisticated ones, everyone concentrated on quality and cost; and various steps were taken to improve them. For example, Tata Iron and Steel Co. in Jamshedpur is among the cheapest producers of steel in the world. This has come about due to the continuous and relentless efforts put in by the management to improve the operating efficiency by reducing energy consumption, raw material consumption, and refracting consumption,- the three important elements in steel production, as well as with full capacity utilization of the plant with optimum labour.

Thus, manufacturing has carved its rightful place in India today, and it is estimated that the exports of manufactured items have grown by 16% in the last decade. The fact that manufacturing in India is rapidly achieving international standards is borne out by the following :

*(I)* Substantial increase in the export of engineering goods.

*(II)* India being used as a sourcing hub by many international industries

*(III)* Recognition of Indian design capabilities in engineering faculties as well as in IT industries.

(I) As for the export of manufactured products, the classic examples are that of automobile and automobile ancillaries.

In the export of **automobiles,** our exports have been as follows over a period of four years.

**Table 2.10**

**VEHICLE EXPORTS**

| *Product* | *1999-2000* | *2002-03* | *2007-08* |
|---|---|---|---|
| Two wheelers | 83237 | 179568 | 819847 |
| Three wheelers | 17725 | 43443 | 141235 |
| Commercial vehicles | 9912 | 10704 | 58999 |
| Cars and utility veh. | 28420 | 71653 | 215910 |
| TOTAL | 139,294 | 305,368 | 1,235,991. |

The increase in the exports of cars are very significant indeed. A car, in many countries is a symbol of sophistication, and the buyers are proud of their new cars which they have acquired after a great deal of enquiry and study. To penetrate such markets is a very commendable achievement. In 2002-03, the export of Indian cars was 71653 units, whereas in 2007-08 it was of the order of 215910, and had more than trebled. The Korean major, Hyundai has already set up its Indian plant as an exclusive source for some of its models. From an export of just 20 cars in 1999, its exports were 144,439 units in 2007-08.

The exports of all categories of automobiles have increased appreciably. In commercial vehicles, the total export was of the order of 58999 vehicles in 2007-08, as against 49537 vehicles in 2006-07, an increase of about 20%. In 2007-08 Tata Motors were the highest exporters of Commercial Vehicles clocking an export of 39,462 vehicles. Further, Tata Motors has acquired Daewoo Motors Commercial Vehicle Unit in South Korea which will make it a leading contender for higher payload commercial vehicles in the 200HP – 400HP category in the global market. There are reports that Tata Motors are already working on a new range of trucks in India which will be competitive, have fuel efficiency, and latest emission standards and be suitable to many markets, with a range of payload capacity from 9 tons to 49 tons. Tatas estimate that the export sales of commercial vehicles will contribute a quarter of their commercial vehicle business by the year 2010/2012.

Another notable development in the Automobile field is the announcement by Tata Motors in early 2008 that they will produce their small car 'Tata Nano' and initially sell it at a price of $2500. This is a great revelation to the entire automotive industry of the world that s modern car can be produced with latest emission standards in India and sold at that price.

The exports of automobile ancillaries is a still more striking example of how Indian manufacturing industries in this sector have repositioned themselves as suppliers of high quality auto components at competitive prices and other delivery parameters expected of international suppliers. This is remarkable indeed!

The entire automobile ancillary industry was supplying mostly to the needs of Indian automobile manufacturers. When the domestic industry went into recession in sectors where they supplied, the ancillary industry faced serious problems. They also realized that with the import duties decreasing due to WTO guidelines, the country would be swamped by foreign ancillary producers who were waiting for an entry into the Indian market.

From the middle of the nineties, more and more International Automobile majors set up their assembly/production facilities in India, and tried to procure components locally. The turning point came when the ancillary manufacturers embarked upon a journey to decrease costs, improve quality and competitiveness. Having made a good beginning in meeting the demands of the multinationals in India, they were ready for the big league of international buyers and also attracted the global auto majors who are always looking for new suppliers meeting their quality and prices.

The potential in the international market for auto ancillaries is enormous. It is estimated to be very much more than a hundred times that of the Indian market which is Rs.20,000 crores per annum.

As per the Automobile Component Manufacturers' Association, the export of auto components in the last few years is as follows:

**Table 2.11**

**EXPORT OF AUTO COMPONENTS**

| *Year* | *Value* |
|---|---|
| 2001-02 | $ 578 million |
| 2002-03 | $ 800 million |
| 2007-08 | $ 3000 million (P) |

All the above developments till the middle of 2008, has to be tempered with the global financial crisis which is shaking the foundations of auto majors all over the world. It will take quite some time for the industry to get its equilibrium, and when it does India is bound to play a very significant role, as envisaged above.

(I) The other areas of engineering capabilities of India which have attracted the attention of the world majors, and which will considerably enhance the exports are the following:

India is being made the **hub of outsourcing** for finished products and components by many international organizations. This is of great importance to India not only from the point of view of increasing exports substantially, but also due to the fact that the international majors feel that India would be a dependable source to get quality and price wise competitive production on a long term basis. In shifting the source of manufacture, industries will always look for dependable supplies, capacity to redesign a product at a short time-frame, and be competitive over a reasonably long period of time. This is because there is bound to be considerable investment in various areas of quality and high volume products.

(a) Hyundai and Suzuki are endeavouring to make India the hub of specific small car production. Ford also exports from India. Similarly, many in the automobile component field in India have also become outsourcing centers. Mercedes Benz has firmed up 25 auto component and ancillary manufacturers to supply products directly to them globally. Another such unit is Toyota Kirloskar Auto Parts Pvt. Ltd. which has been chosen to make the entire Manual Transmission System(Type R 150) for a new platform of the auto giant called Innovative Multipurpose Vehicle(IMV). They will be acting as a global source for IMV Transmission, making and supplying to seven vehicle assembly plants around the world. The Indian unit won the project against close competition from Thailand and Philippines. Delphi, the biggest automotive component company in the world has concluded an outsourcing deal worth $140 million from Indian automotive manufacturers. These consist of products like forged engine parts, machined castings, intricate plastic mouldings and value added ancillary products.

The fact that Indian manufacturing is well recognized is evident from the outsourcing not only in the automobile sector but also in other sectors.

(a) NEG Micon(India) Ltd., a wholly owned subsidiary of NEG Micon(Denmark) is planning to become a global hub for export of wind energy turbines with a capacity of up to 1.65 MW. Suzlon, another international supplier in the field is also making India its base.

(b) Deutz of Germany announced that they have signed an agreement with Rane Engine Valves of Chennai for the supply of engine valves valued at 2 million Euros. This will ultimately result in Rane emerging as a single supplier of engine valves, when values will increase substantially.

(c) Samsonite, the luggage maker has decided to make India one of the key global sourcing hubs for luggage and travel footwear. After Belgium, India is the second largest sourcing hub for luggage for the $ 1.3 billion company.

**(II) Research and Development Centres**

Many international companies are convinced of India's capacity to manufacture quality products at competitive prices. They have also discovered that India possesses very good skilled technical personnel who can design and introduce new innovations in manufacturing. Many companies are now establishing their own Research and Development Centres to exploit the high technical potential of the country. This will lead to India becoming a center for design capabilities as well, apart from being a base for manufacturing.

General Motors Corporation, the world's largest car manufacturer has set up an R & D Lab in Bangalore. It is the first such center for GM outside its headquarters in Michigan, USA. The Centre will focus on software and control systems, with the increasing use of electro-mechanical parts in automobiles. They will work on design testing, modeling and simulation. Already they have spent $21 million on the building and infrastructure.

Suzuki Motors Corporation has decided to make India a base for research and development of new models of cars for the Asian market. This will be the second R&D Centre in Asia, and the first outside Japan.

Asia Brown Boveri (ABB) the German-Swedish power giant has already established an R&D Centre in Bangalore. It is establishing another Global Technology Centre in Nashik for power technologies especially in engineering design and development of medium voltage outdoor products. The reason for choosing India is to leverage the high level of technical expertise, competence and experience available here.

The above are some examples of how India is embarking on a higher level on the value chain. India's edge over China in manufacturing is not only in creating low cost products, but in engineering design which will be the driving force in outsourcing manufacture. Many Indian companies that are successfully getting export orders in manufacturing over low cost countries like China are doing so because of the engineering design capabilities. International customers want their suppliers to not only supply cheaper parts, but also create the best possible designs. The part manufacturer has more expertise in the design of his parts, and international buyers are happy to outsource not only the product but its design as well, and it helps them to freeze the cost of the product. Such moves also cut down the time taken in testing and checking prototypes.

Many design and consultancy organizations abroad are establishing their subsidiaries in India. A typical example is Invensys, a global leader in Production Technology Solutions which has set up an Indian Development Centre in Hyderabad. It is going to be the biggest center outside the USA, even though they have branches in all continents. They have established the center in India as they found very good design engineers and technically skilled personnel. They will be adding 400 more technical personnel to their center in the next year, and the investment will be in the order of $25 million.

All the above go to show that 'manufacturing' has woken up in India, and are rising to their full capabilities. If the government helps by its policies of improving infrastructure and also reduces transaction costs, and gets rid of 'red tape' at all levels, India in the new century can hope to be the world supplier and source for many of the manufacturing products. Then engineering exports can increase by leaps and bounds and be the real engine of export growth

**8. Marine Products Export**

India's exports of marine products was of the order of 387830 tonnes, amounting to Rs.4,313 crores in 1997-98 and increased to Rs. 7890 crores by 2006-07.

The trends in the exports are significant as borne out by the Table 2.12 below:

**Table 2.12**

**EXPORT OF MARINE PRODUCTS**

| *Year* | *Value (Rs. Crores)* |
|---|---|
| 1997-1998 | 4313 |
| 2001-2002 | 5897 |
| 2002-2003 | 6790 |
| 2006-2007 | 7890 |

The Indian marine products industry exports a wide range and variety of fish, including shrimp, mackerel, tuna, squids, cattle-fish, sardines, dried fish and lobster tails. Shrimp has been the mainstay of our exports, and amounts to 60% of our total exports.

The major export countries for the marine products are, European Union amounting to 33%, USA and Japan amounting to 16% each, China amounting to 14%, Middle East 5%, and South East Asia 7%.

One significant feature is the increase of aquaculture and their fast growth in export. However, there have been some complaints from the environmentalists. They claim that

(1) the industry some times takes away even fertile land, affecting food grain cultivation, and (2) that the pollution and after-effects of such intensive aquaculture affects the surrounding lands considerably.

The export of shrimp from India consists of the 'wild caught', as well as the above 'farm raised'. The share of the 'land farm bases' shrimps in the total exports of shrimps is approximately 33% and this figure is rising.

Aquaculture is attractive to marine exporters, and new entrepreneurs are entering the field for the following reasons:

(a) Shrimps are high value, high volume items readily traded in the export markets.

(b) The demand is steadily growing, and the profits are good.

(c) They have a short growing period (120-135 days) and it is possible to take 'two crops' a year.

(d) It has excellent low-feed conversion ratio of 1.5:1. In other words 1.5 units of feed is required to produce 1 unit of shrimp as compared to 4:1 for fishes and still higher ratios for other farm species.

(e) India has vast tracts of land for aquaculture.(one estimate puts it as 1.2 million hectares suited for brackish water aquaculture of which only 77000 hectares is under use)

(f) India has a suitable climate and also abundant labour required for this endeavour.

In spite of all these advantages, the growth of aquaculture has been only in two states - Andhra Pradesh and Tamil Nadu. Even though West Bengal and Gujarat have the largest brackish water area available in the country, aquaculture has not been significant, but is bound to improve as it is manpower intensive.

The expansion in Andhra Pradesh is very fast. They have brought coastal lands, previously barren, under cultivation.

But in its exports there are quite a few problems. USA imports 80% of its shrimp consumption. An anti-dumping petition has been filed by the US Southern Shrimp Alliance against the Indian exporters. The Alliance consists of shrimp sellers and processors from eight US states including North Carolina. They claim that US shrimp harvest dropped by more than half, resulting in 40% unemployment in the shrimp factories of southern US.

The case is that the US industry mostly harvests its products from the sea, as against the farmers in China, India, Brazil, Vietnam and Thailand who raise shrimps in ponds.

The Marine Products Export Development Authority (MPEDA) established by the government has taken many steps to increase exports. Some of these are:

(1) With a view to developing Marine finfish farming through cage culture in the country, an MOU has been entered into with Norway to get technical assistance. Earlier, a technical feasibility of this method was established by the Rajiv Gandhi Centre for Aquaculture.

(2) MPEDA has entered into a MOU with the Swiss Import Promotion Programme to promote Organic Aquaculture in India.

(3) MPEDA Labs at Kochi, Nellore, and Bhimavaram obtained certification under ISO 9001 : 2000 and accreditation by NABL (National Accreditation Board for Testing and Calibration Laboratories) under ISO: 17025:2005. By this recognition the test results of the laboratories will be accepted by the importing countries without further verification

(4) The present exploration of Tuna Fish is negligible; commercially important species of Tuna are generally found in the deep sea level between 100 and 500 metres depth. To exploit such Tuna resources, MOEDA is implementing a subsidy assistance scheme for modifying existing fishing vessels to Tuna long liners. Recently 22 trawlers which had undergone conversion to Tuna long liners were launched from Vishakhapatnam. In this connection a Tuna expert has been hired from Australia to impart training on conversion of the vessels, fishing, on board handling and processing. As tuna is the third largest globally traded fish item behind shrimps and cephalopods, it is expected to create major waves in the marine industry.

(5) Another important problem in marine products exports is that the shrimp market mainly consisting of Mondon species( such as Black tiger) is gradually declining. In 2007 exports to US were around 2000 tons as against the 27000 tons earlier. One of the important reasons for this decline is the advent of a new shrimp variety 'Vannamei' This variety today accounts for 90%

of the global shrimp aquaculture. Vannamei grows to full size in 60-90 days whereas the average period for the full growth of Black Tiger is 90-120 days. One important reason why this species has not come to India is the fear of the various government departments, of the possibility that it may bring some 'new virus' which may affect the existing crop. The brood stock (brought for breeding) should be 'specific pathogen free' (SPF) and should come from known and reputed sources. The Hawaiian Shrimp Institute, Honolulu is acknowledged worldwide as a reliable supplier of SPF brood stock. Government has given a green signal to two pilot projects in Andhra Pradesh, which are doing well. It is hoped that this breed when it comes to full production will augment our main exports substantially.

## Future

A vision document to step up the country's marine product exports from $ 1.7 billion to $ 4 billion in five years and ensuring additional employment of one million people was unveiled by the government recently. The five planks of the vision document are,-

1. product diversification,
2. focus on potential brackish water aquaculture in Maharashtra, Gujarat, and Orissa.
3. a substantial increase in value addition of marine product exports from 15% to 75%,
4. making India a major hub for outsourcing and reprocessing of marine products and
5. creating a bio-security zone here.

## Aquaculture

A serious effort has to be made by the government immediately to find a fair solution to the various issues raised. We should have an impartial Experts Committee who should draw fair guidelines addressing the reasonable environmental concerns, and also the constraints for the industry, to enable the industry to grow in a healthy manner. Thereafter both legislation and voluntary action would be needed to guide the industry on healthy lines. This is a labour oriented industry and has employment potential which India can ill-afford to ignore.

Doing the above will lead to:

(1) Identifying suitable lands for aquaculture, and their clear demarcation in all states.

(2) A clear policy on the allotment of government lands for aquaculture on a fair basis, with clear guidelines. There should also be constraints on the aqua farms, in not locating them near habituated villages, not locating them near any drinking water sources, or near areas where natural drains exist. There should be permission from designated local authorities for setting up aqua farms.

(3) Making water treatment facilities compulsory, so that water pollution is considerably reduced from settling tanks for effluents from aqua farms - removing many suspended impurities and organic components.

(4) Making independent Environmental Impact Assessment Studies mandatory for farms exceeding certain size, and suitable legislation to this effect.

(5) Increasing manpower training courses, and also evolving suitable syllabus in the university/school curricula to make the study optional.

(6) Setting up Brood stock banks - with the number of hatcheries increasing. The demand for parent stock shrimps will increase and there will be need to set up region wise brood stock banks for ready availability of quality stock of hatcheries.

Developments like these are welcome but a quick legislation, and guidelines from government is an immediate necessity.

### 9. Gem and Jewellery

**Table 2.13**

**INDIA'S EXPORTS OF GEM AND JEWELLERY**

| *Year* | *Value (Rs.Crores)* |
|---|---|
| 1997-1998 | 19014 |
| 2001-2002 | 34845 |
| 2002-2003 | 40558 |
| 2006-2007 | 70524 |

India used to dominate the glittering galaxy of cut and polished diamonds. About 85% of the world diamond market in terms of caratage, 60% in value terms and about 90% in terms of pieces or numbers, came from India. The 'roughs' are imported from diamond producing countries, cut and polished in India and exported.

India's Gem and Jewellery exports grew 22.7% to touch $21 billion (Rs.95000crores) in 2007-08. Since India imports key raw materials such as gold and diamond, the exports in this sector are highly import-intensive. In 2007-08, the industry imported $18.5 billion worth of raw materials. The value addition is $2.5 billion. Apart from this the domestic market of jewellery also sustains the livelihood of approximately three million people involved in this trade.

According to the Gem & Jewellery Export Promotion Council(GJEPC), India has ten percent of the world market and has a huge potential to export more. Towards this end the GJEPC has taken steps to develop India as a trading hub. Today Israel and Hong Kong are leading trade centres in the world. Another promotional activity is to build "India Brand' in the world market. A 'trend cell' has been created to keep a close watch on the international market and forecast the trends. The council is also working with the National Institute of Designs and National Institute of Fashion Technology, for enhancing the design capabilities of the Indian artisans.

Another development has been the withdrawal of GSP tariff benefit enjoyed by India in USA. Hence the duty free import of jewellery has been removed and a duty of 6.5% has been imposed, the same as the duty imposed on jewellery from any other source. According to GJEPC Indian jewellery amounted to 33% of jewellery imports in the US. The exporters feel that the duty would not seriously affect our exports. As an experienced exporter remarked " It all boils down to the product itself – the quality and design "

In the exports in this sector, diamonds dominate over all other products. India imports, as is referred to in the industry, 'diamond roughs'. These are cut and polished in India. Even here, India specializes in what is referred to as single and double cuts. In terms of carat-weights processed, and the number of pieces worked, the industry has come to occupy the first rank in the world. We specialize in this area. The industry estimates that there are 25000 diamond cutting and polishing units in India. Half of the cutting activity is concentrated in and around Navasari and Surat in Gujarat. The other traditional centers where this industry is concentrated are Palanpur, Bhavnagar and Mumbai.

World trade in cut and polished diamonds is estimated to be $35 billion. In view of the fact that the segment of the market held by India is of low value, India's share in world trade is not high. Our major markets are USA, Belgium, Japan and Hong Kong. These four markets together account for 80% of our exports.

We have to keep our lead in the 'smalls' segment of diamond export, increase the export of gold jewellery as India has excellent artisans and designers, and also get into the area of bigger diamond processing. This employment-intensive sector has very good prospects as long as glamour and glitter rule the world.

### 10. Leather and Leather Manufactures

Around one-third of leather and leather manufacture exports is accounted for by footwear. Most of the leather products are exported to developed countries such as Germany, USA, UK, France, Italy and Japan. Export of this sector has undergone a structural transformation with value added products contributing around 80% of exports. Leather garments, leather footwear and leather goods constitute major items of exports.

**Table 2.14**

**EXPORTS OF LEATHER AND LEATHER MANUFACTURE**

| *Year* | *Exports in Crores* |
|---|---|
| 1999-2000 | 6952 |
| 2001-2002 | 9212 |
| 2006-2007 | 13272 |

India accounts for a share of 2.5% in the global leather trade. In leather footwear, India's export is hardly 1.41% of the global leather footwear import. There is enormous scope for furthering our export in this sector. This is very evident if we compare India with China's progress in the field. China's exports were $1 billion; double that of India in the late eighties. But by the year 2000, China's exports had surged to $12 billion, whereas India's exports were hardly $2 billion.

The main reasons for China's galloping exports are:

(a) world class infrastructure

(b) substantial foreign investment

(c) a disciplined workforce at competitive wage levels.

In the Greenfield Special Economic Zones(SEZ) established at six different locations in China, a host of leather related industries are flourishing. They get water and power at competitive rates, excellent communication facilities and well developed infrastructure. Further, the FDI is actively encouraged in export oriented industries such as leather and 57% of the total exports are from FDI related industries.

Apart from local raw materials available, China imports raw materials to sustain its spectacular export growth in this sector. China's exports meet about 20% of global import of leather and leather products.

India can compete with China in production systems but in labour productivity there is scope for improvement. India can match China in prices and has advantages in the banking system and English language familiarity. But what it lacks is the enormous capacity available in China in various product segments, which are being expanded further. China's capacity to get large orders and execute them with timely delivery and quality consistency is propelling them fast in their export growth.

If the government helps the Indian leather industry at least three of its important clusters namely Kanpur and Agra in Uttar Pradesh, Jalandhar in Punjab, Ranipet-Ambur Vaniambadi belt in Tamil Nadu, with excellent infrastructure facilities, then India can look forward to a very bright future. It could increase the exports in this sector three fold in the next three to four years.

The industry welcomes foreign direct investment for capacity expansion in Tamil Nadu.

During 2001-02, the exports of leather and leather manufactures amounted to Rs.9212.2 crores. And in 2006-07, the exports were Rs.13272 crores, registering an increase of 44%.

## EXPORT OF SERVICES

Export of Services is growing in importance globally. India's revenue from services which was around $20.9 billion in 2001-02, has increased to $ 76.3 billion in 2006-07.

The prominent services are Banking, Insurance, Telecom, Consultancy services, Travel, Tourism, IT and allied services, and BPO. Out of these, growth has been particularly rapid in software services, business services, financial services and communication services, which was the order of 70% in 2004-05, 37.5% in 2005-06 and 36.7% in 2006-07.

**1. Tourism**

Tourism occupies a very important place in the economies of several countries. Some claim it to be the world's largest industry. It is estimated that the world's earnings in tourism in the year 2005 was $787.3 billion, and India's earnings from tourism is estimated to be hardly 0.73% of this amount. It gives us an idea of the tremendous scope India has in increasing its earnings from tourism.

A study conducted by the Confederation Of Indian Industries says that by the year 2020 India could get 40 million tourists if the necessary spadework is done in getting our act together by increasing hotel capacity, roads and transport facilities up to international standards, and have well educated and trained guides. It also states that the industry could employ 50 million people. In addition, we should ensure international standards of hygiene in all the locations and also health facilities of high quality.

India's record in tourism in the recent past is as follows:

**Table 2.15**

| Year | *Tourists* | *Foreign Exchange Earned US billion $* |
|---|---|---|
| 1999 | 2.48 million | 3,036 |
| 2001 | 2.54 million | 3,042 |
| 2002 | 2.38 million | 2,923 |
| 2003 | 2.75 million | 3,603 |
| 2005 | 3.91 million | 5.730 |

India, as stated earlier, gets less than 1% of the total tourist arrivals in the world.

Among the developed countries, the world's number one earner from tourism is the United States which earns more than $75 billion, practically 50% of the annual merchandise exports of India. Among the top foreign exchange earners in this sector are Italy, Spain, France and U.K. Among the developing countries those who figure are Thailand, Philippines, Malaysia, Kenya Sri Lanka and India.

India has a long way to go in developing tourism as a foreign exchange earner and generator of employment. The lack of infrastructure and a peculiar mindset in India hampers the increase in tourism.

(1) There is an unknown fear lurking in many people in India that once we develop tourism in the country, it will affect our cultural heritage, and will have an adverse effect on the younger generation.

But if we develop tourism on the right lines, this will not happen. On the other hand we can expose all the good aspects of our culture and traditions to tourists, so that many of them carry some of its messages with them.

(2) It is essential that the tourist accommodation be increased suitably. In India this is usually taken as the accommodation in five star hotels. Of course their increase also should be nurtured, but more important is the development of comfortable cheaper accommodation, with the main accent on cleanliness of a high order, and availability of hygienically prepared food.

(3) The internal travel of tourists is of paramount importance. Well equipped comfortable buses, taxis and other means of transport at predetermined and reasonable prices are equally important for the present day tourists.

Of late a major portion of tourists the world over, are of the younger generation who want to travel and see different countries and observe the culture and traditions firsthand.

(4) A determined effort is required on the part of the government, of training tourist guides whose knowledge of our history and traditions should be authentic. Apart from English, they should be conversant in other foreign languages also. One can take a leaf out of Egypt's record on this score, where tourist guides have to study at special institutions, pass examinations and be multilingual and have a permit to become tourist guides, and it is a pleasure to hear them narrate the history, and also answer all queries and give clarifications, patiently and convincingly.

(5) The last and most important aspect lies with the government in developing the infra-structural needs such as an excellent network of road, rail and air transport.

The primary health care of people, and competent and adequate health facilities for the visitor, have a great impact on the tourists. Keeping the city clean, and the effective removal of all garbage lying on the roadside can no longer be ignored as mere stale statistics to be shown in municipal reports. Active policies should be pursued by elected governments and local bodies with zeal and enthusiasm and should reflect in the cleanliness and disease-free cities and towns. They have as great an impact on tourism export earnings as any other export policy.

## 2. Software, IT and IT Enabled Services

One of the fastest growing divisions of the Information Technology field is Computer Software, and allied services. India entered the field in the eighties, but the regulatory framework imposed by the government in the imports and exports of the hardware and software had an adverse impact on the growth of the industry. Since big strides were being made in these sectors in the west, India's contribution was not much at all, in spite of proven abilities in the field.

It will be interesting to record here the circumstances under which the government looked at computer software as an important growth area in exports. In 1983, the author of this book was the Chairman of the Engineering Export Promotion Council. At that time one of the panels under the council was Computer Hardware and Software, and the convener of the panel was Dr.Nirmal Jain (The Electronics and Software Export Promotion Council was not yet born). A delegation was taken by the Chairman to the Commerce Minister in 1983, with members of the software exporting community, to impress upon him the potential of software exports, and what the government can do to help. In the meeting convened in the minister's chambers, there were the Minister of Commerce and the Minister of Science and Technology, Secretaries to the Government of India in the ministries of Commerce, Industry and the Department of Electronics, and a host of other officials. The delegation gave a professional presentation to the gathering, on the potential available for exports in the software industry, the enormous capabilities of the Indian software industry, and the draconian regulations of the government which were coming in the way of exports. Of course there were some bureaucrats in the gathering, who explained vividly the misuse the industry is capable of, if the regulations were relaxed and expressed their views against the move.

The minister remarked candidly that the meeting had helped him to realize the potential and assured the delegation that he would look into it and provide the industry with suitable help. Accordingly, in the next Export–Import Policy of the Government of India announced in April 1984, many of the provisions were relaxed, and enabled free import of software and hardware for export purposes etc, and paved the way for increased exports in this sector. After that the government had taken many other measures to help the software industry, and has never looked back.

What is the position today ?

Nasscom, the professional body representing the industry has declared that in 2007-08, the Software and services export surged 29%, and was of the order of $40.4 billion. This has been done in a year when there was a severe financial sector crisis in USA, a slowdown in the economy, as well as currency fluctuations. The domestic market also continued to gain the momentum, growing 28% to register a revenue of $11.6 billion. This took the overall IT industry revenue - export and domestic, combined – to $52 billion, a growth of 28% compared to the previous year, The overall employment in the IT field also touched 2 million.

Within the export segment, geographical diversification, maturity in services and operating efficiencies, helped the IT Services exports to increase by 28% to $23.1 billion, while the BPO exports increased by 30% to $10.9 billion. Engineering Services and product exports clocked $6.4 billion. As stated earlier the year 2007-08 was difficult with currency fluctuations, sub-prime crisis shaking the industry in US and elsewhere. The IT sector has shown tremendous resilience in keeping up our exports. According to Nasscom, the industry is focusing on improving productivity, efficiency, as well as opening up new markets, such as Continental Europe and Japan and they are confident of achieving the target of $60 billion in exports by 2009-10.

**Table 2.16**

**SOFTWARE AND IT ALLIED EXPORTS**

| | |
|---|---|
| 2002-03 | $ 9.56 billion |
| 2007-08 | $ 40.4 billion |

In 1998-99, India's software exports amounted to 4.5% of India's Total Exports. In 2006-07, Software and IT Allied services exports from India accounted for 20% of India's total exports, emerging as the largest exporting sector of the country.

India is quietly but quickly emerging as one of the leaders in the field. India is emerging as a country that offers cost-effectiveness, great quality, high reliability, rapid delivery, and above all, state-of-the-art technologies in software development. It is no wonder that more than 200 of 'Fortune 500' companies outsource their software requirements to India.

Another enabling factor for the dynamic growth of the software and allied industry is the government's realization of its export potential, and its willingness to go all out to help the industry in its endeavors.

The Indian IT industry is growing fast. The first-mover advantage we had gained over a decade has certainly helped us to come to the center of the world IT operations. Our performance has proved that the world cannot ignore Indian IT capabilities that achieve high quality with comparatively low cost.

The growth to the next stage is very important and crucial. Over the years we have been targeting only the Application Development Market which normally constitutes one third of the total spending on IT by a customer. Though this is still the core revenue source for IT companies, if Indian companies are to scale up further, they have to build capabilities not only in software but also in the area of overall IT infrastructure management, and various other areas as demanded by the customers.

The Indian software companies are growing their knowledge capabilities and are winning new deals, beyond the traditional technology service domain. In other words, Indian companies are going in for more than IT services and BPO combination. For example, in one of the biggest IT deals for an Indian company, Tata Consultancy services has signed a $1.2 billion , ten year agreement with Ac Nielson, the global information and media company,. It is said that TCS will assume responsibilities for important IT and operation processes and help Nielson integrate and centralize multiple systems, technologies and processes, on a global scale. TCS will also assume responsibility for certain finance and human resources, business processes, which will be executed on new BPO platforms built by TCS.

According to Mr Ravi Viswanathan, Vice President of TCS, Indian IT companies have had a tremendous record in bringing efficiency to the business processes of customers. A combination of process efficiency and quality has been the brand dimension of Indian IT companies. A deal like the one with Nielson shows the ability of not only understanding the processes of Nielson, but also applying technology to drive new business models that makes the difference. It is the ability to look at how we can use business process outsourcing, knowledge process outsourcing, and IT Services to help the customers' business.

Similarly Sathyam of India has signed a long term contract with FIFA, the international body controlling Football all over the world. Genpact, Cognizant and TCS have teamed up in a multi-vendor strategy, with 'Kimberly Clark' the US based health and hygiene company.

Any outsourcing services to another country, obviously reduces jobs in the parent company and other service providers in the countries concerned. Even though the business interests in the countries which outsource, understand the advantages and profitability to the organizations concerned, these issues are often politicized and become an election rhetoric during an election year. But this will pass. Over a period of time not only are Indian IT companies growing in the countries from which we outsource, but have also created big establishments and employ 'locals' in those countries in a large measure.

In a slightly different context, the recent acquisitions of foreign companies by Indian corporate houses, like Tata Steel acquiring 'Corus' the Anglo Dutch steel conglomerate; Tata Motors acquiring Jaguar and Land Rover of England from Ford Motors, we have given assurance on the continuous employment of the existing staff. In these endeavours, by showing our desire to expand in these countries with local talent, we have established our intentions and outlook and have given tremendous confidence to international industry and governments.

Mr. Partha Iyengar, Regional Director of Gartners, a premium research organization, says that 'Indian companies will increasingly be in line for new orders, as they expand their domain capability (and credibility) in various verticals. They have to take up such work, if they are to move up to higher profitability/higher revenue opportunities, away from the 'utility' business, that is their bread and butter.'

This is essential since the main concern of any Chief Information Officer who is in charge of IT operations in any company, is to avoid over-investing in the IT infrastructure of the company. He has to ensure the company's IT service capability without enhancing the budget and respond proactively to all the problems.

Out of this arises the question as to whether the company builds the competency internally or out-sources to a specialized service provider. Outsourcing reduces costs considerably. Many established companies abroad have opted to outsource the entire IT operation to an 'outsourcer' who manages the infrastructure from an Operations Management Center set up separately. This enables big companies abroad to focus on their core business, and also get 'round-the-clock' service from the outsourcing. The companies also benefit by gaining access to latest technology developments without investing in infrastructure.

Another development has been that the major IT companies have found the Indian environment of highly skilled personnel and reduced cost very attractive and are setting up their own offshore bases in India. They will aggressively compete with the well-established Indian companies for their outsourcing business.

Gartner, a premier research organization has said that it is possible to simplify procedures with 24-hour 7-day remote infrastructure support from India with necessary cost benefits.

The Indian companies are moving up the value chain with the emergence of new services such as package software implementation, systems integration, network management, R & D services, knowledge services and engineering design.

India has already established itself well in the areas of financial services, telecom and manufacturing and is entering into new verticals such as retail, healthcare, utilities etc.

Added on to this is the emerging competition from newer players in the market like Philippines, Ireland and China and the East European countries which India has to face.

There has been significant growth in software and services companies all over the world. It is estimated that the industry which was around $175 billion in 1990, has grown to nearly $700 billion by now.

As far as India is concerned, we are getting only a small share, but it has been continuously rising and stands today almost at $40 billion for the year 2007-08.

Having seen the healthy growth of the industry, a word of caution on a few areas are in order.

(1) The Nasscom has indicated that having had an increase of 29% to register revenues of $40 billion in 2007-08, the growth in the years following will be less and indicated 21-24% as the expected growth for 2008-09.

(2) The Banking, Financial Services and Insurance (BFSI) contribute about 35 to 45% of the revenue of Indian software companies. Customers in this segment which include big Wall Street banks like Citigroup, and Merril Lynch are still reeling under the bad loan and credit related crisis in the United States. This has forced the management of top Indian software companies to remain guarded and immediately look for alternate opportunities.

(3) Having seen the advantages of outsourcing, many of the big players in the IT services field such as IBM, Accenture, HP, Ernst & Young etc. have their own fully owned subsidiaries in India, to utilize the large technical/skilled personnel available here and provide competitive services to their clients abroad, and some of the big ticket contracts have gone to them.

In view of their considerable experience abroad and the advantages they have in India, they have developed a well rounded global delivery network as opposed to just an offshore model. The MNCs have learnt a lot from India, and their offshore delivery model spans not only India, but also Philippines, Vietnam, Russia, China etc., and they are in a position to leverage strengths that other destinations offer in a way that Indian companies cannot yet do. The competitive edge India had, in terms of low-cost high value offering is now being matched in equal measure by these MNCs. Further, they say that they sell a superior value proposition to the customer due to their deep domain knowledge and ability to provide end to end services that cover the entire gamut from transformational IT services to BPO.

In the final analysis, it is pretty much a level playing field now both for Indian and foreign players. When all things are equal – cost, quality, people, delivery capability – whoever offers a superior proposition will get the business. It is time that the Indian IT majors accelerated their shift to a better integrated global delivery network and offer a superior value proposition. They have to keep transforming themselves. But considering the way they have come and their robust size, there is no reason why they will not be able to meet the challenge ahead in the next ten years.

Finally, in software and allied exports, the confidence of the country is very high, and if the right environment and encouragement is given, experts predict that India can achieve a target of $ 100 Billion by 2020. Let us hope that we can do this.

The trained manpower requirement is enormous for this industry, and good training facilities are not adequate in India. Even though every college has computer education as a course, there are only a few which can train world class software professionals. The industry and the government should put their heads together, and should raise the quality of computer education, while weeding out the inefficient ones.

The quest for new developments and training in the newest skills and tools in the industry should be done systematically. We should always engage ourselves in the leading edge of the industry, so that we are able to increase exports substantially.

Manpower requirement could be dealt with in the following manner:

(a) Finding individuals within the organization with potential for international careers.

(b) Reassigning staff internationally to meet the demand.

(c) Recruiting new staff and training them for international trade.

### 3. Business Process Outsourcing (BPO)

In the area of IT enabled Services, BPO is very important and is growing. It seems to be India's sunrise industry, and as they say 'it is an idea whose time has come'.

What exactly is BPO? It is the act of transferring some of the organisation's repeated non-core and core business processes to an outside provider to achieve cost reduction while improving service quality. If done well BPO results in increasing shareholder value. The main difference between BPO and more traditional outsourcing is that BPO offers companies a way of achieving transformation outcomes more quickly.

The BPO industry is growing very fast at almost 60% to 70% annually. While it has taken almost 20 years for the IT industry to make its presence felt in the export trade, BPO industry has forged ahead in hardly 5 years. Indian BPO exports are as indicated below:

**Table 2.17**

**INDIAN BPO EXPORTS 1999 – 2003**

| *Year* | *Revenue (US $ million)* |
|---|---|
| 1999-2000 | 565 |
| 2002-2003 | 2400 |
| 2006-2007 | 10100 |

*Source:* Nasscom

The BPO industry was nothing very new, for in the early nineties, Swissair established an in-house BPO which dealt with most of the back office billing, ticketing etc. Later, British Airways followed with its in-house BPO for most of its work. GE and American Express followed suit. It looks as if the Nasscom-McKinsey Report of 1999 which outlined the suitability of India and its resources in the field, perhaps opened the flood gates, and a major BPO industry took shape in India. It has amazed everybody including those who followed the Indian Information Technology success story.

The fact that outsourcing reduces costs considerably, and the technology needed – viz. telecommunications, internet, networking and computerization – are all in place makes India the ideal location. Another interesting factor is that the personnel in India who do the work are well educated. Further, India has established itself well due to the success it has achieved in managing the outsourcing of IT services, and this has given it good credibility.

The BPO industry in India consists of –

(a) MNCs establishing their BPOs.

(b) BPO companies from USA and UK setting up their operations in India

(c) Indian BPO companies started by renowned IT firms and others in India.

It is possible that there might be some competition between them but the ultimate beneficiary will be India.

Call Centre Business (which basically amounts to Indians at a center in India, taking care of all customer queries across the globe through phone lines) is also a part of BPO. Today there is a clear shift from Call Centres to Transaction Processing Systems like cheque-clearing, banking transactions, insurance transactions etc. Many units which first started as Call Centres, are going up the value chain to do high end cutting edge work. It is no longer low cost manpower but increasingly brainpower that is making India the preferred destination.

For example, IBM set up the Indian Research Lab in 1998 which produces 38 patents a year and has a large contingent of employees with doctorates. They also produce around 75 research papers which are published in international journals.

GE's second largest R&D Centre is located in Bangalore, and they produce 240 patents a year. All these are staffed by high quality Indian technical personnel

According to the Nasscom-McKinsey report, the total opportunity for BPO is around $ 140 billion, and if India captures one sixth of it, it would translate into 500,000 jobs by 2020 with a revenue of US$ 24 billion.

Though India BPO business does not have much of governmental work, it is not seriously affected at present. But we should be prepared for periodic slowdown due to political reasons. As long as the economy is going well there will not be many obstacles, but if there is a recession and job losses, BPO business will slow down. We should also be prepared for competition from other countries like Philippines and China.

To go up the value chain, India has to enter into new areas such as Insurance, Telecom, Animation, Material research, Health care, engineering, bio-technology research, data analysis, legal database etc. India has expertise in these areas with trained personnel, and BPO in these will flourish.

It should be remembered that this outlook was relevant till August 2008, and thereafter with global financial crisis adversely affecting all countries' economies and exports, a new situation has arisen whose full effects will be known only by the end of 2008-09.

## IMPORTS

India's imports of principal products and commodities for the years 2001-02 and 2006-07 are given in Table 2.18 below

**Table 2.18**

**PRINCIPAL PRODUCTS OF INDIA'S IMPORTS**

| *S. No.* | *Products* | *2001-2002* | *2006-2007* | *% Change* |
|---|---|---|---|---|
| *1* | *2* | *3* | *4* | *5* |
| I. | Bulk Imports | 90700 | 375843.32 | 314.38 |
| 1. | Cereals & Prepara tions | 87 | 1618.40 | 1760.22 |
| | a. Rice | 0.41 | 0.41 | |
| | b. Wheat | 1 | 1473.35 | 1472.35 |
| | c. Other Cereals | 4 | 11.62 | 190.50 |
| | d.Cereal Preparations | 82 | 133.03 | 62.23 |
| | 2. Fertilizers | 3239 | 14222.84 | 339.11 |
| | a.Crude | 796 | 1632.13 | 105.04 |
| | b.Sulphur & Unroasted Pyrites | 274 | 493.59 | 80.14 |
| | c.Manufactured | 2169 | 12097.13 | 457.72 |
| | 3. Edible oil | 6465 | 9416.27 | 45.64 |
| | 4. Sugar | 33 | 3.49 | 89.42 |
| | 5. Pulp & Waste Paper | 1405 | 2875.02 | 104.62 |
| | 6. Paper Board & Manufactures | 961 | 5622.60 | 485.07 |

| | | | | |
|---|---|---|---|---|
| | 7. Newsprint | 1170 | 2407.17 | 105.74 |
| | 8. Crude Rubber incl. Synthetic | 831 | 2840.49 | 241.81 |
| | 9. Non-Ferrous Metals | 3086 | 11791.80 | 282.10 |
| | 10. Metalliferrous Ore & Scrap | 5455 | 37709.90 | 591.29 |
| | 11. Iron & Steel | 3976 | 29076.29 | 631.29 |
| | 12. Petroleum Crude& Products | 66769 | 258259.05 | 286.79 |
| III. | Pearls, Precious, Semi-Precious stones | 22046 | 33880.13 | 53.67 |
| IV | Machinery | 23405 | 147961.30 | 532.17 |
| | 1. Machine Tools | 920 | 6700.94 | 628.26 |
| | 2. Non-Electrical Machinery $ | 14168 | 62665.43 | 342.30 |
| | 3.Electrical Machinery $ | 2835 | 8849.30 | 212.14 |
| | 4.Transport Equipment | 5482 | 69745.63 | 1172.26 |
| V | Project Goods | 2714 | 7938.38 | 192.49 |
| VI. | Others of which | 106334 | 296678.38 | 179.00 |
| | 1.Cashew Nuts | 431 | 1820.75 | 322.44 |
| | 2.Fruits & Nuts | 757 | 1911.75 | 152.54 |
| | 3.Wool Raw | 624 | 1077.45 | 72.66 |
| | 4.Silk Raw | 625 | 673.37 | 7.73 |
| | 5.Synthetic & Regenerated Fibres | 272 | 439.15 | 61.45 |
| | 6. Pulses | 3160 | 3851.45 | 21.88 |
| | 7. Raw Hides & Skins | 311 | 314.99 | 1.28 |
| | 8. Leather | 714 | 1307.13 | 83.07 |
| | 9. Coal,Coke & Briquettes | 5452 | 20794.04 | 281.40 |

| | | | |
|---|---|---|---|
| 10. Non-Metal mineral Manufactures | 1049 | 3584.87 | 241.74 |
| 11. Other Raw Minerals | 489 | 1086.17 | 122.12 |
| 12. Organic&inorganic Chemicals | 13352 | 35345.74 | 164.72 |
| 13. Dyeing,Tanning Material | 1132 | 2727.54 | 140.94 |
| 14. Medicinal&Pharma products | 2027 | 5867.25 | 189.45 |
| 15. Artificial Resins etc. | 3215 | 11773.21 | 266.19 |
| 16.Chemical Products | 2120 | 6005.43 | 183.27 |
| 17.Textile Yarn, Fabrics,Made-up, Art. etc. | 3392 | 4079.73 | 20.27 |
| 18.Metal Manufactures | 1941 | 7257.75 | 273.91 |
| 19.Professional instruments etc.* | 4965 | 10538.52 | 112.25 |
| 20.Electronic Goods incl. Computer Software | 19070 | 72156.30 | 278.37 |

NB * = Other than Electronic

***Source:*** Ministry of Commerce

The import policy regime has been substantially liberalised in keeping with the logic and tenor of the economic reforms. Import substitution as an obstinate obsession is no longer the guiding principle of the trade policy.

The mindset which ordained the import controls in the past was almost synonymous with the myopic concept of self- reliance which fed into a wide range of uneconomic domestic production exercises in the name of import substitution. The dictates of a growth-oriented trade policy are such that an increasing volume of imports is not to be considered as economic adversity at all. On the contrary, a system of nearly uninhibited imports of capital goods and consumer goods alike, subject to suitable import duties consistent with the country's strategic economic security interests, would not only promote exports, and industrial production capable of global competition, but also employment generation, both as a direct and indirect consequence.

## Future

India's merchandise exports in the financial year 2007-2008 were of the order of US $ 150 billion. This was an increase over the export of the previous year (of US $ 126 billion) by 19%. This is indeed a commendable achievement considering the fact that the US dollar is the currency in which a majority of Indian Exports are denominated, and that the dollar has lost its value compared to the Indian Rupee in 2007-08 thus reducing the margins of the Indian Exporters.

Our total trade (exports and imports together) in the year 2007-08 is almost $ 500 billion, accounting to 1.5% of world trade.

We have established the need for a fast-growing export trade and have analysed some of the important sectors of the export trade which have led to the growth so far. We now have to take stock of the existing exports, product wise and economy wise, so as to consolidate them and move in a direction that would increase the level of exports to facilitate growth of the economy.

It is difficult to find a single solution to the question of future direction. Especially at a time like this, when oil prices are fluctuating wildly, inflation at its highest in recent times, and all input prices are on the increase the world over. International trade calls for short-term, as well as long-term, plans. We should capitalise on our current strengths in products and services, where we have an edge, to maximise our exports, while simultaneously monitoring the international scene to devise long-term plans for the growth of existing and new sectors.

In today's context the fast growing sectors in exports, which India should concentrate on and build a strong infrastructure for its continued growth are Engineering Goods and Project Exports, Leather and Leather Products, Marine exports, Gem and Jewellery Exports, Chemicals, Textile Exports, Software and allied services, and Agricultural Exports. This list has been selected keeping in view the direct and indirect employment it will generate.

There should be an in-depth study and debate by the academic, industrial and business communities, and an on-going dialogue with the government to identify the scope, the problems and a SOLUTION TO THE PROBLEMS, to enable the Government and Industry to take short term and long- term steps to make India a premier exporting country.

A discerning reader may note that in the previous paragraph capital letters have been used for the "solutions of problems". Why? It is because, of late in India a tendency has arisen to totally condemn any 'new measure', if it has certain features which they do not like. A campaign is built up, and two sides emerge - one strongly advocating and another condemning the measure. Before long it is politicised, and the public and perhaps the government is also confused, and everything stagnates. The tendency to have a balanced approach to the problems, controversy, and implement the same based on a consensus is not given the importance it deserves in a democracy. We must get out of this mindset and any measure which will help the country in its development should be debated positively and a consensus should be built up, if India has to become a mature nation in international business

A classic instance is the allotment of land by the government to new industries and manufacturing enterprises which have good employment potential. Since our independence, all governments have a healthy policy to provide land, electricity and water for new industries at reasonable prices. But for this policy, India would not have attained the tremendous progress it has. But of late, there is a tendency to politicize the issue and opposition parties use all their influence to oppose this without realizing that they are coming in the way of development of their own state.

The question arises whether it is not possible to come to a consensus/ compromise in this issue. Also, the government should evolve a policy in acquisition as well as land allotment fair to all concerned.

There are certain areas in export where the potential for exports is high, provided we plan ahead and nurture it well. One such area is software and allied IT services, which we have dealt with in detail. There are also other areas, which deserve special attention.

We have made a bold attempt to look far ahead, given conducive conditions, on the Export Potential in the next chapter.

❖ ❖ ❖

3

# INDIA'S EXPORT POTENTIAL

## FUTURE

The export of any country depends not only on its own economy and growth but also on the international trade pattern of the rest of the world. To predict these conditions over a longer period of time is indeed very difficult. At the same time a country like India which has tremendous potential, and has succeeded in various other fields should have a long term objective based on its core strengths, and the technological advances it is envisaging. If the country braces itself to make the best possible efforts, what is it we can expect from the export trade in a fixed time frame?

One can perhaps state that this is the most audacious chapter in the book. It looks at India's potential in the future and where we can stand in 2020.

However, the serious financial crisis sweeping the world is going to affect the economy and exports of all countries enormously. We do expect that in 2009/2010 there will be great turbulence and thereafter hopefully things will change and settle down. India's potential that we have outlined will be reached only with some extra effort.

In this chapter, an effort is made to look at the future in a rational manner, if that is possible. Of course in this year there have been many factors outside India, such as the price of crude oil, raw material prices, food grain prices, and U.S. financial crisis, which can completely distort international trade. But it is hoped that all this will settle down at a new equilibrium, and world trade will continue, perhaps at a lesser pace.

## ORIGIN OF THE DREAM

In India where cynicism abounds, there are a few who can rise above it, and show us, by virtue of their own experiences and achievements, the potential that lies within the nation, and also how, if nurtured properly, can make this country a great one. One such voice in our generation is that of Bharat Ratna Dr. A.P.J.Abdul Kalam, the renowned engineer-scientist, and former President of India.

Dr.Abdul Kalam together with Mr.Y.S.Rajan, has published a brilliant book called 'India – 2020 – A Vision for the New Millennium'. The main theme of the book is that if technology is used effectively, and the country tries hard in all fields, India can become A DEVELOPED COUNTRY by 2020, and can be among the first five economic powers of the world. That book is my inspiration, to attempt to discuss in this chapter, what our export trade can be like in 2020.

The book mentioned above draws heavily on the reports of the various task forces set-up by TIFAC. TIFAC or Technology Information Forecasting and Assessment Council was set up in 1988 to look at the technologies emerging world-wide and identify those relevant to India. It also looked at the possibility of making India a developed country by 2020, and the task forces set up by TIFAC involved all sections of society – government, industries, users, scientific and technological institutions, and other intellectuals; and a series of reports were published in all the disciplines. Hence the conclusions drawn by Abdul Kalam and Rajan have a solid base.

Let us look at the broad parameters, and the growth and development envisaged.

## THE ECONOMY: – THE GDP GROWTH ENVISAGED

The first parameter taken up is the **growth pattern of the economy.** The indicator for the state of the economy is always Gross Domestic Product or GDP.

The book 'India 2020' was published in 1995, at which time the world GDP was \$ 25,854 billion. Based on the best possible estimates on the growth at that time, the GDP in 2020 was arrived at, at \$55,452 billion.

But there have been considerable changes in the world economy and trade, and in 2008, we had the unprecedented rise in the price of crude oil going up to \$145 per barrel, and again the huge increases in the cost of raw materials and food grains. In this context what will be the growth of the world economy in this year and subsequent years? Based on the best possible expert advice available one can reasonably assume 2% growth till 2011 and thereafter 3% till 2020. The reasons given for this assumption are as follows:

(a) After every 'Oil Shock' the world has witnessed from the early seventies to date, the price rise initially affects all the countries to various degrees (the developing countries are very hard hit, compared to developed countries) and after a difficult period of adjustment some balance is achieved and the world economy gradually grows.

(b) Most of the countries have embarked upon alternative energy projects and to the extent they succeed, the oil consumption will come down. Already there are reports that in USA, which consumes almost 25% of the oil supplies, the consumption is going down after the gasoline price became \$4 per gallon this year.

(c) Experts feel that Asian growth, especially China and India will continue, albeit less than expected, and that will propel world economy.

If India has to be within the first five of the world in economic power in the new millennium, its growth plan should be kept up even if it slows down temporarily.

As against a GDP growth rate of 9.4 in 2005-06 and 9.6 in 2006-07, we expect India's GDP growth to go down for a while. But based on the advice of experts, we have assumed the growth in future as follows:

8% till 2011, and

9% from 2012 to 2020.

On this basis, India's GDP, which was \$906 billion in 2006 will rise to Us \$2800 billion by 2020.

Hence, if the nation really gears itself to the task in the various fields as outlined later, it is not impossible to achieve the goal set for us.

The second important parameter assumed in the book is that the **population of the country** would be 1.4 billion by the year 2020. The change in the demographic pattern of the country with the increase in literacy, suggests that this assumption is reasonable.

How then do we plan such a rapid growth rate to achieve a GDP of $ 2810 billion? It is possible to achieve it if we concentrate on

(a) rapid growth of manufacturing and service sectors,

(b) technical upsurge in manufacturing and R & D, and high productivity with new methods and processes, thus making India the world hub for producing not only small cars, wind turbines and various engineering products but a host of other products.

(c) complete modernisation of agriculture in various areas, such as better seeds, better utilization of water, and selective use of bio-technology, with the specific object of increasing the productivity. In this we should closely follow the example of China, which has much less arable land but produces much more, and productivity is twice that of India in grains. This will give rise to a host pf food processing industries, which will have a good domestic as well as export market.

(d) improve our technology and production of added value products in steel and aluminum where we are endowed with the minerals in abundance.

(e) involve in the latest research to produce new 'molecules' and endeavour to get a leading position in drugs and pharmaceuticals for which there is a huge demand all over the world.

(f) get involved in the latest cutting edge technologies and be a strong player in IT and allied services, (this has been dealt with in great detail in the second chapter of this book).

The above list is neither complete nor is it wishful thinking, but based on core-competencies exhibited by Indians in India and abroad in the recent past. However these changes require dedicated and committed personnel, who have faith in their capacities and in the country, and a government which is practical and realistic and supports the national effort with all its resources.

## EXPORT TRADE

Normally international trade consists of both exports and imports of a country. The capacity of a country to earn enough foreign exchange resources for getting adequate imports into the country consistent with the demands of the economy as well as other requirements, depends mostly on the EXPORT TRADE of the country.

Hence one of the benchmarks of a country's sustained growth, high GDP etc. is primarily its exports. Once the growth of exports of a country is on the increase as required, and well planned, other things will automatically fall in place.

Let us now study our country's exports. Here we would look at it in terms of American Dollars, since worldwide the figures for exports and GDP etc. are always mentioned in US Dollars and will be easy for comparison.

Our merchandise exports during the last few years were as follows:

**Table 3.1**

| *Year* | *Exports*<br>*US Dollars Billion* |
|---|---|
| 2003-04 | 68.8 |
| 2004-05 | 83.5 |
| 2005-06 | 103.1 |
| 2006-07 | 126.3 |

If this has been the pattern of exports in this decade, what volume of exports can we anticipate in the years ahead and particularly by 2020? Further, based on the economic growth we assumed, which would give us a GDP of US $ 2800 billion by 2020, what exports can sustain that growth and also the GDP?

## GUIDELINES FOR EXPORT GROWTH

We have a few guidelines to go by:

*(a)* The first is the ratio of exports to GDP of a country. In the last few years the trade in commercial services has grown rapidly, and there are predictions that their growth will be faster in the future. For example for India, in 2006-07, the merchandise export was $126 billion, whereas

the exports in Services was $76.2 billion and the total exports in goods and services amounted to $202 billion.

*(b)* If we take important developed countries and look at the total exports (Merchandise and Service exports), they are as follows : In USA the merchandise exports was $1038 billion, and commercial services export was $388 billion in 2006. In Japan it was $650 billion in merchandise trade and $123 billion in commercial services in 2006. In the case of USA, the ratio of their total exports to GDP is 10.7 and in the case of Japan the ratio of total exports to GDP amounts to 17.7 in 2006. So one can state that statistically the average ratio of total exports to GDP should at least be 14.2% in a developed country. We have not taken the countries of Europe in this comparison, since the intra-trade between the countries in European Union is high. There are practically no import duties among them, and their trade is complementary. Hence they cannot constitute a model for India.

*(c)* Another aspect we have to bear in mind is that as per the model of growth we envisage for India, the domestic market will also be quite large and demanding, and hence the ratio that the total exports will bear to the GDP cannot be unduly high.

However, with these parameters, one can reasonably state that the ratio that India's total exports should bear to its GDP should not be less than 14.2% in 2020.

Since the GDP calculated earlier for India in the year 2020 would be US $2,800 billion, the exports should be not less than $ 400 billion in the year 2020.

In other words, our total exports, which is of the order of US $ 126 billion in merchandise exports and US $ 76 billion in commercial services exports in 2006-07, has to increase at least to US $ 400 billion by 2020. It is a quantum jump in the exports of any country. How do we achieve this objective? Is this within our grasp? Or are we dreaming of the impossible? What are the steps that the country as a whole has to undertake? These are the fundamental questions we have to address. Knowing today's economic conditions of the country, and the world, it is very easy to advance a hundred arguments to say that this is not possible. But it will be against the spirit of this chapter, where we have acknowledged the tremendous potential of this country and how, if the right steps are taken, it is possible to make this a developed country by 2020, and also achieve the export target needed.

By using technology as the main driver, and using all the research work done and the remarkable achievements of Indians in this country and abroad, one can certainly be optimistic about achieving the goal. Let us see how this can be achieved.

Our endeavor in projecting our exports by 2020 will be based on:

*(a)* Today's exports – The normal growth in exports assuming the anticipated growth of international trade, and our economy.

*(b)* Certain identified sectors where the technology missions have indicated that the potential can be considerably increased by taking suitable steps.

*(c)* The new and fast growing sectors which are opening up in the new millennium, and where we can excel, based on our core-strength.

## ANALYSIS OF EXPORTS FROM INDIA

Let us analyze our export trade as it exists today. We have taken the year 2006-07 for reference. The broad picture of the exports in 2006-07 is given in Table 3.2.

Agriculture and primary products constitute 25% of our total exports, and manufactured goods amount to 71%. The rest are minerals and various other products whose export potential is inelastic in nature.

In the case of agricultural and allied products in India, the pull/demand of the domestic market is very high, and has to be fulfilled and only the surplus can be exported. However if we implement the recommendations of the TIFAC technology mission, which has given concrete proposals of the products, the locations in India where these can be developed, and the infra structural needs of the same, we should be able to meet this challenge and can well be on our way to achieve the required surplus for exports, and achieve our goal.

Similarly in the manufacturing sector, we are inhibited by factors such as lack of modernization with increased productivity, no improvement of infrastructure, and inability to compete because of the higher cost of production due to sudden increase in the cost of raw materials and other inputs. But these can be overcome if government and the industry take necessary steps (as outlined in the second chapter under 'engineering exports').

After a careful study of various reports, the views expressed by many experts, of our core-competencies and capabilities, and today's trends, we have forecast what our exports can be in 2020, with a breakup under various categories in Table 3.2.

Let us look into these in greater detail:

1. In **agricultural products**, which consist of a whole range of products, including tea, coffee, rice, wheat, tobacco, spices, cashew, oil meals, processed foods etc., as against $9 billion in 2006-07, we have projected $15 billion,– hardly 66% over a period of 13 years. This can be easily achieved and exceeded.

The main bottleneck here is low productivity and poor infrastructural facilities.

According to the FAO, the average yield of rice in India is 3004kg per hectare, whereas in China it is 6233 kg per hectare,–more than double. For wheat, the corresponding figures are 2688 kg per hectare for India compared to 4155 kg per hectare for China. Further, according to The International Rice Research Institute, India produced 124 million tons of rice compared to China's 186 million tons in 2004, despite having almost double the area under paddy cultivation (42 million hectares for India versus 28 million hectares for China). China says that it is mainly due to research and development, whereas it is reported that India has the largest number of agricultural scientists on the government payroll in the world – 30,000.

If the central and state governments bestow sufficient attention, this area alone can give us more than adequate food grains for the country, and for exports.

In the field of horticulture, especially fruits and vegetables, China produced 60 million tons versus India's production of 55 million tons in 1980. In 2003 China produced 450 million tons versus India's 135 million tons.

It is noteworthy that China does not provide its farmers with subsidies for fertilizers or power, but believes in building suitable rural infrastructure.

Let us hope we will wake up to the possibilities in all sectors of agriculture and other allied areas to improve our exports substantially.

As explained earlier, the increase here is kept small since the domestic demand will also be high due to increase in the population as also the increase of the standard of living of our people. Our agricultural scientists should concentrate on better yields per hectare, continuous research in biotechnology to get better seeds, and better utilization of water resources etc. to increase the production.

2. In **cereals**, such as rice, wheat etc. the present level of exports of $1.5 billion is projected to increase to $ 3 billion. This is indeed a sensitive area. Today the food production in our country is around 210 million tons, and the population is about a billion. We have accepted the projection of our population in the year 2020 as 1.4 billion.

If we plan for the export of cereals to the extent of $ 3 billion in the year 2020, while at the same time fulfilling the domestic demand, how much of food grains production should we have, to achieve this objective? This is where the TIFAC vision on agriculture is very revealing. They have stated that our food production can increase easily to 270 million tons by 2020, and the total value of food grains turnover will increase from today's Rs.90,000 crores to Rs.1,50,000 crores by 2020.But as stated earlier China's productivity in rice and wheat per hectare is twice that of India. If we improve our productivity at least by 50% we should be able to produce 300 million tons by 2020. Here again we should involve our technologists to come up with solutions to improve the seeds, improve the yields in the field, better pest/rodent control, better storing facilities and improved post-harvest practices, using proper inputs suitable after testing our soil, etc. All these are within our capabilities but a determined time-bound programme should by made by the government fully involving the scientists, technologists and genuine agriculturists.

Today, the international prices of cereals are increasing due to various factors. A major portion of the heavy subsidies in this sector given by western countries, have to go sooner or later, and definitely by 2020. Then India's cost of production will also be low and a healthy export market can be envisaged.

A very low target of $3 billion by 2020 is projected in this sector, as the increase in population and domestic demand will also reduce the potential to an extent.

More countries are becoming conscious of pollution and adulteration, and there is an increasing demand for organically produced foods. This is indeed a niche product and market. India can use its inherent strengths in this area by going back to its traditional agricultural systems based on organic farming, cultivation in varied agro-climatic regions, local self-sustaining agricultural systems and methods, cheap labour etc., and get an excellent lead in this sector. Today the global market for organic products is around $ 25 billion and it is estimated to grow at an encouraging annual rate of 15% to 20%. Now India's organic farming is restricted to about 2200 hectares, and the production is also low at around 14,000 tons. There is tremendous scope for increasing this substantially.

3. In **fruits and vegetables** our export was $ 0.68 billion in 2006-07. Let us look at this scenario in a little detail. The world production of fruits and vegetables is estimated to be 1158 million tons, out of which vegetables alone amount to 610 million tons. India is the second largest producer in the world, next only to China, accounting for 120 million tons. However, Indian productivity levels are low – 40% less than the world's best. Further it is estimated that 30% of production is lost due to poor post-harvest handling/management. If, as recommended, India focuses on this sector by resorting to precision farming, hybrid seed technology, post harvest management, processing and value addition, our exports can increase considerably. Also if more areas in Central India suitable for producing fruits and vegetables are brought under cultivation, the exports will increase enormously. Though the exports have been projected to be only $3 billion by 2020, it can be much more.

Here again the TIFAC technology vision report gives suggestions as to what has to be done to achieve this objective. The important suggestions are: The post-harvest losses of about 30% should be brought down by introducing proper post-harvest treatment, providing cold storage at suitable locations, developing other infrastructure and transportation facilities so that the time taken between the harvest and the products reaching the consumption centers are reduced to the barest minimum. They have also suggested that Central India is an ideal location for growing fruits and vegetables in large quantities and work on providing suitable facilities should be taken on hand immediately. It is estimated that the production of fruits and vegetables can be increased practically threefold by a diligent and dedicated programme.

4. In **processed foods,** India has not even scratched the surface. In 2006-07 the exports amounted to $ 1.26 billion. But what are required here are imaginative steps to be taken by the government and the industry. India has no dearth of land. It is stated that 50% of our land area is cultivable, whereas it is very much less in China. Adequate areas of fallow land should be leased out on long-term basis to the private sector. This should be done on the strict understanding that they should cultivate the produce for processed foods in these areas, provide state of the art factories to process, and package the processed foods to the highest standards of

safety and hygiene demanded internationally, and export the same. If this is done, the exports of processed food will increase substantially as the world demand of such goods is always on the increase. A modest target of $4 billion of exports in 2020 can be exceeded substantially, not to speak of the employment potential.

In a FAIDA(Food and Agriculture Integration Development Action Report) prepared by McKinsey & Co. for CII, it has been estimated that the potential for food processing industry is Rs. 2,50,000 crores or $ 50 billion based on positive trends and practices. Hence if this sector is given adequate encouragement by the government, and the industry develops international standards of hygiene and quality, we can reasonably expect that $4 billion or more can be exported by 2020. But we have cautiously assumed an export of only $2 billion.

5. The total export of **marine products** today is around $1.9 billion. In India marine product export is centred around the West and East Coast. In collecting the products, traditional fishermen as well as mechanized trawlers are used. We mostly exploit the areas close to our coasts. It is found that huge mechanized fishing trawlers of countries like Japan and Taiwan do extensive fishing in the deep seas of the Indian Ocean and Arabian Sea. We should guard against exploitation of our marine products within our territorial waters.

Internationally a stretch of 200 miles from our coast is referred to as our territorial waters, and any vessel apart from regular liner vessels can come into the area only after due notification to the government. We can impose restrictions on foreign fishing vessels coming into this area and ensure that our sea wealth is not depleted by them. We should go for deep sea fishing by powerful well-equipped trawlers. These should be state-of-the art trawlers which will have cold storage facilities, processing facilities and packaging as well, so that when the trawler comes back to shore the products can straightaway be exported. We should also make systematic efforts to improve, very considerably, the hygiene and cleanliness in our off-shore facilities to reach the highest standards as demanded by the foreign countries. Then we cannot only reach the target of $5 billion by 2020, but also improve the employment potential substantially.

6. The position in the field of **textiles** is explained in detail in the previous chapter. As stated, the Multi Fibre Agreement (MFA) was dismantled in 2005 and India could export textiles and garments without any restrictions. This is an ancient industry in which Indians have excelled.

For growing cotton, weaving fine fabrics and making garments, we have enough raw material, and skilled hands available. For meeting the demands of the international market, all that is required is to build immediately the infrastructure for producing very high volumes of garments of excellent quality and competitive prices. The export of readymade garments has increased by six times in the last decade. When we talk of textiles we refer not only to garments, but also to cotton yarn and fabrics, man-made textiles, silk, woollen garments, and jute mfrs. Textile Exports in 2006-07 amounted to $17.5 billion, and with all restrictions having been removed by 2005, and international volume buyers like Wal-Mart, J C Penny, Sears Roebuck etc establishing their joint venture or buying operations in India already, we can reasonably expect this to increase to $40 billion by 2020. As raw material is produced in India and as it is a labour intensive industry it will be a great boon to farmers as well as trained labour, to increase the production to meet domestic and export demands.

7. **Gem & jewellery** exports is well suited to India, as it is manpower intensive. The work essentially consists of cutting and polishing small diamonds to the finish required. We have developed excellent expertise in this area. With the world population increasing, the demand will also increase substantially. The Government should give all possible support to encourage this sector of exports from India.

The Indian gem and jewellery export has already crossed the $16 billion mark in 2006-07, and the exports touched $21 billion in 2007-08 according to The Gem & Jewellery Export Promotion Council. The Council has recently set up The Indian Institute of Gem and Jewellery as well as Jewellery Product Development Centers that offer courses in jewellery crafting and manufacture.

Suitable encouragement should be given for the rapid increase in the export of gold jewellery. We export today gold jewellery worth $ 2 billion which constitutes 5% of the world market. With the abundance of gold artisans in India from time immemorial, India should be able to increase the exports significantly. What would be required is a mechanism to know about world trends in new designs for jewellery. The artisans should update their products accordingly.

There have been a few developments in this field which require close attention – China investing heavily in the polish of mid-sized stones, and Angola, Namibia and Botswana developing a polishing industry with local stones. Traditionally in this industry De Beers had a monopoly, controlling the trade of the bulk of the world's rough diamonds from its mines in South Africa. In the last decade, its mining rivals have found diamond deposits in Russia, Australia and elsewhere. India should negotiate with mining countries like Russia to buy rough diamonds directly. It has become all the more important, since trade circles say that De Beers has reduced the amount of rough diamonds it sells to India. As the gem and jewellery export has doubled in the last five years to reach $ 21 billion in the year 2007-08, it will definitely achieve $ 40 billion if not more by 2020, as the world's demands for gem and jewellery can never be satisfied.

8. Our **engineering goods** export is of the order of $ 31.2 billion in 2007-08. India has a reasonably strong industrial base. The technology up-gradation in some industries are very good, and the industries which are exporting are raising themselves to international standards. Further, we have one of the largest and well trained labour forces, which has been appreciated by all the foreign experts who have come to India. So, what is needed is technology up–gradation in all industries by means of joint ventures or outright purchase of the technology needed to make our factories capable of producing world class products. The productivity in India in the industrial sector is low, and determined efforts have to be taken to improve it substantially. Once this is underway, we should encourage the world majors to use India as the base for their worldwide production. Of course in this endeavor we have to have the full backing of the government in removing infrastructural bottlenecks. If we succeed in this, the exports in engineering goods will increase substantially.

The tremendous strides in engineering goods exports, and particularly in the area of manufacturing and design have been dealt with extensively in Chapter 2 under 'engineering exports'.

With the recent developments in the various sectors of engineering, India has become a hub for outsourcing manufactured products. Tata Motors, by buying a Daewoo Motors Heavy Vehicle plant in South Korea with a view to increasing their world wide coverage, and buying Jaguar and Land Rover factories and research establishment from FORD recently, have established a solid base for international sales, apart from being the largest Indian Automotive Company. Further, their unveiling of Tata Nano this year, a car meeting latest emission norms at a price $ 2500 dollars has taken the car manufacturing companies all over the world by surprise, and many international companies are rushing to India for their small car manufacture and before long India will be the world hub for the manufacture of such cars.

In the field of Auto components and spares exports also, India has obtained a preeminent place and the exports are over $ 3 billion in 2007-08.

The export of engineering goods is $ 31.25 billion and the Engineering Export Promotion Council has drawn up a growth strategy. It proposes to increase the exports by 20% till 2009-10 and thereafter by 14%, and hope to reach $ 100 billion by 2016. Hence our estimate of $ 100 billion by 2020 is much below the actual possibility in this area.

9. **Software, IT and IT Enabled Services:** The rapid growth of this industry and its full ramifications have already been dealt with in the previous chapter. The growth potential is enormous and every year it exceeds the expectations of the industry. In a study conducted by IDC for Microsoft, it was reported that India has emerged as the fastest growing IT industry, ahead of all the other Asian countries. The number of IT companies in India which grew from 8082 to 16530 between the years 1995 and 2001 is nearly 26000 by now.

The number of jobs created in the IT sector had grown to almost a million and is projected to grow substantially.

Of late, the Government has also woken up to the potential in this sector, and every state in India is competing to provide the right infrastructure. The Industry and Government should concentrate on providing excellent institutions of a high standard to train the budding software engineers since it is expected that by 2020, almost 30% of all those employed will be using some kind of software, and the knowledge and usage will be widespread.

10. In the last few years **Business Process Outsourcing** has grown very fast and this will also add to the total exports. The BPO exports increased by 30% to $ 10.9 billion in 2007-08. It is expected to grow very rapidly even though there is an outcry in some countries to ban outsourcing. But BPO is a process whose time has come and cannot be reversed against the wishes of business and industry which have experienced its benefits. So there will be growth in all sectors.

Software and Services exports surged 29% during 2007-08 to $ 40 billion dollars, according to NASSCOM. This consists of IT services exports of $ 23.1 billion and BPO exports of $ 10.9 billion.

We have projected that the total IT Services exports by 2020 will be $ 100 billion, which looks reasonable taking into consideration their growth in this decade and the new areas they are trying to conquer.

11. **Engineering designs, CAD, CAM manufacturing programmes etc:** This is a new avenue opening up for us. In western countries they identify a problem or a new use expected out of a product. They would like to off load the entire exercise on a design agency which would do the necessary changes in design and devise efficient production methods to be adopted in the manufacture. The design agency should do all the work and enable prototypes to be produced and also help implement the changes in the system. As mass production is going out of vogue, and as customer preference is given high priority, situations arise when batch production is taken up. Hence such engineering design centers in India, preferably as joint ventures to start with, can grow very fast and bring in a lot of export business. An export of 5 billion dollars in the year 2020 is an easy possibility.

12. **Consultancy:** Management, Reengineering, production marketing etc: This is an area where western countries are investing heavily to enable their organisations to meet the challenges of the present day world. Organisatios such as Mckinsey & Co., and Accenture have been in India and have also trained a large number of Indians who have proved themselves to be outstanding. There are a large number of Indians who have been working abroad in these consultancy firms and many of them have reached the top of their organizations as well. This area is expanding very fast in a world where there are such dynamic changes, and the companies are increasingly relying on experts in this field to help them overcome their problems, and grow. This is an area where Indians have proved their skill, and the potential is high.

13. **Service Sector:** The service sector is growing very fast. There are important areas where they have to employ highly skilled and technical personnel to give the service needed. One such area is Ship Maintenance and Ship Repair. These are time bound, and highly skilled, manpower-intensive jobs. A very modern, state of the art shipyard and dry dock which can take small as well as big vessels in India should generate excellent export earnings.

Similarly aircraft maintenance and repair is regular and compulsory for all aircraft as per strict standards of the makers' recommendations. Indian air travel today extends to private sector also, and is on the increase. All of them are in dire need of maintenance services. It is a time bound, highly skilled and manpower-intensive work. India has excellent trained personnel. All that is needed are modern state of the art workshops spread all over India, (as the airlines are also spread all over India), to undertake the work. It will be easy to have even a joint venture where technical know how is needed, and the Indian services would be cost-effective and of high quality in these areas. Many international airlines would be happy to get such services and the export income would be phenomenal. An export turnover of $15 billion by 2020 is easily achievable.

14. **Financial Services:** These are sought after all over the world. It is not for routine work but for such specialized work like Mergers and Acquisitions, Currency Planning, Accounting work, Legal work, Printing and Publishing work etc. There are numerous Indians in India and abroad working in world famous organizations who are experts in their fields. India is today deeply involved in many of these financial services. It will perhaps need an institutional back-up, and encouragement to develop it further. There is a great demand to start Development Centers in India where the entire gamut of financial services for MNCs the world over can be done in a cost effective manner. This is an avenue which is waiting to be exploited. The top Indian firms specializing in this field will be in great demand. An export earning of $10 billion is envisaged by 2020 in the financial sector.

15. **Tourism:** It is needless to state that this has tremendous potential in earning foreign exchange for the country. The primary needs in the area are the improvement of the infrastructure, and suitable facilities. There are few countries which can match India in the diversity of tourist interest. By 2020 we should be able to earn easily $15 billion or even more, out of a total world revenue of $900 billion. It will still be hardly 2% of the total tourist earnings all over the world by then.

Thus you see the vision of a prosperous India, an India strong in trade and commerce, strong in many fields of science and technology, an India with innovative industry, and with health and education for all.

This can be achieved only by utilizing technology and making it the core strength of the nation. Without the pervasive use of technology we cannot achieve overall development of our people in the years to come. Whether it is for creation of large scale employment or for ensuring nutritional and health security, or for better living conditions, technology is the only answer. Hence mastering of technologies is the key task to which the country and its people have to give the greatest importance. This can be considered to be the very essence of development. And if we become technologically strong, we have every chance of achieving the goal – the vision for 2020 – in the field of international trade and commerce also.

So let us all accept the call given by Dr. Kalam – **"It is a mission we can take up – and accomplish"**, and move forward steadfastly.

In the table below we have given the exports in 2006-07 and what can be achieved in 2020. Even if there are set- backs, the total value of exports should be at least $400 billion.

**Table 3.2**

**INTERNATIONAL TRADE – INDIA**

**EXPORTS - $ BILLION**

**PRESENT VS FUTURE POTENTIAL**

| *Exports* | *2006-07* | *2019-2020* |
|---|---|---|
| 1. Agriculture And allied products | 9 | 15 |
| 2. Marine Products | 1.9 | 5 |
| 3. Ores & Minerals | 7.5 | 12 |
| 4. Leather & Manufactures | 3.2 | 6 |
| 5. Gems & Jewellery | 16.7 | 35 |
| 6. Chemicals & Allied Products | 19 | 30 |
| 7. Engineering Goods | 28 | 100 |
| 8. Electronic Goods | 3 | 8 |
| 9. Textiles | 17.25 | 40 |
| 10. Cotton, incl waste | 1.44 | 4 |
| 11. Petroleum Products | 19.8 | 40 |
| 12. Consulting Services (Eng design, CAD CAM Management & manufacturing) | | 5 |
| 13 Ship Repairs, Aircraft Maintenance & Repaira, Healthcare etc | | 15 |
| 14. Financial Services | | 10 |
| 15. Tourism | | 15 |
| 16. IT Services and BPO | | 100 |
| | | 429 |

In order to emphasise the recent excellent developments in India which make us confident of our growth potential, we have given certain striking examples of our achievements as reported in the media.

We have given below some striking developments and achievements in India, which reinforces our confidence that in export, India will achieve in the year 2020 its rightful status as a **DEVELOPED COUNTRY**.

1. Moser-Baer in Noida is the world's third largest optical media manufacturer, and the lowest cost producer of CD Records. Its exports are close to Rs. 1000 crores. It sells data-storage products to seven of the world's top ten CD-R producers. And, it produces them so efficiently that to shield themselves, European competitors filed an anti-dumping case to stop India exporting CD-R's to Europe. Moser-Baer fought on its own and won the case.

It has acquired Capco Luxemborg, a firm that owns 49% of a Netherlands based CD-R distributor. It has also set up Glyphics Media Inc. in the USA for the markets in North and South America.

It is entering the field of solar energy and is in the process of establishing one of the biggest solar energy production centres in India.

2. Bharat Forge in Pune has the world's largest single location forging facility of 1.2 lakh tons per annum. Its client list includes Toyota, Honda, Volvo, Cummins, Daimler-Chrysler. It has been chosen as a supplier of small forging parts for Toyota's global transmission parts' sourcing hub in Bangalore. Its exports in the year 2002-03 was Rs. 271 crores ( 145% growth) and 40% of its production is exported.

Bharat Forge has also acquired a forging company in Germany, Carl Dan Peddinghaus GMBH at $115 billion. This meets its demands globally and has added BMW, Volkswagon and Audi to its list of customers.

3. Chennai based Rane group is one of the oldest automobile ancillaries companies established in India, and is a major supplier to all Indian manufacturers. It also supplies engine valves, steering assemblies etc. to many automotive manufacturers abroad.

4. Asian Paints of India has production facilities in 22 countries spread across five continents. It has acquired Berger International which gives it access to many other countries, and also SCIB Chemical SAE in Egypt. Asian paints is the market leader in 11 out of 22 countries in which it is present, including India.

5. Hindustan Ink has the world's largest single stream, fully integrated ink plant of 100,000 tons per annum in Gujarat. It has a manufacturing plant and a 100% subsidiary in the USA, and another 100% subsidiary in Austria.

6. Essel Propack is the world's largest laminated tube manufacturer. It has a presence in 11 countries including China. With a global manufacturing share of 25%, it caters to Proctor & Gamble's laminated tube requirements in the USA and 40% of Unilevers.

7. Europe's leading tractor maker Renault has chosen India's International Tractors Ltd. as its sole global sourcing hub for 40 to 85 horsepower tractors.

8. Tyco Electronics India bagged its first outsourcing contract in 1998-99.It has been so successful that components and products which it has contracted since then account for 50% of its total sales. It also supplies to its parent company Tyco.

9. The generics drug market is growing very fast.

'Generics' are cheaper copies of medicines that have gone off the patent list. In the USA alone 200 drugs are coming off the patent over the next few years. It is estimated that the world's top 20 pharmaceutical companies are set to lose patent protection on products whose total sales value would be $36 billion by 2007. The US is keen on easing the entry of generics in order to bring down the healthcare costs which are increasing.

The new President elect Mr Barak Obama has pledged to expand the healeh-care, and this will enable large import of generic products into USA so as to bring down the cost of drugs.

Indian companies, both by virtue of cost competition and reverse engineering skills are one of the main contenders to enter the generics market. Many Indian companies have already increased their R&D expenditure and are well placed to grab a good share of the market.

❖ ❖ ❖

4

# GLOBAL FINANCIAL CRISIS AND CONSEQUENCES

We have seen, in the earlier chapters, India's export record over the last few years. Taking into consideration India's potential, we have hazarded a guess as to how our exports can increase, and in 2020 it will be of an order that will befit a developed country, other things being 'normal'.

But there are a few developments on which an exporter, a company or even a nation has no prior knowledge or control which can upset all well laid out plans of exports. One such development which shook the whole world is the Global Financial Crisis which suddenly erupted in September 2008 in USA.

## I. GLOBAL FINANCIAL CRISIS

All analysts the world over say that it was set off by the 'sub-prime loan crisis' of USA. Even though the 'sub prime crisis' is referred to as the trigger which brought down banks, financial institutions and the entire financial system, there were other factors which contributed to this 'catastrophe', which we shall refer to later.

**What is the 'subprime crisis' and how did this originate?**

Subprime lending is the practice of making loans to borrowers who do not qualify for market interest rates owing to various risk factors, such as income level, size of the down payment made, credit history and employment status.

The crisis began with the bursting of the United States housing bubble and high default rates on "subprime" and adjustable rate mortgages (ARM), beginning in approximately 2005–2006. For a number of years prior to that, declining lending standards, an increase in loan incentives such as easy initial terms, and a long-term trend of rising housing prices had encouraged borrowers to assume difficult mortgages in the belief they would be able to quickly refinance at more favourable terms. However, once interest rates began to rise and housing prices started to drop moderately in 2006–2007 in many parts of the U.S., refinancing became more difficult. Defaults and foreclosure activity increased dramatically as easy initial terms expired, home prices failed to go up as anticipated, and ARM interest rates reset higher. Foreclosures accelerated in the United States in late 2006 and triggered a global financial crisis through 2007 and 2008. During 2007, nearly 1.3 million U.S. housing properties were subject to foreclosure activity, up 79% from 2006.

The subprime mortgage crisis is an ongoing financial crisis characterized by contracted liquidity in global credit markets and banking systems triggered by the failure of mortgage companies, investment firms and government sponsored enterprises which had invested in subprime mortgages. The crisis, which has roots in the closing years of the 20th century but has become more apparent throughout 2007 and 2008, has passed through various stages exposing pervasive weaknesses in the global financial system and regulatory framework.

Major banks and other financial institutions around the world have reported losses of approximately US$435 billion as of 17 July 2008. The liquidity concerns drove central banks around the world to take action to provide funds to member banks to encourage lending to worthy borrowers and to restore faith in the commercial paper markets. The U.S. government also bailed out key financial institutions, assuming significant additional financial commitments.

The risks to the broader economy created by the financial market crisis and housing market downturn were primary factors in several decisions by the U.S. Federal Reserve to cut interest rates and the economic stimulus package passed by Congress and signed by President George W. Bush on February 13, 2008. During the week of September 14, 2008 the crisis accelerated, developing into a global financial crisis. Following a series of ad-hoc market interventions to bail out particular firms, a $700 billion proposal was presented to the U.S. Congress in September, 2008. These actions are designed to stimulate economic growth and inspire confidence in the financial markets. On 3 October 2008, President George W. Bush signed the amended version of the bill into law. The following week the Dow-Jones index of the largest companies traded on the U.S. stock market declined 22%, the worst week in the index's 118-year history. Since 1 January, 2008, owners of stocks in U.S. corporations have suffered about $8 trillion in losses, as their holdings declined in value from $20 trillion to $12 trillion. Losses in other countries have averaged about 40%.

The value of U.S. subprime mortgages was estimated at $1.3 trillion as of March 2007, with over 7.5 million first-lien subprime mortgages outstanding. Approximately 16% of subprime loans with adjustable rate mortgages (ARM) were 90-days delinquent or in foreclosure proceedings as of October 2007, roughly triple the rate of 2005. By January 2008, the delinquency rate had risen to 21% and by May 2008 it was 25%. The U.S. mortgage market is estimated at $12 trillion with approximately 9.2% of loans either delinquent or in foreclosure through August 2008. Subprime ARMs only represent 6.8% of the loans outstanding in the US, yet they represent 43.0% of the foreclosures started during the third quarter of 2007. During 2007, nearly 1.3 million properties were subject to foreclosure filings, up 79% versus 2006.

Traditionally, banks lent money to homeowners for their mortgage and retained the risk of default, called credit risk. However, due to financial innovations, banks can now sell rights to the mortgage payments and related credit risk to investors, through a process called securitization. The securities the investors purchase are called mortgage backed securities (MBS) and collateralized debt obligations (CDO). This new "originate to distribute" banking model means credit risk has been distributed broadly to investors, with a series of consequential impacts. There are four primary categories of risk involved: credit risk, asset price risk, liquidity risk, and counterparty risk.

There is a greater interdependence now than in the past between the U.S. housing market and global financial markets due to MBS. When homeowners default, the amount of cash flowing into MBS declines and becomes uncertain. Investors and businesses holding MBS have been significantly affected. The effect is magnified by the high debt levels maintained by individuals and corporations, sometimes called financial leverage.

Credit default swaps, a type of non-regulated and non-collateral "insurance" for speculating financial institutions contributed to the international scope of the crisis. It led to a virtual credit system, that was virtually insulated from market valuation. The smaller subprime mortgage crisis revealed the hollowness of credit default swaps, which led to a larger loss of confidence inside the banking and insurance sector.

A combination of low interest rates and large inflows of foreign funds helped to create easy credit conditions for many years leading up to the crisis. Subprime borrowing was a major contributor to an increase in home ownership rates and the demand for housing. The overall U.S. home ownership rate increased from 64% in 1994 (about where it was since 1980) to a peak in 2004 with an all-time high of 69.2%.

This demand helped fuel housing price increases and consumer spending. Between 1997 and 2006, American home prices increased by 124%. For the two decades until 2001, the national median home price went up and down, but it remained between 2.9 and 3.1 times the median household income. By 2004, however, the ratio of home prices to income hit 4.0, and by 2006 the ratio was 4.6. Some homeowners used the increased property value experienced in the housing bubble to refinance their homes with lower interest rates and take out second mortgages against the added value to use the funds for consumer spending. U.S. household debt as a percentage of income rose to 130% during 2007, versus 100% earlier in the decade. A culture of consumerism is a factor "in an economy based on immediate gratification". Americans spent $800 billion per year more than they earned. Household debt grew from $680 billion in 1974 to $14 trillion in 2008, with the total doubling since 2001. During 2008, the average U.S. household owned 13 credit cards, and 40 per cent of them carried a balance, up from 6 per cent in 1970.

Overbuilding during the boom period eventually led to a surplus inventory of homes, causing home prices to decline, beginning in the summer of 2006. Easy credit, combined with the assumption that housing prices would continue to appreciate, had encouraged many subprime borrowers to obtain adjustable-rate mortgages they could not afford after the initial incentive period. Once housing prices started depreciating moderately in many parts of the U.S., refinancing became more difficult. Some homeowners were unable to re-finance and began to default on loans as their loans reset to higher interest rates and payment amounts.

An estimated 8.8 million homeowners — nearly 10.8% of total homeowners — had zero or negative equity as of March 2008, meaning their homes are worth less than their mortgage. This provided an incentive to "walk away" from the home, despite the credit rating impact.

Increasing foreclosure rates increased the supply of housing inventory available. Sales volume (units) of new homes dropped by 26.4% in 2007 versus the prior year. By January 2008, the inventory of unsold new homes stood at 9.8 months based on December 2007 sales volume, the highest level since 1981. Further, a record of nearly four million unsold existing homes were for sale, including nearly 2.9 million that were vacant.

Speculation in real estate was a contributing factor. During 2006, 22% of homes purchased (1.65 million units) were for investment purposes, with an additional 14% (1.07 million units) purchased as vacation homes. During 2005, these figures were 28% and 12%, respectively. In other words, nearly 40% of home purchases (record levels) were not primary residences. NAR's chief economist at the time, David Lereah, stated that the fall in investment buying was expected in 2006. "Speculators left the market in 2006, which caused investment sales to fall much faster than the primary market."

While homes had not traditionally been treated as investments like stocks, this behavior changed during the housing boom. For example, one company estimated that as many as 85% of condominium properties purchased in Miami were for investment purposes. Media widely reported the behavior of purchasing condominiums prior to completion, then "flipping" (selling) them for a profit without ever living in the home. Some mortgage companies identified risks inherent in this activity as early as 2005, after identifying investors assuming highly leveraged positions in multiple properties.

This coincided with a slowdown in the US economy, and this made matters worse. Some of the estimates indicated that housing prices had dropped upto 50% from their peak in 2006. Thus the declining value of the collateral meant that the lenders were left much less than the value of their loans, and have had to bear huge losses.

Then the question arises as to how this loan default became a systemic crisis, and affected many banks and many countries. It is because the original lenders had sold their portfolios (of loans/mortgages) to other players in the market. In many cases, the portfolio also contained complex derivatives evolved by financial institutions, which were sold repeatedly by all banks since they were termed as 'good assets'. As a result, nobody is absolutely sure about the extent of the losses and will not know until the dust ultimately settles down.

As explained earlier, because these loans/mortgage portfolios were widely sold and bought by international banks(it is also reported that many credit agencies have given good credit ratings for these), the crisis was felt world wide. It is estimated that a little more than half of these losses (US $ 260 billion) were supplied by US based institutions , and US 207 billion by European banks, and a relatively moderate US $ 24 billion by Asian ones. These were the first estimates, and as it is an ongoing saga, the full extent will be known by and by.

The American government has come to the rescue of many banks and financial institutions in USA by inducting fresh capital into them. (This introduction technically amounts to part nationalization , as the bank's equity will be owned by the government and will be affected to that extent).

## OTHER FACTORS

Apart from the sub prime crisis there were other factors as well:

The US is the biggest borrower in the world since most countries hold their foreign exchange reserves in dollars and invest them in US government securities. Thus, any crisis in US has a direct bearing on other countries, particularly those with large reserves like Japan and China, and to a lesser extent, India.

The equity capital in companies in many markets including India, allow investment by foreign institutional investments as well as direct foreign investment in companies. Hence any crisis overtaking foreign investors will result in the sudden withdrawal of their investment to meet their domestic demands, and affect the share market in the countries concerned.

Another factor which was responsible for the crisis is the role of 'investment banks', another type of financial institution in the USA. These are not covered by the usual banking regulations of scheduled banks. Further, these institutions had great leverage and freedom so that many could raise funds in some cases, equivalent to 30 times their capital. These institutions such as Lehman Brothers, Merryl Lynch, Goldman Sachs etc were also responsible in developing many 'financial instruments' based on loans, mortgages, derivatives etc., which are tradable and helped them to raise more money and make huge profits. But when things such as sub prime mortgages failed, the losses incurred were so huge that they were enough for the collapse of these institutions. Of the five big investment banks, *viz.,* Lehman Brothers, Merryl Lynch, Goldman Sachs, Morgan Stanley, and Bears & Stearns, one has collapsed, one has been merged with Barclays Bank- a scheduled bank, and the others converted themselves into regular scheduled banks. In spite of the transformation, government had to induct huge amounts of capital to keep the bank liquid.

Due to the extensive sub prime loan failures, in which many banking institutions were involved, the American government had to induct capital into them to keep them afloat. Whenever we say that the government has inducted money into the institution, you must remember that it is all tax payers' money. How much the government can give, and how much the banks need, is still hazy. The US government has passed a regulation for US$ 700 billion fund, as sdtated earlier.

Over the last eight years, the rapid decline in international trade shows clearly that America has become the most indebted nation.

**Table 4.1**

**TRADE BALANCE OF USA**

| *Year* | *Exports* | | *Imports* | | *surplus(+)/deficit(-)* | | |
|---|---|---|---|---|---|---|---|
| | *Goods* | *Services* | *Goods* | *Services* | *Goods* | *Services* | *Total* |
| 2000 | 771 | 298 | 1224 | 223 | -452 | 74 | -377 |
| 2002 | 682 | 292 | 1164 | 231 | -482 | 61 | -421 |
| 2003 | 713 | 304 | 1257 | 250 | -550 | 53 | -496 |
| 2004 | 807 | 349 | 1469 | 292 | -669 | 57 | -612 |
| 2005 | 894 | 388 | 1673 | 315 | -787 | 72 | -714 |
| 2006 | 1023 | 422 | 1853 | 342 | -838 | 79 | -758 |

In simple terms, it amounts to the fact that the American consumer, economy and government are all living way beyond their means and it is not sustainable. This is borne out by the fact that for the American consumer, the outstanding credit card balance was on the verge of $1 trillion till early September 2008. The defaulters on this count are on the rise. This also indicates that thrift and savings are no longer the agenda in their households.

The savings as a percentage of disposable income in an American household was around 8% in 1950, and rose to 12% by 1980. It has been on the decline and in 2004, it had plunged to 0% and was close to – 2% in 2007. From the above, the kind of profligacy is obvious.

The credit crunch in the USA is severely affecting industry and commerce. Even healthy sectors are vulnerable and the contagion is spreading to Europe and Asia.

Practically from the end of Second World War, the Automotive Industry in USA was the biggest and was shown as a symbol of their superiority in the industrial sector. There was even a saying then: 'What General Motors think today, America thinks tomorrow.'

Such premier institutions like General Motors, Ford etc were already in trouble due to severe competition in the field and increase in the price of gasoline. But after the Financial Crisis, unless government gives a helping hand, they cannot survive for long.

The unemployment figures for October' 08 in USA was the highest in a decade and layoff of employees has become a wrenching second act in the unfolding crisis. Companies such as Merck, Yahoo, General Electric, Xerox, Pratt & Whitney, Goldman Sachs, Bank of America, Coca Cola, and automotive companies like GM, Ford etc., are retrenching staff. People in general have seen a lot of their wealth wiped out, and as they cut back their spending, companies are responding with reduced production and layoffs. This hurts the economy considerably. Unemployment will become widespread and recession in the economy has already begun.

The worst consequence of this will be that many countries who used to export in large measure to USA will suffer. China, and to a much lesser extent, India will be affected.

In the European Union, a large number of banks have suffered from the exposure to sub prime credit portfolios which were freely bought and held, and also because they have taken oversized risks and are overstretched. In a situation like this where the biggest financial market is doddering, it is needless to say that it spreads panic in all the countries and the banking systems. In end September 2008, governments from Germany to Ireland rushed to prop up five sinking financial institutions with huge cash infusions amounting to almost a full blown nationalization. Even though the governments sent reassuring messages to the public that their money was safe, a lot more convincing needs to be done.

There is another fallout – the loss of confidence of banks with one another. Due to this, they have stopped lending to one another, for fear of financial risks. Further, the USA has the Federal Reserve and Treasury Secretary who can evolve a policy for the whole country, whereas in the 27 nations of the European Union, there is no single bank regulator and no mechanism to draft a comprehensive solution that will apply to all the countries.

The after effects of these are becoming clear. In Europe, a recession is setting in. As America is one of the biggest markets for Europe, their exports to that country will be affected. Consequently, there will be less production of goods and services, resulting in layoffs and all other consequences thereof.

This may result in their efforts to increase exports to Asia, wherever possible. In spite of all their efforts, there will be slowdown in the economy and they will have to endure a recessionary period.

## II HOW THE GLOBAL FINANCIAL CRISIS AFFECTS INDIA

Initially, for the Indian observer, it was a huge unimaginable spectacle. The very big and mighty financial institutions of the West suffered very badly and disappeared. The government and the administration of the Western world fought a grim battle to keep their financial system running. But the crisis had not yet hit the Indian economy in a significant way, namely job losses or income curtailment till the third quarter of 2008.

The future remains to be seen, as the signs are ominous.

The Indian economy was already in a slowdown and the pundits had predicted a growth of 7.5% in the current year 2008-09 as against 9% in 2007-2008.

The choking of credit, combined with elevated risk perception, will lead to lower capital flows and reduced levels of foreign direct investment, lesser exports, and slowing down of the economy. The combined effect will be lesser economic growth. Experts feel that it may slow down to 6% to 6.5% this year from close to 9% in the last four years.

Another interesting feature which came to the help of India is that India's globalization has been in the direction of increasing manufacturing abilities, increasing exports and improving the infrastructure and also to make India the hub of exports in many products and services to the whole world, while nurturing the domestic market. In the financial sector, India had not effected complete convertibility pf the Indian Rupee, and hence the financial institutions and banks had restrictions, which helped.

Further, India was fighting double digit inflation which was showing a gradual decline and with a good monsoon and prices declining, the economy was anticipating decrease in interest rates to help drive the engine of growth.

At this juncture, the global financial crisis hit all the countries including India to present a new picture where the fear of the unknown was predominant.

1. The Global Financial Crisis has injected a huge amount of uncertainty and scarcity of funds. Most of the financial institutions and banks have become extremely risk-averse. Further, there are reports that banks hesitate to finance any expansion programme of companies, and in some cases, do not allow companies to draw credit to the already approved limits. The interest rates are still very high, introduced to fight inflation when it was flaring up.
2. As stated earlier, the Foreign Institutional Investors from abroad, who have pulled out almost $13 billion from the Indian stock market, have given it a big jolt, and the usual fear and frenzy exhibited by the stock markets have brought down the prices of shares considerably, unrelated to the real worth of the companies. This is affecting many companies whose abilities for growth and expansion are getting inhibited, for he simple reason that they cannot raise funds from the market.
3. The heightened risk perception may affect the investments. India is in a state where it needs all types of investments – foreign, governmental and private sectors – for the growth of the economy. It has long been evident that if India has to bolster the economy and continue to grow at the pace of the last couple of years, foreign investment is absolutely necessary. As such, foreign investment in projects or companies may come down drastically in the coming years due to the Global Financial Crisis, and it will affect our growth.
4. Infrastructure spending may be affected. Projects such as highways, airports, ports, electricity generation projects and such other essential needs of the economy may be delayed or postponed. Further, the present high rates of interest will make private infrastructure projects less profitable and private sector investors may look for other types of investments. Projects with larger share of private and foreign funds might suffer badly.

5. The real estate sector which was booming, with many of them having foreign investments through private equity route, will have a tighter fund crunch, and lesser demand, and their growth and expansion will be moderated. This will have an effect on the job creations per se, and also on the sale of steel, cement and other requirements which gave a boost to all those sectors.

6. To cite an example as to how India's Industry will be affected by this crisis, let us look at India's Textile Industry. It accounts for 11% of our exports, and amounts to 4% of our GDP. It is the largest employer in India after agriculture, providing livelihood for 35 million people. It is estimated that 40% of India's textile and apparel output is exported mostly to the USA and Europe. Hence, the sector has become very vulnerable to the recession in the west. It is imperative that suitable steps are taken by the industry with full help and support from the Government to increase its domestic market, and also find alternate export markets. This is going to be very difficult at a time when the Global Financial Crisis is driving a strong recession directly or indirectly in all countries.

7. One of the important driving forces of the economy is consumer demand. This may suffer due to lack of job growth and income growth. The effect of these will be known in the months ahead and is difficult to quantify now.

We have listed above how the Global Financial Crisis may affect Indian economy. It is still early days.

At the same time, it is necessary to point out certain favourable trends in the third quarter of 2008 that may help India's economy in the short-term.

1. India had a good monsoon in 2008. This ensures adequate food production. Good monsoons always increase rural demand, which is another engine of growth of the economy.

2. Crude oil price has dramatically come down. From a high of $147 per barrel it has dropped to $64 per barrel by end October 2008. This will considerably help us as we import around 75% of our petroleum product needs. Further, there is a drop in prices of many commodities and metals.

3. There is still a steady inflow of Foreign Direct Investment in India in the first half of this fiscal amounting to $14 billion,

even though the Foreign Institutional Investments(FII) in the stock market have withdrawn a considerable portion of their investments. FDI will help the economy and the growth thereof.

4. India still has the highest household saving rate (even higher than China) which is a positive factor and we are still a domestic driven economy.

These are a few factors that will help us to weather the Global Financial Crisis engulfing us.

No matter what the consequences and damages of this crisis, according to experts, India is expected to overcome the same much better than the developed world, and come out of it with the least negative consequences.

For this, the government should be very active, listen to the industry and commerce, and take policy decisions at the right time which will help the economy. The government is responding well so far in increasing the liquidity and encouraging banks to assist industry and commerce. But the reluctance of the banks to reduce the interest rates, and expand the credit portfolio as of the first week of November is seriously affecting automobile, housing and consumer durables sectors which are main engines of growth for the economy.

## III. GLOBAL FINANCIAL CRISIS AND ITS IMPACT ON EXPORTS FROM INDIA

Let us see how India's export is faring in the first half of 2008-09.

The cumulative value of exports for the period Apr-Aug 2008 was $81.23 billion, which was an increase of 35% over the corresponding period of last year. However the exports in the month of September 2008 was only $13.4 billion, which was 10.4% over the same month last year. It is significant to note that that this monthly increase was the lowest in almost the last three years. It also indicates that a steady and commendable increase in the past few years has started to decline, appreciably.

Another disturbing factor is the trade deficit. The imports during Apr-Sep 2008 was $154.7 billion whereas the exports in Apr-Sep 2008 was of the order of $94.9 billion. Hence, the trade deficit (the excess of imports over exports) in Apr-Sep 2008 is $59.8 billion. This is much higher than $39 billion which was the trade deficit in Apr-Sep 2007. If the present trend continues, experts predict that we will have a trade deficit of over $100 billion in 2008-09, which will result in an ultimate trade and fiscal deficit of a high order.

The country's export sector assumes very great importance in a situation like this. So far India has had the advantage of reducing fiscal deficit by invisible incomes such as tourism and travel, the remittances of the Indian diaspora abroad, as well as the FDI and FII inflow into India.

Already signs are evident in the reduction in tourists coming to India. Of the total number of tourists who visit India, 65% come from the USA and the European Union. Needless to say that this will reduce immediately. In the case of air travel, the public and private sector airlines are in the red in India. They are curtailing many of their schedules indicating a serious drop in occupancy rates. Due to the serious financial crisis in the USA and EU, foreign capital inflow into India will be drastically curtailed for quite sometime, at least for a couple of years according to experts.

Under circumstances like these, the nation can depend only on the Exports of the country (both merchandise and services), which can reduce the trade as well as fiscal deficit. Hence, the Exports of the country assume great importance and top priority , and the government should keep a very close watch and have a proactive approach. This is worth reiterating, because in India government wakes up to the importance of exports only after it is affected. As exports is the most important lifeline at this juncture, policy measures wherever needed should be brought in very quickly to sustain and improve the situation.

1. Of the total exports from India, 41.2% (around Rs. 235,563 crores in 2006-07) went to OECD countries (which are all developed countries, Further) 35% (out of the 41.2% mentioned above) are being exported to European Union and USA. For these exports, the writing on the wall is clear. When most of the developed countries from America to Japan go into recession, it is needless to say that their capacity to import will be constrained greatly. Our exports are going to suffer, and to what extent and in which sector is a little difficult to predict at the moment.

2. Of all the exporters, the Export Oriented Units or those situated in Special Economic Zones with a commitment to export will be affected considerably. Further, there are other joint ventures who have made India as the base for world production and exports and they will also be affected. There are many units in the industrial sector who have a large domestic market as well as export market. If due to recession abroad, the export markets of these units suffer badly, their production will be reduced and consequent problems on profitability, cost of product, excess labour etc. will surface.

3. Many organization which export from India have improved their quality and competitiveness considerably, based on the premise that the whole world is their market. This trend is also due to the fact that there were fluctuations in demand in the domestic market. Such units will be affected due to the sudden fall in the demand abroad as well as a contraction in domestic demand due to the seeping financial crisis. For example, the Automobile Ancillary Units in India achieved exports of over $3 billion in 2007-08. Most of these exports were to developed countries. Due to serious recession in western countries, many of them will drastically reduce their purchases and also bargain more for reduction of prices. This will seriously affect their exports.

Our exports in the software sector and BPO grew to a healthy $40 billion in 2007-08. The majority of our exports were to US (almost 60%) and most of it was in the financial sector. As the financial services sector is in a tailspin in USA, and the slowdown in the economy is spreading to Europe, our IT and allied exports will be affected sooner or later. To what extent, and for how long, are matters which will be clear only in 2009.

Of course our IT sector is trying to diversify from banks and financial sectors to other sectors such as manufacturing. Perhaps the reason for their concentration on the financial sector was because the financial sector spends an average of 10% of its earnings on IT, whereas the average spending of other sectors was around 3.5%.

Indian IT companies should get away from project based contracts (which are short term with a better profit) and try to obtain annuity contracts on a long term.

Indian companies should also improve their on-shore delivery capability by having suitable establishments abroad. This is also essential from the point of view that MNCs from abroad have developed a huge base in India and thereby furnish good competition to Indian IT vendors.

It short, Indian IT Export needs to broad base its revenue, geographical areas, expand global delivery capability and more, develop a non-linear business model where the direct link between revenue and head count is broken. The same should be priced on revenue share or outcome based model. Such an approach will considerably help.

It is still early to give an estimate of how much the export in this sector will be affected.

## CONCLUSION

It is needless to state that in India the export sector as a whole will be seriously dented, because of the recession in the major importing countries, and government should immediately help the exporting sector in finding alternate markets/products and finance this effort at low interest rates and commitments.

For many exporters, the basis for exports is and will always be a strong domestic market. Serious production cuts, job losses, and financial bottlenecks are around the corner. The government should immediately bring down the interest rates and encourage demand in the automotive, retail and consumer durables sector in the domestic market to start with, and in other sectors later.

It is also essential that government treat the Global Financial Crisis as a warlike situation and devise suitable (if necessary absolutely unconventional) policies to help exporters and the domestic industry to withstand the most serious onslaught after Independence on our growth and all that we have built over the last decades, until we get out of this mess, which is not of our making. The best way to do this is for the government to form a group of both government representatives and the export sector, and review the needs of exporters/economy almost on a daily basis. All proactive decisions should be taken in time, and implemented forthwith.

It is quite instructive to see what Chinese government is doing to meet the Global Financial Crisis head on. China has always fully supported its exports as very vital for its growth. The exports which were growing at an average of 20% is fast going down to zero or negative growth. The government greatly concerned with this, has already cut the interest rate three times in the last two months. The government has come out with a programme to bolster the economy in ten areas, chief among them being infrastructre real estate, domestic growth and exports. They have pledged an amount of $ 580 billion for this effort.

It is often pointed out to exporters and industry in India about what China does, and how we should emulate them, to be on top. It is interesting to note what China is doing to meet the GFC. Quoting a report from the press: 'The Chinese Government is preparing a large economic stimulus package, pushing new infrastructure products, offering aid to exporters and finding new ways to prop up the nation's depressed stock and real estate markets.'

Knowing the Chinese government, these steps should already be under implementation. It will not be too much to ask the Indian government to emulate the Chinese to the maximum extend possible to safeguard our economy and exports.

❖ ❖ ❖

# 5

# INTERNATIONAL MARKETING

## GENERAL

As we are at the commencement of the new Millennium, what will be the nature of marketing, especially international marketing, in the new century?

This of course depends upon the economic and political conditions prevailing in the world. Most of the experts believe that globalisation will be pursued, and there will be a tremendous exchange of goods, services and capital among all the countries. History has shown that competition has always spurred organizations to do better and cheaper, and movement of people and ideas across the borders have provided creativity and innovation.

The world's exports of goods and services were $ 12643 billion dollars by 2002, amounting to almost 40% of the world GDP. It is interesting to note that the world trade's share of the GDP twenty years ago, was a mere 9.3%.

Even today we see many strands of the transformation of the future taking place. Some of these are:

(1) As globalisation will be on the increase the world over, organizations will be forced to look at marketing in a holistic manner. The trend towards global manufacturing will increase, while at the same time offering country-specific and innovative solutions for each country. The ability to supply customized products and services will be enhanced.

(2) Another aspect is that the pace of technology development will accelerate and transform many of the traditional industries. Like other sectors, the impact of Information Technology on industry is quite great. It has made the manufacturing of machine tools highly sophisticated. Most of the products produced will have microchips in them, so as to make them very efficient and user-friendly, with faster market adaptation.

Because of the fast pace of technology development, it has brought to fore the need to have strong R & D Centres, company wise and country wise. The high cost of developing modern R & D Centres, may perhaps price it beyond the reach of many countries in the world. Will it lead to Techno-nationalism? No one knows. But India has some very strong players in the IT field as well as in design and R & D, and they will certainly keep us upfront, since many of the innovations are based on IT research.

(1) Internet and telecom technology advances will transform all aspects of international marketing. The developed world says that e-business, and especially e-commerce is going to affect marketing in a way that nothing else has done in the past fifty years. The communication revolution which is on, will enable individuals to carry their data and communication medium with them. As they say, the competitors' specifications and prices will only be a 'click' away. Hence, an international marketer should be abreast of all these, and have the ability to react and reach his buyer immediately to clinch his deals.

(2) The importers are expected to be more sophisticated and demanding about their requirements. The wide choice and options they have from different countries, and the ability to get the latest quotes instantaneously, and compare different offers will make them quite formidable. Hence the marketer who is knowledgeable as to what his competitors can offer, and who can convince the buyer that his product, its delivery and service facilities are better than the competitors, will be the winner.

(3) The demand for human resources or human capital for international marketing, is going to be the topmost priority in an organization. We should be able to get people, who are quick on the uptake, can learn

new skills fast, and who can work in the above milieu. As they say in the export trade, they should be able to interact and work with personnel in corporations without national boundaries or borders. Companies should be able to combine the respective strengths of different cultures into productive teamwork. Continuous investment in human resources will become one of the most compelling and competitive factors in the globalised market.

(4) Service Industries are developing fast in all the international markets. There is going to be fierce international competition, facilitated by internet and worldwide data exchange facilities. It will need in-depth knowledge of different market segments, which will provide them fast and customized responses to obtain a good share of this market.

This is of particular importance to India. India's service exports in 1997 were $ 9.3 billion as against its merchandise exports of $32.3 billion. India's service exports increased in value in 2002 to $23 billion. Out of this, software and services exports are increasing at the rate of 40% every year, and is expected to exceed $15 billion in 2004-05.

(5) The primary role of marketing is to design and execute effective and appropriate market programmes which will help to market the goods and services. The task is complex enough when the organization serves a single national market. It becomes much more complex when we have to market in several countries, or export to new international markets.

It is amazing to see how many considerations come into the picture, and some though looking innocuous, can completely set aside all the basic systematic hard work done. One is, by compulsion, an eternal student of marketing, learning all the time. Hence an attitude of mind and approach to the problems – one of strong determination, capacity for quick and imaginative responses, with an array of contingency plans and programmes all the time, are some of the traits needed.

The marketer primarily concentrates on the customer's needs, and the quality, price and delivery of the product. True, these things are equally important in an international market. But in an international market some other considerations take overwhelming importance. When we are trying to market our product or service in a new country, in practically all the cases, we are fulfilling a need and 'replacing an existing supplier', who is performing the task. The ties, the traditions, the business and other aspects, which are binding the supplier and the buyer have to be unraveled. This becomes paramount in Gulf countries where the buyer, invariably a government department, and the supplier are bound by traditions and considerations about which we can write a whole book. In such cases a new strategy has to be evolved which would take strong perseverance and a long time to succeed. Do the individual and the organization have the determination and the sustaining power for such a program is an important question that the international marketer has to ponder over.

(1) Many organizations do not squarely face or go deeply into the fact that international marketing is a COSTLY PROCESS. They feel that it is an extension of the domestic market, and lay no stress on market study and analysis. They feel that a visit or two by their capable salesman can land them with good orders. It might, in some cases, but they forget the fact that many salesmen of this ilk have already visited these countries before and done the same things, and unless they have a different product or service, their sales effort will be a hit and miss affair.

If one wants to establish oneself in the international market, he should have, not only the product and capable staff, but also a capacity to bear the upfront expenditure. The visits, surveying the market, meeting all customers, and getting market intelligence are all very costly compared to the domestic market, and unless one has a product or service which can withstand international competition, and is prepared to budget these expenditures, one should not venture into international markets.

(2) More than 50% of India's exports are to developed countries, and that is where its future exports are going to be for large volumes and sizable increases in exports. These countries which trade among themselves largely, have also formed themselves into groups like EU, NAFTA etc.

They are all keen on entering the markets of countries like India which are large. But they have an agenda of their own, and they decide the extent to which they would give an entry into their markets. The Indian exporter has to face this and other hidden agendas.

An example of this would be: European countries have given the developing countries GSP considerations which helps them to sell many of their goods without any import duty. These European countries are threatening to withdraw this facility.

Hence, apart from all the rules and regulations of the World Trade Organisation which has come into existence recently for fair play and justice in international trade, one will always find new problems and obstructions. International trade is likened to a war, and no quarter is given or taken, and we as a country should steel ourselves for this.

(3) As India exports and gets an exposure to the various countries, marketing is going to bring in its wake, new opportunities. An alert international marketer should grab these opportunities as they come along. They will be in the form of the following:

*(a)* existing products/services India can supply,

*(b)* new products/services which India can produce and supply competitively,

*(c)* joint ventures with collaboration and buyback,

*(d)* relocating of industries from developed countries to India, to produce goods economically and establish India as a source for supplying internationally.

The essence of international marketing is to identify new opportunities and increase trade on the one hand, and on the other hand to study all the regulations and new barriers which will come up in the various countries and find ways and means to overcome the same, apart from attending to other aspects of marketing which are well-known.

## MARKETING PROCESS

A simple definition of international marketing is,' an effort to find a global customer whose needs can be satisfied by an exporter in a way better than the competitor, and coordinating the entire marketing activities in consonance with the rules and regulations of both the countries.'

In the very definition of this we find many features which are unique to international marketing. Let us analyse these:

1. 'Needs of a global customer' – This requires extensive market research to enable one to arrive at the right product or services which can be exported on a long-term basis.
2. 'In a way better than the competitor' – One should realize that the existing needs of the customer are probably met by another supplier, and the international marketer selling a new product has to replace that. Unless the product is superior to the existing one, it cannot make headway.

The means of doing this are:

*(a)* If possible, introduce one extra quality or advantage in using the product, or some such value addition.

(b) Adopt better distribution methods so that the buyer gets the product easily, in the numbers he needs.

(c) Use better packaging or presentation, and better promotion methods like advertising or better servicing.

As to which of these methods will have the best effect can be known only by market research.

3. 'Co-ordinating Market Activities'–This would primarily amount to ensuring that the product is made available in time and shipped in consonance with the delivery committed, and the realization of export proceeds and incentives if any. It also includes other activities such as product adaptation that will be appreciated by the customer. Or in some cases like export of machinery, one can establish an excellent after sales service, which will attract the customer. An exporter can also improve the method of production so as to reduce the manufacturing costs and meet the competition. This is where marketing skills will be in evidence.

4. 'Market the product in consonance with the rules and regulations of both the exporting and importing country'-

The very definition of **international marketing** implies that goods and services are marketed across national boundaries. This calls for special efforts and the means of implementing them.

(a) The first element in this is **export finance.** The currency in which the export invoice will be made may be different, and foreign exchange rules have to be adhered to, both in the exporting and importing country.

(b) The second is the **documentation.** When sales invoices are made in export, a host of documents have to accompany the invoice to the bank (the details are dealt with in another chapter) and any discrepancy in this area will delay the receipt of the export proceeds.

(c) The third issue is the **rules** administrated by the customs and port authorities in the country of export as well as in the importing country. As these are complicated and also change periodically, the help of an experienced clearing agent is required by both the exporter and importer in their respective countries.

Hence it is evident that a series of efforts are required to succeed in international marketing. Indian exports in the year 2002-2003 reached $ 50 billion, and it is a credit to the international marketing skills of India's exporters.

Let us see how an export company goes through the process of international marketing.

The world market is made up of a number of countries with different groups of people, each with its own life style, standard of living, habits, preferences and inclinations. For a given product, therefore, a number of markets exist with different characteristics, which may be looked upon as individual markets similar to the domestic market. On the other hand, for a given market, a company might identify the different types of products it might possibly market, keeping in view its objectives. Both these decisions would entail a commitment of a large amount of resources. Since a company has limited resources at its disposal, these should be deployed in such a manner as to maximize their advantage.

Ideally a company would like to utilize its resources in a few markets where its sales and profits are maximal. It is therefore essential for it to obtain as much information on the market as possible so that it may be in a position to set clear-cut aims and objectives. Once these objectives are set, a market strategy may be worked out. Strategic planning is absolutely essential. Specifically, answers to such questions as the following should be obtained:

*(a)* Which of its products can it sell in a foreign market?

*(b)* For a given product, which market should it concentrate on in order to achieve optimum result?

*(c)* What kind of strategies should be followed to ensure the success of the marketing plan?

The answers to these questions would enable one to arrive at a decision, which would help in the effective deployment of available resources.

## INTERNATIONAL TRADE

If we attempt to list the **various steps** involved in the exploration of the international market, we would arrive at the following:

**1. Survey of the market:** Market survey is a means of obtaining maximum information which would help one identify the markets where a particular product may be sold, or identify the products that may be sold in a given market.

**2. Decide on market product configuration:** Based on the data available from the market survey, a decision has to be taken by the management about the product it would like to promote in a particular market, as also the markets to which a given product may be exported.

**3. Draw up a marketing strategy and plan:** A plan is a group of decisions taken by the management about the various aspects of the marketing scenario – product, price, delivery, packaging, promotion, distribution etc. A marketing strategy is usually drawn up by the management for a pre-determined level of sales volume and profit in accordance with the data obtained by it from the market survey.

**4. Implement the Market Plan:** The implementation of the market plan would also involve the identification of various sales promotion strategies, which would create a need for the product in the market and consequently result in a sale. The effectiveness of sales promotion strategies would determine the volume of sales and the market share obtained by the company for a particular product.

## MARKETING STRATEGY/MARKETING PLAN

Once the market product configuration has been identified, the next step is to draw up a marketing strategy for the promotion of a product in a particular market. The marketing strategy is nothing but a combination of decisions based on the various aspects of the marketing mix. These are:

*(a)* Product

*(b)* Pricing

*(c)* Delivery

*(d)* Distribution

*(e)* Promotion

*(f)* Packaging

The marketing plan clearly stipulates decisions about each of these variables *vis-à-vis* the competition faced by the company in that market.

### (a) Product

The market product configuration has already established the type of product that can be sold in the market. Once this has been identified, the other decisions relating to the product and the product features will have to be incorporated to make it more acceptable to the target customers. A comparison is always made between the product we are endeavoring to promote in the market and the competitor's product, to determine which one is the most acceptable to the target customer. Depending on whether it is an industrial product or a consumer product, the comparison may relate to a variety of features and specifications. For instance, in the case of a consumer product like hair oil or toilet soap, its colour, fragrance and the appearance may possibly influence customer acceptability. In the case of an engineering product, the technical specifications and the optional equipment that is provided along with the product may be the deciding factors, which influence its marketability. The product decision with regard to its marketability should cover all the aspects of product specifications, appearance and other related features *vis-à-vis* those provided by the best competitor. In recent times, the most important factor determining the sale of engineering products to developing countries is the after sales service rendered by the manufacturer.

**(b) Pricing**

The price at which the product is sold in the market exerts considerable influence on its marketability. It is a simple truth that the higher the price, the lower the volume of sales and *vice versa*. At the same time a company has before it, the objective of recovering at least the cost involved in the manufacture and marketing of the product. In view of this fact, it has to make a conscious decision to fix the price which is most advantageous for it in terms of profitability and the volume of sales. In fact the pricing policy is decided on the basis of the market share which the company decides to achieve. When it introduces its product in a new market in competition with established brands, it is quite likely that the company will make some sacrifice in price, even if it means incurring losses in the initial stages. Once the product is established and accepted by the customer, an increase in the price may be considered. The pricing decisions may therefore be altered if the company tries to introduce a product in a new market against established brand leaders.

**(c) Delivery**

The availability of goods in the market when a customer decides to purchase them, is an important criterion for enhancing sales. In the case of consumer products and consumer durables, it is essential that one should avoid stock-outs in the market. There is a definite element of impulse buying, and this should not be sacrificed, particularly when a product is introduced for the first time. In the case of engineering items, which are manufactured for a particular use, quick deliveries definitely ensure better marketability.

**(d) Distribution**

Distribution decisions relate to the appointment of agents and distributors, with the provision of warehouse for stocks, depending on the product handled by the company. Agents or distributors perform a definite function in the entire marketing set-up, for they ensure that the product is made available to the ultimate customer at the right time. In addition, they are in direct contact with the target customers and are therefore an important link in the entire marketing process. The appointment of an agent for distribution and establishing a distributorship network are very important contributory factors in the marketability of a product.

Apart from the decision about the appointment of a distributor, physical distribution of the product is an important factor in a distribution policy. Physical distribution relates to decisions directly connected with the movement of goods from the point of manufacture to the point of sale so as to ensure the availability of the product at the right place at the right time. When a company is exploring the international market, where manufacturing units and selling points are separated by long distances and where communication facilities are inadequate, certain problems may arise. That is why distribution decisions about the actual distributorship as well as physical distribution should clearly be spelt out while drawing up a market plan.

**(e) Promotion**

This decision refers to the sales promotion to be adopted in achieving the marketing objectives. The decision covers all the aspects of advertising, visual aids, provision of show windows, promotional shows and other sales promotion activities. A combination of these methods is usually adopted to achieve the best results.

**(f) Packaging**

The packaging decision usually plays a role in the marketing of consumer goods like cosmetics, toiletries etc. Attractive packaging enhances the marketability of the product.

The foregoing paragraphs have broadly described the marketing decisions necessary for effectively exploring an export market. A detailed analysis of each of these decisions with reference to the competition and its intensity to be faced is to be undertaken by the exporter before he commits his marketing resources. In fact, the nature of attaining a definite percentage share of the market or the extent of market penetration, largely influences the content of each marketing decision detailed above. For instance, if an exporter wants to market his brand of toilet soap in a new market in competition with a number of popular brands already on sale in that market, he should be prepared to sell his toilet soap at a price lower than those of his competitors, offer larger discounts to agents or distributors, and perhaps, incur heavy expenditure on advertising and sales promotion until his brand is well established. Once this has been achieved, he would be in a better position to raise his prices and gain a larger market share.

But when one plans to enter a new market for export, with no previous experience, there is a need for a preliminary market research by way of desk research and market survey of the new market before the product is decided upon. This has been described in detail in Chapter 3 on 'Problems of Starting an Export Business'.

## NEW PRODUCT PLANNING FOR EXPORT MARKETS

### 1. NEED AND IMPORTANCE

The need for an exhaustive and detailed study of the product/services one plans to export to a market, is of great importance in export marketing. It can be for an existing product produced by the exporter, or for an altogether new design of a product which the exporter is capable of producing, to export.

Let us examine how one goes about this task.

#### (a) Research

As a first step, the exporter has to do some detailed study or 'research' as it is called. In the case of domestic marketing, one can go to the market straightaway, and do all necessary studies. In the case of export where one is exporting to a foreign country about which his knowledge may be very inadequate, one is advised to do initially, 'desk research'.

**Desk research** simply means studying about the market from one's own office, by collecting all available data from various sources, and known published data. The sources of published or available data are varied. Some of them are:

*(a)* International Agencies, such as UNCTAD, UNIDO, WORLD BANK, ECAFE etc who all have available economic and social data about almost all the countries.

*(b)* Chambers of Commerce of the respective countries and also specific country trade bodies such as Indo-American Chamber, Indo-Australian Chamber etc who always provide all the information required to develop trade between countries.

*(c)* Embassies of foreign countries in India – Their primary task is to develop the trade between the two countries and usually the commercial counselor in the embassy will be a very good source to give all import policies of the country concerned and also a possible list of buyers who will be interested in the product.

*(d)* Indian Embassies in the country to which export is envisaged may also be able to provide information on the possibility of exports, possible agent/agencies who would be interested in the product, and what kind of safe financial arrangement has to be made for the export trade.

*(e)* Foreign banks in India – Many of them have a lot of data with them on a whole lot of countries, and may also get further data if required, through their counterparts in that country.

*(f)* A few public sector agencies, like MMTC, STC also possess a wealth of information which will be of help.

*(g)* Export Promotion Councils and Statutory Trade bodies like Coffee Board, MPEDA etc also have a lot of information and commercial data in their respective product groups and will be able to help.

After collecting all the available data from sources mentioned above or from other sources as well, the exporter can tentatively come to the conclusion on an export product and decide on the market he feels confident of exporting to.

**(b) Market Study**

It is at this point that the exporter has to make a visit to the country concerned, and conduct a personal field survey to get detailed information on the following areas:

(1) **Market Profile** – Apart from demographic details and product preferences in the market, he will get a clear picture of the demand in the market and its viability.

(2) **Product profile** – all details of the product preferred, whether any modification is necessary, the demand for the present and future, local practices etc. can all be obtained.

(3) **Competition** – He can ascertain the nature of the competition, their strengths and weaknesses, the type of arrangements they have in the market with the dealers, payment terms etc.

(4) **Distribution** – the kind of distribution channels available in the country, whether dealings are through an agent/dealer or directly, the wholesaler/retail network etc. should all be ascertained and which one of the available facilities can be used by the exporter.

(5) **Pricing and financing** – From the currency in which the goods are to be sold, the market practice in realizing sales proceeds, credit needs and how it is fulfilled, the banking practices, how soon the exporter can realize the proceeds of his sale are all relevant data required.

After the desk research and a personal visit, the exporter will be in a position to identify one or more of the products and the market, the prospective buyer and the payment terms.

This is all the more true if the exporter is entering a new market.

## DESIGNING PRODUCTS FOR THE EXPORT MARKET

This requires considerable experience of the market, knowing the likes and dislikes of the buyer and his clientele, to assess the immediate need for a new product, and bring it to the market at the right time. The timing is extremely important. Let us take a couple of practical instances which exemplify this.

The author of this book has been in the field of exports for over three decades, and in his experience, 'product planning' is designing a product for a market, and normally comes about when one is already in an export market with a successful product and knows the contours of the market. Then a planned effort to introduce a product modified to suit the demand always succeeds.

Let us take two case studies:

A commercial vehicle exporter from India had been successful in a market where he had sold a number of trucks and buses. He had established an excellent after-sales service set up with workshops, spare parts and trained service personnel. By virtue of these, the exporter had a good share of the market.

The exporter found that this oil rich country suddenly went in for a lot of construction work in building roads, bridges, buildings etc. and the best builders from various countries were competing for the construction work.

At this point, he made a quick survey of the needs of the construction companies. He sent a marketing executive to the various countries where construction was being done in a big way by these companies who wanted to enter the market, and found out that the most important product used was the tipper truck. The exporter did not have such a tipper truck in his production line. But his Research and Development department was able to assure the exporter that they could adapt their truck to become a tipper truck by attaching a suitable hydraulic mechanism, the controls and a suitable tipping body.

Knowing the country, the topography and the kind of loads they would carry in a tipper truck, the exporter had the tipper truck designed and produced in a month.

As a marketing strategy the exporter contacted a construction company to which he offered the tipper truck. As the exporter was not known for his tipper trucks, the company hesitated to buy from him. The exporter then offered one truck free of cost to them, and requested them to try it out for a month on condition that his service engineer would be with them for the period to look after the maintenance of the vehicle.

They agreed and started using the tipper truck. The service engineer who was attached to the buyer company helped with the maintenance and dealt with problems as they arose.

With his experience with the new tipper truck, the service engineer was also able to suggest changes in the design of the tipper body and controls to increase its efficiency. With this, the exporter was able to produce a reasonable quality of tipper trucks suited to the work and contractor. At the end of the month, when the construction company was satisfied with the tipper truck, they placed an order for 20 such trucks which the exporter was able to supply, and capture a share of this new market.

The exporter, being an experienced person in export marketing, got a testimonial from the first construction company to which he gave the tipper truck free, stating that under the conditions in the country the truck performed very well with good maintenance and no breakdown. He also increased his service facilities in that country by placing a few more service engineers there. As there was a boom in construction work in the country, and many companies got huge contracts, the exporter was able to show his testimonial to acquire large orders for his trucks. His sale of tipper trucks alone was, in a couple of years, to the extent of Rs. 4.5 crores.

This is a practical example which shows the need and importance of designed products and services in export marketing.

Another such instance refers to textile and garment export. An exporter was exporting workshop uniforms to quite a few companies in a country. He had established himself as a reliable supplier with a good competitive price, and his customers were very happy.

His agent in that country requested him to supply shirts, as there was a good demand. Since he was not producing shirts, he hesitated. But he sent one of his executives to study the market, obtain samples of the complete range of shirts sold in the market. After that the exporter visited some garment companies producing shirts and noted the kind of expertise and machinery that was needed.

The exporter found that (a) He had to expand his unit by adding more machinery and (b) get some experienced workmen who could do the cutting and stitching of shirts. He evaluated the total cost of such a step, and took up initially the production of the easiest shirts (those sold to the poorer sections of society with much less sophistication). After calculation of all the costs, he arrived at a particular price at which he could export the shirts. He informed the agent in the country of his decision and the price at which he would be able to export.

The agent at the other end worked out the landed cost, duties to be paid, margin required for the seller etc. and he found that the price quoted by the exporter was workable only if the shirts had a well known brand name.

This made the exporter think again, and as he did not want to lose a new market for shirts, he gave an alternate suggestion. He would sell his shirts at 10% less than the price indicated for the first six months, and if the market accepted the product, and the buyers were happy, he would revise the price later.

After checking with the buyer, the agent agreed to this proposition and requested him to send samples first. The exporter got a lead time of three months, within which he got the machinery, necessary skilled labour and supplied the trade samples. It was accepted and he started supply of shirts on a regular basis under his own brand name at a price 10% lower than the first intended price. He took very special care on the designs, selection of shirt material, finishing and packing. As there was a good demand in the market, he was able to increase his price by 10% after six months, and sold the shirts at the original price offered.

One interesting point to note here is that when the exporter gave his first quotation to his agent, the price included a profit of 10% for himself. When the need arose to reduce the price, he agreed to reduce the price for six months by 10%. It was a clever move, since he figured that he would sell at cost price (usually referred to as 'no profit no loss price') for six months, and thereafter sell it at the original quoted price and get his profit.

These are some of the strategies one has to adopt to get into the export market.

## Product planning

Product planning for export markets goes beyond the product itself. Attributes such as branding, packaging, labelling, advertising etc. are also important components in the sale.

## Branding

The purpose of branding is to give a product an identity and helps to establish a reputation for quality. The major brands in the international market such as Liptons, Coca Cola, Gillette etc. have been there for more than 70 years. The main advantage in brand recognition is that it is an assurance to the buyer that the quality, services, customer satisfaction and value for money are inherent in an internationally branded product. It is assumed that a brand name under which a product sells in the domestic market has been registered with the authorities. Similarly, the exporter should check whether the country to which he exports can register his brand name. If his brand name is already registered for some other product in that country or export market, or by some other exporter, then he has to think of a different name altogether to register. This is necessary for him to establish his brand as one of quality and service in the export market.

## Packaging

The purpose is to protect the product, preserve it in a good condition and also make it attractive to the buyer. More importantly, it becomes easy to handle when packaged properly. In India, the Indian Institute of

Packaging or the Package Industry can advice the exporter on appropriate packaging.

## Labelling

This refers to the printed material that appears on the package. This is of great importance as it indicates the details of the product, the quantity, date of manufacturing and expiry date if required by the importing country.

The language on the label is also considered in consultation with the buyer. The label is also a part of advertising appeal to the buyer, and has to be designed carefully with pleasing colours, and the brand name in an attractive presentation. The same design has to be used wherever the brand name is used. However in the case of industrial products, the manufacturer's logo should be prominently displayed.

## Marking

When exporting a product in suitable containers like wooden cases, or as individual items like tractors, the marking has to be prominently displayed. Marking refers to the country of origin, handling details and the destination of the product. It should be done in such a manner that even if it is handled roughly or is damaged by natural elements in transit, the marking remains clear.

## Advertising

This is a means of communication by the company through the media such as newspapers, magazines, television and hand outs. It is an important element of sales promotion and is essential for a new product introduced in the export market. Even for established brands and products, it serves as a reminder to the customer.

The type of advertisement has to be done as per the local practice and perception. For example, the language is an extremely important component. The psychological and cultural distance to the markets have to be bridged.

One should bear in mind that advertisement costs vary widely in different countries and the volume of sales expected for the product is the main factor which will decide the advertising costs one can bear.

In some cases, the exporter himself plans for a certain quantum of advertisement and chooses the medium and duration for such advertisement. In some cases, the distributor in the country concerned takes upon himself the role of advertiser and bears the cost of advertisement.

It is advisable to entrust the advertising to a successful advertising company in the country concerned. However, the exporter should get involved in this activity so that his product and brand are projected in a proper manner.

In other words, the 'communication intensity' is important. Apart from promotion campaigns, the exporter should try and have direct contact with end-users as well as personal contact with the middlemen.

## PRODUCT POSITIONING IN OVERSEAS MARKETS

When we are planning to introduce a product in an export market, the positioning of the product is extremely important.

'Positioning' simply means the way the product will be projected, so that it can be differentiated from other competitive products in the market. The essential ingredient in positioning in the market is the buyer's perception of the product based on the way it is projected. For this, the exporter should have a clear picture of the market, the buyer, his perceptions and what he values most in the product.

The uniqueness the exporter brings to the product in terms of qualities that a buyer would appreciate is very important. For example, if it is a food item, the quality of ingredients, hygiene in the workplace and the tests of international standards employed, will all be differentiating factors.

One can also differentiate the product by way of a longer period of guarantee, providing centers where the product can be tested and replaced if necessary, and providing service engineers when required for products like heavy machinery. Service benefits play an important role in positioning in the export market.

The basic requirements which we have referred to earlier such as packaging, labelling etc. should be made in such a manner that will attract customers to the product.

Depending upon the market, and the perception of the buyer, the exporter should position his products so that the purchaser is happy in buying the product.

The advantages are:

*(a)* By creating a distinct image of the product in the mind of the buyer, one increases the appeal of the product, sales and the market share.

*(b)* By careful positioning, the exporter can overcome the competition in the initial stages, and increase sustainability so as to bring greater profitability and cover all the initial costs of entering the market.

## PRODUCT SERVICING

This is a very important element of export marketing. The first aspect of this is the warranty given for the product at the time of sale. Similarly there are other guarantees given such as product life, prospective use etc. In all these cases, the exporter should make suitable arrangements with his agent/distributor to fulfil these requirements immediately and as quickly as the customer expects it.

There are many ways of doing this. In the case of a consumer product of low value, the exporter leaves a few extra products with the agent/distributor to fulfil the warranty requirements. The exporter, on his next visit to the country will make sure that the claims were just and properly attended to.

In some cases, where the product is essential in the business such as a battery in a car, the agent will have to supply spare ones to replace the battery that may have to be repaired or replaced.

Another aspect of servicing is referred to as 'After Sales Service'. This is better understood in terms of bigger machinery or automobiles supplied by the exporter. A typical example will help to understand this.

Tata Motors is one of the largest exporters of commercial vehicles (trucks and buses) from India over the last three decades. These vehicles may need maintenance as also trouble-shooting when the need arises. Tata Motors have a separate Service Department, which has experienced Service Engineers who will be rushed to any market where there is a need.

However as the export of vehicles to a particular country increases, they station their Service Engineer in that country, to provide regular after-sales service to their vehicles. One of the duties of these resident service engineers is to train the local engineers in maintenance and repair, so that eventually large buyers of Trucks and Buses will have their own trained engineers to look after their vehicles. The engineers posted abroad will contact all the customers/buyers in the country to ensure that the vehicles are maintained as per company advice, and also make sure that sufficient spare parts are available in the country for maintenance jobs.

This kind of planned after-sales service pleases the customer and he becomes loyal to the exporter. It is interesting to note here that the excellent after sales service of TELCO (as it was then known) helped it to export over 2000 transport buses to Kuwait in a span of eight years.

Good after sales service provided by the exporter will result in the following:

*(a)* Timely repair and maintenance of products thus increasing their life.

*(b)* Builds the confidence of the buyer and enables repeated purchases. Ensures brand loyalty.

*(c)* The exporter's reputation for good after sales service spreads in the market, and a lot of new customers get interested in the products.

It should also be emphasized here that having a fully equipped Sales and Service Department, and frequent visits to export markets by service personnel, or posting them in the country of sales are all costly propositions. The exporter should plan the expenditure and strategies in advance and be able to control it properly.

## PRODUCT LIFE-CYCLE

Those who are concerned with marketing are aware that every product introduced in the market has distinct stages in its existence. These are:

(a) **The Introductory Stage:** when the product will have an entry into the market, the sales will be low and the promotional cost will be high.

(b) **The Rapid Growth Stage:** During this period the product will be well accepted by the market, and the sales will increase rapidly, and will build a good profile and reputation to the exporter.

(c) **Maturity Stage:** The product will be well established and will have steady sales. But by this time competition will increase and newer products will come into the market.

(d) **Stage of Decline:** The product sales will reduce as also the profit. Other competitive products may take its place.

These four stages together are referred to as Product life-cycle. This is true for many products but not all. For example, products like tea, coffee etc. in the export market depend on the supply and demand, whereas products like handicrafts, garments of a particular style are all products that have their own life-cycle.

The export marketer can and should use product life-cycles to his advantage. When exporting to many countries, a product such as a particular design of a cotton garment can be introduced at different times in different countries, so that when the product is in the last stage of decline in one market, it may be in the growth and expansion stage in another market. This will help the exporter to have steady production, and export for as long a time as there is demand in different markets.

## CONCEPT OF MARKETING MIX

Apart from the normal functions of selling, advertising and other promotional efforts, there are other important factors which persuade customers to buy the product. Marketing mix dwells on four P's – product, price, promotion and place.

**(a) Product** – It is wellknown that the quality of the product is the most important element. The consumers' desire for the same product may vary from country to country. The same product in an affluent country may demand a different style, or power in the case of a vehicle, as compared to a poor country where they would prefer a smaller size, durability and simplicity. The product will have to be suitably adapted to the country.

**(b) Price** – This is also a very important factor, as many countries are price sensitive. If the product sells at different prices in different countries the exporter should adjust the price as per the price sensitivity of the country if the cost of the product can accommodate the same. If the product has special features of a high quality, the exporter can price it slightly above the competitor's price. In countries where the purchasing power is low, prices can be reduced by modifying the product by perhaps using fewer features and of greater simplicity or using smaller sizes.

**(c) Promotion** – This covers the whole area of promotion of the product such as advertising, sales literature, distribution of pamphlets etc. Apart from the above for many consumer products, sampling, premium, prize contests, festival discounts etc. may be introduced. These various promotion measures will entirely depend upon the normal practices in the respective countries, and what the buyer would value most. There are promotional organizations in every country which are well versed in conducting promotions, and their help can be sought.

**(d) Place** – This is a general term which refers to the logistics and the manner of availability of the product and its location. It covers the channel of distribution (whether it is a wholesaler or retailer), and the location. (There should be a convenient place where the majority of people can easily buy), and the amount of stock to be kept, so that at the height of the promotion the agent does not run out of stock of the product.

The importance of marketing mix should be understood properly. Apart from a suitable product with good demand which is chosen for a market, a whole range of other activities which come under the heading of marketing mix should also be properly chosen as part of one's strategy to export a product to a market. Sometimes, other elements such as branding, display, servicing etc. are also added as components of marketing mix. It is only the correct choice and proper application of the various elements of the marketing mix that will make the exporter successful in his exports.

## AGENT

In international marketing, the exporter is separated from his customer by a considerable distance. Successful marketing operations demand constant contact with the customer by the exporter. Besides, an exporter has to obtain continual feedback information on a variety of marketing details that would help him to keep the customer's interest alive in his product. In addition, there are certain essential functions that need to be carried out in a foreign country before a product is made available for the customer to buy. For instance, the goods shipped by an exporter have to be cleared out of the customs and port area, transported and stored in a warehouse. If necessary, they may have to be packed before they are distributed to retail outlets for sale to customers. A host of other functions related to promotion of product sale have to be necessarily performed in a foreign country. An exporter cannot perform these functions himself unless he has established his own office for this purpose. An agent or a distributor is an ideal alternative to the establishment of a foreign office.

An agent performs functions similar to those of a foreign office of an exporter. He arranges for the clearance of goods from the port area, for the payment of duties and other incidentals at the time of clearance, for the transportation and storage of goods in a warehouse and their distribution to various retail outlets in the market. He also supervises their sale in their outlets on behalf of the exporter, especially in connection with the distribution of the product. In addition he also performs the basic marketing functions of sales promotion, advertising, customer contact, physical distribution, etc., and obtains for the exporter valuable feedback information on competitive activity, customer reaction to product specification and product use, pricing, discount schemes, and other related matters that would help the exporter in sustaining this market.

Depending on the product exported, and the services expected by the exporter from his agent, he may appoint any one of the following types of agents:

**(a) Commission Agent:** A commission agent acts as an intermediary between the exporter and the buyer. The agent himself will not handle the product, which will be shipped direct to the customer. The payments for the export would be made directly by the buyer. The agent only helps in bringing together the buyer and the exporter, besides helping the buyer in arranging for payment, clearance of goods, and rendering such other services. He also follows up potential enquiries before they mature into a concrete order. Sometimes, he provides valuable market information to the exporter. The agent is compensated for all these services; he receives a commission, which is usually a percentage of the f.o.b. value of the goods exported.

**(b) Sole Distributor:** A sole distributor is one who has exclusive responsibility for the marketing and distribution of a product in a foreign country. His involvement in promoting its sale is therefore deeper than that of the commission agent. A sole distributorship arrangement is more common in connection with the export promotion of engineering goods. The selected distributor should, therefore, be in a position to provide essential after-sales service once the product is sold to customers. An enormous amount of effort and evaluation are essential in the selection of a distributor in a foreign market.

**(c) Sole Importer:** The functions of a sole importer are similar to those of a sole distributor. He enjoys the exclusive right for the import of a product into a foreign market. Usually, sole importers are appointed in connection with the export of such products as raw materials, steel, food articles, etc.

**(d) Del Credere Agent:** For all practical purposes, a Del Credere Agent is functionally identical with a commission agent. However, this type of agent undertakes to indemnify the exporter for any bad debts incurred owing to default on the part of a customer. In view of this, these agents are paid a special rate of commission, which is higher than that received by conventional commission agents.

**(e) Retail Agents:** Retail agents and stockists are normally appointed by exporters dealing in hardware and spare parts of motors cars. Where an exclusive arrangement exists, the exporter, in consultation with the sole distributor, appoints these agents; otherwise the exporter directly appoints these agents and advises the distributor about their appointment. The number of agents appointed depends on the volume of sales and coverage of territory. A suitable discount on the price list is offered to these agents for stocking and selling the goods.

## Selection of an Agent

An agent or a distributor represents an exporter in a foreign country. It is therefore essential for the exporter to select the right person to represent him. An exporter, while selecting an agent, always looks for a person who has been engaged in a business similar to the one he wants him to promote. In addition to this relevant experience, the agent should possess an adequate financial standing which can be certified by a reputed bank. Since the main function of an agent is to promote the sale of a product, it is essential that he should be a person with considerable influence with wide and varied contacts.

Besides these basic qualifications, an agent should have adequate sales staff to promote sale of the product, to provide enough storage facilities for it, to create an effective after-sales service facility together with the necessary personnel and should be willing to participate in the advertising and sales promotion campaign. In addition, he should be equipped to provide essential feedback information on the market situation to the exporter.

It is always preferable for an exporter to appoint a person as an agent who does not deal in a competing range of products. Divided loyalties do no pay dividends in the long-run.

An exporter looks for an agent or a distributor when he is comparatively new in the export market. A number of institutions would be in a position to guide him and direct him to potential agents. Government departments are one of the main sources of information on known and established agents. Trade associations, by virtue of their contacts with the business community, can suggest potential agents. Banks and financial institutions are, perhaps, one of the best sources available to the exporter on agents and distributors. Chambers of commerce can also provide valuable information on this subject to the exporter.

A shrewd exporter usually collects information from different sources before evaluating and deciding on the selection of an agent. After obtaining information from various sources, he visits the foreign country to acquire first-hand knowledge of the status and reliability of his potential agent distributor. On the basis of his visit and his discussions with various financial institutions, he selects an agent best suited for the promotion of his product. The agent thus selected, could be an individual, a company or an organization.

Once an agent is appointed, he has to be supported with extensive assistance. After all, the agent may be new to the exporter's product even though he may have been dealing with similar products for a long time. He may not be aware of the special features of the product. An exporter should consider him as a vital member of his marketing team and a part of his marketing family, and train him. Such an attitude helps him to put across to the agent his ideas and market strategies in the right perspective. The agent should be encouraged to visit the offices and manufacturing facilities in India, so that he may develop a sense of involvement. Periodic visits by him to the exporter's country, would moreover, help promote better understanding. In his marketing effort, the exporter should be willing to provide all the assistance, administrative and technical, that may be required by the agent. Periodic visits by the exporter to the foreign market can also help him to appreciate, at first hand, the problems of his agent.

Regular evaluation of the agent's performance is essential for the successful marketing of a product. If the agent appointed is also an agent of various other products, it may happen that he is not devoting enough time and attention to the exporter's products. The criteria followed for evaluating agents are basically their skills in promoting a product and their willingness to give complete satisfaction to customers in the marketing of the exporter's product. Sometimes it may happen that the force behind an agency is a single individual, and if he were to leave, then the agency would collapse. It is absolutely essential to assess the credit-worthiness of the agent prior to his appointment.

Once an agent has been selected, an agency agreement is drawn up between the exporter and the agent. Though the various clauses in the agency agreement will fall within the realm of legal experts, the exporter should keep in mind a few of the important clauses while drafting the agreement. He should normally obtain the help of his legal department for this purpose. Some of the more important points that should form part of the agreement are:

*(i)* Parties of the agreement on both sides;

*(ii)* Purpose of the agreement;

*(iii)* The product/products covered by the agreement;

*(iv)* Jurisdiction of the agent, namely, the territory in which the agent is permitted to sell;

*(v)* The responsibilities of the exporter;

*(vi)* The responsibilities of the agent;

*(vii)* Payment of compensation or commission to the agent;

*(viii)* Duration-period for which the agreement is valid;

*(ix)* Breach of agreement;

*(x)* In some agreements the price at which the products are supplied to the agent is also specified; and

*(xi)* The law governing the agreement and a specified suitable clause for arbitration, if a dispute arises.

A marketer, be he international or domestic, is often faced with the question, 'Can an agent be dispensed with?' When we speak of an agent or an agency agreement, we do not refer to an individual, but rather to a group of functions in the marketing chain. Even if we accept that an agent can be dispensed with, it does not mean that the functions of an agent can be dispensed with. Whether an agent is present or not, the functions performed by him exist, and form an important part of the entire marketing chain. This should always be borne in mind and hence, while changing an agent or dispensing with his services, we must seek and ensure the continuity of the functions of the agent.

## SOME FEATURES OF INTERNATIONAL TRADE

Beyond the export market process and new product planning for export, there are quite a few specific practices, formal groups, and institutions with their rules and regulations in international trade. One should have knowledge of these and also be able to foresee how it will affect the export of goods and services in the short-term as well as the long-term.

**1. Anti-dumping duties:**

Often times, exporters from developed countries, in their eagerness to capture a large market for a particular product, arrange to sell it at a very low price, lower than the price at which it is sold in the country of origin. This attempt at introducing a product in a large quantity into a market at a price which is even lower than its cost is known as 'dumping.' To counteract this unfair competition effectively, most countries have introduced legislation providing for antidumping duties, which take the form of special additional import charges over and above the custom duties, if any. The additional charges would cover at least the difference between the export price and the normal price, or the price the consumer usually pays in the exporting country. This increases the cost for the buyer and he rejects the product.

**2. Countervailing Duties:**

These are similar to the antidumping duties, and are charged on goods imported from countries where the manufacturer-exporter is paid, directly or indirectly, a subsidy as an incentive for export. The amount of duty normally does not exceed the estimated amount of subsidy.

**3. Non-tariff Barriers:**

Over the last few decades, GATT has been endeavouring to achieve a reduced and rationalized tariff structure for trade among its members so that "Most Favoured Nation" treatment is accorded to all the members of the group. Any attempt at deviation from the norms accepted and the settlement reached by mutual negotiation, is discouraged by GATT. At the same time, importing countries, especially developing countries, desire to protect their own domestic industry against unfair competition and dumping with a view to giving the domestic industry a fair chance for survival. To effectively combat these limitations, more and more countries have been adopting a number of non-tariff measures aimed at regulating their import trade.

Some of these measures are:

*(a)* Quantity restrictions, quotas and licensing procedures;

*(b)* Foreign exchange restrictions;

*(c)* Technical and administrative regulations;

*(d)* Consular formalities;

*(e)* State trading; and

*(f)* Preferential arrangements.

**(a)Quantity Restrictions:** The quantity restrictions fall into two categories – the quota system for the import of commodities and the licensing procedure for regulating the import of goods.

Under the quota system, the importing country specifies the quantities of a commodity that would be allowed to be imported from various countries. The quotas fixed normally depend on the relationship of the importing country with the supplier of the commodity. Sometimes, historical data are also used as a justification.

Licensing procedures are more systematic in their methods of controlling imports into a country. Depending on its total requirements of a particular commodity, as also on the consideration of total domestic production, the government of a country allows the import of a balancing quantity to match domestic need. The balancing quantity allowed to be imported is either imported through a canalizing agency, which is usually a State enterprise, or through a number of importing agents. A licence or a permit to import the commodity is obtained from the Government. Only after obtaining the import licence specifying the quantity that may be imported, can the importing agent conclude the contract with the supplier.

Some countries use a special form of quantity restriction while regulating their import trade. They stipulate that, in order to allow import of a certain quantity of a commodity, the importing agent should buy a definite pre-determined quantity of the commodity manufactured domestically. This type of controlled regulation of imports is usually applied to such commodities as agricultural products, minerals etc.

**(b)Foreign Exchange Regulations:** Exchange control methods have been widely used by a number of countries to regulate imports, and are usually adopted by most of the developing nations who experience an unfavourable balance of payment. Under this scheme, the importer has to ensure that adequate foreign exchange is available for the import of goods by obtaining a clearance from the exchange control authorities prior to concluding a contract with the supplier.

**(c) Technical and Administrative Regulations:** The imposition of certain standards of technical production, technical specification, etc., to which an imported commodity should conform is another method of regulating imports into a country. In the case of pharmaceutical products, the importing countries normally specify the pharmacopic standards that should be satisfied before their import is permitted. Such specifications exclude the import of products which, though of good quality, and satisfying the pharnacopic standards, do not conform to other details called for. Besides these, sometimes adherence to certain documentary procedures are adopted to regulate trade. These measures impede the free flow of international trade to a large extent.

**(d)Consular Formalities:** A number of importing countries demand that consular documents – such as certified invoices, import certificates etc. – must necessarily accompany shipping documents. Sometimes, they even insist that such consular documents should be drawn in the languages of the importing countries. The fees payable for such documentation are often quite high, varying up to 3% of f.o.b value of a product. Heavy penalties are levied by importing countries if there are any errors in documentation.

**(e)State Trading:** In most socialist countries, export/import trade is exclusively handled by certain specialized agencies which are normally State enterprises. All the items imported into such a country or items exported from it are canalized through these agencies. A number of such agencies are established, each of which deals exclusively with a specific group of products. The nature and extent of international trade, both import and export, is influenced by governmental policies, on the basis of which targets are set for achievement. International trade by and large, is carried on through bilateral arrangements with a number of countries, the commodity and the quantity to be exchanged with each of the bilateral partners being predetermined at the governmental level.

A few other countries of the world follow state trading in a restricted sense to achieve certain desired results, especially where bulk imports are needed. The entire range of imports is canalized through a single agency so that the country may enjoy the benefit of price and delivery terms.

**(f) Preferential Arrangements:** Within the multilateral trading system that is evolved, a few member countries tend to look inwards by forming themselves into small advantageous groups for their mutual benefit. The main objective in the formation of these small groups is to negotiate and to arrive at a settlement of a preferential tariff rate to carry on trade amongst themselves. These preferential tariff rates are applicable exclusively to the small group of nations, and are lower than conventional tariff rates which are outside the purview of GATT. Some of these small groups are the EU, ASEAN, NAFTA etc. These are dealt with later in this chapter.

This refers to certain conditions or restrictions imposed by a government in respect of foreign investment in a country.

It has been agreed that any conditional ties imposed on TRIM should not be inconsistent with WTO articles. The agreement now in existence also provides for the adoption of the WTO consistent TRIMS in a period of five years by developing countries. The transition period can also be extended if there are difficulties in implementing this.

India used to employ TRIM earlier with restrictions such as local content requirement in manufacture etc. Many of these have been phased out now.

## Trade Related aspects of Intellectual Property Rights (TRIP)

Usually the intellectual property rights are legally protected by patents, copyrights, trademarks etc. TRIP agreement covers copyright and related rights, Trade marks, Geographical indicators, Industrial designs, Patents, Layout designs etc.

India has been amending its laws to fall in line with TRIP requirements. However there is a significant difference between Indian Patent Law and the Patent Laws in Western countries.

The Indian Patent Law protects only the process. This means that one can make a product similar to any patented product if he can produce it through a different process. This has been prevalent in the Pharmaceutical Industry. The WTO insists on both product and process patents.

## Most Favored Nation Clause (MFN)

This arises from the GATT rules, and is centered around non-discrimination and reciprocity. The rule of non-discrimination suggests that no member country shall discriminate between the members of GATT in the conduct of International Trade. The essence of MFN is that if a member country gives tariff concessions to another member country, then the same concessions become applicable to all other member countries. This is the essence of MFN.

But the later developments such as trading blocks, the formation of EU providing free trade among members and free movement of labour and capital have all made the MFN Clause ineffective.

## Genaralised System of Preference (GSP)

The European Union members have adopted a generalized system of preference towards developing countries. Under this system, countries like India will be entitled to a concessional rate of import duties when exporting to these countries. However, a 'certificate of origin' should accompany the exports and should have been given by an authorized agent. For this, the government of India has authorized the Export Promotion Councils of India, Export Promotion Offices, FIEO, and Chambers of Commerce and Industry to give the necessary certificate of origin to the exporters.

## BILATERAL TRADE

Both UNCTAD & WTO are opposed to any system of bilateral trade arrangements which, according to them, are discriminatory in character and violate the fundamental principle of free multilateral trade. The market forces of supply and demand, they contend, are effectively curbed by such arrangements. However, of late, a softening of attitudes is visible among these international forums especially towards bilateral arrangements concluded by developing countries which after all, help to expand their international trade and therefore fulfil at least some of the objectives of these multilateral arrangements.

The Government of India has done pioneering work in establishing bilateral trade arrangements. It has finalized over 25 trade and trade payment agreements in the past. The main objectives of the Government of India in organizing these bilateral trade arrangements are:

*(a)* As a developing country, India has been aspiring to a greater share in world trade. By securing for itself bilateral trade arrangements with East European countries and other nations, it has acquired a firm base on which it can build its exports to other world markets.

*(b)* Since Independence, India has been chronically plagued with adverse balance of trade and balance of payments. By balancing its trade at least with its bilateral trade partners, it has managed to limit the trade gap only to essential imports that are not available from its bilateral partners. Of late, India has been increasingly looking to these bilateral partner countries even for the import of such essential items as crude oil, food items, etc. These bilateral trade agreements have thus reduced its balance of trade and balance of payment liabilities to a large extent.

*(c)* Owing to an assured volume of trade, which is pre-determined in these bilateral arrangements, India has been in a position to stabilize its exports trade to a larger extent.

*(d)* From the very beginning, the Government of India has been committed to a policy of industrialization. This policy formulation demanded the import of a huge quantity of machinery and capital equipment for India's nascent industry. During the fifties, when the export trade of India was not impressive, its foreign exchange reserves were not adequate for the large import demand. Trade agreements with USSR and East European countries came in handy, for these countries offered to supply the machinery and capital equipment required for industrialization against bilateral trade arrangements.

Bilateral trade agreements are based on mutual trust and the political relationship between the two countries. The signatories to the agreements are aware that the document is an instrument for closer economic and commercial co-operation. As such, a spirit of give and take should prevail. Further, it is also recognized that export from either side are essential for the fulfillment of the agreement. It also provides for a progressive relaxation of import restrictions, so that a smooth flow of trade may be possible between the contracting countries within the ambit of the provisions of the agreement. Efforts are constantly made by both the parties to satisfy as much of these requirements as possible through bilateral trade agreements. The countries involved in the agreement usually set up a joint commission to oversee and nurture the trade agreement.

While concluding trade agreements, the parties to them should clearly spell out the details regarding the following:

*(a)* The duration for which the agreement is operative.

*(b)* The mode and currency of payment for commercial and non-commercial transactions.

*(c)* The agreement sometimes stipulates the balancing of bilateral trade after a fixed period of time. Trade balance at the end of this stipulated period is wiped out by making equivalent payment in free foreign exchange. The agreement usually stipulates the currency and mode of payment of the balancing trade.

*(d)* The exchange rate applicable for trade balances between the two countries is an essential clause of agreement.

*(e)* The agreement should cover the list of items available for export from either country and the list of items that can be imported.

(*f*) Sometimes, export quotas with reference to certain commodities are specified in the agreement. Such restrictions are imposed particularly when one of the countries to the agreement is in a position to export goods which are in great demand elsewhere in the world. Usually, such merchandise is kept outside the purview of the trade agreement. In the event of this being included in it, the quota for export is specified.

(*g*) Most trade agreements stipulate that the "MFN" status be accorded to the contracting parties.

It is interesting to note that over 220 trade agreements are presently operating among the various countries of the world. A majority of these, as many as 200, are agreements with centrally-planned economies and account for over 50% of the total world trade.

## Joint Commissions

It is the aim of almost all governments to achieve a balanced trade pattern by equalizing their imports and exports, so that unfavourable balances do not hinder economic progress. With this end in view, developing countries in particular enter into bilateral trade agreements wherever possible. While trading with countries where the possibility of bilateral trade does not exist, developing countries nevertheless organize trade with them by setting up what are called Joint Commissions which would study the problem of trade in depth with a view to arriving at a mutually acceptable solution. The main objectives in establishing such joint commissions are:

(*a*) To develop close economic and commercial co-operation leading to a better understanding of the policies related to them;

(*b*) To identify areas of co-operation and spell out the steps to be taken to effectively implement mutually beneficial schemes;

(*c*) To seek to facilitate efforts to meet each other's requirements in the light of their respective priorities;

(*d*) To guide and regulate the trade flow by negotiating and setting quotas for export/import where required, so that no unfavourable balance of trade occurs for either of the countries without their consent; and

(*e*) To sort out all other trade problems that may arise from time to time through negotiation in a spirit of accommodation and goodwill.

## TRADING BLOCKS

Trading Blocks are a kind of regional economic coordination by countries adjacent to one another so as to increase their trade.

Initially it started in the following manner:

**(a) Free Trade Area:** Here the main aim is to eliminate tariff among the countries of the group, whereas each will have its own tariff rates with outside countries.

European Free Trade Union EFTA, is one such group.

**(b) Custom Union:** This is an extension of FTA in that the members eliminate tariff among themselves but agree to have a uniform customs tariff against all other countries.

**(c) Common Market:** This is an improvement over the earlier agreement in that member countries abolish tariff among themselves, and permit free flow of all factors of production capital, labor, and technology among themselves. The EU is a good example of this.

One of the important post war phenomena, starting from the early fifties, is the setting up of the regional economic cooperation. In a broad sense this takes the form of unification of the separate individual economies into a larger single economy. In order words it is aimed at closer economic ties within a region of several politically independent countries, which in effect help to minimize the economic consequences of political boundaries.

## EU – European Union

This was originally established as European Common Market by the Treaty of Rome in 1957, and came into operation in 1959. The founder members of the community were France, West Germany, Italy, Belgium, The Netherlands and Luxembourg. In 1973 UK joined the community. Today it is known as EU, and comprises Belgium, Denmark, France, Greece, Ireland, Italy, Netherlands, Portugal, Spain, United Kingdom, Germany, Luxembourg, Finland, Austria and Sweden.

The association has advanced to the extent of removing most trade barriers and allowing free movement of persons and goods within the union. They have also established a European Parliament for which members are selected from each country on a proportionate basis, and are given powers to legislate many issues which are then ratified by the governments.

They have a common currency which is the Euro.

## Association of the South East Asian Nations (ASEAN)

ASEAN stands for the Association of South-East Asian nations. It is a loose economic union of five South-East Asian nations namely, Malaysia, Thailand, Singapore, Indonesia and the Philippines. The main aim of ASEAN is to promote economic interdependence among member countries. ASEAN nations meet periodically to formulate their strategies. In these meetings, they present a united front with a view to obtain concessions and favorable terms for the products exported by them to other countries, particularly to the developed countries. Like other economic unions, ASEAN aims at political understanding among member countries with a view to strengthening their economic interdependence. They have included Vietnam also in the group.

## North American Free Trade Agreement (NAFTA)

This is a group consisting of Mexico, USA and Canada. NAFTA was formed after long deliberations and serious arguments in USA whether including Mexico would affect seriously the manufacturing base as well as jobs in the USA. This is a justifiable fear as Mexico offers all the advantages of a base for production where the labor wages are extremely low as compared to the US. However, after much debate, this has been ratified, and NAFTA was formed.

But the serious problems faced by Mexico in 1994, when there was a run on their currency, resulting in devaluation, affected their economy and therefore affected the members of NAFTA. It will take long for NAFTA to revive and become a strong unified market so as to counterbalance the effects of a strong EU.

There have also been other efforts for groupings. It is always tempting for a marketer to think that a region as a whole can be treated as a single market for his product. Sooner or later, he finds that the separate markets within the region do not cease to exist. The relevant demographic characteristics like social, cultural, legal and traditional influences which define a market do not change just because a country becomes a part of a group with free internal trade, and free movement of resources.

The classic example of this is the UK, which in spite of being a member of EU, finds it difficult to agree to a common currency, or submerge its strong individuality in the EU.

The lesson that we have to draw in international marketing from all these groupings is to learn to evaluate how it will affect our exports, and plan a strategy to overcome them. Perhaps, one way will be to have a production or operation base within the groups concerned by means of a joint venture or own establishment. Our government regulations today allow this easily.

**SAARC** – Seven nations in the region of the Indian subcontinent came together to form the **South Asian Association for Regional Cooperation (SAARC)** in 1985. SAARC members are India, Pakistan, Sri Lanka, Bangladesh, Nepal, Bhutan and Maldives.

The agreement establishing the SAARC Preferential Trading Agreement (SAPTA) was signed in April 1993 in Dhaka by all the seven countries. It provides a framework for the exchange of tariff concessions with a view to promoting trade and economic cooperation among the SAARC countries.

The final objective of SAPTA is the ultimate achievement of South Asia Free Trade Association (SAFTA).

## Effects on Exports by this Development

(1) This helps to eliminate trade barriers completely between the countries in the region, so that the market available increases considerably for an exporter in any of the countries within the group.

(2) For an exporter outside the region, there will be a decrease in the exports to the region, because of the preferential treatment given to exporters within the region. The only way to overcome this is to have a production base within the region.

(3) This also helps units manufacturing in a country within the region. Suddenly, the market for them enlarges several times, with the availability of inputs from other countries in the region without any levies. They also benefit from the economies of scale, and cumulative clout.

This, therefore, calls for a change in the marketing strategy, so as to get a foothold within the region.

The nature of the union differed in its concept in the early years. It could be in the form of a free trade union as European Free Trade Association EFTA, or Customs Union as in the case of Benelux countries – Belgium, Netherlands and Luxembourg – where the main aim is to eliminate all customs and other duties and encourage free trade as if it is a single country.

This has another effect on the production within the region. Suddenly the market enlarges several times. The producer has also available, raw materials and other inputs from the various other countries of the region at lost cost, since there are no duties leviable on them.

A trading block which has fully matured now is the European Union. Apart from banishing tariffs among themselves and allowing free flow of capital, labor and technology, they have for over two years, a common currency, the EURO.

Common currency when adopted by all the countries, completely eliminates the problems of exchange conversion among various currencies in the countries, in the group.

They are going through the initial problems still, as UK has not yet made the Euro the common currency.

But the Euro has grown rapidly and it is emerging as a counterweight to US in industrial trade. This may help to an extent, the balancing of industrial trade and perhaps countries may become more considerate to one another, as any unilateral dominant currency will have a strong repercussion among members of the group.

## THE GENERAL AGREEMENT ON TARIFFS AND TRADE (GATT)

The General Agreement on Tariffs and Trade known as GATT, was set up on October 30, 1947 in Geneva with 23 countries as its founder members, and India was one of them. It was originally set up as a temporary arrangement to bring about trade liberalization. India has always been an active champion of multilateral trade negotiations. GATT later became an important and permanent organization to attend to all trade issues among member countries. Its membership also got enlarged to practically all the members of the United Nations, except the communist countries and East European countries at that time.

The broad goal of GATT has been to reduce the trade restrictions put up by individual nations in pursuit of their narrow national interests. The goal was to achieve through multilateral negotiations, settling of all trade disputes through a set of rules and regulations evolved by GATT for its members.

The other objective was to aim at tariff concessions for exports and imports among the countries, with a view to aim at developing the full use of the resources of the expanding world trade. GATT always permitted exceptions to its general rules which require the eventual elimination of all import restrictions. It was always subject to safe guard intended to protect legitimate interests of other trading nations. The most important exceptions given by GATT were the special protection given to agriculture by most nations and allowing many import restrictions to protect the farmers. Their rules also made exceptions in the case of countries which were in 'balance of payments' difficulties. It also allowed developing countries to protect infant industries.

From 1947 to 1967, GATT sponsored six rounds of multilateral trade negotiations mainly with a view to bring down the trade barriers by persuading countries to bring down their import levies to allow greater exchange of goods and more trade flow. The sixth round brought the weighted average tariff of major trading nations to be reduced by 2% on raw materials and 7.7% on industrial products.

GATT played a prominent role in the settlement of trade disputes. Before GATT there was no way of resolving the trade disagreements between two countries.

It should be remembered that the period between 1947 and 1973 was one of steady economic growth in the developed and developing countries, and the volume of international trade increased six fold. GATT certainly played a useful role in this period. But in the seventies there were many changes which occurred in the world economy. The fixed system exchange rate was moving towards a floating system of exchange parity. The oil prices quadrupled in 1973, and threatened to increase further. There was a world-wide economic recession in 1974-75. Many of the developing countries had diversified their export base, and were becoming competitors to developed countries in the field of steel, shipbuilding and some manufactured goods. Whenever there was a recession or economic slowdown, the western countries resorted to rising protectionism.

In 1973 the next round of multilateral negotiations were commenced by GATT, and it was concluded in 1979 at Tokyo, and was referred to as the 'Tokyo Round of Negotiations'. Here, tariffs were lowered by 27% to an average level of 5%. Certain non-tariff barrier agreements and codes were also agreed to.

It should be remembered that GATT was not a statutory organization like the World Bank or IMF. Many also questioned its appropriateness to the changing world economy. Meanwhile many developed countries forsook the open market commitment of GATT and entered bilateral and multilateral arrangements outside of GATT, referred to as 'market sharing agreements' which covered a good part of the world trade in steel, cars, consumer electronics and textiles. The GATT 'wisemen' group assembled in 1985 to study the trading system, said, 'today the world market is not opening up. It is being choked by a growing accumulation of restricted measures. Demands for protection are heard in every country for one industry after the other.'

An eighth round of trade negotiations under the auspices of GATT was launched in the mid-eighties. This was known as the Uruguay Round. Apart from the usual exercise to bring down the trade barriers it also attempted to draft trading rules to cover four major sectors not previously regulated. These were agriculture, services, investment, and intellectual property rights (patents, trade marks, copyrights etc) It was also decided that an institutional framework was to be given to GATT, and thus was born the World Trade Organisation (WTO) which was to replace GATT as an apex trade policy body.

The discussions, many times very vociferous, continued for eight long years. Many of the developing countries put forward their view strongly to protect their economies, and in the Intellectual Property Rights discussion, India played a prominent role and changed many of the original stringent changeover measures for the developing countries. It also protected the age-old traditions of the farmers to have the right to their own seed protection and various other clauses, which may have a bearing on our agriculture.

The discussions dragged on and ultimately a deadline was given that it should be completed at a conference in Morocco and the new organization – WTO – should come into existence on 1st January 1995. Accordingly, all the countries who are members of GATT signed the WTO agreement and lodged the instrument of ratification on 1st January 1995. India was one of them.

## WORLD TRADE ORGANISATION (WTO)

The establishment of WTO is a watershed in the history of multilateral trade relations. In the fast changing global environment WTO will work as an apex body at par with other multinational organizations like IMF and World Bank.

### The functions of WTO are:

1. To administer the trade policy mechanism.

1. To achieve greater coherence in global economic policy-making in cooperation with World Bank and IMF.
2. To provide a forum for negotiations among its members concerning their multilateral trade relations in matters dealt with in the agreements.
3. To administer the understandings on rules and procedures governing the settlement of disputes.
4. To introduce the idea of 'sustainable development' in relation to the optimal use of world resources and the need to protect and preserve the environment in a manner consistent with the various levels of national economic development.
5. To recognize that there is a need for positive effort to ensure that the developing countries, especially the least developed countries, secure a better share of the growth in international trade.

More than all this, for the first time there is an organization to which countries can take their disputes for a redressal. Since this organization is set up on the lines of international institutions like the World Bank, the developed countries cannot ignore it as they did GATT which was just an 'arrangement' extended indefinitely.

The WTO has also been entrusted with non-trade related issues like the social cause. It is for the first time that the developed countries spearheaded by USA have raised the issue in a multilateral forum. Developed countries are of the view that the WTO should, apart from trade, look into issues relating to Forced labour, Child labour, Toxic substances and Export processing zones.

Earlier, issues like labour standards, child labour and trade unions were looked after by the ILO with the full backing of all the countries. But due to an ineffective mechanism to deal with these issues, developed countries feel that the ILO is not competent to set universal standards on labour and child labour and want to delegate the responsibilities to the WTO to set universal norms with regard to these, and link these with trade.

Apart from the above, the introduction of Intellectual Property Rights also has certain implications for India.

There has also been a debate in the national press, and some public figures have suggested that we should not subscribe to any of the regulations which may affect us even remotely, and if need be defy WTO and opt out of it.

This approach is economically shortsighted because:

1. In a sense, international trade is equated to a war, and quite rightly so. Apart from price, quality, and delivery, every country tries to manage the trade in a way, which will benefit its perceived interests, but in the process bring about a host of problems and bottlenecks. We have to devise a strategy to overcome these and try to win over them, and get the better of them.
2. WTO will not allow us to pick and choose what regulations we want, without agreeing to the others. When all the members of GATT – both developed and developing countries – have agreed to be signatories and become members of WTO, India alone cannot take a stand to be outside. It would be suicidal to remain outside WTO, since any country can bring about any unilateral step to stop our trade and we will have no recourse at all.

It is high time that we set aside this futile controversy and make vigorous efforts to protect our interests in all areas, and find ways and means to increase exports.

## The Functioning of WTO

WTO has been in existence for well over ten years. It is time to look at its functioning.

When it came into existence, according to its secretarial study, the post-WTO era was expected to generate annual trade of US$510 billion, and India would benefit to the extent of at least US$ 15 million in trade.

Its functioning has been eventful in the sense that its main activity has been mostly in the area of resolving disputes, and every dispute brought before it has raised passion and strong arguments on either side.

The perception of equitable, fair and free trade varies from country to country. Most countries were happy to strengthen and increase their trade and access to new markets through WTO. At the same time, they were not inclined to further open up their market to others.

Of the total members of WTO almost three fourths are from developing countries, whose combined share in world trade is only 26%, compared to 70% from developed countries. Any effort at harmonization was bound to be in favour of the stronger partners in the trade. Hence one of the difficult problems has been the allowable tariffs to protect the domestic industries. This is further complicated in countries like India due to huge unemployment problems, and a guarantee of social justice according to the Constitution.

Many of the disputes coming up in WTO pertain to the developed countries. Some of the disputes which surfaced were:

1. The EU in an effort to give a fillip to the exports of some of the countries like Jamaica had a policy of importing bananas at concessional duty rates compared to higher duties for bananas imported from elsewhere. US protested against this, and the US government took the matter to WTO. In spite of the many entreaties to both sides to settle the dispute amicably, they were adamant. In the end, US decided to levy additional duties on specific imports amounting to US$ 520 million from EU, so as to retaliate against its banana import policy. After deliberating over this, WTO ruled that additional levies need to be slapped on the imports from EU of US$191 million.

2. Another bone of contention was the ban on the hormone-treated beef by EU. WTO ruled that EU should lift its ban on hormone-treated beef by May 13, 1999, as there was no convincing scientific evidence that hormones were harmful. America was planning to impose sanctions on around US$300 million worth of imports from EU, mainly on foodstuffs (and motor cycles) The EU in its turn hit back with a new scientific report claiming that hormones could cause cancer.

Looking at the overall picture of post-WTO era, one can say:

(a) Trade is far too close to the political system and economic well being of the countries, that no country is prepared to give up its advantages. And more so if powerful groups like US and EU are pitted against each other, the disputes last longer.

(b) WTO is largely reactive rather than proactive. It has to strengthen its machinery to anticipate problems in advance, and devise a consensus or a compromise acceptable to both sides so that the main goal of WTO of reducing protectionism and increasing world trade is achieved.

## CHALLENGES FOR THE INDIAN ECONOMY

What is of great concern to India and many developing countries is the tendency of the developed countries to drag in many extraneous issues into the WTO, which indirectly would affect their exports.

One such move was to bring into WTO the need for uniform labor standards among the members. The issue was that with liberalization of trade, developing countries whose wages are comparatively lower, would have an edge in the competition with the developed countries. They forgot that international trade is basically built upon comparative advantages and cost differences. India and other countries have taken a strong stand against this for the simple reason that having labor standards which are not in tune with the standards of the other sections of society will create chaos in the economy and social unrest.

It is essential that India's concerns be articulated well in these deliberations, and preliminary spadework with as many countries as possible, who agree with our point of view, has to be done. Food security for a massive population like ours, at the present stage, demands appropriate use of subsidies, state procurement systems, pricing of agricultural products, public distribution systems, and import restrictions. This system cannot be disturbed in a hurry in the name of liberalization. Trade negotiations in the agricultural sector have to accommodate these legitimate concerns.

We should also take care to negotiate properly in the services sector, for it holds out great promise for Indians by virtue of the large pool of technical and professional people available in India.

Our interest lies not in blindly opposing the multilateral trade regime, but in designing intelligently a plan of action for the country, taking full advantage of the favourable provisions, preventing adverse consequences as far as possible. This requires deep commitment from the government, industry and all the people involved. They should gather considerable data from all over the world and have meaningful meetings with the experts to evolve our approach and arguments to protect the national interest.

In these trade negotiations, countries like America bring in hundreds of experts, each a specialist in his area so that they get the best benefit in the negotiations. But countries like India send perhaps half a dozen people who are expected to be the repositories of all knowledge available in the country. This has to change.

After WTO was formed, there have been three important ministerial rounds, as they are called, in Seattle, Doha and Cancun. The purpose of these meetings was to discus pending problems so as to smoothen out trade prospects for all the countries.

The Cancun Ministerial round was meant to carry forward the earlier Doha agenda with a view to arrive at a consensus on many issues. But it turned out that both developed countries and developing countries took stands that could not be resolved, and the meeting ended without any major outcome.

The main objection of the developing countries was the reduction of the agricultural subsidies as well as high tariff barriers of developed countries. They could not give any commitment on reducing the subsidies. The developing countries were also against the introduction and discussion of new issues ( referred to as 'Singapore Issues') without a prior resolution of the various issues raised by the developing countries earlier.

Cancun will be remembered for the ability of developing countries to hold together despite the severe pressure being exerted by global economic powers. Multilateral trade negotiations were conducted on more even terms for the first time in WTO. India, China and Brazil stood together in this effort.

But the problems do not end there. The entire history of GATT and WTO shows that the developed countries always get together and try to see that their markets expand and try to get unfettered entry for their products and services. As the eminent trade economist Mr. Jagadish Bhagwati says, all trade negotiations whether in WTO or bilateral between two countries, are always political. Every country tries to get the best possible openings for its trade and services to expand.

Even though we can show solidarity with the developing countries in these meetings, we should not lose India's main interest and advantage.

There are critics who say that the WTO meetings and discussions are all not completely friendly to us, but mostly help the developed countries; and even go to the extent to say that we should opt out of it. It is an impractical and dangerous suggestion, since as a member, we have recourse to the WTO for any patent injustice we may face in the trade. Once we are out of WTO we will have no protection, and will be completely at the mercy of other trading countries.

We should also acknowledge that India's exports have increased in a little over a decade to $ 150 billion in 2007-08, from $ 26.3 billion in 1994-05.

India's share in the total world exports of goods and commercial services has gone up to over 1% in 2007 from 0.61% in 1995.

It is only the deliberations of GATT and WTO that enabled the Multi Trade Agreement, which restricted our exports of textiles and garments to be dismantled, and from 2005 onwards, textile exports have increased.

Another important aspect of WTO process is that it allows bilateral negotiations between two countries. This will be made use of by developed countries, and get their entry into the market by giving in exchange some benefits as reduced tariff or entry into areas where developing countries have an edge.

We should get into these bilateral negotiations whenever needed, to get specific entries and increased exports for our goods and services to developed countries and in the process concede tariff reductions in areas where it will not affect us seriously and in a time frame which will suit us.

Hence the sum and substance of WTO negotiations are that we have to oppose any unfair demands in the ministerial discussions and show solidarity with other countries which do so, while at the same time continue negotiations indirectly with the countries to improve our trade. The developments in the last few years exemplifies this stand.

An important landmark of WTO was the Ministerial Conference in Doha in November 2001, which provided a mandate for negotiations including those on agriculture and services. It also approved linked decisions that developing countries face in implementing the current WTO agreements.

The original mandate has now been refined by work at Cancun in 2003, Geneva in 2004, and Hong Kong in 2005.

The entire discussion in various meetings, both formal and informal, is for the ultimate objective of member governments to cut tariff and subsidies. With 153 members of WTO, and thousands of products, the effort has been to arrive at a formula to cut various tariffs and subsidies and set new ceiling commitments.

Leaving the vast verbiage on WTO negotiations in round after round, the main obstacles as they seem to an observer are:

(1) NAMA or Non-Agricultural Market Access is a big bone of contention. It is the effort of aggressive tariff liberalization that developed countries seek from the developing countries, which needs modifications in the interest of the developing countries.

(2) The issue of the vast subsidies given to agriculture by the developed countries such as America and the EU, and their reluctance to abolish or reduce them drastically.

Agriculture is of prime importance to India and China. In India, practically 60% of the population is dependent upon agriculture for its livelihood, and is characterized by small holdings of less than five acres. The Indian farmer has progressed, but not sufficiently to compete with USA and Europe whose farmers have substantial subsidies from their governments. The US has a million people engaged in farming which is nearly 200 million, in India.

Indians live off agriculture. It is important for India to be sure that its international commitments do not put its farmers (most of them engaged in subsistence farming) at the risk of forces beyond the governments' influence. Cheap imports may bring down prices in the domestic market and may trigger a collapse of local produce. The consequences would be extremely serious.

❖ ❖ ❖

**6**

# EXPORT MANAGEMENT

Of all the innovations of the last century, the innovation of the 'discipline of management' – the vast storehouse of knowledge and experience which is at the root of the success of an organization, is the most important one. During the past many decades, this discipline has helped organizations to be successful, however advanced they are, and however complex and specialized their fields are.

It has been so important that we can say that it is the fulcrum around which industry, trade and commerce revolves. If we want to start, or invest in or even join an organization, the primary concern would be about the kind of management it has, and how good it is.

Despite its role in the success of many organizations, management, apart from the serious who study or practise it successfully, is the least understood profession. Many have a cynical view that it is a need that has arisen because we have inherited a lot of organizations that have grown without professional expertise, and hence we need modern management to manage them. But in actual fact, we have created organizations that meet a vast array of the needs of society by applying the 'discipline of management'. This could not have been done by any other means.

Of late the 'New Economy' as it is christened has come into being. It claims that (a) it will do away with all the appendages of management and traditional organizations, (b) the technology and the so called virtual organization will make the organisations transform completely, (c)organized groups or work teams will take their place, and there will not be a hierarchical relationship, and (d) a large number of people will work independently, may be from their homes, and management will become everyone's responsibility.

But the premise on which the above claims are made is flawed. Management as a discipline is primarily not about supervising others, or hierarchy in a chain of commands. The discipline of management is about getting the performance and desired results out of the complexities and the specialized knowledge and skills of many people. This is the hallmark of the 'New Economy'. One can go to the extent of saying that as the Global Economy is becoming more knowledge-based, work will become very specialized and complex, and hence the 'discipline of management' has to play a bigger role in getting optimum performance. Even though the New Economy makes the knowledge-workers think that they live in a world of their own and tend to contribute as individuals, it is only because of the 'discipline of management' that their specialized work and skills are made very productive and performance-oriented. As the old adage goes 'The more things change, the more the fundamental principles matter.'

Management as is known and understood by us has evolved considerably over this century. The latter day gurus of management have emphatically claimed that each of the theories they brought forth could alone answer the needs of the day. All these theories had certainly some relevance at the time, and touched upon one or more important aspects of management, and certainly helped in the evolution of management. However they could never cover the entire spectrum of management, and in the fast moving world, new situations always arose which the erstwhile theories could not address comprehensively.

From the early part of the century till perhaps the oil boom of 1973, when oil prices began to escalate, 'scientific management' as propounded by Fredrick Winslow Taylor (1856-1917), and the various improvements brought on by subsequent practitioners, held ground. It also helped for a rapid and orderly growth of the economy and world trade. Though the core discipline of management was still in tact, there were two very important developments in the latter part of the twentieth century, which were quite fundamental and very swift in their occurrence. As a result, the old framework of 'management' that was propounded, needed new innovations to suit the fast changing world.

The first was the fourfold increase in oil prices in 1973, which affected the economies of all the countries of the world and it took the world quite some time to get adjusted to the change.

The second was the cataclysmic change that came about in 1990 – breaching of the German wall and the fall of the communist regimes the world over.

These two developments were unprecedented, and the economy of each and every country was affected by them. Questions such as, whether the free-market led economies are the best answer for all the ills of the Universe which loomed large, had no definite answers. Meanwhile the changes on the ground in all the economies and countries gave rise to problems needing radical changes, and the governments and the corporates tried to tackle them in the best possible ways known to them.

This was also the period when a large number of 'Management Gurus' appeared on the scene, each one evolving his own theory and solutions to the problems faced by management. Without going into great details of who proclaimed what, let us look at the ideas they proposed that were of utmost importance in moving ahead in management.

These were, 'Strategic Planning', 'Total Quality Management', 'Bench Marking', 'Core Competencies', 'Reengineering', 'Value Chain Analysis', etc.

Each one of these had its own effect on management practices. They had their own success stories as well as failures, but none could be claimed as a complete panacea for all the ills of management.

But after all these, where do we stand at the end of one millennium and the beginning of a new one? Are we in a position to recommend to the students of business in the world, a truly tried and tested 'management theory', which will withstand all the tests, and be relevant for the present time?

As they say, the jury is still out on this.

But what we seem to have realised is this:

(1) In the 'management', we practise in business, there are no readymade answers to all the new situations we encounter. As every new change occurs, we have to adapt ourselves to the new situations with the

help of perhaps a bit of one or all the old theories practised earlier, and if need be evolve something of our own, based on our experience, to meet the situation.

(2) Whatever theory (or fad as some like to call it) held good and successful at one particular point of time need not necessarily be the answer for all time to come.

In this situation how do we look at 'export management' in India today? It is indeed an amalgam of the old as well as the new. For all the new export organizations coming into being now, they have no choice but to follow the tried and tested discipline of management, and improve upon the actions to be taken.

But the merchandising exporters of the country, who form a majority of the exporting community, have to sustain and improve their exports in sectors where we have core-strengths and capabilities and new areas where the future demands of the world lie. They have to adapt their export management techniques to meet new challenges.

In India, apart from applying the various new theories which are relevant and help to improve the export management of the organization, there are two fundamental factors which should not be forgotten.

(1) The export organization should be kept 'lean and hungry' – this should never be forgotten. Primarily successful export performance is expense-intensive, as the markets are abroad and overseas set-up as well as travel, consume a large part of the budget, and hence the need to keep the home base as compact as possible.

(2) The 'discipline of management' should not be forgotten, and should be practised well. The details of the discipline are given later in the chapter.

The evolution of export management organizations in India is given with reference to the challenges they face, how they deal with them and how to tackle the problems at the basic levels of planning and execution.

## EXPORT MANAGEMENT

Management in India today faces new challenges after the recent reforms, which have not only made the market place competitive with many new players, but also with the latest technologies becoming prominent.

Export Management organisations have faced some of these challenges in the past as well, since their marketplace was the world arena, where they had to face the best in the world, and local inhibitions were irrelevant.

Today there are more business opportunities and also new challenges. How far are the companies able to adapt themselves to the radical and fast changes which are taking place due to the revolution brought about by the Information Technology in all aspects of business – supply chain management, new materials used, new production techniques, distribution, service etc? Are we able to match the expectations of our customers abroad in these areas?

It is no longer the financial parameters alone which are enough in evaluating an organization and its growth. They are indeed essential. But what differentiates a company which wants to be in the forefront, from the others, are its forward looking management polices, the choice of personnel, and building a good team with complete support. Only then can it achieve its goals.

The areas of constant review in the export field of management are:

*(a)* Is the present export of goods and services sustainable over the next few years? If not, what else, and how to prepare the organization to face the new needs and changes.

*(b)* What are the changes taking place in the international arena, and are we equipping ourselves to meet the new challenges?

*(c)* What kind of new technological changes affect our business and have we initiated the process of building the necessary infrastructure and personnel to meet these challenges ahead?

*(d)* The need for adequately qualified manpower is very great. It is said that in most knowledge-based companies, Human Resources Management plays a vital role. And this trend is occurring in export organizations as well. There is always fast mobility of managerial staff in the corporate sector, and much more so in the export field, where qualified and experienced professionals are few and far between. What are the plans of organizations to keep ahead of this phenomenon?

There should be serious deliberation on all these in a company and it should evolve its own answer to these challenges. The answers will revolve around the commitment to customers, teamwork of a high order, increased employee participation in the decision making processes, introduction of adequate rewards for performance, motivating the staff, realigning staff so as to take up the challenges of technology improvements, exposure to international marketplace, etc.

The above should be an ongoing process, and should exercise the attention of top management. It is an ever changing and dynamic scene in exports. The development in the international market place is so swift and unexpected, that unless one manages to get the necessary inputs in time, be alert and also observe the changing needs of the society and the customers very carefully, one would lose out.

Assuming that the management applies itself to all the above, it becomes equally important to have a tight-knit management structure, with clear goals and objectives and well-defined functions, so that the work is carried out efficiently, is successful and gets the appreciation of the customers.

There is no other way than to go to the fundamentals, which we refer to as the 'discipline of management' which has stood the test of time, and which can be suitably adapted to each company depending upon its size, nature of business and needs. Let us also see how export management has evolved in our country.

Export activity in our country in the fifties and sixties centered on traditional and primary products. In the case of many primary products such as cotton, jute, tea, etc., the pattern and direction of trade was well established and the emphasis was on an increase in the volume of trade and diversification of products to new markets. It is only in the late sixties and the early seventies that industrial activity switched over to non-traditional exports and export-oriented industries to cater to specific needs of the world market. This welcome and necessary change in emphasis, brought in its wake a host of problems, the most important of which was the need for a trained professional management cadre to take up the challenge. A challenge it was, there is no doubt, since India found that it was up against well-organised and very well-managed international organizations whose efficiency and quickness to react to situations was of a high order.

Therefore, a dire need arose for professional management practices in export management.

One should have a clear picture of the 'discipline of management' as it is called in order to appreciate the role of export management.

There have been innumerable books on management which emphasis the need for professional managers who will be able to put into practice this 'discipline of management'. Before we proceed further, we should have an idea of what this is all about, and the best method is to try to understand the system through the "manager", who is the kingpin of this system.

Simply defined, a manager is a person who has the responsibility and authority for getting results through others who report to him. A manager is first a leader. He gets his results, not primarily by what he can do himself, but by what he can accomplish through others. This is an important distinction. The definition tells us that the results a manager can achieve are defined, not by his personal abilities as a finance manager, engineer or expert salesman but by the extent to which he can get a finance manager, engineer or an expert salesman to secure results for him.

A professional manager performs a special kind of job, just as does an engineer, a doctor or a lawyer. Many managers fall short of expectations and use an excessive proportion of their time and energy in non-managerial activities because they fail to recognise their own shortcomings. Our initial assumption in identifying the work of a professional manager is that it is different from the work performed by the people he manages. Obviously, if an export Sales Manager concentrates only on selling, he is not managing but selling. Our question now is: What work must a professional manager do that cannot be performed effectively by those he leads?

This question can be answered very precisely if we recognise that a manager has a unique organisational placement. Because he is the leader of a group, only he can be objective and look with balance and perspective upon the needs of his subordinates as well as that of the organization.

For example, consider the question of who is to set goals or targets for one of the export divisions in an export organization. If the manager allows a sales executive to set the target of exports for the division as a whole, we can expect that the individual sales executive will set the export target to satisfy the selling conditions in the countries he covers and will have only secondary consideration for the needs and problems of his fellow sales executives, or the organization's needs. Only the export manager can make a decision in the light of the needs of the division as a whole, because he does not specialise in single areas or products, but has an overall picture of the division.

## MANAGEMENT SKILLS

**(a) Transferable:** An engineer ordinarily does not have the skills necessary to perform finance work nor can a tool dresser perform the work of a salesman. However, an individual who is an expert in managing one activity or function can, to a high degree, transfer his managerial skills to another activity or function. The higher on the managerial scale a manager is, the more will he be expected to spend his time on managing. Further, the more expert a manager is in managing, the greater are the range of activities he can manage.

This is why the Chief Executive or an Export Manager is expected to be able to manage effectively not only finance, export sales, overseas operations, shipping and documentation, but also employee relations and other functions, without necessarily being an expert in any of them.

**(b) Measurable:** Management is as much a specialised kind of job as is engineering or production; and it is also measurable. That is, we can determine how much of this work has to be performed, and whether or not the pre-determined quantum is carried out effectively. This is a vital consideration. If a manager can measure his work, he can also realise where he is strong and where he is weak in his performance, and what steps he should take to improve himself. This periodic self-assessment is very necessary.

Before we go to the 'discipline of management' we have been referring to, we should briefly review the essential characteristics of export management where it differs from a domestic activity of a similar kind.

Where export activity differs:

When we talk about business potential, targets, sales, etc., we refer, basically, to our activities in countries other than our own. Hence, it is axiomatic that the management should have,

*(a)* Keen perception and understanding of the economy of the country to which we export, the state of development of the manufacturing and services sector, and other trade activities as well as export/import regulations and long-term national plans. All these have a definite bearing on our export trade.

*(b)* The political developments in a country in many cases affect economic activity and trade. Hence, a reasonable understanding of the political climate and likely developments is essential, especially in drawing up long-term plans.

(c) A deep understanding of the financial aspect of export trade is essential. One should have a clear concept of the mode of payment through letters of credit, international codes and practices for such documentary credits, pre-shipment and post-shipment financial facilities, deferred payment facilities, etc. These are explained in the chapter on "Export-Finance". These demand specialised knowledge and expertise to a great extent. One should not only know the details of all this in his country, but also in the countries to which he exports.

(d) The expertise needed extends also to such other activities as shipping, insurance, and export control regulations in our country as well as in the country to which we export. All these have a set pattern of rules and regulations, and in many cases so different from domestic trade, that it calls for special knowledge and diligent application.

(e) The various governmental regulations and policies, for example, *(i)* on procedures and documentation, *(ii)* on import license and its implications, *(iii)* on trade agreements with various countries and *(iv)* on periodical governmental notifications thereof, call for trained and professional expertise of a high order. This is necessary so that one is able to take full advantage of the markets and, more particularly, is able to anticipate some of the policies to be adopted.

## DISCIPLINES OF MANAGEMENT

If we study export management in detail, we can identify five clear-cut categories of management activity, which we refer to as the 'discipline of management', and around which the process of management revolves. The principles involved in these processes are the basis of management, and a professional manager in the field of exports should master them. These activities may be classified as:

(I) Planning (II) Organization (III) Building a team (IV) Executive Action (V) Management Control.

### (I) Planning

Planning is the pre-determination of a course of action. It has conscious thinking through every aspect of the work the manager expects to do. The concrete result of planning is a series of decisions arrived at beforehand to enable the manager to undertake his tasks in an orderly and fully effective fashion.

Planning for export, even though extremely difficult, is the most important and often neglected function.

Planning helps an organization to make the most effective and economical use of manpower and resources. It provides an overall plan which offers individuals an opportunity to participate in the decisions that are made, thus getting total involvement of the staff. To come to specifics in export, planning involves, first, forecasting. In the light of the forecast, the objectives or goals can be set. Thereafter, it helps the manager to develop his programme which is a step-by-step sequence of the activity he expects to undertake. It is also essential to set time limits for the completion of the different phases of the programme by establishing an operating plan. The plan will envisage the work to be done in a uniform manner, which calls for development of procedures. Finally, the management must allocate the resources available to carry out these plans. The last step is referred to as budgeting.

Planning is broadly divided into:

**(a) Short-term:** This will comprise an export plan of one to two years, indicating the volume of export, cost, profitability, and indicating also the infrastructure one has to develop, and personnel needs.

**(b) Long-term:** This will comprise an export plan of 3 to 5 years or, in some cases, up to 10 years, which will include diversification into new products and markets, export-oriented industries, joint ventures, new innovations etc., to sustain export on a long-term and substantial scale.

In the above framework of planning, **forecasting** of exports is crucial. It encompasses the following:

(1) Accurate evaluation of market requirements.

(2) Evaluation of competitive challenges and their impact; New processes or innovations which would come to the market in competition to ours.

(3) A clear comprehension of the political developments in the importing countries which will have a direct bearing on one's exports.

(4) A clear picture of the economic and trade activities of the importing countries and anticipation of the developments during the year which may affect exports.

(5) The infrastructural needs, such as shipping, finance, production capacity, etc; required for effective exports.

(6) Governmental policies which have a direct bearing on exports.

This indicates how much data, information and knowledge one has to gather to attempt realistic planning of exports.

In view of the possibility of sudden and absolutely unexpected developments, both national and international, there should always be a contingency plan to achieve one's objectives.

**Objectives:** Forecasting leads to the objectives or goals which, in the case of an export organization, would amount to export target sales set for it on a country-wide basis; these objectives are based on past performance and current potential in the export market. One should aim at setting objectives which are capable of being realised. If the target is set too high, it will eventually frustrate those held accountable for achieving it. If, on the other hand, it is too low, it will lack challenge and fail to spur one to higher achievement.

Further, the objectives should be stated in measurable terms. It is normal practice for many export organisations to state that their objective is to "increase exports" or to get "a larger share of the market." But a better approach is to state in specific terms that the objective is to "increase the volume of sales from 10,000 to 15,000 units" or "increase the export turnover from Rs.10 crores to Rs.12 crores." This facilitates an easy evaluation of the objective in terms of the resources required to achieve it.

It is also essential that the personnel held accountable for accomplishing the export targets should participate in these exercises, for it has been found that objectives are easily accepted as management goals only when they are fully understood by the people who have to execute them. This indirectly means that the export manager has the primary responsibility of securing the participation of his subordinates in the objectives he establishes for them.

This participation may be secured in several ways. One approach is to ask the executive covering each area to set an export target for his area of operation.

The other approach is to set the target on a group basis, the executives covering different areas working together. In either case, the export manager discusses the target in detail and the objective is arrived at after mutual discussions.

The objectives should be reconciled to the limitations of different groups in the organisation. Thus, while a specific figure may be arrived at as an export target for an area or for the entire organization, this may have to be suitably altered in some cases because of the infrastructural facilities available. For example, there may be a demand at good prices for machine tools of a particular type. It may perhaps be possible to achieve an export target of Rs. 10 crores. On the other hand, the production capacity in the country, after meeting the domestic demand, in this particular category may be not sufficient to meet the export demand. Or, the shipping freight or inadequacy of sailings may render it impossible for us to cater to the demands of certain countries.

It is possible that the design and supply of a particular type of software is well within the capability of an organization, provided it can deploy a suitable number of software engineers. Due to other prior commitments, the organization will not be able to spare the number of engineers required. Therefore, objectives have to be reconciled to a realistic figure in a practical manner in line with the facilities available.

**Programming:** While the objective spells out what you expect to accomplish, the programme outlines how you expect to do it. It is natural that a programme is built around an objective, for it serves as an overall planning guide, presenting a total picture of what the management aims at over a specified future period. A properly prepared programme becomes an administrative tool of great value, for it will enable the management to foresee the uncertainties and problems which will arise in its implementation. This helps the manager to evolve, ahead of time, alternatives and marshal the resources and facilities with a view to achieving his objective.

A programme also acts as a basis for effective control. By evaluating progress against the programme that has been outlined, he obtains a measure of the target achieved.

Programming cannot be static. It should be a continuous function and should provide for individual divisions. It should be periodically reviewed to provide improvement factors, wherever possible. Any change should be supported by carefully investigated and justified reasons, and the change itself should be in line with the export potential and facilities available.

**Procedures** have an important role to pay in an export organization. Basically, they help in the performance of work in a uniform manner, no matter in which location the work is undertaken. Further, in export activity, many of the procedures followed have been laid down in accordance with governmental, banking, legal and other regulations, and a strict adherence to those formal procedures is essential. The procedures are laid down in such a manner that a close observance of them will automatically ensure financial security and protection of one's goods and rights in international trade. This aspect will be dealt with in detail in the chapter on Export Procedures.

**Budgeting**, especially in export marketing, is a vital element in planning. In simple terms, it is a process of estimating what resources in manpower, materials, and facilities will be required to carry out a planned programme, and of allocating those resources in the best possible manner. Since the resources, such as manpower, materials and facilities are dissimilar, a common denomination for budgeting is used whereby all elements of cost are converted into money.

To outline the whole process of budgeting in exports, we should start with the forecast on export targets as a means of what probable level of income we anticipate under given conditions. In other words, it is the total amount we expect to have over a given period. To accomplish this export objective, we undertake a definite sequence of activities or a programme which becomes the basis for our budget.

If we simply pay our expenses as they occur without setting definite limits as to what we can afford to spend, we shall have little chance of achieving our profit objectives. If we figure out beforehand how much it would cost us for materials, facilities, salaries, overheads and other expenses, we will be able to calculate whether we can make our desired profit in terms of the programme. If we know the amount we expect to realise by way of export proceeds, and if we have also established a definite profit objective, it is obvious that our operating expenses, including depreciation and taxes, will be no more than the difference between our anticipated income and desired profit.

Budget is an effective tool in regulating income and expenditure. If it is discovered that we cannot attain our profit goal with the programme we have planned, we can take immediate steps to cut back on some programmed activities which, without affecting the turnover, would reduce expenses and enable us to reach a position as close to our profit objective as possible.

In the expense budget of the nature described above, there are fixed and variable costs. The fixed costs are such items as rent of a building, insurance, salary outgo, etc., while variable costs are those incurred on transport, clearing and forwarding, purchase, consumable items and other recurring expenditure directly proportional to our activities. In an export organization, the aim is to keep the fixed costs exceptionally low so that effective cost control can be exercised on the total budget.

## (II) Organization

This refers in brief to the means by which the programme mentioned earlier is carried out by the export manager who arranges the work to be done by various groups most effectively. A sound organization largely determines the economy and effectiveness with which the business is both managed and operated.

Organization consists of three basic activities:

(1) Designing organization components; that is, identifying the work that has to be performed to reach the objectives, and grouping this in well-balanced jobs, territories, division and other organisational units.

(2) Defining and delegating responsibility and authority.

(3) Establishing relationships.

An export organization has to be kept lean, fit and streamlined so that it may do its job most effectively and quickly at the lowest cost. It is well known that, in India, export activity produces only marginal profits. Further, the fluctuations in export turnover even in established export organizations are at times considerable for reasons beyond their control – such as international recession and competition, governmental policies, etc. Hence, there is the need to have a lean organization commensurate with the size of trading activities. The most economical circumstances of operation for an export division would be the possibility of inducting more people from the domestic operations when the situation demands.

Notwithstanding what has been stated above, there are certain basic organization principles with respect to an export organization which should be thoroughly understood before we set about the actual task of organization.

*(i)* Work assigned to an individual should be specialised so far as it is consistent with effective human effort. People perform work more efficiently and learn faster if they specialise in one kind of work. Specialization is a means of increasing efficiency up to a point.

*(ii)* Each employee or executive should be assigned the maximum work load that he can handle. Under-utilisation of a man's capacity to work is as harmful as overloading. People work at their maximum capacity if they have a sizeable quantum of work in front of them, but not one that is overwhelming. It is usually true that a comfortable organization in terms of workload which is not challenging, is never an economical one.

*(iii)* The span of supervision should be limited in terms of the diversity, dispersion, complexity and volume of the work being managed. The span of supervision refers to the number of people reporting directly to one manager. The four factors which determine the number of people who can be effectively supervised by a manager are:

*(a)* **Diversity:** The more dissimilar the work being supervised, the more effort and attention a manager must devote to planning, organization and control.

*(b)* **Dispersion:** The more widely separated the activities that are to be supervised, the more difficult it is to plan, co-ordinate and control.

*(c)* The Complexity of the work being performed will render it more difficult to plan, coordinate and control in view of the breadth of knowledge and information required to do an effective job.

*(d)* Volume is not very significant, but if it is accompanied by any of the above factors, it may affect the span of supervision.

## Types of Organisation

We can next examine the different ways in which functions can be combined to form organization components. Basically, there are two types of organizations – functional organization and divisional organization. The former is made up of positions and groups doing similar work. It encourages specialization.

Divisional organization is the process of organising in terms of the end-results to be accomplished. It is essentially a process of grouping different types of work together to accomplish a common end result.

**Delegation:** A professional manager must possess the ability to delegate his work, reserving for himself only that which is organisationally so placed that he can perform it effectively.

Delegation, in simple terms, is the process of entrusting a part of one's work to others for performance. However, skill in delegation requires the observance of certain key principles:

*(a)* The responsibility and authority of each person should be written down. Only when it is put in writing is the work clearly defined and also indicates whether the workload is balanced or not.

*(b)* Authority should always be delegated to the extent to which it is commensurate with responsibility. When responsibility – that is, the work to be performed – is delegated to an employee, he should also have the power and the right or authority he needs to carry out his duties. For example, we may entrust an export salesman with the task of exporting our products to customers. However, to get the best performance from him we should also give him the right to decide how much time he needs to spend with the customers to get the job done, the power to commit the company to delivery promises and the right to travel and incur sales promotional expenses within an overall limit. To the extent to which we refuse to delegate such authority to him, we lessen his ability to perform effectively.

Development and training of subordinates is essential to enable them to perform the work delegated. It is also necessary to provide effective controls. This is best achieved by establishing appropriate performance standards and then providing for accurate reporting against these standards to enable effective monitoring of delegated duties.

In all matters of delegation, it should be borne in mind that even though responsibility is delegated to a subordinate, the accountability is still that of the manager, and this cannot be delegated.

Establishing Relationship: The organisation chart provides a clear picture of the reporting relationship of all the employees. It shows the various levels of authority and who is reporting to whom in the organisation. It also shows the individuals responsible for specific functions and the manner in which the various functions are grouped.

## (III) Building a Team

It is essential for an export organisation to have the right people to build a team. In India, in many of the organisations, we find persons in the export department who have neither training nor experience. They are usually employees of the company who are transferred to the export department because no one else is available.

However, if one gets an opportunity to build an organisation afresh, utmost care should be bestowed on selecting appropriate personnel for the export department. The top management should get involved in this selection since a great deal rests on the type of person who is best suited for the job. Even though candidates are chosen primarily on the basis of educational qualifications, previous experience, personality and aptitude, a thorough screening and a detailed personal interview are essential to determine the right candidate for the job.

Apart from initial selection, the other major requirement is executive development which enables an organization to develop the members of the team to the limit of their potential effectiveness. This is an area where many export organisations in the country are not doing enough.

Whenever an employee or a group of employees is not effective, they are either transferred to other jobs or their functions are diluted by augmenting the staff in the department. The correct procedure would be to study in depth the reasons for inefficiency and take corrective action. This will take the form of:

**(a) Performance Appraisal:** This has to be done objectively. A good deal of time should be spent on considering an employee on what he has done and on what you think he can do with proper help and encouragement. There is often a tendency to rate a man on what he did two or three years earlier, or to permit past performance to colour current appraisal. This should be avoided.

**(b) Counselling:** The full value of performance appraisal can be realised only if we discuss the findings with the person involved, and use them as a basis for developing a programme for improvement. To render effective counselling, one should be frank with the employee, establish a friendly relationship with him and create confidence in him by listening to his point of view very carefully, which will give an opportunity to the employee to analyse his own performance. This will result in a mutual effort in charting out a programme for improvement.

**(c) Coaching:** This is a process carried out on the job to help employees improve their performance. It should not be a haphazard approach, but a programme fitted to each individual's requirement. This involves creating on-the-job opportunities for him with a view to helping an individual to build up his strong points and overcome his weaknesses. It also requires creating developmental opportunities. As a result, employees will be assigned to new and different tasks or may be given a special problem to work out on their own initiative. Coaching may take the form of in-company or outside training and development courses.

In the field of exports, periodic appraisal, counselling and coaching are extremely important. As stated earlier, export being a marginal profit activity, it will be a burden to carry an "ineffective" employee with low productivity.

## (IV) Executive Action

Executive action as a management process consists of those activities which a professional manager undertakes to put his plans, organization and controls into operation. This is of paramount importance in the export field where the management will be called upon to take action at short notice.

*(a)* The first and the most important executive action in this connection is what is popularly referred to in management parlance as decision-making. In simple terms, decision-making is defined as a logical process consisting of four steps, namely,

*(i)* identifying the problem;

*(ii)* securing the available facts;

*(iii)* analysing the possible alternatives; and

*(iv)* deciding upon a course of action.

However, in export activity, situations which call for quick decisions are numerous and frequent. They arise not because of subjective factors (falling within the scope of the export organization) but because of other considerations, such as developments in other countries, including new government regulations, banking regulations and restrictions, an export buyer's creditworthiness which sometimes fluctuates etc., not to speak of political developments which affect government buyers abroad. In all such situations, complete data may not be immediately available; and the export manager will be expected to take decisions based on his past experience and knowledge of the problems. A wrong step may result in a serious set-back for his organisation and loss of foreign exchange earning for the country.

(b) **Motivation:** is also an essential part of executive activity. It is a process of inspiring, impelling and encouraging people to work at their best. In motivating people, the management should recognise the basic need of every human being, which psychologists call "ego recognition".

In simple terms, this is the desire to feel important. It is a need to be recognised as a worthwhile individual doing necessary and meaningful work.

(c) **Leadership:** This is necessary to motivate people and to get the best out of them. Export business, especially for the export executive who is on tour most of the time to explore new markets, is no bed of roses; many a time, the set-back one gets after working hard on a proposal for months and years, is such that even the best of men may give up. A good leader is one who motivates people and inspires them to do better.

(d) **Communication:** The effectiveness of a professional manager rests in a large measure upon his skill on communication. Plans can be acted upon, organization can be made effective, motivation can take place, controls can be exercised only if he can convey his conception of these activities to others, and also understand what they are trying to convey to him. To be an effective communicator, a manager has to be a good listener too.

In an organization, constant communication between the various groups at all levels is vital. As in the export trade one deals with other countries, and as situations in many developing countries change from day to day, a clear appraisal of the situation as it affects our trade should be communicated to the employees involved.

The practical manner in which this is done is to have frequent group meetings, as also frequent meetings at the highest level. At the operating level, it may be on a daily basis and at higher levels on a biweekly/weekly basis. Such meetings will help one in analysing specific situations to arrive at the best possible executive action. Even though a professional export manager may be adept at communication with his team, at a lower level, inter-group/inter-departmental communication may be ineffective. Hence, such meetings offer an excellent opportunity for correcting such situations and also for effective communication at all levels. It should also be borne in mind that since it is not always possible to put in writing all the information one wishes to convey, meetings serve a very important purpose.

## (V) Management Control

This refers to the process of evaluating the completed work, and the work in progress, to ensure that it is carried out according to the plan and programme envisaged at the commencement of operations. The earliest form of management control is personnel inspection and supervision. This limits one to a relatively small span of control. Far more effective is the development of a system of control that alerts the manager when things are not going according to plan.

Control involves a sequence of activities. It begins with the setting of performance standards which serve as yardsticks against which performance is measured. Once the work is under way, it is measured by appropriate recording and reporting procedures. The results secured are then compared with the standards established. The resulting variances are then identified with a view to taking corrective action.

In an export organization, care should be exercised in establishing control. The points to bear in mind are:

(a) Since accountability can be exercised only in terms of the formal organisation, control channels must follow organisational lines, that is, a subordinate's activities can be controlled only in terms of what has been formally delegated to him.

(b) As real control occurs at the point of action, the first line supervisors should be trained to spot the variances and take immediate corrective action.

A reporting system should be evolved. This may be in terms of daily meetings of an export organization referred to earlier, which may provide an immediate opportunity to take remedial steps. Or it may be in the form of daily/weekly reports on pre-determined lines. Timely submission of reports and the action taken thereupon are extremely important, for in matters of export even a day's delay may create problems of a serious nature. There is a tendency among many export executives to take simple corrective action as an immediate remedial effort. They do not go deeper into the problem with a view to changing the procedures to prevent such occurrences in future, which is very vital.

## EXPORT ORGANISATION

Having studied the various principles of professional management, as applicable to exports, we shall now turn our attention to the growth of an export organization in India.

In many cases, exports have originated from the desire of two or three persons working in an organization, or running a company of their own, to trade in overseas markets. By their efforts, they generate a few orders and these are handled more or less in the manner of domestic trade. The new problems which arise, such as documentation and shipping, are solved with the help of bankers and clearing agents.

In the second phase, as exports increase in volume, a fairly simple form of administration evolves. This will be the appointment of an export executive, not necessarily experienced or specially trained. Usually, he is from another division of the company itself, and is given the job because he is the only candidate readily available. He is assisted by a stenographer and a clerk who looks after the banking and shipping aspects of exports.

In the next stage, as the exports grow, a formal export department is established, where the objectives of the department and its functions are clearly defined. The export executive in charge becomes an export manager, who may have to concentrate on selling and also undertake travelling abroad fairly often. The other important additions will be *(a)* a sales assistant, who will attend to sales correspondence and office work, *(b)* a shipping assistant who, with the help of the clearing and forwarding agent, will organise the movement of goods from the production centre to a port, arrange for shipment and documentation, *(c)* an accounting assistant, who will take care of negotiation of documents, financial requirements, bank dealings, etc.

Depending upon the volume and nature of exports, the sales, accounting and other service sections will be suitably strengthened with adequate personnel.

This set-up is referred to as the Basic Export Organization.

Finally, in the last phase of evolution, a full-fledged export division or export company takes shape. It will assume complete responsibility for all aspects of the export activities and function as a well-oiled machine.

The organizational set-up will be headed by an export manager or general manager or director, as the case may be. He will be assisted for export sales by a sales manager and a group of sales executives who will be responsible for generating sales. The other areas which have to be suitably strengthened with adequate personnel to cope with the increased volume of work will be finance and marketing services, consisting of supply co-ordination, shipping and after-sales service. In addition, the necessary expertise will be drawn, either from within the company or with the help of consultants on advertising, publicity, legal matters, market research, recruitment and training of personnel etc. At this stage the stationing of representatives abroad for sales and services and joint ventures in other countries may also become part and parcel of export activities.

This is the usual pattern of growth of an export organization. It may help us to understand the organisational set-up and personnel interrelations if we have an organization chart, which shows the activities, and the reporting relationships in the organization. One or more activities may be handled by one individual. The chart on the next page has been drawn on the basis of practical experience in the export field over a period of years in India. It indicates all the important functions of an organization. The chart is mainly drawn to indicate the variety of activities involved. It is for the management to decide as to what activities can be combined, what activities can be outsourced, and what level of manpower is required to take care of all the functions which are essential for a successful export management.

As for the export of 'services' the organization has to be suitably modified deleting the functions not needed, and adding those which are necessary.

## ORGANIZATION CHART– EXPLANATION

**General:** The chart has been drawn with a view to emphasise the functions which are vital to an export organization. Obviously the chart is for a large export organization which deals in new products, services and markets and is liable to expand fast.

In the case of smaller organizations many of the functions can be combined, to be dealt with by one officer. The personnel required depends upon the volume and the variety of exports being carried out. As stated earlier, the organization has to be kept lean. The tendency now is to outsource quite a few functions, depending upon the savings and efficiency. The obvious areas for outsourcing in a small organization are the legal, human resources and such areas.

Another development in recent times is to organize a small group (consisting of a technical, marketing and financial person within the organisation) and entrust them with the sale of a product or services to a market. In such cases the preliminary survey of a market is already done and a definite possibility of exports to it is indicated. The team may modify the product if necessary, with the help of the technical person, based on the marketing feedback, and the financial person will check on the costs and viability of the exports. In such cases a definite market, a target date and volume of exports expected is given to the group, and they work towards that goal.

**A TYPICAL PRODUCT EXPORT ORGANISATION**

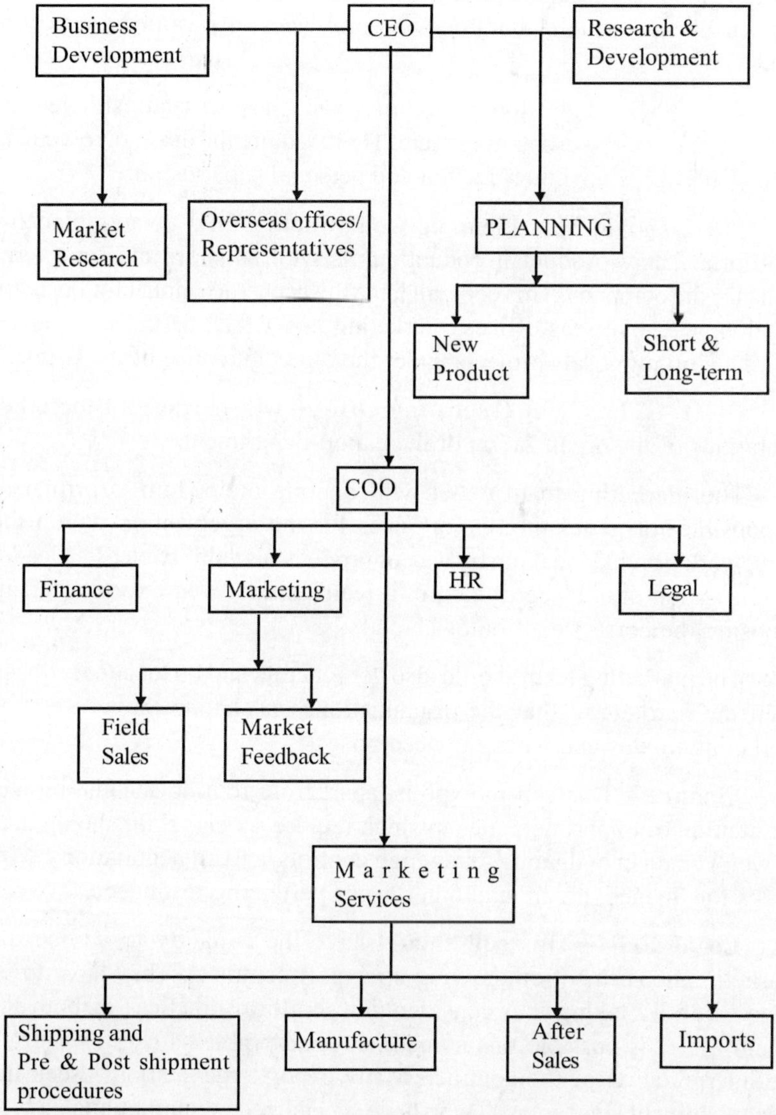


**CEO – The Chief Executive Officer** is the one who formulates the policies and sets the objectives of the organization. The sections handling Business Development, Research and Development and Planning, report to him directly. He should have leadership qualities and the capacity to assess the markets correctly. Through the Research and Business

Development Department, he should work out the export potential in the changing market place. This may be a department in his own organization or a consultant research laboratory whose services are obtained for specific needs.

When exports develop, it becomes necessary to establish overseas offices and place representatives there. These require the direct involvement of the Chief Executive in selection and personal supervision.

There should be a Planning Cell which should always plan for appropriate new product introduction, as well as short and long term plans for the company. This cell will have the necessary inputs for business development, overseas offices, marketing and R&D, based on which it will develop proposals/projects under the direct guidance of the CEO.

**COO – The Chief Operating Officer** will oversee all the other operations of the organization or the export department.

The marketing team which will operate under him is primarily responsible for generating export sales for the organization within the framework provided to them by way of product availability etc. The leader of this group should be dynamic, a team builder and experienced in choosing the correct distributor abroad.

The marketing team should also get accurate and up to date feedback from the market, so that the organization can change the strategy or marketing mix as and when the need arises.

**Finance** – This cell in exports, apart from routine accounting and negotiation of export documents which require special skill, should also be well versed in budgeting, budgeting controls, and all negotiations with banks for finance, credit, and other needs pertaining to finance.

**Legal Cell** – This cell should have the capacity to advise the marketing department on drawing up export contracts. They have to be done carefully taking into consideration the legal practices of both the countries. It is possible that sometimes legal problems may arise from the interpretation of the contract. Many export organizations seek the help of eminent legal counsel who have specialized in international law, to advise them.

**Human Resources** – The one in charge of human resources though reporting to the COO, will also be accountable to the CEO for duties like new recruitments. In exports, more than in other business, the personnel chosen are the key to success. Evaluating their work, organizing specialized training where necessary, weeding out the inefficient ones, and keeping the personnel highly productive and counselling them when necessary are all functions of this section. It is possible to outsource the entire operation, having only one personnel manager to co-ordinate.

**Overseas Offices/Representatives** – Their responsibility is mainly to select and get new orders and to provide complete customer satisfaction. They should have a thorough knowledge of the administration and technical process of the organization to enable them to identify and sort out field problems. They are also the eyes and ears of the organization and their market reports should be comprehensive. In many organizations, they report directly to the CEO.

**Marketing Services** – This section takes care of all the operations needed to deliver the products as contracted to the supplier. The functions under marketing services will become very important in the case of merchandise exports or manufacture exports. These consist of manufacturing or procurement of the product as per specifications of the contract, providing import inputs if necessary, shipment of the final product and after-sales service to be provided in the country of import. If the export organization is small, these functions can come under the CEO or even an administrative officer well versed in export trade.

The chart drawn for Product Export Organisations above is for a large export firm. In the case of smaller export organizations, many of the functions are combined and given to one sector which handles them. Smaller organizations can also contract (outsource) agencies which can do many of the functions in a cost-effective manner.

The chart is drawn to cover comprehensively all the functions needed, and it is upto the management to suitably alter it to its specific needs.

The essential difference between product and services export organization is the nature of the business. The services sector normally works in the manner of one 'project' to the next, compared to product exports which concentrate on a set of products to be exported on a continuous basis.

In the case of the services sector, each 'project' is obtained based on the experience and track record of the export services unit. When a project of such a nature is negotiated and obtained, the entire project is given to a cell referred to as Strategic Business Unit (SBU). The number of people working in the SBU will be the minimum needed for optimum results.

**A TYPICAL SERVICES EXPORT ORGANISATION**

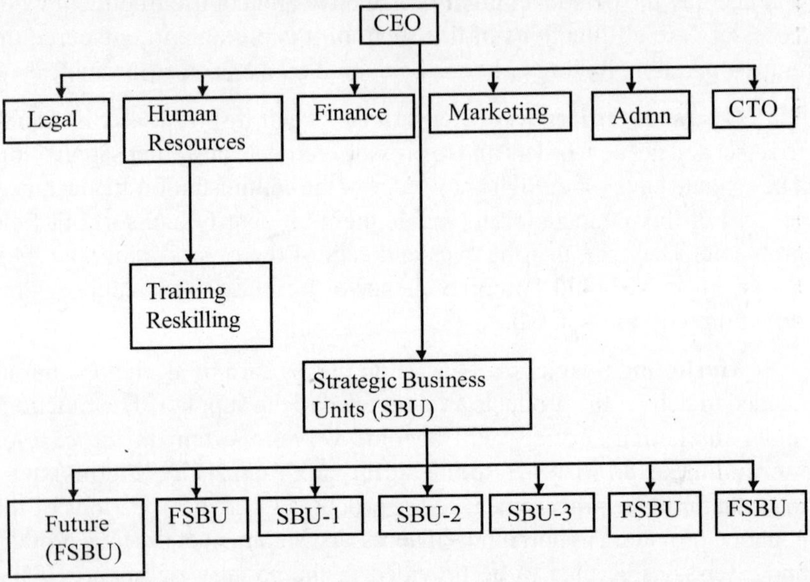


It will have a Project Leader who is an experienced person who has negotiated and obtained the project, and he will coordinate with the customer. He will draw upon the necessary technical and administrative help to complete the project to the satisfaction of the customer by the target date.

It is possible that the project is such that the implementation of the same at the premises of the customer is part of the contract. In that case, the same people who worked on the project will be required to go to the site to implement the same.

The number of SBUs depends on the business contracted. It is possible that one SBU will be asked to take up two or three small projects of similar nature.

One will also note that the legal, finance, marketing, administration, and human resources all come under the CEO. It is upto the CEO to outsource some of the functions to save cost. As most service exports have a technical component, a Chief Technical Officer with sufficient experience has to work under the CEO and he will be asked to help all the SBUs.

The essence of the service organization is its elasticity. It should have the minimum required personnel on its payroll and should be able to outsource with suitable supervision, or increase the personnel required on a contract basis. Only after a few years of experience can an organization be able to arrive at an optimum level of staffing needed.

Here again the need to be lean and efficient is of paramount importance, and the induction of additional manpower should be judicious.

There is no such thing as an ideal export set-up because, however efficient an organization or the people in it, there is always room for improvement. There is always more knowledge to be gained about the various export markets because of the continual political, economic and social developments which often take place and which can baffle the most experienced export department personnel.

These and other developments should be the kind of things an efficient export team discusses continuously and tries to deal with effectively.

In the Indian context, the various types of exporters have been identified traditionally in the classification given below. This mainly arises out of the fact that this has been historically followed in the export-import trade policy. This classification was used in the policy to give them specific advantages/incentives, which will help them increase their exports in the particular categories. After the new export-import policy announced by the government in April 1992, these distinctions have lost their significance, except for Export Houses, Trading Houses and Star Trading Houses.

Exporters can be classified as:

**(1) Merchant Exporters:** This group consists mainly of traders who buy products from the market and export them against orders they have got, by virtue of their contacts developed over a period of years. They identify a supplier who can provide the product with the specifications, quality, delivery schedule and price quoted by them. The merchant exporter takes all the responsibility for exporting the product and realising the proceeds; and practically insulates the supplier from any claims from abroad. In addition, in many cases he helps the supplier by way of finances, import licences, shipping etc.

**(2) Manufacture Exporters:** Any manufacturer who exports his product is included in this category. He can export directly, or through an Export House, Trading House or merchant exporter. Normally a manufacturing exporter develops a good domestic base and markets his products successfully in India, and then seeks an export market in countries where he feels his products will sell.

Initially he prefers to do this through a merchant exporter or Export House or Trading House. All he would need is a liaison man who can co-ordinate manufacture and supply to the export market. But as his export volume increases, the manufacturer feels the need to be directly in touch with the market in order to assess the potential and needs correctly, so that he can increase his exports. At this juncture, he establishes an export department in his company, and either trades directly or goes through a Trading House. The Trading House will provide him with all the facilities to visit the export markets, arrange for after-sales services abroad if necessary, and work closely with him to increase exports.

Apart from the above categories, there are Export House, Trading House, and Star Trading House. The criteria for selection of these organisations have been given in Chapter 7.

The main thrust of these is to provide:

*(a)* marketing overseas,

*(b)* sales promotion of the products,

*(c)* identify dealers with after-sales services facilities abroad,

*(d)* quote for tenders abroad,

*(e)* provide facilities for finance, import licence and other needs of the supporting manufacturer.

In all the above categories of organizations described, the principles of management are the same as outlined in the earlier part of this chapter. They have to be modified only in application, depending on the needs of the market.

❖ ❖ ❖

# 7

# EXPORT POLICY, PROMOTION AND REGULATIONS

Export Policy is two fold. The first is the policy which an organization or an exporter has to adopt for his own organization, and the second is the larger Exim Policy adopted for the nation by virtue of the annual Exim Policy announcement by the Ministry of Commerce in March/April of every year.

The policy to be adopted by an organization, if it wants to be in the field of exports, should be well thought out and have clear goals. The organization should identify products, or projects or services which it would take up for exports, based on the inherent strength it has in producing them or sourcing them. In other words, exports should be based on specific areas where one would have the capabilities to supply to other countries at a competitive price and quality.

Once these are identified, the organization should have a plan to commit resources, both human and financial, for achieving the goals. Thereafter, systematic export marketing efforts can be undertaken which will yield results.

There should be conscientious commitment by the top management in this process. These are being emphasized here, because in India, many people take up exports casually, simply because an enquiry has been directed to them, without thinking through the proposition thoroughly, and end up in problems which could have been avoided. One of the common problems they encounter is that they take up an order based on certain promises of price and quality, and find that these cannot be met at the time of dispatch, and lose in the bargain financially, or get a bad name for themselves and the country for not fulfilling the order.

Now, let us look at the Export/Import Policy of the government, which influences to a considerable extent the exports of the country. It is useful to know that the export policy of the country is not of recent origin, and dates back to 1970 when the government accorded exports its due importance by formulating the policy. This was known as 'Export Policy Resolution, 1970, and tabled in the parliament.

The Export Policy Resolution, 1970 may be considered as a landmark in the history of exports in our country. Its importance lies in the fact that it was perhaps the first time, government has stated clearly the kind of policies it will pursue, in order to increase the exports. Some of the important features of this policy are: *(a)* making Indian products competitive, *(b)* modernizing industry *(c)* improving quality control, *(d)* providing marketing support, *(e)* providing adequate and timely finance, and *(f)* providing adequate shipping facilities at reasonable freight rates.

It would appear that the policies laid down in this resolution are as valid and relevant today – 38 years later – as it was then.

The 'Export Policy Resolution 1970' is reproduced in **Annexure I,** as it is a historical document of importance in the evolution of Indian Exports.

The Export/Import Policy is a necessary instrument of a government to regulate the exports and imports of the country to ensure the balance of trade. As stated earlier, one important source of foreign exchange available to the government is by virtue of the export proceeds apart from the Foreign Direct investment into the country, and the remittance of Indian nationals from abroad. The entire import needs of the county have to be managed accordingly. Even though there may be deficits and surpluses in balance of trade in some years, the endeavour will be to balance it out over a period.

The primary object of the policies is not only to regulate the exports and imports, but to spur economic growth.

It is customary to announce the Export/Import Policy of the Government in the Budget Session of the Parliament and publish the same as public notices in the Gazette of India Extraordinary. The Export/Import Policy is issued in two instalments. The Handbook of Export/Import Procedures is published as a supplement to the Import/Export Policy of the Government and contains all the relevant procedures. Recently, these have been published simultaneously.

These publications are available for sale with the Controller of Publications, Delhi, and other authorized dealers in government publications.

There have been tremendous changes in the Export/Import Policy from 1991 onwards which can be termed as a landmark year in Indian Economy, with a devaluation of the currency, the Trade Policy reforms and other far reaching reforms in policies, all announced in July 1991. Over and above this, the government also announced a new Industrial Policy which changed the very concept of regulated industrial licensing, foreign investment and collaboration with foreign industries.

All these had a tremendous impact on the economy and finally in 1992 government introduced a New Export/Import Policy for the country for five years from 1992 to 1997.Of course every year in March/April government announces various changes and new features even though the broad canvas of a 5 year policy is kept active. At present, the export/ import policy currently pursued is the 2004-09 policy adumbrated when a new govt came into being in 2004.

Accordingly in the year 2008, the current annual supplement to the Foreign trade policy of 2004-09 was announced by the government in April 2008.

An effort is made in this chapter to give a summary of important aspects of this policy. But it should be borne in mind that any exporter who wants to utilize the provisions of this policy should check with the office of the Director-General of Foreign Trade pertaining to his location, and confirm his course of action since numerous changes by way of notices are periodically issued by the ministry on the Export/Import Policy.

## HIGHLIGHTS OF THE EXPORT-IMPORT POLICY (2004 to 2009) - (amended as of 11-4-2008)

The Central Government has notified the Export and Import Policy for the period 2004-2009. This is being done under The Foreign Trade (Development and Regulation) Act, 1992. Every year in April, the amendments and changes made in the Policy are consolidated together with the new changes proposed by the Government and the same is published. Some of the important and salient features of the Policy as on 11-4-2008 are summed up below.

## 1. Objectives:

The principal objectives of the Policy for 2004-09 were:

*(i)* To facilitate sustained growth in exports to attain a share of at least 1% of global merchandise trade.

*(ii)* To stimulate sustained economic growth by providing access to essential raw materials, intermediates, components, consumables and capital goods required for augmenting production and providing services.

*(iii)* To enhance the technological strength and efficiency of Indian agriculture, industry and services, thereby improving their competitive strength while generating new employment opportunities, and to encourage the attainment of internationally accepted standards of quality.

*(iv)* To provide consumers with good quality goods and services at internationally competitive prices while at the same time creating a level playing field for the domestic producers.

The objectives will be met through the coordinated efforts of the State Governments and all the departments of the Government of India in general and the Ministry of Commerce and Industry and the Directorate General of Foreign Trade and its network of Regional offices in particular, with a shared vision and commitment and in the best spirit of facilitation, in the interest of promotion of trade in goods and services.

## Some of the innovative steps in the new policy are:

(1) To promote modernization of our manufacturing and service exports, the import duty under the EPCG scheme is being reduced from 5% to 3%.

(2) Refund of tax on a large number of services relating to exports has already been announced by the Government. A few remaining issues regarding refund of service tax on exports would also be resolved soon.

(3) Income tax benefit to 100% EOUs available under Section 10B of Income Tax Act is being extended for one more year, beyond 2009.

(4) Sports goods and toys are mainly produced by our unorganized labour intensive sector. To promote export of these items and also to compensate disadvantages suffered by them, an additional duty credit of 5% over and above the credit under Focus Product Scheme is being provided.

(5) Our export of fresh fruits and vegetables and floriculture suffers from high incidence of freight cost. To neutralize this disadvantage, an additional credit of 2.5% over and above the credit available under VKGUY is proposed.

(6) Interest relief already granted for sectors affected adversely by the appreciation of the rupee is being extended for one more year.

(7) The DEPB scheme is being continued till May 2009.

## (1) Annual Supplement to Foreign Trade Policy 2004-09

**(a) Duty Entitlement Passbook Scheme (DEPB)**

To impart continuity and stability to our foreign trade regime, DEPB scheme is being extended till May 2009.

**(b) Refund of Service Tax**

The Government has already announced refund of service tax on almost all the services, which are directly relatable to export production and supply.

Some services related to export, which do not attract service tax have also been clarified through a Circular. A few remaining issues regarding refund of service tax will also be resolved shortly.

**(c) Income Tax on EOUs**

Income tax benefit to 100% EOUs under Section 10B of I.T. Act., being extended by Govt. for one more year, beyond 31.3.2009.

**(d) Sectoral Initiatives**

*(i)* IT hardware sector as Special focus initiative – Specific items to be included for benefits under High Tech Product Scheme. There will also be earmarked funds for this sector under the MDA and MAI Schemes.

*(ii)* Setting up a new Export Promotion Council for Telecom Sector to provide institutional support to exports from telecom sector.

*(iii)* Export of Toys and Sports Goods will be given an additional duty credit scrip @ 5% (in addition to the existing benefits under Focus Product scheme). Separate funds for market promotion activities will also be given for promoting these exports under ongoing MDA Scheme and MAI Scheme.

*(iv)* Additional duty credit scrip of 2.5% over and above the normal benefit available under VKGUY, for export of certain flowers, vegetables and fruits.

## (e) Relief to Sectors affected by Rupee Appreciation

*(i)* Interest subvention provided last year to sectors affected by rupee appreciation and to SMEs, has been extended by one more year.

*(ii)* Reduced average export obligation under EPCG, for sectors, which have witnessed decline in exports in the previous year.

## (f) Promotion of High Value Added Manufactured Products

An enhanced duty credit scrip of 2.5% (instead of the normal 1.25% under FPS) would be allowed for export of High Value Added Manufactured Products. The list of products will be notified separately.

## (g) Export Promotion Capital Goods Scheme (EPCG)

*(i)* The customs duty payable under EPCG Scheme has been reduced from 5% to 3%.

*(ii)* To improve export competitiveness of Indian exports, all exports made towards fulfillment of export obligation under EPCG scheme will not be eligible for incentives/rewards under promotional schemes.

*(iii)* Average export obligation under EPCG for Premier Trading Houses shall, as an option, be calculated, based on the average of last 5 year's export, instead of the present 3 years.

## (h) Focus Market & Product Schemes

*(i)* Coverage of FMS has been increased and additional 10 countries have been included. These are Mongolia, Bosnia-Herzegovina, Albania, Macedonia, Croatia, Honduras, Djibouti, Sudan, Ghana and Colombia.

*(ii)* FMS/FPS would also be calibrated, so that products of general high export intensity, presently not covered under FPS, but

which have low penetration in countries, not covered under FMS, would be considered for export incentives as a focus product for that particular country.

## (i) Substantive Measures Taken to Facilitate Exports

*(i)* To ensure that terminal excise duty and CST refund is made to the exporters in time, it has been decided that interest @ 6% per annum shall be paid to the exporter, in case refund is not made within one month of the due date. This interest on delayed refund will be paid on all such claims that have become due on or after 1.4.2007.

*(ii)* The facility of export on consignment basis has been extended to the export of coloured gem stones.

*(iii)* In case of textile and granite sector EOUs, payment of only excise duty on DTA sale, in case the use of duty paid imported inputs is upto 3% of the FOB value of exports.

*(iv)* Any waste or scrap or remnant generated during manufacturing or processing activities of an SEZ Unit/Developer/Co-developer to be disposed in DTA freely, subject to payment of applicable Customs Duty.

*(v)* Withdrawal of the requirement of submission of non-availment of MODVAT certificate in case of quantity based advance licence issued prior to 1.4.2002. This step is likely to lead to closure of approximately 7000 old advance licences.

*(vi)* Surat Hira Bourse recognized as port of export for jewellery, in addition, to the existing facility for export of diamonds from the Bourse.

*(vii)* A few additional ports have been included under Export Promotion Schemes. This will help in reducing costs and adhering to delivery schedules. Some more ports are also under consideration.

## (j) Measures to reduce transaction cost to exporters

*(i)* Advance Authorisation Scheme and EPCG Scheme will be EDI enabled through the electronic message exchange with effect from 1.7.2008. This will do away with the present requirement of physical verification and registration at Customs end.

*(ii)* W.e.f. 01.01.2009, all existing EDI ports will be treated as a single port and there will be no requirement of TRA under Advance Authoriztion Scheme.

*(iii)* Payment of duty under EPCG scheme through debit of duty credit scrips under the promotional schemes or DEPB w.e.f. 1.1.2009.

*(iv)* Application fee for duty credit scrips and for EPCG Authoriztions reduced from Rupees 5 per thousand to Rupees 2 per thousand. The application fee for Importer-Exporter Code number has been reduced from Rupees 1000 to Rupees 250.

*(v)* Reduction of fee in case of supplementary claims from 10% to 2%.

## (k) Procedural simplification

*(i)* EOUs shall be allowed to pay excise duty on monthly basis, instead of the present system of paying duty on consignment basis, subject to conditions/documentation to be notified by Dept. of Revenue.

*(ii)* Prorata enhancement/reduction in CIF value or duty saved amount beyond 10% has been allowed under EPCG scheme, by Regional Authorities under DGFT.

*(iii)* In respect of duty free import of R&D equipment, units not registered with Central Excise will be allowed to give installation certificate issued by an independent Chartered Engineer in place of excise authorities.

*(iv)* Certificate of Registration as Exporter of Spices (CRES) issued by Spices Board shall be treated as Registration-Cum-Membership Certificate (RCMC) for all purposes under this Policy.

*(v)* Central Excise to issue installation certificate under EPCG Scheme within 30 days of intimation by the exporter.

*(vi)* To facilitate faster clearance of deemed export benefits, Central Excise to endorse supply invoice within 21 days of supply.

*(vii)* Split-up facility under DFIA Scheme introduced.

*(viii)* Export of sawn timber processed from imported logs made easier from select Customs ports.

*(ix)* The limit of duty free import of samples has been increased from Rs.75,000 to Rs.1,00,000.

*(x)* The time period for re-import of branded jewellery remaining unsold, has been extended from 180 days to 365 days.

*(xi)* Value of jewellery parcels, through Foreign Post Office, raised from US$ 50,000 to US$ 75,000.

## (2) Promotional Measures

## Assistance to States for Infrastructure Development of Exports (ASIDE)

Scheme for Assistance to States for Infrastructure Development of Exports (ASIDE) is formulated to encourage State Governments to participate in promoting exports, and is administered by Department of Commerce (DoC).

Objectives of ASIDE include:

(1) Developing infrastructure such as roads connecting production centers with ports,

(2) Setting up Inland Container Deposits (ICD) and Container Freight Stations (CFS),

(3) Creation of new State level export promotion industrial parks/zones,

(4) Augmenting common facilities in existing zones,

(5) Equity participation in infrastructure projects,

(6) Development of minor ports and jetties,

(7) Assistance in setting up of common effluent treatment facilities,

(8) Stabilizing power supply, and

(9) Any other activity as may be notifies by DoC.

Details of ASIDE are available at http://commerce.nic.in

## MARKET ACCESS INITIATIVE (MAI)

MAI Scheme is intended to provide financial assistance for medium term export promotion efforts with sharp focus on a country/product, and is administered by DoC.

Financial assistance is available for Export Promotion Councils (EPCs), Industry and Trade Associations (ITAs), Agencies of State Governments, Indian commercial Missions (ICMs) abroad and other eligible entities as may be notified.

A whole range of activities can be funded under MAI scheme. These include, amongst others,

(1) Market studies,

(2) Setting up of showroom/warehouse,

(3) Sales promotion campaigns,

(4) International departmental stores,

(5) Publicity campaigns,

(6) Participation in international trade fairs,

(7) Brand promotion,

(8) Registration charges for pharmaceuticals, and term export promotion efforts with sharp focus on a country/product,

(9) Testing charges for engineering products.

Each of these export promotion activities can receive financial assistance from Government ranging from 25% to 100% of total cost depending upon activity and implementing agency.

Full text of guidelines is available at http://commerce.nic.in

## MARKETING DEVELOPMENT ASSISTANCE (MDA)

MDA Scheme is intended to provide financial assistance for a range of export promotion activities implemented by EPCs, ITAs on a regular basis every year. The scheme is administered by DoC. Assistance includes, amongst others, participation in

(1) Trade Fairs and Buyer Seller meets abroad or in India, and

(2) Export promotion seminars.

Financial assistance with travel grant is available to exporters traveling to Latin America, Africa, CIS region, ASEAN countries, Australia and New Zealand. In other areas, financial assistance without travel grant is available.

MDA assistance is available for exporters with annual export turnover upto Rs.15 crores. Full text of guidelines is available at http://commerce.nic.in

## MEETING LEGAL EXPENSES FOR TRADE RELATED MATTERS

DOC would provide financial assistance to deserving exporters on recommendation of EPCs for meeting cost of legal expenses for trade related matters.

## TOWNS OF EXPORT EXCELLENCE (TEE)

A number of towns have emerged as dynamic industrial clusters contributing handsomely to India's exports. It is necessary to grant recognition to these industrial clusters with a view to maximizing their potential and enabling them to move higher in the value chain and tap new markets.

Selected towns producing goods of Rs.1000 crore or more will be notified as TEE based on potential for growth in exports. However for TEE in Handloom, Handicraft, Agriculture and Fisheries sector, threshold limit would be Rs.250 crores.

Recognized associations of units will be able to access funds under MAI scheme for creating focused technological services. Common service providers in these areas shall be entitled for EPCG scheme. Further such areas will receive priority for assistance under ASIDE scheme.

Notifies TEE are listed in Appendix 7 of HBP v1.

## BRAND PROMOTION AND QUALITY

Central Government aims to encourage manufactures and exporters to attain internationally accepted standards of quality for their products. Central Government will extend support and assistance to Trade and Industry to launch a nationwide programme on quality awareness and to promote total quality management.

## TEST HOUSES

Central Government will assist in modernization and upgradation of test houses and laboratories to bring them at par with international standards.

## QUALITY COMPLAINTS / DISPUTES

Regional Sub-Committee on Quality Complaints (RSCQC) set up at Regional Offices of this Directorate shall investigate quality complaints received from foreign buyers. Guidelines for settlement of quality complaints, in particular, and such other complaints, in general, are given in Appendix-16 of HBP v1.

## TRADE DISPUTES AFFECTING TRADE RELATIONS

If it comes to DGFT notice or he has reason to believe that export or import has been made in a manner that

(1) is gravely prejudicial to trade relations of India with any other country; and/or

(2) is gravely prejudicial to interest of other persons engaged in exports or imports; and/or

(3) has brought disrepute to the country;

DGFT may take action against such exporter or importer in accordance with FT (D&R) Act, Rules and Orders made there under and FTP.

## EXPORT AND TRADING HOUSES

Merchant as well as Manufacturer Exporters, Service Providers, Export Oriented Units (EOUs) and Units located in Special Economic Zones (SEZs), Agri Export Zones (AEZs), Electronic Hardeare Technology Parks (EHTPs), Software Technology Parks (STPs) and Bio-Technology Parks (BTPs) shall be eligible for Status.

## STATUS CATEGORY

Applicant shall be categorized depending on his total FOB (FOR – for deemed exports) export performance during current plus previous three years (taken together) upon exceeding limit given below. For Export House (EH) Status, export performance is necessary in at least two out of four years (i.e., current plus previous three years).

| Status Category | Export Performance FOB/FOR Value (Rupees in Crores) |
|---|---|
| Export House (EH) | 20 |
| Star Export House (SHE) | 100 |
| Trading House (TH) | 500 |
| Star Trading House (STH) | 2500 |
| Premier Trading House(PTH) | 10000 |

**Note:**

1. Exporters in Small Scale Industry (SSI)/Tiny Sector/Cottage Sector, Units registered with KVICs/KVIBs, Units located in North Eastern States, Sikkim and Jammu and Kashmir, Units exporting handloom/ handicrafts/hand knotted or silk carpets, exporters exporting to countries in Latin America/CIS/Sub-Saharan Africa as listed in Appendix-9, Units having ISO 9000 (series)/ISO 14000 (series)/WHOGMP/HACCP/SEI CMM level-II and above status granted by agencies listed in Appendix x-6 or HBP v1, exports of services and exports of agro products shall be entitled for double weightage on exports made for grant of status. Double Weightage shall be admissible to Merchant as well as Manufacturer Exporters. However, a shipment can get double weightage only once in any one of above categories.

2. (a) Transfer of export performance from one to another is not permitted. Therefore, disclaimer system shall not be allowed for counting of export turnover.

(b) Exports made on re-export basis shall not be counted for recognition.

(c) Exports made by subsidiary of a limited company shall be counted towards export performance of limited company for recognition, only if limited company has a majority share holding in subsidiary company.

Status Holder shall be eligible for following facilities:

1. Authorization and Customs clearances for both imports and exports on self-declaration basis;
2. Fixation of Input-Output norms on priority within 60 days;
3. Exemption from compulsory negotiation of documents through banks. Remittance/Receipts, however, would be received through banking channels;

4. 100% retention of foreign exchange in EEFC account;
5. Enhancement in normal repatriation period from 180 days to 360 days;
6. Exemption from furnishing of Bank Guarantee in Schemes under FTP; and
7. SEHs and above shall be permitted to establish Export Warehouses, as per DoR guidelines.
8. For status holders, a decision on conferring of ACP Status shall be communicated by Customs within 30 days from receipt of application with Customs.
9. As an option, for Premier Trading House (PTH), the average level of exports under EPCG Scheme shall be the arithmetic mean of export performance in last 5 years, instead of 3 years.

## SERVICES EXPORTS

Services include all 161 tradable services covered under General Agreement on Trade in Services (GATS) where payment for such services is received in free foreign exchange. A list of services is given in Appendix-10 of HBP v1.

## REGISTRATION CUM MEMBERSHIP CERTIFICATE (RCMC) FOR SERVICE PROVIDERS

Software exporters shall register themselves with Electronics and Software EPC. Exporters of 14 specific services listed in Sl.No. 34 of Appendix-2 of HBP v1 are required to register themselves with Services EPC. Other service exporters shall register themselves with Federation of Indian Exporters Organization (FIEO).

## COMMON FACILITY CENTRES

Government shall promote establishment of Common Facility Centres for use by home-based service providers, particularly in areas like Engineering and Architectural design, Multi-media operations, Software developers etc., in State and District-level towns, to draw in a vast multitude of home-based professionals into services export arena.

## SERVED FROM INDIA SCHEME (SFIS)

### Objective

Objective is to accelerate growth in export of services so as to create a powerful and unique 'Served From India' brand, instantly recognized and respected world over.

### Eligibility

All Service Providers, of services listed in Appendix-10 of HBP v1, who have a total free foreign exchange earning of at lease Rs.10 lakhs in preceding financial year shall qualify for Duty Credit scrip. For Individual Service Providers, minimum would be Rs.5 lakhs.

### Entitlement

All Service Providers (except Hotels, Restaurants and other Service Providers in Tourism Sector) shall be entitled Duty Credit scrip equivalent to 10% of free foreign exchange earned during preceding financial year.

However services and service providers as listed in Paragraph 3.18.1 of HBP v1 shall not be entitled.

### Remittances

Free foreign exchange earned through International Credit Cards and other instruments as permitted by RBI for rendering of service shall also be taken into account for computation of Duty Credit scrip.

### Hotels, Restaurants & Other Service Providers in Tourism Sector

Hotels of one-star and above (including managed hotels) and heritage hotels approved by Department of Tourism (DOT) and other Service providers in tourism sector registered with DOT as well as Clubs having residential facility of minimum 30 rooms shall be entitled to duty credit scrip equivalent to 5% of free foreign exchange earned during preceding financial year.

Stand-alone restaurants will be entitles to duty credit scrip equivalent to 10% of free foreign exchange earned during preceding financial year.

### Imports Allowed

Duty Credit scrip may be used for import of any capital goods including spares, office equipment and professional equipment, office furniture and consumables; that are otherwise freely importable under ITC (HS). Imports shall relate to any service sector business of applicant.

Utilization of Duty Credit scrip earned shall not be permitted for payment of duty in case of import of vehicles, even if such vehicles are freely importable under ITC (HS).

In case of hotels; clubs having residential facility of minimum 30 rooms; golf resorts and stand-alone restaurants having catering facilities, Duty Credit scrip may also be used for import of consumables including food items and alcoholic beverages.

### Non Transferability

Entitlement/goods (imported/procures) shall be non transferable (except within group company and managed hotels) and be subject to Actual User condition.

### Procurement from Domestic Sources

Utilization of Duty Credit Scrip shall be permitted for payment of excise duty in terms of DoR notification issued in this behalf, for procurement from domestic sources of items permitted.

## VISHESH KRISHI AND GRAM UDYOG YOJANA (VKGUY)

## (Special Agriculture and Village Industry Scheme)

### Objective

Objective of VKGUY is to promote exports of

1. Agricultural Produce and their value added products;
2. Minor Forest Produce and their value added variants; for exports w.e.f. 1.4.2004;
3. Gram Udyog Products, for exports w.e.f 01.04.2006;
4. Forest Based Products, for exports w.e.f 01.04.2007; and
5. Other products, as notified from time to time.

Such products shall be listed in Appendix 37A of HBP v1.

### Entitlement

Duty Credit scrip benefits are granted with an aim to compensate high transport costs. Exporters, of products notified in Appendix 37A of HBP v1, shall be entitled for Duty Credit scrip equivalent to 5% of FOB value of exports (realized in free foreign exchange).

However, Duty Credit scrip benefits shall be granted only at a reduced rate of 3.5% of FOB value of exports (realized in free foreign exchange) in such cases where exporter has availed benefits under Chapter 4 of FTP for import of Agriculture Inputs (other than catalysts, consumable and packing materials) relating to export item under this scheme.

However, for exports made w.e.f 1.4.2008, Flowers, Fruits and Vegetable, as listed in Table 13 of Appendix 37A, shall be entitled to an additional duty credit scrip equivalent to 2.5% of FOB value of exports: over and above the 5% / 3.5% VKGUY entitlement.

Period of exports for which entitlement is granted is given in Appendix 37A of HBP v1. However, new additional products notified/clarified in Appendix 37A of HBP v1 shall be entitled for Duty Credit Scrip on exports, w.e.f 1.4.2008, unless otherwise specified

Exports made by EOUs/BTPs who do not avail direct tax benefits/ exemption shall be eligible, provided the same is not covered.

Following exports shall not be taken into account for Duty Credit scrip entitlement.

1. Export of imported goods covered under Para 2.35 of FTP;
2. Exports through transshipment, meaning thereby that exports originating in third country but transshipped through India;
3. Deemed Exports;
4. Exports made by SEZ units; and
5. Items, which are restricted or prohibited for export under schedule-2 of Export Policy in ITC (HS).

For exports during 2008-09, all Status Holders (having status recognition w.e.f 1.4.2008) exporting products covered under ITC HS Chapter 1 to 24, shall be incentivized with duty credit scrip equal to 10% of FOB value of agricultural exports (including benefits entitled under paragraph 3.8.2) provided that the total benefits for all status holders put together does not exceed Rs.100 Crores (i.e. Rs.50 Crores for each half year) and the conditions specified in Para 3.19.10 of HBP v1 (RE2008) are satisfied. Zonal Office CLA, New Delhi shall be licensing office for grant of the benefit to all status holders.

The following capital goods/equipments shall be permitted for import:-

1. Cold storage units including Controlled Atmosphere (CA) and Modified Atmosphere(MA) Stores, Pre-cooling Units and mother storage for onions etc.;

2. Pack Houses (including facilities for handling, grading, sorting and packaging etc.);
3. Reefer Van/Containers; and
4. Other Capital Goods/Equipments as may be notified in Appendix 37F

Imported capital goods/equipment shall be utilized for storage, packing etc. (as in (2) above) and transportation of agricultural products (including agro-processed perishable products).

This additional benefit shall be subject to actual user condition and hence non-transferable.

## FOCUS MARKET SCHEME (FMS)

### Objective

Objective is to offset high freight cost and other externalities to select international markets with a view to enhance our export competitiveness in these countries.

Exporters of all products to notified countries (as in Appendix 37C of HBP v1) shall be entitled for Duty Credit scrip equivalent to 2.5% of FOB value of exports for each licensing year commencing from 1st April, 2006.

However New additional Markets notified in Appendix 37C of HBP v1 shall be entitled for Duty Credit scrip on exports w.e.f. 1.4.2008.

Exports made by EOUs/EHTPs/BTPs who do not avail direct tax benefits/exemption shall be eligible, provided the same is not covered under Paragraph 3.9.2.2.

Following exports shall not be taken into account for computation of entitlement:

(a) *(i)* Export of imported goods covered under Para 2.35 of FTP; *(ii)* Exports through transshipment, meaning thereby that exports originating in third country but transshipped through India;

(b) Export turnover of SEZ units or supplies made to such units or SEZ products exported through DTA units;

(c) Deemed Exports;

(d) Service Exports;

(e) Diamonds and other precious, semi precious stones;

(f) Gold, silver, platinum and other precious metals in any form, including plain and studded Jeweller;

(g) Ores and Concentrates, of all types and in all forms;

(h) ugar, of all types and in all forms;

(j) Crude/Petroleum Oil and Crude/Petroleum based Products covered under ITC HS codes 2709 to 2715, all types and in all forms;

(k) Items, which are restricted or prohibited for export under Scheduel-2 of Export Policy in ITC(HS);

(l) Cement, all types and in all forms; and

(m) Primary Steel Products as listed Public Notice No.130 (RE2007)/2004-09 dated 27.03.2008, as amended from time to time.

## FOCUS PRODUCT SCHEME (FPS)

### Objective

Objective is to incentivise export of such products, which have high employment intensity in rural and semi urban areas, so as to offset infrastructure inefficiencies and other associated costs involved in marketing of these products.

### Entitlement

Exports of notified products (as in Appendix 37D of HBP v1) to all countries (including SEZ units) shall be entitled for Duty Credit scrip equivalent to 1.25% of FOB value of exports for each licensing year commencing from 1st April, 2006.

However, for exports made w.e.f. 1.4.2008, Toys and Sports Goods as detailed in Table 2 of Appendix 37D shall be entitled to duty credit scrip equivalent to 6.35% of FOB value of exports, Further, for exports made w.e.f. 1.4.2008, High Value Added Manufactured goods, as notified in Table 9 Appendix 37D, shall be entitled to duty credit scrip equivalent to 2.5% of FOB value of exports.

However, New additional products notified/clarified in Appendix 37D of HBP v1 shall be entitled for Duty Credit scrip on exports w.e.f. 1.4.2008.

Exports made by EOUs/EHTPs/BTPs who do not avail direct tax benefits/exemption shall be eligible, provided the same is not covered under Paragraph 3.10.2.2.

Following exports shall not be taken into account for computation of entitlement.

(a) *(i)* Export of imported goods covered under Para 2.35 of FTP; *(ii)* Exports through transshipment, meaning thereby that exports originating in third country but transshipped through India;

(b) Export turnover of SEZ units or SEZ products exported through DTA units; and

(c) Deemed Exports.

## MARKET LINKED FOCUS PRODUCT

For exports w.e.f. 1.4.2008, Products of high export intensity (which are not covered under present FPS List) but which have a low penetration in countries (which are also not covered under present FMS list) would be incentivised and entitled to a duty credit scrip equivalent to 1.25% of FOB value of exports, provided that the product/sector are destined to specified linked markets for that particular product/sector. Such products/sectors, along with their linked markets, shall be notified in Table 10 of Appendix 37D of HBP v1.

## HIGH-TECH PRODUCTS EXPORT PROMOTION SCHEME (HTPEPS)

### Objective

Objective is to incentivise export of High Technology products.

### Entitlement

Exports of High Technology products (as notified in Appendix 37E of HBP v1) in free foreign exchange to all countries, shall be entitled for Duty Credit Scrip equivalent to:

(a) 1.25% of FOB value of exports; or

(b) 5% of incremental growth in FOB value (realized as per BRC/FIRC) of exports of notified products for current year (i.e. 2008-09) over previous year (i.e.2007-08) (all taken together) and similarly for each subsequent licensing year.

Exporter may opt for either (a) or (b) above. However, applicants with 'nil' exports in base year shall not be eligible.

Exports made by EOUs/EHTPs/BTPs who do not avail direct tax benefits/exemption shall be eligible, provided the same is not covered under paragraph 3.11.4.

## CEILING

Duty Credit Scrip shall not exceed Rs.15 Crores for an exporter for all shipments done in a licensing year put together, for which benefit is being claimed under this scheme.

### Ineligible Exports/Categories

Following shall not be counted for entitlement

(1) Export of imported goods covered under Para 2.35 of FTP;

(2) Exports originating in third country but transshipped through India;

(3) Exports of SEZ units or SEZ products exported through DTA units: and

(4) Deemed Exports.

## ADVANCE AUTHORISATION SCHEME

An Advance Authorisation is issued to allow duty free import of inputs, which are physically incorporated in export product (making normal allowance for wastage). In addition, fuel, oil, energy, catalysts which are consumed/utilized to obtain export product, may also be allowed. DGFt, by means of Public Notice, may exclude any product(s) from purview of Advance Authorisation.

Duty free import of mandatory spares upto 10% of CIF value of Authorisation which are required to be exported/supplied with resultant product are allowed under Advance Authorisation. Advance Authorisations are issued for inputs and export items given under SION. These can also be issued on the basis of Adhoc norms or self declared norms as per para 4.7 of HBP v1.

Advance Authorisation can be issued either to a manufacturer exporter or merchant exporter tied to supporting manufacturer(s) for;

(1) Physical exports (including exports to SEZ); and/or

(2) Intermediate supplies; and/or

(3) Supply of goods to the categories mentioned in pararagraph 8.2 (b), (c), (d), (e), (f), (g), (i), and (j) of FTP;

(4) Supply of 'stores' on board of foreign going vessel/aircraft subject to condition that there is specific SION in respect of item (s) supplied.

In addition, in respect of supply of goods to specified projects mentioned in paragraph 8.2 (d), (e), (f), (g) and (j) of FTP, an Advance Authorisation can also be availed by sub-contractor to such project provided name of sub contractor(s) appears in main contract.

Such Authorisation can also be issued for supplies made to United Nations Organisations or under Aid Programme of the United Nations or other multilateral agencies and which are paid for in free foreign exchange.

Advance Authorisation are exempted from payment of basic customs duty, additional customs duty, education cess, anti dumping duty and safeguard duty, if any. However, imports for supplied covered under paragraph 8.2 (h) and (i) will not be exempted from payment of applicable anti-dumping and safeguard duty, if any.

Advance Authorisation and/or materials imported there under will be with actual user condition. It will not be transferable even after completion of export obligation. However, Authorisation holder will have option to dispose off products manufactured out of duty free inputs once export obligation is completed.

Advance Authorisations necessitate exports with a positive value addition. Exports to SEZ units/supplies to Developers/Co-developers, irrespective of the currency of realization, would also be covered.

For physical exports for which payments are not received in freely convertible currency, same shall be subject to value addition as specified in Appendix – 11 of HBP v1.

Similarly, in case of spices (covered by Chapter 9 of ITC (HS), duty free import of spices shall be permitted only for value addition purposes, like crushing/grinding/sterilization, or for manufacture of oils and oleoresins, and not for simple cleaning, grading, repacking etc. and minimum value addition shall be 15%.

Advance Authorisation shall be issued in accordance with Policy and procedure in force on Authorisation issue date.

Validity period of Advance Autorisation for import shall be as prescribed in HBP v1.

## Free of Cost Supply by Foreign Buyer

Facility of Advance Authorisation shall also be available where some or all inputs are supplied free of cost to exporter by foreign buyer.

In such cases, for calculation of value addition, notional value of free of cost inputs along with value of other duty-free inputs shall be taken into consideration. However, if all inputs are supplied free of cost, exporter shall also have option to follow provision prescribed by DoR.

## Export Obligation

Period for fulfillment of export obligation under Advance Authorisation shall be as prescribed in HBP v1.

## Provision for BIFR units

Any firm/company registered with B1FR or any firm/company acquiring a unit, which is under B1FR shall be allowed Export Obligation Period (EOP) extension as per rehabilitation package prepared, subject to approval of B1FR, or 5 years if not specified, without payment of composition fee.

Above provisions apply also to SSI units as per rchabilitation scheme of concerned State government.

## Advance Authorisation for Annual Requirement

Advance Authorization can also be issued for annual requirement. Status Certificate holder and all other categories of exporters having past export performance (in preceding two years) shall be entitled for Advance Authorization for annual requirement.

Entitlement in terms of CIF value of imports shall be up to 300% of the FOB value of physical export and/or FOR value of deemed export in preceding licensing year or Rs. 1 crore, whichever is higher.

## Advance Release Orders (ARO) and Invalidation Letter

Holder of Advance Authorisation, Advance Authorisation for annual requirement, Diamond Imprest Authorisation and Duty Free Import Authorisation intending to source inputs from indigenous sources/State Trading Enterprises in lieu of direct import, has option to source them either against Advance Release Order (ARO) or Invalidation letter denominated in free foreign exchange/Indian rupees. However, supplies may be obtained against Authorisation from EOU/EHTP/BTP/STP/SEZ units, without conversion into ARO or Invalidation letter.

Transferee of DFIA shall also be eligible for ARO/Invalidation letter facility.

Validity period of ARO shall be as prescribed in HBP v1.

## Back-to-Back Inland Letter of Credit

Holder of Advance Authorisation, Advance Authorisation for annual requirement, EFIA and Diamond Imprest Authorisation may, instead of applying for an ARO or Invalidation letter, avail of the facility of Back-to-Back Inland Letter of Credit in accordance with procedure specified in HBP v1.

## Prohibited Items

Prohibited items of imports mentioned in ITC(HS) shall not be imported under Advance Authorisation/EFIA. Further items reserved for imports by STEs cannot be imported against Advance Authorisation/DFIA. However, those items can be procured from STEs against ARO or Invalidation letter.

STEs are also allowed to sell goods on High Sea Sale basis to holder of Advance Authorisation/DFIA holder

In addition, STEs are permitted to issue "No Objection Certificate (NOC)" for import by Advance Authorisation/DFIA holder. Authorisation Holder would be required to file Quarterly Returns of imports effected against such NOC to concerned STE and STE would submit half-yearly import figures of such imports to concerned administrative Department for monitoring with a copy endorsed to DGFT.

Similarly prohibited items of exports mentioned in ITC(HS) shall not be exported under Advance Authorisation/DFIA scheme. Export of restricted items shall be subject to all conditionalities or requirements of export Authorisation or permission, as may be required, under Schedule II of ITC (HS).

## Admissibility of Drawback

In case of an Advance Authorisation, drawback shall be available for any duty paid material, whether imported or indigenous, used in goods exported, as per drawback rate fixed by DoR, Ministry of Finance

(Directorate of Drawback). Drawback allowed shall be mentioned in Authorisation.

## DUTY ENTITLEMENT PASSBOOK (DEPB) SHCEME

Objective of DEPB is to neutralize incidence of customs duty on import content of export product. Component of Special Additional Duty and customs duty on fuel shall also be allowed under DEPB (as brand rate) factored in DEPB rate in case of non-availment of CENVAT credit. Neutralisation shall be provided by way of grant of duty credit against export product.

An exporter may apply for credit, at specified percentage of FOB value of exports, made in freely convertible currency or payment made from foreign currency account of SEZ unit/SEZ Developer in case of supply by DTA.

Credit shall be available against such export products and at such rates as may be specified by DGFT by way of public notice. Credit may be utilized for payment of customs duty on freely importable items. DEPB scrips can also be utilized for payment of duty against imports under EPCG Scheme w.e.f. 1.1.2009.

DEPB holder shall have option to pay additional customs duty in cash as well.

### Validity

Validity period of DEPB for import shall be as prescribed in HBP v1.

### Transferability

DEPB and/or items imported against it are freely transferable. Transfer of DEPB shall however be for import at specified port, which shall be the port from where exports have been made.

Imports from a port other than the port of export shall be allowed under TRA facility as per terms and conditions of DOR notification.

### Applicability of Drawback

Additional customs duty/Excise Duty and Special Additional Duty paid in cash or through debit under DEPB may also be adjusted as CENVAT Credit or Duty Drawback as per DoR rules.

## DUTY FREE IMPORT AUTHORISATION (DFIA) SCHEME

### Scheme

DFIA is issued to allow duty free import of inputs, fuel, oil, energy sources, catalyst which are required for production of export product. DGFT, by means of Public Notice, may exclude any product(s) from purview of DFIA. This scheme is in force from 1st May, 2006.

### Entitlement

Provisions of paragraph 4.1.3 shall be applicable in case of DFIA. However, these Authorisations shall be issued only for products for which standard input and output norms (SION) have been notified.

In case of post export DFIA, a merchant exporter shall be required to mention only name(s) and address(s) of manufacturer(s) of the export product(s). Applicant is required to file application to concerned RA before effecting exports under DFIA.

Pre-export Authorisation shall be issued with actual user condition and shall be exempted from payment of basic customs duty, additional customs duty/Excise duty, education cess, anti-dumping duty and safeguard duty, if any.

In case of actual user DFIA and where CENVAT credit facility on inputs have been availed for the exported goods, even after completion of export obligation, the goods imported against such DFIA shall be utilized in the manufacture of dutiable goods whether DFIA shall be utilized in the manufacture of dutiable goods whether within the same factory or outside (by a supporting manufacturer).

### Import Items

Provisions of paragraphs 4.1.11, 4.1.12, 4.1.13 abd 4.1.14 of FTP shall be applicable for DFIA holder.

### Value Addition

A minimum 20% value addition shall be required for issuance of such authorization except for items in gems and jewellery sector for which value addition would be as per paragraph 4A.2.1 of HBP v1. Items for which higher value addition is prescribed under Advance Authorisation Scheme, shall be applicable.

## Export Obligation

Procedure and time period related to fulfillment of Export obligation have been laid down in Chapter 4 of HBP v1.

## Transferability

Once export obligation has been fulfilled, request for transferability of Authorisation or inputs imported against it may be made before concerned RA. Once transferability is endorsed, Authorisation holder may transfer DFIA or duty free inputs, except fuel and any other item(s) notified by DGFT. However, for fuel, import entitlement may be transferred only to companies which have been granted authorization to market fuel by Ministry of Petroleum and Natural Gas.

Once transferability is endorsed, imports/domestic procurement against authorization or transfer of imported inputs/domestically procured inputs shall be subject to payment of applicable additional customs duty/ excise duty. While endorsing transferability, authorization would bear a note as to liability of such additional customs duty/excise duty. However, in case where CENVAT facility has not been availed, exemption from additional customs duty/excise duty would be available even after endorsement of transferability on DFIA.

Wherever SIONs prescribe actual user condition and in case of Acetic Anhydride, Ephedrine and Pseudo Ephedrine, DFIA shall be issued with actual user condition for these inputs and no transferability shall be allowed for these inputs even after fulfillment of export obligation.

However, for authorizations issued prior to 1.4.2007, exemption from Additional Customs Duty/Excise Duty shall continue to be available even after endorsement of transferability, as provided in FTP (RE-2006).

## CENVAT Facility

CENVAT credit facility shall be available for inputs either imported or procured indigenously.

# GEMS AND JEWELLERY

Exporters of Gems and Jewellery can import/procure duty free inputs for manufacturing.

## Replenishment 8Authorisation

Exporters may obtain Replenishment (REP) Authorisations from RA in accordance with procedure specified in HBP v1.

Replenishment authorization may also be for consumables as per paragraph 4A.28 of HBP v1.

## Schemes for Gold/Silver/Platinum Jewellery

Exporters of gold/silver/platinum jewellery and articles thereof may import their essential inputs such as gold, silver, platinum, mountings, findings, rough gems, precious and semi-precious stones, synthetic stones and unprocessed pears etc. in accordance with the procedure specified in this behalf.

## Nominated Agencies

Nominated agencies are MMTC Ltd., Handicraft and Handloom Export Corporation (HHEC), State Trading Corporation(STC), the Project and Equipment Corporation of India Ltd (PEC), Premier Trading House under Paragraph 3.5.2 of FTP and any other agency authorized by RBI. Exporters (except EOUs and units in SEZ) may obtain gold/silver/platinum from nominated agency(s).

A bank authorized by RBI is allowed export of gold scrap fro refining and import standard gold bars as per RBI guidelines.

## Items of Export

Following items, if exported, would be eligible for facilities:

1. Gold Jewellery, including partly processed jewellery and articles including medallions and coins (excluding legal tender coins), whether plain or studded, containing gold of 8 carats and above;
2. Silver Jewellery including partly processed jewellery, silverware, silver strips and articles including medallions and coins (excluding legal tender coins and any engineering goods) containing more than 50% silver by weight;
3. Platinum jewellery including partly processed jewellery and articles including medallions and coins (excluding legal tender coins and any engineering goods) containing more that 50% platinum by weight.

# VALUE ADDITION

Value Addition (VA) for gems and jewellery sector shall be as per paragraph 4A.2.1 of HBP v1. It would be calculated as under;

$$VA = \frac{A - B}{B} \times 100, \quad \text{where}$$

A = FOB value of the export realized/FOR value of supply received.

B = Value of inputs (including domestically procured) such as gold/silver/platinum content in export product plus admissible wastage along with value of other items such as gemstone etc. Wherever gold has been obtained on loan basis, value shall also include interest paid in free foreign exchange to foreign supplier.

## Wastage Norms

Wastage or manufacturing loss for gold/silver/platinum jewellery shall be admissible as per paragraph 4A.2 of HBP v1.

## Export against Supply by Foreign Buyer

Where export orders are placed on nominated agencies/status holder/exporters of three years standing having an annual average turnover of Rs. Five crores during preceding three licensing years, foreign buyer may supply in advance and free of charge, gold/silver/platinum, alloys, findings and mountings of gold/silver/platinum for manufacture and export.

Such supplies can also be in advance and may involve semi-finished jewellery including findings/mountings/components for repairs/re-make and export subject to minimum value addition of 10% However, if so imported semi finished gold/silver/platinum jewellery is exported as studded jewellery, value addition of 15% shall be achieved. In such cases of export, wastage of 2% may be permitted.

Exports may be made by nominated agencies directly or through their associates or by status holder/exporter. Import and Export of findings shall be on net to net basis.

## Export Against Supply by Nominated Agencies

Exporter may obtain gold/silver/platinum as an input for export products from nominated agencies in advance or as replenishment after exports, in accordance with specified procedure.

## Export Against Advance Authorisation

An Advance Authorisation may be granted for duty free import of:

1. Gold of fineness not less than 0.995, and mountings, sockets, frames and findings of 8 carats and above;

2. Silver of fineness not less than 0.995 and mountings, sockets, frames and findings containing more than 50% silver by weight;

3. Platinum of fineness not less than 0.900, and mountings, sockets, frames and findings containing more than 50% platinum by weight.

Such authorization shall carry an export obligation to be fulfilled as per procedure specified in paragraph 4A of HBP v1.

Advance Authorisation holder may obtain gold/silver/platinum from nominated agencies in lieu of direct import.

## GEM REPLENISHMENT AUTHORISATION

Gem Replenishment (Gem and Jewellery REP) Authorisation may be issued as given in paragraph 4A.8, 4A.9 and 4A.10 above.

In case of plain or studded gold/silver/platinum jewellery and articles, value of such Authorisations shall be determined with reference to realization in excess of prescribed minimum VA.

Such Gem REP Authorisations shall be freely transferable.

### Gem REP Rate and Item

Replenishment Rate and item of import will be as prescribed in Appendix 12B of HBP v1.

### Export Promotion Tours/Export of Branded Jewellery

Nominated agencies and their associates, with approval of Department of Commerce, and others, with approval of Gem and Jewellery EPC (GJEPC), may export gold/silver/platinum jewellery and articles thereof for exhibitions abroad.

Personal carriage of gold/silver/platinum jewellery, precious, semiprecious stones, beads and articles and export of branded jewellery is also permitted, subject to conditions as in HBP v1.

### Personal Carriage of Export/Import Parcels

Personal carriage of gems and jewellery export parcesl by foreign bound passengers and import parcesl by an Indian importer/foreign national may be permitted as in HBP v1.

## Export by Post

In case of exports through Foreign Post office (including via speed post), value of jewellery parcels shall not exceed US $ 75000 and 20 kg. by weight.

## Private/Public Bonded Warehouse

Private/Public Bonded Warehouses may be set up in SEZ/DTA for import and re-export of cut and Polished diamonds, cut and polished coloured gemstones, uncut and unset precious and semi-precious stones, subject to achievement of minimum VA of 5%.

## Diamond and Jewellery Dollar Accounts

Firms and companies dealing in purchase/sale of rough or cut and polished diamonds/precious metal jewellery plain, minakari and /or studded with/without diamond and/or other stones, with a tract record of at lease 3 years in import or export of diamonds/coloured gemstones/diamond and coloured gemstones studded jewellery/plain gold jewellery, and having an average annual turnover of Rs.5 crore or above during preceding three licensing years, may also carry out their business through designated Diamond Dollar Accounts (DDA).

Dollars in such accounts available from bank finance and/or export proceeds shall be used only for:

(1) Import/purchase of rough diamonds from overseas/local sources;

(2) Purchase of cut and polished diamonds, coloured gemstones and plain gold jewellery from local sources;

(3) Import/purchase of gold from overseas/nominated agencies and repayment of dollar loans from the bank; and

(4) Transfer to Rupee Account of exporter.

Details of this DDA Scheme are given in HBP v1.

A non DDA holder is also permitted to supply cut and polished diamonds to DDA holder, receive payment in dollars and convert same into Rupees within 7 days. Cut and polished diamonds and coloured gemstones so supplied by non-DDA holder will also be counted towards discharge of his export obligation and/or entitle him to replenishment Authorisation.

Gems and jewellery exporters shall be allowed to export cut and polished precious and semi-precious stones for the treatment and re-import as per customs rules and regulations. In case of re-export, the exporter shall be entitled for duty drawback as per rules.

### Import of precious metal scrap/used jewellery for melting and re-export of jewellery

Import of precious metal scrap/used jewellery shall be allowed for melting, refining and re-export of jewellery as per the procedure laid down in HBP v1. However, such import shall not be allowed through hand baggage.

### Re-import of rejected jewellery

Gems and Jewellery exporters shall be allowed to re-import rejected precious metal jewellery as per para 4A.32 of HBP v1.

### Export on consignment basis

Gems and Jewellery exporters shall be allowed to export diamond, gemstones and jewellery on consignment basis as per HBP v1 and Customs rules and regulations.

## EXPORT PROMOTION CAPITAL GOODS (EPCG) SCHEME

EPCG scheme allows import of capital goods for pre production, production and post production (including CKD/SKD thereof as well as computer software systems) at 3% Customs duty, subject to an export obligation equivalent to 8 times of duty saved on capital goods imported under EPCG scheme, to be fulfilled in 8 years reckoned from Authorisation issue-date.

In case of agro units, and units in cottage or tiny sector, import of capital goods at 3% Customs duty shall be allowed subject to fulfillment of export obligation equivalent to 6 times of duty saved on capital goods imported, in 12 years from Authorisation issue date.

For SSI units, import of capital goods at 3% Customs duty shall be allowed, subject to fulfillment of export obligation equivalent to 6 times of duty saved on capital goods, in 8 years from Authorisation issue – date, provided the landed cif value of such imported capital goods under the scheme does not exceed Rs.50 lakhs and total investment in plant and machinery after such imports doe not exceed SSI limit.

However, in respect of EPCG Authorisations with a duty saved amount of Rs.100 crores or more, export obligation shall be fulfilled in 12 years.

In case CVD is paid in cash on imports under EPCG, incidence of CVD would not be taken for computation of net duty saved, provided the same is not CENVATed.

Capital goods shall include spares (including refurbished/ reconditioned spares), tools, jigs, fixtures, dies and moulds.

Second hand capital goods, without any restriction on age, may also be imported under EPCG scheme.

However, import of motor cars, sports utility vehicles/all purpose vehicles shall be allowed only to hotels, travel agents, tour operators or tour transport operators and companies owning/operating golf resorts, subject to the condition that:

(a) total foreign exchange from hotel, travel and tourism and golf tourism sectors in current and preceding three licensing years is Rs.1.5 crores or more.

(b) 'duty saved' amount on all EPCG Authori-sations issued in a licensing year for import of motor cars, sports utility vehicles/ all purpose vehicles shall not exceed 50% of average foreign exchange earnings from hotel, travel and tourism and golf tourism sectors in preceding three licensing years.

(c) Vehicles imported shall be so registered that the vehicle is used for tourist purpose only. A copy of the Registration certificate should be submitted to concerned RA as a confirmation of import of vehicle. However, parts of motor cars, sports utility vehicles/all purpose vehicles such as chassis etc. cannot be imported under the EPCG scheme.

Import of Restricted items of imports mentioned under ITC(HS) shall only be allowed under EPCG scheme after approval from EFC at Headquarters.

Spares (including refurbished/reconditioned spares), tools, spare refractories and catalyst for existing plant and machinery (imported earlier, under EPCG or otherwise) shall be allowed to be imported subject to an export obligation equivalent to 8 times of duty saved to be fulfilled in 8 years reckoned from Authorization issue date.

## EPCG for Projects

An EPCG Authorization can also be issued for import of capital goods under Scheme for Project Imports notified by the Central Board of Excise and Customs under S.No.441 of Customs Exemption Notification NO.21/2002 dated 01.03.2002.

Export obligation for such EPCG Authorizations would be eight times of duty saved. Duty saved would be difference between the effective duty under aforesaid Customs Notification and concessional duty under the EPCG scheme.

## EPCG for Retail Sector

To create modern infrastructure in retail sector, concessional duty benefits under EPCG scheme shall be extended for import of capital goods required by retailers having minimum area of 1000 sq meters. Such retailer shall fulfill export obligation, i.e., 8 times of duty saved in 8 years.

## Eligibility

EPCG scheme covers manufacturer exporters with or without supporting manufacturer(s)/vendor(s), merchant exporters tied to supporting manufacturer(s) and service providers.

## Conditions for import of Capital Goods

Import of capital goods shall be subject to Actual User condition till export obligation is completed.

## Export obligation

Following conditions shall apply to the fulfillment of the export obligation:-

(1) Export Obligation shall be fulfilled by export of goods manufacture/services rendered by the applicant.

Export obligation under the scheme shall be, over and above, the average level of exports achieved by him in the preceding three licensing years for the same and similar products within the overall export obligation period including extended period, if any; except for categories mentioned in paragraph 5.7.6 of HBP v1. Such average would be the arithmetic mean of export performance in the last three years for the same and similar products. Provided that Premier Trading House (PTH) shall have option of fixing average level of exports based on arithmetic mean of export performance in the last five years instead of three years.

Upto 50% Export Obligation may also be fulfilled by exports of other good(s) manufactured or service(s) provided by the same firm/ company, or group company/managed hotel, which has the EPCG authorization. However, EPCG authorization issued prior to 1.4.2008 will be governed by earlier policy provisions.

However, in such cases, additional export obligation imposed shall be over and above average exports achieved by the unit/company/group company/managed hotel in preceding three years for both the original and the substitute product(s)/service(s), despite exemption in Para 5.7.6 of HBP v1.

(2) Shipments under Advance Authorization, DFRC, DFIA, DEPB or Drawback scheme, or incentive schemes under Chapter 3 of FTP; would also count for fulfillment of EPCG export obligation.

(3) Export obligation can also be fulfilled by the supply of ITA-1 items to DTA, provided realization is in free foreign exchange.

(4) Exports shall be physical exports. However, deemed exports as specified in paragraph 8.2(a), (b), (f), (g) and (j) of FTP shall also be counted towards fulfillment of export obligation, along with usual benefits available under paragraph 8.3 of FTP.

Royalty payments received in freely convertible currency and foreign exchange received for R & D services shall also be counted for discharge under EPCG. Payment received in rupee terms for port handling services, in terms of Chapter 9 of FTP shall also be counted for export obligation discharge.

## Provision for BIFR units

Any firm/company registered with BIFR or any firm/company acquiring a unit, which is under BIFR shall be allowed EO extension as per rehabilitation package, subject to approval of BIFR, or 12 years if not specified.

Above provisions apply also to SSI units as per rehabilitation scheme of concerned State Government.

## EPCG for Agro units

LUT/Bond or 15% BG (as applicable) may be given for EPCG Authorsation granted to units in Agri Export Zones provided EPCG Authorisation is taken for export of primary agricultural product(s) notified in Appendix 8 or their value added variants.

## Indigenous Sourcing of Capital Goods and benefits to Domestic Supplier

A person holding an EPCG Authorisation may source capital goods, from a domestic manufacturer. Such domestic manufacturer shall be eligible for deemed export benefit under paragraph 8.3 of FTP. Such domestic sourcing shall also be permitted from EOUs and these supplies shall be counted for purpose of fulfillment of positive NFE by said EOU as provided in Para 6.9 (a) of FTP.

## Fixation of Export Obligation

In case of direct imports, export obligation shall be reckoned with reference to actual duty saved amount. In case of domestic sourcing export obligation shall be reckoned with reference to notional customs duties saved-on FOR value.

## Technological Upgradation of existing EPCG machinery

EPCG Authorisation holders can opt for Technological Upgradation of existing capital good imported under EPCG Authorisation.

Conditions governing Technological Upgraqdation of existing capital goods are as under:

1. Minimum time period for applying for Technological Upgradation of existing capital goods imported under EPCG is 5 years from Authorisation issue-date.
2. Minimum exports made under old capital goods must be 40% of total export obligation imposed on first EPCG Authorisation.
3. Export obligation would be refixed such that total export obligation mandated for both capital goods would be sum total of 6 times of duty saved on both the capital goods, to be fulfilled in 8 years from new authorization issue-date.
4. Facility for technological upgradation shall be available only once and the minimum imports to be made shall be at least 10% of the existing investment in plant and machinery by applicant.
5. Capital Goods to be imported must be new and technologically superior to earlier CG.

## Incentives for Fast Track Companies

To incentivise fast tract companies with a view to accelerate exports, in cases where Authorization holder has fulfilled 75% or more of export obligation (including average level of exports) in half or less than half the original export obligation period specified, remaining export obligation shall be condoned and the Authorization redeemed by RA concerned.

However no benefits under Para 5.12 of HBP v1 shall be available in such cases.

**(i) Exports and Imports:**

Exports and imports shall be free, except in cases where they are regulated by the provisions of this Policy or any other law for the time being in force. The item-wise export and Import policy is specified in a separate book "ITC (HS) classification of Export and Import Items", published by Director General of Foreign Trade, as amended from time to time.

**(ii) Procedure:**

The Director General of Foreign Trade also publishes The Hand Book of Procedures containing relevant procedures and other details to be followed by an exporter or importer or other authorities for the purposes of implementing the provisions of the policy.

**(iii) Restricted goods:**

Any goods, the export or import of which is restricted under the policy may be exported or imported only in accordance with a licence/certificate/permission or a public notice issued in this behalf.

**(iv) State Trading:**

Any goods, the import or export of which is governed through exclusive or special privileges granted to state trading enterprise(s) may be imported or exported by the state trading enterprise(s) as specified in the policy subject to the conditions specified therein.

**(v) Importer–Exporter Code Number:**

No export or import shall be made by any person without an Importer – Exporter Code (IEC) number unless specifically exempted. An Importer-Exporter Code Number will be granted on application by the competent authority in accordance with the procedure specified in the Hank Book.

**(vi) Actual user condition:**

The goods that are importable without any restriction, may be imported by any person. However, if such imports require a licence/ certificate/permission, the actual user alone may import such goods unless the actual user condition is specifically dispensed with by the licensing authority.

**(vii) Second Hand goods:**

All second hand goods shall be restricted for imports and may be imported only in accordance with the provisions of the policy.

**(viii) Realisation of Export Proceeds:**

If an exporter fails to realize the export proceeds within the time specified by the Reserve Bank of India, he shall, without prejudice to any liability or penalty under any law for the time being in force, be liable to action in accordance with the provisions of the Foreign Trade (Development & Regulation) Act, 1992 and this policy.

**(ix) Registration–cum–membership certificate:**

Any person applying for (i) a licence/ certificate/permission to imports/ Export (ii) any other benefit or concession under the policy shall be required to furnish Registration-cum-membership certificate (RCMC) granted by the competent authority. Usually, the RCMC is granted by the concerned Export Promotion Council.

## 3. Export Oriented Units (EOU's)

## Electronics Hardware Technology parks (EHTPs)

## Software Technology Parks (STPs)

## Bio-Technology Parks (BTPS)

**(i) Eligibility and Ivnestment Criteria:**

Units undertaking to export their entire production of goods and services (except permissible sales in the Domestic Tariff Area), may be set up under the Export Oriented Unit (EOU) Scheme, Electronic Hardware Technology Park (EHTP) scheme or Software Technology Park (STP), schemes or Bio-Technology Park (BTP) Scheme, for manufacture goods, including repair, remaking, reconditioning, re-engineering and rendering of services. Trading units, however are not covered under the scheme.

Only projects having a minimum investment of Rs.1 crore in plant and machinery, shall be considered for establishment as EOUs under the scheme. This shall however not apply o existing units and units in EHTP/STP/BTP, Handicrafts/Agriculture/Floriculture/Aquaculture/Animal Husbandry/Information Technology, Services, Brass Hardware, and Hand-made Jewellery sectors. The Board of Approval (BOA) may also allow establishment of EOUs with a lower investment criteria.

**(i) Export and Import of Goods:**

(a) An EOU/EHTP/STP unit may export all goods and services except items that are prohibited in the policy.

(b) An EOU/EHTP/STP unit may import without payment of duty, all types of goods required by it for its activities for manufacture of goods, repair, remaking etc. provided they are not prohibited items of Imports as per the policy.

(c) EOU gem and Jewellery units may also source gold/silver/platinum through the nominated agencies.

**(ii) Second Hand Capital Goods:**

Second hand capital goods may also be imported duty free without any age limit.

**(iii) Net Foreign Exchange Earnings:**

EOU/EHTP/STP unit shall be a positive net foreign exchange earner. Net Foreign Exchange Earnings (NFE) shall be calculated cumulatively for a period of five years from the commencement of production. The formula for net Foreign Exchange Earning (NFE) takes note of the foreign exchange outflow and inflow as detailed in the Hand book.

**(iv) Sale in Domestic Tariff Area (DTA):**

The general rule is that the entire production of EOU/EHTP/STP units shall be exported. However, sale of finished products, rejects, waste/scrap/remounts and by-products are permitted to be sold in Domestic Tariff Area subject to a number of conditions depending upon the categories of such goods sold in DTA. Such conditions speak of the percentage of sale permitted, achievement of NFE, quantum of duty payable in each case, import policy for such goods etc. In most of the cases up to 50% of the FOB value of goods can be sold in Domestic Tariff Area. This is a great boon to many such units which gives them flexibility in fulfilling the stipulated export obligation.

**(v) Entitlement for supplies from the DTA:**

Supplies from the DTA to EOU/EHTP/STP units will be regarded as "deemed exports" and the DTA supplier shall be eligible for the relevant entitlement under the Policy. Others concessions to DTA units are:

(a) Reimbursement of Central Sales Tax.

(b) Exemption from payment of Central Excise Duty on all goods.

(c) Reimbursement of duty paid on fuels procured from domestic oil companies.

(d) Suppliers of precious and semi-precious stones, synthetic stones and processed pearls from DTA to EOU shall be eligible for grant of Replenishment Licences.

**(vi) Other Entitlements of EOU/EHTP/STP Units:**

(a) Exemption from payment of Income Tax as per the provisions of Income Tax Act

(b) Clubbing of FOB value of export of an EOU/EHTP/STP units with FOB value of export of its parent company in the DTA or vice versa for the purpose of according Export House, Trading House, Star Trading House or Super Star Trading House status.

(c) Foreign Direct Investment (FDI) up to 100% in the manufacturing sector is permissible, as per the guidelines of Department of Industrial Policy and promotion on the subject.

(d) Software units are also allowed to use the computer system for training purposes (including commercial training) subject to the condition that no computer terminal shall be installed outside the bonded premises for the purpose.

(e) Exemption from Industrial licensing for manufacture of items reserved for SSI sector.

(f) State Trading Regime shall not apply to EOU manufacturing units subject to certain exceptions in respect of certain products.

**(vii) Inter Unit Transfer:**

(a) Transfer of manufactured goods from one EOU/EHTP/STP unit to another such unit or to SEZ (Special Economic Zone) unit will be allowed.

(b) Capital goods may be transferred or given on loan to other EOU/SEZ/EHTD/STP units with prior permission of the concerned Development Commissioner and customs authorities.

**(viii) Sub-contracting:**

EOU/EHTP/STP units may sub-contract production process in DTA through job work by units in the DTA. Such sub-contracting of both production and production process may also be undertaken through other EOU/EHTP/ STP/SEZ units. Such sub-contracting of part of production process may also be permitted abroad. EOU may undertake job work for export, on behalf of DTA exporter. In all these cases suitable permissions are to be obtained from the Development Commissioner/Customs Authorities. Scrap/waste/ remnants generated through job work may either be cleared from the job worker's premises on payment of applicable duty or destroyed in the presence of customs/Excise authorities or returned to the unit.

**(ix) Sale of Unutilized Material:**

In case an EOU/EHTP/STP unit is unable for valid reasons to utilize the goods and services imported or procured from DTA, it may be transferred to other EOU/SEZ/EHTP/STP units, or disposed off in the DTA on payment of applicable duties and submission of import licence by DTA unit, wherever applicable or exported. Capital goods and spares will be allowed depreciation, as applicable, in case of disposal to DTA. No duty shall be payable in case the goods are destroyed with customs concurrence.

**(x) Reconditioning, Repair and Re-engineering:**

EOU/EHTP/STP units may be set up to carryout reconditioning, repair, remaking, testing, calibration, quality improvement, upgradation of technology and re-engineering activities for export, in freely convertible foreign currency. However, some of the concessions given to EOU/EHTP/STP units are not available to these units.

**(xi) Exit from EOU Scheme:**

(a) Subject to the approval of the Development Commission, EOU/EHTP/STP units may opt out of the scheme. Such exit from the scheme shall be subject to payment of duties of customs and Excise and the industrial policy in force at the time of exit.

(b) If the unit has not achieved the obligations under the scheme, exit from the scheme shall also be subject to penalty as may be imposed by the competent authority.

**(xii) Conversion:**

(a) Existing DTA units may also apply for conversion into an EOU/EHTP/STP unit, but no concession in duties and taxes would be applicable under the relevant scheme for plant, machinery and equipment already installed.

(b) The existing EHTD/STP units may also apply for conversion/merges to EOU Unit and vice versa. In such cases the units will continue to remain in bond and avail the permissible exemption in duties and taxes as applicable under the relevant scheme.

**(xiii) Approvals: Exception:**

In the case of units under EHTP/STP schemes, necessary approval/permission shall be granted by the officer designated by the ministry of communication and information technology, Department of Information Technology instead of the Development commissioner of SEZ and by the Inter-ministerial Standing Committee (IMSC) instead of BOA.

## 4. Special Economic Zones Scheme

***Definition:*** Special Economic Zone (SEZ) is a specifically delineated duty free enclave and shall be deemed to be foreign territory for the purpose of trade operations and duties and tariffs.

(a) Status: Goods and services going into the SEZ area from DTA shall be treated as exports and goods and services coming from the SEZ area into DTA shall be treated as if these are being imported.

(b) Setting up of SEZ: A SEZ may be setup in the public, private or joint sector or by State Government. Project proposals for setting up of SEZ recommended by the concerned State Government, shall be considered by the Board of Approval in the Department of Commerce. On approval of the proposal, a letter of permission shall be issued to the developer for development, operation and maintenance of SEZ.

(c) Entitlements of SEZ Developer: For development, operation and maintenance of infrastructure facilities in SEZ's the developer shall be eligible for the following entitlements:

*(i)* Income tax exemption *(ii)* Import/procure goods without payment of customs/excise duty *(iii)* exemption from service tax and iv) exemption from CST.

(a) Eligibility of SEZ units: SEZ units may be set up for manufacture of goods and rendering of services.

(b) Export: SEZ units may export goods and services including agro-products, partly processed goods, sub-assemblies and components except prohibited items of exports in the Policy. The units may also export by-products, rejects and waste scrap arising not of the production process. Software units may undertake exports using data communication links or in the form of physical exports, including export of professional services.

(c) Import/Domestic procurement:

(i) SEZ unit may import/procure from the DTA without payment of duty all types of goods and services, including capital goods, whether new or second hand, required by it for its activities or in connection therewith, provided they are not prohibited items of imports in the policy. However, any permission required for import under any other law shall be applicable. Goods shall include raw material for making capital goods for use within the unit.

(ii) SEZ units may import /procure from DTA, without payment of duty, all types of goods for creating a central facility for use by units in SEZ. The central facility for software development can also be accessed by units in the DTA for export of software.

(iii) SEZ units may import/procure goods and services from DTA without payment of duty for setting up, operation and maintenance of units in the zone.

(iv) Goods, except capital goods and spares shall be utilized within the approval period of 5 years.

(d) Net Foreign Exchange earnings:

SEZ unit shall be a positive net foreign exchange earner. Net Foreign Exchange earnings (NFE) shall be calculated cumulatively for a period of five years from the commencement of production according to the following formula:

Positive NFE $= A - B > 0$

Where,

A: Is the FOB value of exports by the SEZ unit; and B: Is the sum total of the CIF value of all imported inputs and the CIF value of all imported capital goods, and the value of all payments made in foreign exchange by way of commission, royalty, fees, dividends, interest on external borrowings during the first five year period or any other charges. "Inputs" mean raw materials, intermediates, components, consumables, parts and packing materials. For annual calculation of NFE, the value of imported capital goods and lump sum payment of foreign technical know-how fee shall be amortized as under:

$1^{st}$ -$10^{th}$ year : 10% each year.

(e) Monitoring of performance:

Failure to ensure positive NFE or to abide by any of the terms and conditions of the LOP/LUT shall render the unit liable to penal action under the provisions of the Foreign Trade (Development & Regulation) ACT, 1992 and the rules and orders made there under without prejudice to action under any other law/rules and cancellation or revocation of LOP (LOP: Letter of Permission and LUT: Letter of undertaking; The former issued by the appropriate Government authorities and the latter given by the SEZ unit)

(f) DTA sales and supplies:

(a) SEZ unit may sell goods, including by-products, and services in DTA in accordance with the Import Policy in force, on payment of applicable duties.

(b) DTA sale by service/trading unit shall be subject to achievement of positive NFE cumulatively. Similarly for units understanding manufacturing and services/trading activities against a single LDP, DTP sale shall be subject to achievement of NFE cumulatively.

(c) Scrap/waste/remotes arising out of production process in connection therewith may be sold in the DTA on payment of applicable duty.

Entitlement for supplies from the DTA: DTA supplier to SEZ shall be entitled for:-

(i) Drawback or DEPB in lieu of Drawback

(ii) Discharge of export performance, if any

(iii) Supplier of precious and semi-precious stones, synthetic stones and processed pearls from DTA to the SEZ units shall be eligible for grant of Replenishment Licences.

Entitlements for SEZ units: SEZ units shall be entitled for:–

(i) Exemption from Central Sales Tax

(ii) Exemption from payment of Central Excise Duty on all goods eligible for procurement

(iii) Reimbursement of Duty paid on fuels or any other goods procured from DTA as per the rate of drawback notified by the Directorate General of Foreign Trade.

(a) Inter-Unit Transfer: SEZ units may transfer manufactured goods, including partly processed/semi-finished goods and services from one SEZ unit to another SEZ/EOU/EHTP/STP unit. Goods imported/procured by a SEZ unit may be transferred or given on loan to another unit within the same SEZ. Capital goods imported/procured may be transferred or given on loan to another SEZ/EOU/EHTP/STP unit. Some of these transfers need permission from appropriate authorities while some other need no such permission.

(b) Other Entitlement for SEZ units:

(i) Units set up in SEZS established by the Government will be charged rent for lease of industrial plats and standard design factory buildings/sheds as per rates fixed from time to time.

(ii) Exemption from service tax.

(iii) Exemption from Income Tax as per the provisions of the Income Tax Act.

(iv) Foreign equity up to 100% is permissible for most of the manufacturing activities under automatic route.

(v) SEZ units may retain 100% of their export proceeds in their EEFC account.

(vi) Export value of goods, software and services by SEZ units may be realized and repatriated to India within 12 months from the date of export or within the time extended by Reserve Bank of India.

(vii) Software units may, in addition, also be allowed to use the computer system for training purposes (including commercial training) subject to the condition that no computer terminal shall be installed outside the zone premises for the purpose.

(viii) Procurement of raw materials and export of finished products shall be exempt from central levies.

(ix) Exemption from industrial licensing for manufacturers of items reserved for SSI sector.

(x) State Trading Enterprises Policy shall not apply to SEZ manufacturing units (with certain exceptions to certain products).

(xi) SEZ unit may install one fax machine at a place of its choice, outside the zone.

(xii) SEZ units may, temporarily take out of the zone duty free laptop computers and video projection systems for working upon by persons authorized by unit.

(xiii) SEZ units may install personal computers not exceeding two in number imported/procured duty free in the registered/administrative office subject to certain guidelines.

(c) Sub-contracting:

(i) SEZ units may sub-contract a part of their production or production process through units in the DTA or through other SEZ/EOU/EHTP/STP units. Sub-contracting of part of production process may also be permitted abroad. Permission of appropriate authorities are required.

(ii) All units may sub-contract part of the production or production process through other units in the same SEZ without permission of Customs authorities subject to records being maintained by both the supplying and receiving units.

(iii) Scrap/waste/remnants generated through job work may either be cleared from the job worker's premises on payment of applicable duty or destroyed in the presence of customs/excise authorities or returned to the unit.

(iv) SEZ units may undertake job work for export on behalf of DTA exporter provided the finished goods are exported directly from SEZ units.

(v) SEZ units may be permitted to remove moulds, jigs, tools, fixtures, instruments, and drawings to the premises of sub-contractors subject to the condition that these shall be brought back to the premises of the units on completion of the job work within a stipulated period.

(d) Sale of unutilized material/destruction:

(i) In case a SEZ unit is unable, for valid reasons, to utilize the goods, and services, imported or procured from DTA, it may be transferred to other EOU/SEZ/EHTP/STP units or disposed off in the DTA on payment of applicable duties and submission of Import licence by DTA unit, wherever applicable or exported. Such transfer from SEZ unit to another SEZ/EOU/EHTP/STD unit would be treated as import for the receiving unit.

(ii) Capital goods and spares that have become obsolete/surplus may either be exported, transferred to another SEZ/EOU/EHTP/STP unit or disposed of in the DTA on payment of applicable duties. The benefit of depreciation, as applicable will be available in case of disposal in DTA.

(iii) SEZ unit may be allowed by customs authorities concerned to donate imported /indigenously procured computer and computer peripherals, including printer, plotter, scanner, monitor, key board and storage units without payment of duty, two years after their Import/procurement and use by the units, to recognized non-commercial institutions, registered charitable hospitals, public libraries, public funded research and development establishments, organisations of the Government of India or Government of a state or union territory as per notification issued in this regard.

(iv) No duty shall be payable in the case of capital goods, raw materials, consumables, spares, goods manufactured, processed or packaged and scrap/waste/remnants/rejects are destroyed within the zone after intimation to the customs authorities or destroyed outside the zone with the permission of customs authorities.

(e) Self-certification: All activities of SEZ units within the zone unless otherwise specified, including export and re-import of goods shall be through self-certification procedure.

(f) Distinct Identity: If an industrial enterprise is operating both as a domestic unit as well as an SEZ unit, it shall have two distinct identities with separate accounts, including separate bank accounts. It is, however, not necessary for it to be a separate legal entity, but it should be possible to distinguish the imports and exports or supplies effected by the SEZ units from those made by the other units of the enterprise.

(i) Exit from SEZ Scheme: SEZ unit may opt out of the scheme with the approval of the Development commissions. Such exit from the scheme shall be subject to payment of applicable customs and Excise duties on the Imported and indigenous capital goods, raw materials etc. and finished goods in stock. In case the unit has not achieved positive NFE, the exit shall be subject to penalty, that may be imposed by the adjudicating authority under, Foreign Trade (Development and Regulation) Act, 1992.

The Policy relating to all aspects of the working of Special Economic Zones are governed by the SEZ Act of 2005, and the rules framed there under.

## STRUCTURE OF THE NEW EXPORT-INPORT POLICY

The Export Import Policy of India has changed considerably over the years. In spite of all rules and regulations therein, one can boldly say that an exporter will be able to import anything he needs for his export endeavour, be it know-how, technology, production machinery, components or any other needs for exporting his goods or services.

### Import Policy – Structure:

Before liberalization of the Export and Import policy in a regime of strict controls, there used to be a negative list of imports. Since the policy was liberalised, 6 years ago, the Commerce Ministry has given a detailed item-wise policy in the book, "ITC (HS) Classification of Export Import items." In the last 6 years there has been a paradigm shift in the import policy regime. All the Quantitative Restrictions (QRs) maintained in the earlier years on account of Balance of Payment (BOP) reasons have been progressively removed. A number of such restrictions have also been removed to comply with WTO requirements. A common classification was required for purposes of imposition of customs duty, determination of the Import Policy and collection of import statistics. This is also a *sine-qua-non* for effective computerization and Electronic Data Interchange (EDI) A large number of quantitative restrictions and similar restrictions on exports have also been removed. In effect, today, we have only three categories of items:

(a) Prohibited

(b) Restricted

(c) Free

The prohibited items cannot normally be imported. The restricted items can be imported after obtaining an import license or as per the special instructions announced by the Ministry of Commerce. Some of the items are exclusively allotted to State Trading Organisations for import purposes. All items other than the ones indicated above belong to the category of freely importable items. In other words, the bulk of these items are not subjected to any restrictions by the Ministry of Commerce in their importation.

Certain other restrictions, however, still exist in the importation of various commodities in the form of provisions in other enactments. These are broadly summarized below:

(a) Export of beef in any form and import of products containing beef in any form are prohibited.

(b) All packaged products, which are subject to provisions of the Standards of Weights and Measures (Packaged Commodities) Rules, 1977, when produced/packed/sold in the domestic market, shall be subject to compliance of all provisions of the said rules, when imported into India.

(c) Import of certain specified products in the ITC (HS)book shall be subject to compliance of the mandatory Indian Quality Standards as indicated, and these are applicable to domestic goods as well.

(d) Import of meat and poultry products will be subject to the compliance of conditions regarding manufacture, slaughter, packing, labeling and quality conditions as laid down in Meat Food Products Order, 1973.

(e) Import of all such edible/food products, domestic sale and manufacture of which are governed by Prevention of Food Adulteration Act, 1954 shall be subject to all conditions laid down in the aforesaid Act. Import of all these products will have to comply with the quality and packaging requirements as laid down in the Act.

(f) Import of all primary agricultural products will be subject to a Bio-security and Phyto-sanitary Import Permit, issued by the Department of Agriculture and Cooperation, as per condition s of Plants, Fruits and Seeds (Regulation of Import into India) Order1989.

(g) Similarly the provisions of the Tea Wastage (Control) Order 1959 is applicable to import of Tea Waste.

(h) Import of textiles and textile articles is permitted subject to the condition that they shall not contain any of the hazardous dyes in terms of the Environment (Protection) Act,1986.

(i) Import of alcoholic beverages shall be subject to compliance of various mandatory requirements as stipulated by various State Governments.

(j) Import of meat and meat products shall be subject to a sanitary import permit issued by the Department of Animal Husbandry and Dairying, Government of India as per Livestock Importation Act, 1898.

## Export Policy – Structure

In the export policy published in the ITC (HS) Book of the government of India, all goods other than those specified in Table A and B are freely exportable. This is however subject to any other law for the time being in force.

Exports subject to control have been listed in Table A and B.

Each Table gives details of code, item description, policy and nature of restriction. As regards export policy there are four policy categories:

(a) Prohibited

(b) Restricted

(c) State Trading Enterprises

(d) Free with conditions.

In some cases, restricted entries also show conditionalities. In all cases of restrictions, licenses are required to be taken. The nature of restriction in each case is also detailed. The prohibited items are not permitted to be exported. Exports through TTE are permitted without an export license through designated STEs only, and subject to the conditions in the policy. The freely exportable items can be exported without an export license/permission from the DGFT.

Some examples are:

(a) Marine Products can be exported freely subject to pre-shipment quality inspection by the government, through a notification.

(b) Tallow, Fat and Oils of any animal origin, excluding Fish Oil is prohibited.

(c) Finished Leather of all kinds are Free subject to the definition of Finished Leather, notified by the DGFT from time to time.

(d) Crude Oil can be exported under STE through the Indian Oil Corporation Ltd.

A comprehensive account of the Export Import Policy of the Government of India is given in this chapter. However, it is essential to keep abreast of the various notifications issued by the government periodically, to be fully informed on the rules and regulations for export. An export organization in India should have at least one person trained in the field of these policies and their official jargon to guide the company in its efforts, and the steps to be taken. Many organizations outsource this work to consultants who have specialized in this field and are available in India.

The Policy as given by the Government is given above. All doubts/ clarifications should be referred to the Joint Director General of Foreign trade of the region, who is authorized to provide the same.

## EXPORT ASSISTANCE AND PROMOTIONAL MEASURES

There is an entire range of assistance given by the government but all of the schemes or incentives may not be useful to all exporters. Market Development Assistance (MDA) was used mainly for the purpose of market studies, exhibitions, approved tours abroad, publicity etc. for which the government would bear a portion of the expenses. Even though it exists, fewer and fewer exporters resort to it, but the government has enlarged the scope and shifted the emphasis in the new policy calling it as Market Access Initiative and applies it to a whole lot of activities in the country and for the initiatives of the states as well.

The Schemes available are:

### Duty Exemption/Remission Scheme

The Duty Exemption Scheme enables duty-free imports of inputs required for export production. An Advance License is issued under the duty exemption scheme. The Duty Remission Scheme enables post-export replenishment/remission of duty on inputs used in the export product. Duty Remission Scheme consists of:

(a) DEPB: The DEPB Scheme allows drawback of import duties on imports used in the export product.

(b) Advance License (now referred to as Advance Authorisation Scheme).

The full details of the scheme in provided earlier in this chapter.

(c) Duty Entitlement Pass Book Scheme: The full details of the scheme in provided earlier in this chapter

(d) Gem and Jewellery Scheme: Separate schemes of incentives are available in the policy for exporters of gem and jewellery. Such schemes provide Replenishment License, Advance License, Diamond Imprest License etc. as well as permit gold imports.

The full details of the scheme in provided earlier in this chapter.

(e) Export Promotion Capital Goods Scheme (EPCG): The full details of the scheme in provided earlier in this chapter

## ELECTRONIC DATA INTERCHANGE

In an attempt to speed up the transactions, reduce physical interface and to bring about transparency in various activities related to exports, electronic data interchange would be encouraged. Applications received electronically shall be cleared within 24 hours. Such applicants shall be required to furnish a fee equivalent to 50% of the prescribed fee.

## THRUST SECTOR

With a view to achieve the share of 1% of global trade and accelerated growth in exports, the following were declared as the thrust sectors:

(a) Electronic hardware

(b) Textile including garments

(c) Auto components/ancillary

(d) Gem and Jewellery

(e) Agriculture

(f) Service Sector.

The Department of Commerce shall take concerted efforts to promote exports of these sectors by specific sectoral strategy.

## DUTY DRAWBACK

Duty drawback is composed of the customs duty and central excise duty paid on all raw materials, components, and consumables utilised in the manufacture of the end products.

Duty drawback is allowed as per the Customs Act, 1962, under which customs authorities have issued the Customs & Central Excise Duty Drawback Rules. The schedule to these Rules specifies the broad categories of the items on which drawback is allowed. If any item of exports has not been included, the Ministry of Finance should be approached for its inclusion of the item in the schedule.

The rules made by the government of India and published in their notification given forms the basis of drawback of duties. Even though there have been amendments from time to time of these rules, the notification of 1995 is still the basis on which duties are computed and paid.

The rates of drawback are divided into two categories, **the All-Industry Rates** which are applicable to all exporters of such items. These all-industry rates are subject to revision either on the initiative of the Government or of the Export Promotion Councils. The variation of duty incidences may warrant a revision of these all-industry rates.

The other category is the **Brand Rates** which are fixed for a particular manufacturer. Unlike the all-industry rates, brand rates are applicable only to the manufacturer for whom these rates have been fixed. For this fixation, the manufacturer is required to submit date in the prescribed Drawback Proformas-I, II and III. After a verification of these statements and related documents, the Central Excise Commissionerates having jurisdiction over the manufacturing unit will fix a rate/quantum of drawback which will be applicable for all the exports made by the manufacturer of the products for which the rate of drawback is fixed.

No separate application is required for claiming the duty drawback. If an exporter wishes to claim drawback, it is compulsory that he should file a **Drawback Shipping Bill**. A triplicate copy of this Shipping Bill automatically becomes, after shipment, an application for the claim for duty drawback. If the products exported are given under the all-industry rate category, the serial and sub-serial number, together with the amount, should be indicated in the Green Shipping Bill. If brand rates are applicable, the exporter should mention the notification, number and date, and claim the amount as per the rates/quantum indicated in the authorisation. If the product exported does not come under the all-industry rates or brand rates, the exporter can still safeguard his claim for drawback by indicating in the shipping bill "that the claim is made under the provisional claim for drawback."

On receipt of the triplicate copy of the shipping bill from the exporter, duly completed, together with a freighted/signed copy of bill of lading, a photo copy each of the invoice, bank certificate, and insurance premium receipt, the Drawback Department verifies the particulars and issues the cheque to the exporter's bank, under intimation to the exporter, giving the payment details.

## DEEMED EXPORTS

**Deemed Exports** refers to those transactions in which the goods supplied do not leave the country and the payment for such supplies is received either in Indian rupees or in free foreign exchange.

**(a) Categories of Supply:** The following categories of supply of goods by the main/sub-contractors shall be regarded as "Deemed Exports" under this Policy, provided the goods are manufactured in India:

(i) Supply of goods against Advance Authorisation/Advance Authorisation for annual requirement/DFIA under the Duty Exemption/Remission Scheme.

(ii) Supply of goods to Export Oriented Units (EOUs) or units located in Special Economic Zone (SEZs) or Software Technology Parks (STPs) or Electronic Hardware Technology Parks (EHTPs).

(iii) Supply of capital goods to holders of licences under the Export Promotion Capital Goods (EPCG) Scheme.

(iv) Supply of goods to projects financed by multilateral or bilateral agencies/funds as notified by the Department of Economic Affairs, Ministry of Finance under International Competitive Bidding in accordance with the procedures of those agencies/funds, where the legal agreements provide for tender evaluation without including the customs duty.

(v) Supply of capital goods, including in unassembled/disassembled condition as well as plants, machinery, accessories, tools, dies and such goods which are used for installation purposes till the stage of commercial production, and spares to the extent of 10% of the FOR value to fertilizer plants.

(vi) Supply of goods to any project or purpose in respect of which the Ministry of Finance, by a notification, permits the import of such goods at zero customs duty coupled with the extension of benefits under this chapter to domestic supplies.

(vii) Supply of goods to the power projects and refineries not covered in (vi) above.

(viii) Supply of marine freight containers by 100% EOU (Domestic freight containers – manufacturers) provided the said containers are exported out of India within 6 months or such further period

(ix) Supply to projects funded by UN agencies.

(x) Supply of goods to nuclear power projects through competitive bidding as opposed to International Competitive Bidding.

The benefits of deemed exports shall be available under paragraph (iv), (v), (vi) and (vii) only if the supply is made under the procedure of International Competitive Bidding (ICB).

**(b) Benefits for Deemed Exports:** Deemed exports shall be eligible for any/all of the following benefits in respect of manufacture and supply of goods qualifying as deemed exports subject to the terms and conditions as given in HBP v1:

(i) Advance Authorisation/Advance Authorisation annual requirements/DFIA.

(ii) Deemed Exports Drawback.

(iii) Refund of Terminal Excise duty.

## EXPORT PROMOTION ORGANISATIONS

Soon after independence, India embarked upon a huge nation building exercise, when export was only an item on the periphery. Only in the decade of the eighties, Export was recognized as an essential and important activity needed for the economic growth of the country. India being a developing country, it had many hurdles to face in exports. Hence the government devised various Export Promotion Organisations to concentrate on export efforts, help the exporting community and discus the various factors adversely affecting exports. These organizations could then get the help of the government to solve them.

These are specialized trade bodies looking into different groups or services. Some of them are:

## EXPORT PROMOTION COUNCILS

These are non-profit organizations dedicated to the exports of a particular group or products, projects and services. These are:

1. Agricultural and Processed Food Products Export Development Authority – New Delhi.
2. Apparel Export Promotion Council, New Delhi.
3. Basic Chemicals, Pharmaceuticals and Cosmetic Export Promotion Council - Mumbai.

4. Cashew Export Promotion Council, Cochin.
5. Carpet Export Promotion Council, New Delhi.
6. Chemicals and Allied Products Export Promotion Council – Kolkata.
7. The Cotton Textiles Export Promotion Council, Mumbai.
8. Council for Leather Exports – Chennai.
9. Electronics and Computer Software Export Promotion Council - New Delhi.
10. Engineering Export Promotion Council, Kolkata.
11. The Gem and Jewellery Export Promotion Council, Mumbai
12. Export Promotion Council for handicrafts, New Delhi.
13. The Handloom Export Promotion Council, Chennai
14. The Indian silk Export Promotion Council, Mumbai
15. Marine Products Export Development Authority – Kochi
16. Project Exports Promotion Council of India – New Delhi.
17. Council for Leather exports, Chennai.
18. Overseas Construction Council of India, Mumbai
19. The Plastic and Linoleum Export Promotion Council, Mumbai
20. Shellac export promotion council, Kokkata.
21. The Sports Goods Export Promotion Council, New Delhi.
22. The Synthetic and Rayon Textiles Export Promotion Council, Mumbai.
23. Wool and Woollens Export Promotion Council, New Delhi.
24. The Powerloom Development and Export Promotion Council, Mumbai.
25. Export Promotion Council (EPC) for EOUs/SEZ Units, New Delhi.

The Councils look after the interest of the exporters of the product group entrusted to them. They hold periodical meetings of the representatives of the trade to discus their problems and present them to the government to find solutions.

They are in touch with our embassies and various trade sources and gather information regularly regarding export opportunities and circulate them to the members.

They help to conduct exhibitions and fairs and also arrange to send delegations abroad to promote exports.

## TRADE BODIES

There are also some trade bodies established by the government of India to exclusively look after the export trade of some specific groups. These are:

Agricultural and Processed Food Products Export Development Authority (**APEDA**). This looks after the entire range of agricultural products as well as processed foods being exported from the country, and helps to increase exports.

The other one is Marine Product Export Development Authority (**MPEDA**).

These are statutory boards usually headed by a government official. The premier exporters are coopted to the board. They not only oversee the export of the product but also devise plans for the improvement of the industry as a whole so that there is healthy growth for the domestic sector as well as exportable surplus.

## COMMODITIES BOARDS

These have been set up by the government of India to develop and promote production and export of certain traditional commodities. These are:

1. Tea Board
2. Coffee Board
3. Tobacco Board
4. Species Board
5. Rubber Board
6. Coir Board
7. Central Silk Board

The exporters dealing with these commodities can register with the respective boards. The board will supply all the information they have on international markets, and the latest developments. They also conduct exhibitions and fairs, to give publicity to the products.

The Boards take interest not only for exports, but also in cultivation and production of the product, increase in production and processing etc. Further, they interact with the government on behalf of the producers with a view to solving their problems and help them to get remunerative prices.

## M.VISVESVARAYYA INDUSTRIAL RESEARCH AND DEVELOPMENT CENTRE (MVIRDC)

The World Trade Centre in Mumbai is promoted by the MVIRDC. It is a non-profit organization, and in the World Trade Centre offices/cells of agencies and institutions connected with export trade are all located. The MVIRDC center also includes consultancy firms and some government agencies. This is a good location for the exporter to establish contact with all the agencies connected with export.

It also provides exhibition space for Indian goods.

The WTC is also a member of the World Trade Centre Association, New York, with more than 200 members spread over 60 countries, and this happens to be a trade exchange center where the need of many exporters and importers in all the 60 countries will be made available to its members.

If properly exploited this will be an excellent source of information background for many exporters.

Chambers of Commerce and Industry and Associations of Trade and Industry:

These play a prominent role in the export promotion activities of trade and industry. They arrange periodic meetings which help in:

(a) Exchange of information and compilation of data, indicating the present state of the export activities in a particular trade/industry.

(b) Exchange of views and formulation of specific remedies and policies which will be taken up with the government.

Membership of the Chambers and associations is open to all trade and industry. The discussions therein are amongst professional people who have a thorough knowledge of a trade or an industry. This can be an excellent forum to project practical, viable and sound suggestion for removing impediments, or changing policies in the national interest, provided the right persons are at the helm.

Many of these Chambers/Associations have separate sections/cells to deal with the export trade, which are helpful in interpreting government policies to members, disseminating data to them and also in making meaningful representation to government.

## FEDERATION OF INDIAN EXPORT ORGANISATIONS

This was set up in 1965 by the government and industry. It is a common coordinating agency of all Export promotion councils, commodity boards, service institutions, and represents the entire cross section of the exporting community.

It offers its services to all its constituents and members in conducting export promotion activities, representing the problems faced by exporters, to the government with a view to getting solutions, arrange seminars and workshops on export trade etc.

It is also the registered authority for Export Houses and trading Houses.

It also arranges buyers-sellers meets, keeps in touch with all overseas trade and commerce chambers, send trade delegations, and provide trade information to all of its constituents and members.

## INDIAN INSTITUTE OF FOREIGN TRADE (IIFT)

The IIFT was established by the government of India as an autonomous organizations in 1964 to strengthen the country's international business effort by developing human resources, conducting research and providing consultancy services.

It has four foundational programmes and two certificate courses. It undertakes market studies for the exporters or export promotion agencies if called upon to do so.

## INDIAN INSTITUTE OF PACKAGING (IIP)

The Indian Institute of Packaging is a research and development organization set up in 1966. It is also an education and training organization. IT is entrusted with the responsibility of bringing about improvements in the standards of packaging especially for exports.

## INDIAN COUNCIL OF ARBITRATION (ICA)

This was set up in 1965 mainly for promoting and encouraging amicable settlement of commercial disputes by arbitration between exporters and importers. They conduct training courses and seminars on conventional arbitration and international law.

Unless ICA is specifically mentioned in the contract and agreed to by both parties, it cannot play a part in arbitration in disputes.

However in international contracts it is normal practice for the parties to introduce a clause that in case of dispute they will abide by the arbitration procedures of the International Chamber of Commerce, an Indian wind of the International Chamber of Commerce dealing with arbitration proceedings. It is situated in India in the premises of the FICCI in New Delhi.

## 100% EXPORT ORIENTED UNITS (EOU)

These are units undertaking to export their entire production of goods and services; and set up in the exclusive EOU Zones. They are permitted to sell 50% of their production in the Domestic Tariff Area for Indian Consumption subject to certain conditions. These units may be in manufacture, repair, re-engineering, services or agricultural areas.

New EOU are exempted from payment of income tax for a block of 10 years, EOUs are mainly concentrated on textiles and yarn, food processing, electronics, chemicals, plastics, granite and minerals/ores. The majority of the units are located in Tamil Nadu, Andhra Pradesh, Karnataka, Maharashtra and Gujarat.

## INDIAN TRADE PROMOTION ORGANISATION (ITPO)

This came into being in 1992, and is a premier trade promotion agency of the government. It provides a broad spectrum of services to trade and industry so as to promote Indian exports.

Their main services to trade and industry are:

(a) Organising trade fairs and exhibitions in India and abroad.

(b) Arranging buyer-seller meets and contract promotion programmes for the exporting community.

(c) Provide information on export markets and products to the exporters.

They have recently developed a website of their own giving all the details of their activities and allied information.

## ANNEXURE I

## Export Policy Resolution, 1970

(1) India's foreign trade policy has been reviewed in the context of the objectives, strategy and priorities of the Fourth Five Year Plan. Government is of the view that expansion of export earnings in as crucial for financing the Plan as the mobilization of domestic resources to achieve national self-reliance and to reduce dependence on external assistance, export earnings need to be expanded at a high rate. The compound rate of expansion envisaged in the Fourth Plan is 7 per cent per annum.

(2) A steady increase in export earnings is dependent on the continuous development and expansion of export-oriented production. The aim of such development should be the promotion of economic efficiency, diversification of production and better utilization of skilled and unskilled manpower. The development of the economy's export sector has thus a vital role to play in the achievement of the Plan's social and economic goals. The needs of this sector should, therefore, receive very high priority.

(3) The experience of the last few years testifies, on the one hand, to the country's potential for achieving a rising level of exports and on the other, to the need for the adoption of appropriate policies and measures designed to promote investment in an development of the promising sectors of the economy.

(4) In each of the broad lines of production such as agriculture, horticulture, sericulture, forestry, fisheries, minerals, textiles, chemical & engineering industries, electronics, etc., the products having long-term export potential will be identified with greater precision and special measures and programmes will be undertaken to secure their development and improvement. At the same time, like attention and assistance will also be provided for consolidating the position acquired in overseas markets by our traditional products such as tea, jute manufactures, cotton textile, etc and for identifying in these sectors, new areas of growth and production adaptation.

(5) In the agriculture sector, the production of cash crops identified as possessing a promising export potential such as, cashew kernels, oilseeds, raw cotton, raw jute, spices, tobacco, etc. will be developed further through increased provision of requisite inputs including irrigation, fertilizers, improved methods of cultivation. The objective of the development of cash crops would be to promote not only their direct exports but also to augment their availability and improve their quality so as to increase the income from the overseas sales of processed and finished goods based on them.

(6) In horticulture, production of fruits, vegetables and flowers, both in natural and processed forms, will be developed scientifically and on a commercial scale. This would call for not merely the organization of adequate production, but also of processing and transportation facilities. Special measures, including multiplication of silk and to improve its quality.

(7) In view of the recent increase in the export of and demand for sea foods and their abundant availability in the Indian ocean, there is urgent need for scientific exploitation of the potential in its sphere. To this end, appropriate measures for the expansion of the country's deep sea fishing fleet and organization of adequate facilities for processing the catch will be undertaken.

(8) India's forest resources have not yet been fully harnessed for the purpose of exports. Apart from shellac, gums and other resins, there is scope for increasing the export of timber and processed plywood/veneers and minor forest produce. The export potential of our forest produce will be exploited more fully. Similar steps will be taken in regard to livestock, hides and skins, and the processing industries based on them.

(9) In the mineral sector, iron ore is among our principal foreign exchange earners and the country is fortunately endowed with such large reserves that even at a high rate of exports, domestic requirements of ore for steel making can be easily met. Further, investment in the developing of mines and processing the raw ore for export as well as the in the provision of transport and port handling facilities, is called for. Geological exploration and development of other ores, e.g., manganese ore, chrome ore and bauxite is also of other minerals such as mica, cadmium sillimenite, kyanite and fluorspar needs to be encouraged both for direct export and for use in the production of finished products for export. The expansion of the mineral sector would not only keep to augment export earnings but also accelerate the development of backward regions in the country.

(10) In the textiles sector, based on cotton, wool, jute, coir silk and synthetics, there is need for diversification and modernization of industry and for product development. Keeping in view the size of India's textile industry, selective modernization of exporting or export-oriented units will be undertaken so as to equip them with modern machinery, if necessary through imports. The export of yearn, of blended and finished fabrics and of readymade garments will be stepped up. In jute goods, since carpet backing cloth and decorative fabrics hold out the promise of long-term growth, expansion of their production will receive special attention. Expenditure on research and development to adapt traditional fibres to changing consumer preference will be increased and special encouragement will be given to the organization and expansion of production in the product lines for which overseas demand is expected to increase.

(11) The diversification of industrial production and the improvement of its economic efficiency have been assigned an important role in the Fourth Plan. Fortunately, industrial products also constitute the most dynamic component of international trade. The value added to the export of industrial processes is high and the export of industrial products gives expanding opportunities for the utilization of our resources in skilled and unskilled manpower.

Our industrial policy will consequently be guided not only by internal requirements but also by the rising demand for industrial products in overseas fostering the creation of new export capacity. In implementing it, the aim will be to generate expanding surpluses of industrial products. In pursuing this aim, every effort will be made to assist export-oriented units in the private and public sectors to achieve economies of scale, improve efficiency of production, abroad. To this end, the procedures relating to foreign investment, licensing of creation or expansion of industrial capacity, licensing of imports of capital goods and raw materials or other inputs, will be suitably adapted. Every effort will also be made to ensure that indigenous industrial raw materials required for export production are made available in right quality and quantity, and at fair prices.

(12) There is a steady increase in the demand, especially in industrial countries, for labour-intensive products. A number of these products can be manufactured economically in our small or medium scale sectors. Every effort will be made to organize their production and marketing so as to secure quantitative adequacy of their output and sales. Equally, there is growing demand in developing countries for the products of our technology which are more relevant to their needs at the present stage of their development. Special encouragement is intended to be provided to producers and exporters of equipment for the development of infrastructure, industrial machinery, machine tools and consumer durables to meet the emerging requirements of other developing countries. India is also in a position to undertake turnkey projects abroad, including the preparation of feasibility studies, blueprints, supply of machinery equipment and materials and their installation and maintenance. Indian firms, both in the public and private sectors, will be given encouragement to complete for such projects, and to contribute to economic co-operation among developing countries.

(13) The skills of India's artisans and craftsment have made a significant contribution to India's foreign exchange earnings through the export of handicrafts. These will be developed to meet the emerging needs of overseas customers and changing trends in overseas markets.

(14) Indian industries have begun to compete in international markets on the strength of their own inherent efficiency. The main responsibility for the task of further improving their competitive ability naturally rests with producing units. Government will, however, provide the necessary assistance to build up efficient production and, in the meanwhile, endeavour to compensate exports for the temporary handicaps that stem from transitional difficulties inherent in a developing economy and to alleviate disadvantages arising from our domestic fiscal policies or tariff barriers in importing countries.

(15) While rapid growth comparable to that envisaged in the non-tradition sector cannot be expected in the traditional items of exports, it will be Governments' policy to promote measures to improve their competitiveness in

the international market, to defend their unit value and to improve to the extent possible, their export performance. Attention will also be paid to modernizing our marketing and promotional techniques and improving the efficiency of exporting firms engaged in this sector.

(16) As the quality of production for export needs special attention, Government will strengthen, expand and intensify its policy of compulsory quality control and pre-shipment inspection by the Indian Standards Institution and by the Directorate of Marketing and inspection, will endeavour to improve the efficiency of its services so as to reinforce the confidence of overseas importers in the authenticity of its certificates of quality.

(17) Exportable surpluses do not always arise automatically. Sometimes when there is a shortfall in production or indigenous production on an adequate scale is yet to be developed, there tends to be a temporary conflict between domestic consumption and port, Since export markets once lost can hardly be regained, a part of the production must always be made available in consultation with the ministries concerned keeping in view the degree of essentiality of the product in questing for industrial use or consumption at home.

(18) Export marketing and product development have now become highly specialized disciplines. Our efforts to improve marketing research, to build up marketing skills and to train managers will be intensified and expanded. The projections of the expansion of international trade over the seventies will be studied so that new investment effort in the country is directed to areas where we have natural factor endowment advantages and the overseas markets have growing needs for our products.

(19) Product and market research is currently the responsibility of several bodies, official and non-official. Their work will be co-ordinated and the results of research will be pooled so as to promote more effective utilization.

(20) Export Promotion Councils and Commodity Boards are providing export services to producers and exporters and are helping them to co-operate in their promotion endeavours. The effectiveness of the services provided to their members will be improved; and the responsibility for the execution of development programmes and the achievement of time bound targets will be fixed on them.

The world does not yet have an adequate picture of India's recent technological, industrial and commercial resurgence. Our efforts in the field of commercial publicity will be strengthened and the Director of Exhibitions and Commercial Publicity and the Indian Council of Trade Fairs will adopt modern techniques of audio-visual projection.

(21) The role of the public sector in the development and expansion of our foreign trade will be expanded progressively and substantially. Its competence to penetrate new markets and to market new products as well as to provide merchandising service to Indian producers will be built up. Special

attention will be made to forge enduring relationship with procurement authorities and trading firms and organizations in overseas countries. New Patterns of relationship with state trading organizations in other countries will be evolved. This effort will be spearheaded by the State Trading Corporation of India and the Corporations will be organized and new public sector agencies will, wherever and whenever necessary, be crated.

In particular, a new organization is being set-up in the public sector to provide package assistance to individual enterprises to build up their export potential and to earn and sustain the confidence to overseas customers. Manufacturing enterprises in the public sector agencies will provide leadership for the country's commercial effort and will co-operate with other export houses and agencies actively in attaining a standard or commercial efficiency comparable to the best in the world.

(22) Provision of adequate and timely finance is indispensable for both export production and export marketing. Packing and post-shipment credits are already being provided on concessional terms by commercial banks with the support of the Reserve Bank of India, while the Export Credit and Guarantee Corporation provides credit insurance facilities. Every effort will be made to strengthen and expand these credit arrangements and put them on an internationally comparable basis and the framework of financial institutions for the purpose, will be suitably strengthened.

With the nationalization of major Scheduled Banks, it has become possible for the banking system to evolve fresh programmes and new patterns for their financial and technical services to the exporting community. The aim will be to induce entrepreneurs to expand and adapt their production with a view to entering into enduring relationship with overseas importers and to offer attractive terms and conditions to importers and users of our products abroad.

(23) In order to encourage export-orientation of production the investor must have the assurance that export policies shall be reasonably stable and that production for exports would be advantageous to the producer. To this end, export policies should enjoy a degree of stability at lease over the period of the Fourth Plan. There will, however, have to be room for flexibility to take account of charges affecting the competitiveness of our export products.

(24) Among the inadequates of the existing infrastructure for exports, that of shipping facilities need to be emphasized. Government proposes to intensify its efforts to expand the national merchant marine fleet, to start new services and to strengthen the existing ones, as may be necessary for the development of our trade. Government also proposes to strengthen the existing institutional machinery to secure fair freight treatment for our export cargo and to provide improved shipping opportunities for it. Methods for the handling of export cargo in our docks are also proposed to be improved in this connection.

(25) The export of services and development of tourism provide means for a substantial expansion I our foreign income. There are attractive possibilities for the export of consultancy services in the fields of irrigation, power, agriculture, railways and road transport to many countries. Our long experience, established competence and competitive terms enable us to offer these services in pursuance of our programmes for economic co-operation with developing countries. This movement will be actively developed and encourage.

(26) The income from tourism constitutes an expanding source of foreign exchange for a growing n number of countries. Foreign tourists have shown increasing interest in visiting India. The provision of adequate transport and accommodation facilities for them will be accorded a high priority.

(27) The commercial and aid policies pursued by many Governments set limits to the natural expansion of Indian exports. Government proposes to concentrate its efforts on securing speedy modification of these policies in the interest of the general expansion of international trade. These efforts will be vigorously pursued through bilateral negotiations and in UNCTAD and GATT and other international forums.

(28) Early implementation of the Resolution adopted by the Second United Nations conference on Trade and Development in New Delhi for the institution by industrialized countries of a system of generalized non-reciprocal and non-discriminatory preference in favour of the products of developing countries is a matter of high priority. Simultaneously, every effort will be made to promote measures to develop new uses for primary products and to secure stability of prices for them.

(29) The practice of tying aid inhibits the development of mutually beneficial trade among developing countries; there is urgent need for untying it at lease in favour of all developing countries.

(30) The desire of developing countries to concert measures of intensifying mutually advantageous economic co-operation amongst themselves has yet to express itself in practical forms and institutions. Government proposes to play an active role in promoting economic co-operation in Asia and strengthening its economic links with other developing countries in Africa and Latin America.

(31) Efforts will also be made to ensure that the enlargement of European Economic Community, instead of diminishing, expands our trading opportunity in that part of the world. Trade development programmes will be launched and wherever necessary appropriate agreements will be negotiated for the expansion of exports to other industrial countries, including the United States and Japan, Medium-term agreements for the expansion of trade with the Soviet Union and another Socialist countries will be negotiated. Arrangements will also be made to intensify commercial and industrial co-operations with them.

(32) It is to be hoped that the declaration to be adopted by the United Nations on the Second Development Decade will make adequate provision for concerted international measures to secure adequate increases in the export income of all developing countries including India.

(33) While the importance of international co-operation for exports cannot be overemphasized, co-operation within the country in the export effort is no less essential a prerequisite for its success. A steady growth of export earnings at the rate of 7 per cent per year can be achieved only if adequate export performance is accepted as a national goal of very high priority. The Central Government is committed to pursuing vigorously appropriate policies to this end. A similar commitment is necessary from State Governments. Local bodies and all the sectors of the economy and the sections of society are vitally concerned with the export effort. The co-operation of agricultural, mineral and industrial producers in sustaining, expanding and re-orienting production, of the consumers in voluntarily restraining their consumption, of labour and management in maintaining an atmosphere of industrial peace, and of manufacturer exporters in cultivating export markets will be actively sought.

(34) In placing this statement on export before Parliament, Government of India trusts that the exports will be viewed as one of the highest national commitments and that the people will extend to it their whole-hearted support and accord due recognition to those engaged in it.

## ANNEXURE II

### Speech by Commerce & Industry Minister on Release of Annual Supplement April 2008

*(Speech of Shri. Kamal Nath, Union Minister of Commerce and Industry, Government of India)*

Four years ago I had announced India's first ever integrated Foreign Trade Policy for the period 2004-2009. I had then indicated two major objectives, namely (a) to double our share of global merchandise trade within 5 years, and (b) to use trade expansion as an effective instrument of economic growth and employment generation.

I am pleased to say that our achievements have exceeded our expectations. Not only have we fulfilled our promises in substantial measure, but we have achieved these remarkable results in just four years, instead of five.

In 2004 our exports stood at a little over $ 63 billion, In 2007-08, they have exceeded $ 155 billion; our exports are not only just double what they were four years ago, but 2 ½ times that. We have managed an average cumulative annual growth rate (CAGR) of 23%, year on year, way ahead of the average growth rage of international trade.

Our total merchandise trade – exports and imports together – will be almost 400 billion US dollars this year; accounting for nearly 1.5% of world trade. If the trade in services is added to this, our commercial engagement with the world would be in the region of 525 billion US dollars.

We have delivered on our second objective as well; that of fashioning trade into an instrument of economic growth and employment generation. Our total trade in goods and services is now equivalent to almost 50% of our GDP. This is unprecedented in India's modern economic history.

On the issue of employment it is our estimate that during the last 4 years, increased trade activity has created 136 lakh new jobs. I have always maintained that exports are not just about earning foreign exchange but about boosting our manufacturing sector, creating large-scale economic activity and generating fresh employment opportunities.

The Special Economic Zones polity is a case in point. The Government sees SEZs as vehicles of industrialization and employment generation. Till now we have granted 453 formal approvals for setting up of SEZs. 207 out of these have been notified, and are at various stages of implementation and operation. I am particularly happy to say that approvals are not restricted to a few states, but spread over 19 States and 3 Union Territories. SEZs currently provide employment to more than 2.80 lakh people. The incremental employment generated by these SEZs since February 2006 is 1.5 lakh. In the last 3 years, the exports from SEZs have shown an increase of over 150%. It is projected that the exports from SEZs would reach Rs.1,25,000 crores by the end of this financial year. Developments of this nature re-assure us of the validity of the basic policy relating to SEZs, notwithstanding the skepticism expressed by a few persons.

What is more remarkable about all our achievements is that they have been accomplished in the face of appreciation of the rupee (by more than 12% in the last year alone), high interest rates, spiraling oil prices, withdrawal of some GSP benefits to India by other countries and a general international economic slowdown in some of our major trade markets. In spite of all this our exporters have shown great resilience. For this, they deserve our congratulations.

It is in this context that I am happy to present the final Annual Supplement to the Foreign Trade Policy for 2004-2009. In this supplement, we have proposed several innovative steps:

(1) I firmly believe that there must be stable Policy environment for the exporters. Accordingly, we have extended the DEPB Scheme till May 2009.

(2) To ensure that terminal excise duty and CST refund is made to the exporters in time, it has been decided that interest @5% per annul shall be paid by the Government to the exporter, In case refund is not made within one month of its becoming due. I know we have made this announcement last year. Thus, to honour my commitment, I announce that this refund along with interest will be paid on all such claims that have become due on or after 1.4.2997

(3) To become competitive in international markets, our factories and service providers need to have state-of-the-art machinery and equipment. Through the EPCG, the Government has been incentivising exporters to modernize the customs duty payable under EPCG from 5% to 3%. Further, exports made towards fulfillment of export obligation under EPCG shall also be eligible for incentives/rewards under promotional schemes.

(4) Last year Govt. had announced a reduced rate of interest to the exporters in sectors affected by rupee appreciation, and to SMEs. I am happy to announce that Government has decided that these reduced rates shall be continued for another year.

(5) The Average export obligation under EPCG Scheme for the year 2007-08 will be lowered for those sectors or product groups, which have a decline in export of more that 5% in 2007-08. Further premier trading houses would be given the option, on request, to refix their average export obligation based on the average of their exports of last 5 years instead of 3 years.

(6) 100% EOUs have been contributing significantly to our national export efforts. Export by these units has crossed Rs.125000 crores in 2007-08, which is approximately one-fifth of our total exports. The income tax exemption available to these 100% EOUs under section 10B of Income Tax Act is to expire on

31.3.2009. I am pleased to announce that this exemption will be extended for one more year, beyond 2009.

Further, EOUs operating in textile and granite sector shall be required to pay only excise duty on their DTA sale, in case the use of duty paid imported inputs is up to 3% of the FOB value of exports. This measure will provide the EOUs, greater operational flexibility.

(7) India produces 11% of the world's vegetables and 15% of its fruits. Not only are we the second largest producer, but we also produce them at a very competitive cost. According to the World Bank, our cost of vegetables is half the average of global prices, and that of fruits is two thirds of global prices. Unfortunately, our share in world trade in fruits and vegetables has remained dismal at 1.7% and 0.5% respectively. The major handicap suffered by our exporters of fruits, vegetables and flowers is high incidence of transport cost; domestic as well as international. To partially neutralize this disadvantage I announce that for specific fruits, vegetables and flowers, an additional duty-free credit scrip of 2.5% over and above the existing available under VKGUY.

(8) India has a varied toys and sports goods industry, predominantly in the unorganized sector, which is more than 100 years old. The two major clusters of sports goods industry, at Meerut and Jalandhar, provide employment to a large number of people, including those of minority communities. India has a minuscule share of less than 1% in world sports and toys exports. To promote exports from this sector, I announce an additional credit of 5% over and above the credit available under focus product scheme for these products. Further, separate funds shall be marked for this sector under ongoing Market Development Assistance (MDA) Scheme and Market Access Initiative (MAI) Scheme.

(9) Our capability and expertise in IT software is internationally established. Now, there is a need to focus on strengthening our manufacturing and export capabilities in IT hardware sector. We are bringing this sector in Special focus initiative this year. Specific items of this sector shall be made eligible for benefits under High Tech Product. Export Promotion Scheme. Further, funds would be specifically earmarked for this sector under the ongoing MDA and MAI Schemes.

(10) The Government has already announced refund of service tax on almost all the services, which are directly relatable to export production and supply. A number of services related to export, which do not attract service tax have been identified and a Circular is being issued to inform the exporting community. The remaining issues regarding refund of service tax on services linked to exports will also be resolved shortly.

(11) It has been the endeavour of the Government to reach "zero rating" of exports, so far as domestic taxes is concerned. The Government is seized of the issue that a number of State taxes are not being refunded to exporters. The

Government is looking into formulation of a scheme for rebating these taxes. With urgency.

(12) To promote export of high value added manufactured products, I announce an enhanced incentive under focus product scheme @ 2.5% for products, which would be notified separately.

(13) Our exporters are really going places! To encourage them on their voyage of discovery, I announce including of another 10 countries within the ambit of Focus Market Scheme. These countries include Mongolia, Bosnia-Herzegovina, Albania, Macedonia, Croatia, Honduras, Djibouti, Sudan, Ghana and Colombia.

(14) The focus products and focus markets schemes would be calibrated, so that some products of high export intensity (which are presently not covered under FPS) but which have low penetration in countries (which are presently not covered under FMS), would be considered for export incentive as a focus product for that country. We would invite suggestions from the Export Promotion Councils in this regard.

(15) Under the Industrial Park Scheme, administered by the Department of Industrial Policy and Promotion besides manufacturing, it has now been decided to include, IT, ITES and R &D in Natural Sciences and Engineering, as industrial activities permitted in the parks.

(16) Last year I had announced the formation of the Export Promotion Forum for Telecom to boost exports in the telecom sector. The exports from this sector are likely to touch Rs.4,000 crores this year, up from Rs.1800 crores last year. This is likely to exceed Rs.10,000 crores by 2011, To encourage this sector, I am pleased to announce the establishment of an Export Promotion Council for Telecom.

(17) Export Credit Guarantee Corporation of India (ECGC) has completed fifty years of operations. With the establishment of National Export Insurance Account (NEIA), ECGC now provides credit risk insurance cover even to high risk countries where such insurance cover was not earlier provided. NEIA has already provided Rs.396 crores to ECGC and a balance amount of Rs.1704 crores will be provided during the current plan period to enhance ECGC's under-writing capability. ECGC has also reduced its premium by more than 10% to provide relief to exporters affected by rupee appreciation.

(18) The time period for re-import of branded jewellery remaining unsold has been extended from 180 days to 365 days. The facility of export on consignment basis has been extended to the export of coloured gem stones. At present in case of exports through Foreign Post Office, value of jewellery parcels is limited to US $ 50,000. The limit is now raised to US % 75,000.

(19) To curb inflation on essential commodities, Government has banned export of non-basmati rice, edible oils and pulses. Benefits under DEPB Scheme

have been withdrawn on export of rice, cement and primary steel items. We are also withdrawing the incentives under promotional scheme (FMS) on export of cement and primary steel items.

(20) Every now and then I come across surveys by reputed international and domestic organizations pointing out the distressing fact that transaction costs – in both money and time –for exporters in India are very high. In the last four years we have taken a number of steps to reduce these costs. Introduction of e-commerce in Government, removal of controls and simplification of procedure have been pursued relentlessly. Apparently, a lot more needs to be done. In the last year of this Policy period, we proposè additional measures towards this end:

(i) Advance Authorisation Scheme and EPCG Scheme will be brought under the EDI system with effect from 1.7.2008.

(ii) With effect from 1.1.2009, all existing EDI ports will be treated as a single port and there will be no requirement of TRA under Advance Authorisation.

(iii) Payment of duty under ePCG Scheme, through debit of DEPB or other duty credit scrips would be allowed w.e.f. 1.1.2009.

(iv) To facilitate faster clearance of deemed export benefits, Central Excise authorities will now endorse the supply invoices within 21 days.

(v) A few additional ports havc been included under export promotion schemes. This will help in reducing costs and adhering to delivery schedules. Some more ports are also under consideration.

Similarly, a large number of other measures have been announced, details of which are given in the Annual Supplement.

We still face many structural problems which need to be addressed. We have to plan an integrated strategy to tackle these issues. I announce the setting up of a joint task force of representatives of the Central Government,

State Government, Panchayati Raj Institutions, Industry and Exporters to draw up, within six months, a detailed Action Plan as a roadmap to achieve this objective.

The key elements of this strategy that the JTF will be mandated to look at would include:

(a) Development of world-class infrastructure to facilitate trade involving an investment of over $ 800 bn in infrastructure.

(b) Trade facilitation through EDI, such that the waiting periods at ports, airports and ICDs and Land Customs Stations, would match world standards; of 2 hours of less.

(c) The development of global manufacturing hubs in selected sectors like auto components, generic drugs, gems and jewellery, handicrafts, textiles, petro products etc.

(d) The development of global services hubs, not only in IT but also in KPO, industrial design, research and development and product testing.

(e) The development of a chain of sector-specific skill development institutes, so that trained manpower is available for all sectors.

(f) In line with the Government's policy that no duty and taxes should be exported, early implementation of GST and simultaneous reimbursement of the remission or refund of all taxes & levies.

(g) Encouraging e-commerce through robust implementation of e-governance at all levels.

You are aware that negotiations for further liberalization of trade under WTO are continuing since 2001. This indecisiveness at the World Trade Body is not on account of any unreasonable positions of developing countries like India. The negotiations remain inconclusive on account of the recently discovered fear and shyness from trade liberalization by the developed countries. We remain committed to a fair, rule bound international trading order, where the developing countries have an equal say and share. We will continue our endeavour to protect our farmers from the trade distorting subsidies provided in developed countries. We will also ensure adequate safeguards for protection of our small and tiny industries and we will continue to seek enhanced market access for our goods and services.

The remarkable achievements in trade and commerce of the past four years gives me the confidence to spell out an even more ambitious target – that of achieving a 5% share in world trade by the year 2020. In practical terms this means a four-fold increase in our percentage share in the next 12 years. Considering that world trade is itself increasing, this would translate into an eight-fold increase in absolute terms. Ambitious the target may be, but achieving it is not impossible. It means we would have to ensure an average annual growth rate of 25% but achieving it is not impossible. It means we would have to ensure an average annual growth rate of 25% consistently for the next 12 years. To begin with, I set a target of $200 billion for exports during the current year.

The task is difficult, but the prize is great. If we achieve it, India will once more become the trading superpower it was two centuries ago.

❖ ❖ ❖

# 8

# EXPORT PRICING AND COSTING

Pricing decisions play a significant role in the marketing of any product in the export market. Unfortunately, no simple mathematical formula is available for an international marketer in arriving at the right pricing decision. No doubt, as in the domestic market, the interaction of the market forces like demand and supply affect the price at which the product can be sold in the export market.

The conditions obtaining in the export market are entirely different from those in the domestic market. International markets are characterized by the existence of a large number of suppliers, and thus conditions akin to 'Open Market' situations often occur. Given the quality of the product, the market share that an export product is likely to enjoy would largely depend on its price.

Before we go into the area of costing one important factor in arriving at the export price of a product should not be forgotten.

The actual price of the product in the market place – in other words, the price at which a similar product is sold in the international market – will determine the maximum price one can get for the product. Whatever the costing or price build up of a product we do in our calculations, it is essential that the selling price of the product in the country to which it is exported cannot be more than the selling price of a similar product in that market. This will be the ultimate determining factor of the export price of a product.

The manufacturing cost of a product plays an important role in determining its final selling price in the export market. After all, a company or a corporation is in business to earn a reasonable profit, and therefore would, as far as possible, endeavour to recover at least the costs incurred by it in manufacturing and marketing its product, with a margin. It is possible that under certain circumstances, business organizations may decide to sell their products lower than the cost prices. But they would do so with the definite objective of gaining a foothold in a new market, or of sustaining their own market participation for a short while till prices pick up.

## FACTORS INFLUENCING PRICING

A student of international marketing should understand that there are certain costs which are relevant only to export operations. As such, he should be thoroughly familiar with the total composition of the various costs that go to make up the export price of a product. A thorough understanding of the price structure is thus essential for determination of prices in the export market. We deal more with this later in the chapter.

Invariably, prices of different products in international markets are accepted in certain specified forms - f.o.b., c.i.f., etc. which are internationally known. These price quotation terms should be thoroughly understood before prices in international markets are offered or quoted. A detailed explanation of this is also given later in the chapter.

Thus, a combination of factors will have to be considered before a pricing policy is adopted for an export market. We shall discuss in detail these factors in the ensuing pages of this chapter.

Let us see how these factors work out in the field, taking a manufactured product as example.

## COSTING

The cost of a product may broadly be classified into two groups:

*(a)* Ex-factory costs.

*(b)* Sales and distribution overheads.

The ex-factory cost of a product includes all the costs incurred on it till it leaves the factory premises. This cost may be split into the following elements for the purpose of analysis of costs:

(a) The ex-factory cost of a product can be broadly stated as follows:

Ex-Factory Cost = Direct Cost plus Indirect Cost plus Factory Overheads.

**Direct cost or Variable Costs:** This is also sometimes known as "primary cost". All elements of cost that vary linearly with the volume of production are grouped under this category. The various components of costs into which this may be further broken are:

*(i)* Direct Labour Cost: Cost of labour like wages, etc. that are directly related to the production of a product from raw material stage to finished component stage.

*(ii)* Direct Material: All materials that form part of the products including raw materials, components, bought out items, etc.

*(iii)* Direct Expenses: Any other expenditure that can be directly related to the production of goods and which increases proportionately with the volume of production.

**Indirect Costs:** These may also be grouped into:

*(i)* Indirect Labour: Wages and salaries of supporting services like plant maintenance, quality control, etc., functions which are not directly related to production, but essential for production.

*(ii)* Indirect Material: Costs of all materials that do not form part of a product but which, at the same time, are essential for its production. Some examples are cost of lubricants, coolants, oils, and other consumable items used in the manufacture of the product.

*(iii)* Indirect Expenses: All other expenses necessary for the manufacture of the product like lighting charges, heating charges, etc.

**Factory Overheads or Fixed Costs:** These include all other costs not covered by direct and indirect costs. Interest on capital, depreciation, salaries for factory and office staff, rentals, welfare services, etc., are included in this category of costs.

It may be noted that Direct Costs vary with production volume, and every additional unit produced adds to the total cost. As against this, "factory overheads" are more or less fixed and remain constant regardless of the volume of production, or at best vary disproportionately with the volume of production.

(b) Sales and Distribution Overheads: These cover all the costs incurred from the time the product leaves the factory premises - the cost of transportation to the warehouse, salaries in the export department including those of sales personnel, advertising, sales promotional expenses, and establishment expenses of the export office. This cost is fixed and changes little with the volume of sales.

These are all the costs incurred inside and outside the factory before a product is ready for export. In addition to these costs, however, there are certain other cost elements which are exclusively incurred in exporting a product. A few of these relevant costs are enumerated below.

(i) **Export Packaging Costs:** Goods meant for export require special packaging to withstand rough handling in the process of loading and unloading at ports as also during long sea voyages. When goods are loaded, they need to be protected from the harmful effects of exposure to sea water and consequent deterioration. Special preventive treatments are carried out to avoid rusting owing to prolonged exposure to sea-water.

(ii) **Export Handling Charges:** Export handling charges include the cost of transportation of a product from warehouse to port, all storage charges before it is loaded on to a ship, payment of port dues, charges connected with documentation for export, etc. Sometimes, owing to circumstances beyond the control of the exporter, goods may have to lie in the dock premises for quite some time before they are loaded on to a ship. In such circumstances, port authorities, after an initial grace period of 7 days, levy a charge called "demurrage" charge towards storage and protection of these goods in the port premises.

(iii) **Sea-freight/Airfreight Charges:** Depending on the requirements of a customer, goods are shipped or dispatched by air. The freight charges, incurred by an export organisation in shipping or air freighting these also involve a certain amount of incidental charges for the purpose of export pricing. Freight charges are usually recovered from the customer at actuals.

(iv) **Insurance:** Goods for export are usually insured against damage, deterioration and loss during transit. An exporter, at the request of the customer, insures the goods as soon as they are shipped and recovers the charges from him. Insurance charges until goods are loaded are also a part of "direct cost" for the exporter and have to be included in his costing for the purpose of pricing the product.

(v) **Commission Payable to Agents Abroad:** Where the sales promotion of a product is sought to be achieved by the appointment of a suitable agent in the importing country whose function is to promote its sale, a predetermined commission is required to be paid to the agent on the sale price of the product. This commission also forms part of the cost of the product and should be taken into consideration while arriving at the export price.

It may be mentioned here that all the above costs, which are exclusively relevant for export operations, are direct in nature, i.e., they vary with the sales volume.

We have not mentioned the profit element in the cost price calculations. It can be taken as a separate element or included in the sales and distribution overheads.

## Break-even Point

In evaluating the cost of a product, the break-even point is the point where the cost of a product is equivalent to the fixed or variable cost, with little or no contribution to the sale and distribution overheads, and does not include any profit at all. In simpler words, any product sold below the break-even point incurs loss, and when sold above the break-even point makes a profit.

The break-even point assumes importance in the export of a product because in a competitive market, where an exporter wants to make an entry, he may choose to export at break-even point price until the product is well accepted , and then increase the price to get his profit.

After determining the costing, whatever the price at which he ultimately wants to sell the product in the export market, the possibilities are that the price at which a similar product is sold in an export market may be much higher than the price the exporter has arrived at. If this is the case, the exporter can afford to have a price slightly lower than the current selling price of a similar product in the export market.

The point here is that he should sell at a price close to the price of a similar product in the market, and not lower it considerably even if he can afford to.

On the other hand if the prices at which similar products are sold are less than the exporter's calculated price, he has to seriously consider whether it is worthwhile exporting to that country. Otherwise, he will have to reduce the production cost so that the export cost becomes close to the prices prevalent in that country.

## EXPORT OFFER

**Structure of Export Price:** Let us now consider the composition of the export price for a product in a particular market and how an offer can be prepared. We may list all the costs and the data required to be collected for export pricing.

(1) Ex-factory cost of product, plus export duty, if any

(2) Special packaging for export

(3) Transportation from factory to city warehouse

(4) Storage at city warehouse

(5) Inspection of goods by international inspectors or an Export Inspection Agency

(6) Transport from warehouse to docks,/airport

(7) Handling charges inside the port, including port dues, demurrage, if any, etc.

(8) Documentation for exports prior to shipment

(9) Documentation after shipment related to negotiation of documents

(10) Sea freight or airfreight charges

(11) Insurance premium charges

(12) Unloading charges at destination

(13) Import duty and taxes

(14) Clearing charges at destination

(15) Transportation to warehouse of buyers

(16) Buyer's profit margin

(17) Wholesaler's profit margin

(18) Retailer's profit margin

(19) Selling price.

All costs from 1 to 9 comprise the f.o.b (free on board) cost of a product.

If we add sea freight or air freight charges as well as the cost of insurance premium to f.o.b. cost, we shall obtain the c.i.f. cost of the product.

All the cost elements upto 11 comprising the c.i.f. cost of the product have already been dealt with in detail elsewhere in this chapter.

The unloading charges at destination relate to costs incurred in discharging the cargo from a ship to the wharf of a port. It will also include the dues to be paid to the port authorities. Thesc charges are normally included in the freight rate charged by a shipping company and as such, need not be considered separately.

Once the goods are discharged at the port of destination, they have to be cleared out of the customs and port area by the buyer. A certain amount of documentation relating to the clearance of goods is also involved in the process. All the charges incurred in clearing the goods out of the customs and port area - including the cost of documentation, handling inside the port, cost of storage, etc. – are covered by clearance charges at the destination. In view of the expertise required for the purpose of these functions, importers normally employ "clearing agents' who look after the clearance of goods from the ports. Where such agents are appointed, their charges, known as clearing agents' charges usually cover all the expenses coming under "clearing charges at destination.'

Import duties and taxes are usually levies collected at the destination port according to customs tariff regulations prevalent in the importing country. This is an important element in the cost structure of a product. In view of their desire to protect their domestic industries some countries charge high import duties. Hence, the significance of import duties and taxes in the final price of the product.

The c.i.f. cost, together with the import duties and taxes paid at the port of destination as also the clearance charges, constitute the landed cost of a product. In other words, it is the cost incurred in making a product available at the port of destination after clearing it out of the customs and port area, and making it ready for distribution in a market.

The cost elements 16, 17 and 18 relate to distribution costs and profit margins of the various functional groups in making a product available on the shelf of a retail store for the customer to buy.

## Quotation

As the basis of any export transaction is the "Quotation" as it is called, it is worth knowing certain important features of these. An offer or quotation is made in one of the following four ways:

*(a)* A proforma invoice indicating the price as well as other charges incurred in shipment. This invoice normally is an exact duplicate of the invoice which will be sent when the goods are exported. We should remember that proforma invoices are required by the buyers to obtain a letter of credit or allotment of foreign exchange in some countries. They have, therefore, to be very accurate.

*(b)* The quotation may be in response to a public tender floated by a buyer, in which case it should be comprehensive, covering all the conditions of the tender and listing out the prices, together with other charges such as freight, insurance, etc., and also the anticipated escalation, if any, in the price during a prolonged delivery period.

*(c)* The quotation may be in the form of a printed price list where the goods have a standard export price. One should take care to see that the terms and conditions of delivery, payment etc., are either included in the printed price list, or stated specifically in the accompanying letter.

*(d)* The quotation can also be given in the form of a letter indicating the price, terms of payment and the delivery period.

Whatever may be the mode of a quotation, it should be written in a simple and easily understandable style, and care should be taken to ensure that there is no scope for any different interpretation or for misunderstanding.

Delivery dates should be stated clearly. In case this is not done, it is assumed that delivery is made immediately on receipt of the order. One of the most common complaints against exporters is their inability to stick to delivery dates. Extra care should be taken in evaluating the manufacturing period, facilities for internal transport, shipping frequency, etc., so that realistic delivery dates may be offered and met.

## Export Contract

In the case of large exports, the offers given on acceptance are converted into a contract between the exporter and the buyer. The important elements of an **export contract** are:

(1) The specifications and the quantity of an export product

(2) The price

(3) Delivery dates

(4) Terms of payment

(5) Any specific responsibilities and rights of the party, such as inspection, etc.

(6) The law which governs the contract

(7) The provision for arbitration in the event of a dispute.

A contract should not be one-sided. If at all a dispute is referred to a court, the latter normally takes into consideration the intentions of both parties. Where a large and complicated contract is involved, it is better to check if there are legal problems which may arise in the importer's country and also ensure that the exporter is not subjected to any taxes and duties at a future date in the importer's country.

In order to have uniform export terms for delivery, "INCOTERMS" as they are called, are used all over the world. They indicate:

*(a)* The charge and expenses which must be paid by the seller.

*(b)* The place of delivery of the goods.

*(c)* The point in time when the goods and their transit risks are transferred.

Each term used covers these points. The common ones in use are:

Ex-works: Packing costs are paid by the exporter and delivery takes place at the works or a warehouse. The goods and transit risks are transferred to the buyer at the time of notification.

Ex-works price quotations are rarely used in international markets. For most standard products, no buyers would accept ex-works price quotations. However, for products such as complete plant and machinery, when it is difficult to estimate the cost of transportation, shipping freight, etc., in advance, ex-works quotations are usually accepted. Later, charges like transportation, shipping freight and insurance are charged at actuals and recovered from customers.

F.O.R. means "Free On Rail," and the exporter must pay all the costs until the goods are loaded into a railway wagon or a truck. Delivery takes place at the rail siding or at factory gates, while the goods and transit risks pass to the buyers when delivery is made to the carrier.

F.A.S.: This means "Free Alongside Ship" The exporter pays all the charges up to putting the goods alongside the ship, while putting them on the ship is at the buyer's expense. Where shipping companies accept goods "on stream" and where goods have to be moved by barges to the side of a vessel, an F.A.S. quotation should include barge charges as well. The goods and transit risks are transferred when the ship is able to load.

F.O.B. is one of the most common export terms, meaning "Free On Board." F.O.B. would mean that the exporter has the obligation to put the goods on board the ship. This would involve the exporter in the payment of port trust charges and other duties, if any, for completing the documentation and loading the goods on a ship. Delivery takes place when the ship has been loaded, and the goods and their transit risks are transferred when the goods go over the ship's rail.

For Indian conditions, the F.O.B. price of a commodity is significant. Even while price quotations of other types are submitted to foreign buyers, the F.O.B. price of a product should be desirable or at least identifiable in the entire pricing structure because all the export benefits offered by the Government of India are usually related to the F.O.B. price of a product.

C&F: This denotes "Cost and Freight" where, in addition to the responsibility and expenses to be incurred as in F.O.B. above, the exporter has also to pay ocean freight. Delivery takes place when the bill of lading is handed over, and the goods and transit risks are transferred as soon as the goods go over the ship's rails. (In other words, f.o.b price plus freight)

C.I.F means "Cost, Insurance and Freight", and would mean that all the cost, as in C&F above, together with Marine Insurance, are paid by the exporter. Here also delivery takes place when the bill of lading is handed over, and the goods and transit risks are transferred when the goods go over the ship's rails. (In other words, F.O.B. plus freight plus insurance).

FRANCO: In the broadest sense, "Franco" means that all the charges are paid by the exporter up to and including delivery to the buyer's warehouse, and this includes duty as well as landing charges and internal freight cost at the destination. Delivery takes place when the goods arrive at their final destination, and the goods and their transit risks are transferred when delivery is made.

## PRICING STRATEGIES

International marketing is characterised by severe competition among a large number of suppliers of the same product to a select group of customers. A customer thus has the choice of selecting any one of the brands of a product available, according to his taste and need. One's ability to hold one's own prices and still enjoy a good share of the market would depend on one's capacity for meeting and satisfying the customer's needs at the right time and at the right price. Thus, the pricing of a product is influenced by the entire range of marketing mix – the product itself, its quality and specifications, the promotional methods adopted, distribution setup, after sales service, packaging, personal selling, etc.

Most of the products in international markets are well established. Philips, Westing House, Colgate, Siemens, Sony etc, are practically household names and have established their own individual brand images. In view of this brand leadership, it is possible for them to realise a good price for their products. Similar goods from Indian manufacturers are comparatively unknown, (except those manufactured in collaboration with multi-national companies,) and require price support until they establish themselves in course of time.

The selling of certain commodities, like antiques and handicrafts from developing countries like ours, depend little on their prices because these commodities enjoy a fancy and prestige value.

Prompt deliveries and continuity of supplies influence to a large extent the pricing of the product. This is especially so in the case of consumer products, because their shelf life is low, and therefore continuous availability of these products is essential. If a particular brand of soap, tooth paste, or tea is not available when the customer needs it he is likely to change to another brand. Continuous availability may also create brand loyalty and therefore command a premium price as well.

Where a product is an engineering item, the provision of an efficient after-sales service may well become an important factor in its selling. An engineering item, if supported more than adequately by prompt after sales service, may well command a better price than similar items of other makes.

Similarly, ready availability of spare parts for the machinery and equipment which have been sold also influence the price that may be obtained for the product. Efficient and prompt after-sales service and spare parts availability create customer satisfaction and thus generate brand loyalty and confidence in the product.

Attractive packaging for products and impressive advertisement and sales promotion campaigns help to sell consumer products to a large extent.

Given the same condition, an aggressive marketing team with a committed field force would be in a position to evoke more favourable responses from customers and win a greater share of the market.

Sometimes, quick and ready deliveries earn an exporter premium prices for his product. In some products, Indian manufacturers possess the advantage of quicker deliveries compared to those of manufacturers from developed countries in Europe and America. Where Indian products lack the brand image of those of developed countries, they are still preferred and purchased by customers at attractive prices owing to faster deliveries by suppliers.

Very often, the ability to supply the complete range of products is essential for a successful marketing of products. Unfortunately, developing countries are not geared to achieve this simple requirement. For example, a customer in the construction business in the Middle East would like to purchase the entire range of construction equipment from one source. Most manufacturers in India do not produce the entire range and cover only one or two or at the most, a few items. Their inability to offer the entire package limits their chances of marketing their products. On the other hand, a company which offers the entire range is able to obtain good prices for its products.

These are some of the market factors that influence the price of a product.

Profit under certain circumstances, could be the chief motive in exporting certain products. India, with its vast population, offers a very good market for all goods and services, and a company whose management is not keen on export as a policy measure, may set for itself the objective of profit maximisation. In such situations, unless export operations result in profits similar to those made in domestic markets, the company may not be interested in export as a business proposition. There are also other factors which influence the cost.

Increasingly, most of the companies in the organised sector tend to look upon exports as a committed management philosophy. In export markets you are in a competitive environment and your products compete with those manufactured by other world-renowned manufacturers with a vastly superior technologies capability. Under such a competitive environment, you obtain valuable feedback information from the market, which helps you to improve your product and thereby helps you in consolidating your position in the domestic market. It is well worth keeping in mind that product improvement is a continuous process and in India where the entire domestic market for many products is protected, very little incentive is available for product improvement. A compulsion for improvement, however, arises when a management is committed to exporting its product. The sacrifice in time, effort and money towards commitment of resources is more than made up by the resulting benefits which product improvement may bring to the domestic market.

A company may plan to introduce its product in a particular export market. Export marketing usually offers fierce competition; there may already exist a large number of suppliers who have established channels of distribution and who enjoy a good market share, depending on their brand image. A new company has to introduce its product against this competition, and has therefore to make its purchase as attractive a proposition as possible, so that it may generate a certain amount of brand loyalty. In the absence of established channels of distribution and already existing brand image, the easy way in which a company can promote its product is by offering it at a very competitive price, perhaps at a price which is below its cost price. But this cannot last long.

A situation may also arise where a company has got its product well established in the export market. A new entrant arrives with high pressure sales campaign and large price discounts to capture a sizeable share of this market for his product. The existing exporting company, which considers this market a prestigious one, would not like to lose out to the new competitor and may be forced to offer matching discounts in prices to retain its share of the market.

These are some of the management policy decisions that would affect the pricing policy. It would be apparent from the foregoing discussions that management objectives for pricing decisions may vary from market to market.

## IMPACT OF INCENTIVES ON PRICING

In the sixties and seventies there were many hurdles for the export of Indian products. Taking them into consideration, government evolved a system of incentives to exporters to enable them to be competitive in the world market. Hence, it was essential to take the benefit of these incentives in arriving at an export price.

But after the reforms brought about by the government in 1991, it has withdrawn most of these incentives. There are hardly a few left, such as:

(a) Advance license to import raw materials and components without duty.

(b) Duty drawback – under this scheme the exporter gets a refund of duties – import duty on raw materials and components, and excise duty on locally bought out components.

As stated earlier, the effect of these concessions will not be much. In exports, there is always a sudden need for visits abroad, or test marketing products in new markets, or developing new products needed for the market, all of which can wipe away any benefits one gets through incentives.

We are at a stage when the export price is almost the same as domestic price, and it is better to base export pricing on this in the future, since it is government policy to eliminate all incentives.

## MARGINAL COSTING AND EXPORT PRICING

It is likely that, despite the assistance offered by government, the products exported may still not be competitive. In such an event, it is desirable to continue exports if the exporter is in a position to recover at least his variable costs. This is the basis on which marginal costing concept operates. It is in this context that an exporter should have a thorough knowledge of classification of cost into variable costs and fixed costs.

The use of marginal cost in the case of export markets is advocated on the grounds that if manufacturers are able to realize their direct cost and variable cost, they would be able to carry on their export operations without in any way jeopardizing the overall profitability of the company. Thus, in export operations, profitability has to be assessed with reference to variable cost and should constitute export pricing. In other words, profitability should be measured in terms of the contribution from exports.

The usefulness of marginal cost in export pricing is a debatable point. The contribution of fixed cost being a significant factor, it may be argued that the marginal costing system would be relevant only in industries whose capacities are not fully utilized, and the promotion of the exports of these companies would at least ensure for the manufacturer a recovery of a part of his fixed costs.

However, it would not be worthwhile for the manufacturer to sell his products at prices that do not even recover the variable costs incurred by him. Thus, the marginal cost indicates the lower limit of the price which a manufacturer can risk without unduly affecting his overall performance. It is interesting of add here that, for industries which are fully export-oriented, the total cost, including the fixed cost, constitutes the basis of the marginal cost concept.

## EXCHANGE RATES

One can give an export quotation to a foreign buyer either in Indian rupees, in the currency prevalent in the buyer's country, or in a third country currency which is accepted internationally for all export transactions, like the US Dollar.

In the case of the second option, the Indian exporter will be hesitant to give a quotation in the currency of the importing country as he will not be fully aware of the fluctuations in the value of the currency.

In the case of the third option, if it is accepted by the buyer, the exporter can be sure of exactly how many rupees he would get for his product. Most buyers prefer a third country currency such as US dollar as most of the import and export transactions worldwide are done in this currency.

One should know what is floatation in currency. Theoretically, the value of the country's currency is allowed to float in the international market, the rate going up or down *vis-à-vis* other currencies depending upon the demand and supply in the market.

The fluctuation in the exchange rate of the currencies, if it is of a high order, can wipe out all the profits, and even end in a loss for a particular export transaction. In many cases, the central government intervenes buying up the over supply in the market so that the currency does not fluctuate too much. But the ultimate help for the exporter is a forward contract.

Not withstanding all the above, it should be stated that almost 75% of the export – import transactions are usually done in terms of the US dollar. Hence, the price quotation given to a foreign country buyer is normally in US dollar.

Since the exporter from India does all his domestic transactions in Indian rupees, he would want to know what his export realization would be in Rupees even as he quotes in dollars.

# FORWARD CONTRACT

For the exporter's realization, there is a provision in the banks in India to take a 'Forward Contract'. Once an export order is obtained and the delivery of the product and the payment terms are firmly established, the exporter can negotiate with his bank a 'forward contract.' Through this the bank tells the exporter exactly what the rupee value would be when he negotiates his document with the bank after export, and how much in Indian rupees he would get after the export transaction. Whatever be the fluctuation in the value of the rupee *vis-à-vis* the dollar, the bank would give the exporter the money in Indian rupees as per the forward contract.

The exporter should be aware that if the delivery of the product is delayed by him and he is not in a position to complete the document and get it to the bank on the date agreed to in the forward contract, the forward contract becomes invalid, and he has to pay a small penalty.

There are a few terminologies used in export pricing strategies, and it is better to understand what they signify.

**(a) Market Penetrative Strategy:** Here, the aim of the exporter is to somehow get an entry (penetration) into the market. The presumption here is that once the product enters the market and the customers buy and use it, they will know its quality. After a certain period, the exporter can increase the price to his comfortable level. This can be used only if the exporter makes sure that his assessment is correct.

**(b) Market Skimming Price Strategy:** This strategy can be used on new and innovative products entering a market for the first time. The exporter can sell at a very high international price to achieve very good profit. The price can be later reduced to get more market penetration and higher sales.

**(c) Transfer Pricing:** These are prices fixed for intra-company transfers. If the product is produced by a company in country A and sent to its own fully owned subsidiary in country B, the price charged by the parent company to the subsidiary is referred to as Transfer Pricing. It is usually the right of the parent company to decide the price. The company will look at the possibility of making maximum profit, whereas the tax authorities in either country will check whether low or high pricing has resulted in evading taxes.

❖ ❖ ❖

# 9

# EXPORT FINANCE

The financial function in the export department is similar to the financial function in any other organisation, but with this essential difference – that there are a host of governmental, banking and export insurance regulation one should strictly adhere to, and quite a few precautions have to be taken, since the export deal will be in foreign exchange and any inept handling will result in a serious loss of foreign exchange, apart from the other consequences.

## Export Finance Needs

The areas where finance would be needed, after one obtains an export order will be:

*(a)* Procurement of raw materials and components, and manufacture of the product.

*(b)* Refinance facilities so as to get the proceeds of export bills at the time of negotiation of export documents, soon after shipping the goods.

*(c)* Availability of funds until the export benefits are realized.

(d) Refinance facilities for long-term credits offered for the export of products.

The schemes of export financing available to an exporter in India are reasonably liberal and it may be safely stated that no export contract would normally be frustrated for lack of finance. Financial institutions, like commercial banks, require basic procedural formalities to be completed between the buyer and the exporter to enable them to provide the necessary financial facilities to the exporter, whether such facilities extend over a short, medium or long-term.

Before we go into a discussion of the export financing aspect, let us first look at how an exporter gets paid for an export order. An understanding of this is essential because terms of payment between the exporter and the buyer form a significant part of the exporter's ability to obtain the necessary financial facilities from the banks.

## TERMS OF PAYMENT

The following are the usual payment terms in any export transaction:

*(a)* Payment by documentary credit

*(b)* Advance payment

*(c)* Cash against documents (CAD)

*(d)* Documents on acceptance (DA)

*(e)* Consignment basis

**(a) Payment by Documentary Credit** –

Export orders or contracts normally stipulate that the buyer should open a letter of credit in favour of the exporter. Once the goods are shipped, the exporter presents the negotiable documents against the letter of credit and receives payment. A letter of credit is an authority for payment for the exporter provided he does not violate any of its clauses.

Payment by a letter of credit (L/C) is not only one of the most secure methods of payment but also the most widely followed in international marketing.

## Letter of Credit

A letter of credit is a letter of payment authority issued by the buyer's bank at the behest of the buyer in favor of the exporter, and stipulates certain conditions, the performance of which fulfils the contractual obligations of the exporter and entitles him to receive payment. The letter of credit is routed through a bank in the exporter's country referred to as the negotiating bank.

The technical definition of a letter of credit is found in the ' Uniform Customs and Practices for Documentary Credits', where it is defined as "any arrangement, however named or described, whereby a bank (the issuing bank), acting on the request and in accordance with the instructions of the customer (the applicant for the credit), is to make payment to or to the order of the third party (beneficiary) or is to pay, accept or negotiate bill of exchange (drafts) drawn by the beneficiary, or authorizes such payments to be made or such drafts to be paid, accepted by another bank against stipulated documents provided that the terms and conditions of the credit are complied with."

Payment methods through a documentary letter of credit have a number of advantages. These are:

*(i)* Once the exporter fulfils all the conditions of credit and presents the documents for negotiation to his bankers in his own country, he receives his payment as per the terms of the letter of credit and is entitled to receive full payment for the exports he has made.

*(ii)* Once the letter of credit is established, the exporter may be reasonably sure that all the import trade regulations of the buyer have been complied with and that the transfer of funds against payment would not normally pose a problem from the exchange control authorities.

*(iii)* Where the letter of credit is a confirmed and without recourse one, the liability of the exporter ceases, once he has presented the negotiable set of documents and adhered to all the conditions of the L/C.

*(iv)* A letter of credit in India is an important document, for a commercial bank advances pre-shipment finance, such as packing credit, against the letter of credit.

**Parties to the Letter of Credit:** The various parties connected with the letter of credit are:

**Opener:** The buyer who makes application and on whose behalf the credit is opened is called the 'opener" of the letter of credit.

(i) **Beneficiary:** The beneficiary is the person in whose favor the credit is opened; normally the exporter.

(ii) **Opening bank:** The bank in the importing country which establishes the letter of credit on behalf of the opener.

(iii) **Negotiating bank:** Usually beneficiary's bank through which the documents are normally negotiated. It is also called the paying bank.

All the above parties have certain rights and responsibilities, which are enumerated in detail in the "Uniform Customs and Practices for Documentary Credit". Annexure I at the end of the chapter gives the complete details.

A few points must be kept in mind while accepting payment through a letter of credit. The letter of credit asked for should be – Capable of confirmation by the negotiating bank. It should be irrevocable and without recourse.

**(a) Confirmed Letter of Credit:** If the letter of credit by the opening bank is routed through the negotiating bank, which adds its own confirmation to the credit, the letter of credit is called a confirmed letter of credit. Confirmation by the negotiating bank entails a definite commitment on its part to carry out the provisions of payment. A confirmed credit thus carries with it the guarantee for payment from two banks – the opening bank and the confirming bank and is therefore a foolproof method of payment.

It should be remembered that the bank in India adds its confirmation after getting the necessary authorization from the issuing bank. Another method, which is sometimes resorted to, is for the opening bank to route its L/C through an internationally reputed bank abroad, which adds its confirmation when sending it to the negotiating bank.

**(b) Irrevocable Letter of Credit:** This would mean that a letter of credit cannot be modified or cancelled, once it is opened without the consent of the beneficiary. It is thus a firm commitment on the part of the opening bank.

**(c) Without-Recourse Letter of Credit:** Under without-recourse letter of credit, the opening bank cannot have recourse to the drawer of the bill (exporter) in case payment is defaulted by the opener. An irrevocable letter of credit by itself does not permit the opening bank to have recourse to the drawer. However, as an additional precautionary measure, it is advisable to have without-recourse letter of credit.

**(d)** There are two other variations in the letter of credit, which are rarely used but are prevalent in international trade:

1. *Transferable L/C:* In cases where the export product has to be fabricated partially or completely by a party other than the exporter, a portion or the full value of the letter of credit is made transferable to the party by means of the transferable L/C.

2. *Red Claused L/C:* This enables the beneficiary to draw a predetermined value of L/C, as soon as it is established, to enable him to process the product.

**(b) Advance Payment –**

When the buyer pays the export order/contract value to the exporter along with the confirmation of the order, he is stated to have made advance payment – that is, payment is made before the contractual obligations of supplying the goods are fulfilled. The remittance is normally made by a demand draft. This method of payment is rarely adopted, and is essential only when the buyer's credit worthiness is open to question.

**(c) Cash Against Documents –**

In this case, the goods are shipped and the negotiable documents are forwarded to the buyer through a bank and surrendered to him by the bank in his country on his payment for the goods. Until the payment is received from the buyer through his bank, the title to the goods rests with the exporter. Despite this, the exporter runs the risk of the buyer not accepting the documents. Export insurance should always be taken out on such deals. This point is dealt with later in this Chapter.

**(d) Documents on Acceptance –**

As is CAD type of payment, negotiable documents are sent through a bank to the buyer, the buyer signs the documents, accepting liability to pay as per the terms specified, and takes custody of the goods. The exporter runs the risk of the buyer not honoring his commitment even though he has taken possession of the goods. This kind of payment, however, is offered only to well established buyers who are credit worthy and whom the exporter has been dealing with for a long time. In these circumstances, it is essential that export credit insurance through the Export Credit & Guarantee Corporation (dealt with in detail in an earlier part of this Chapter) is always taken out.

**(e) Consignment Basis –**

It is often required that goods should be readily available in a foreign country so that "off-the-shelf" or quick delivery terms may be given to obtain an export order.

This is possible if the exporter can hold "consignment stocks" abroad; and the method by which this is done is as follows.

The exporter has his own establishment or appoints a reliable agent to hold the consignment stocks on his behalf abroad, who sells them as and when the demand arises, and repatriates the amount. It is essential to enter into a legally sound consignment contract with the agent, and get the Reserve Bank's approval for it. It is also necessary to take appropriate export credit from ECGC for such an operation.

In this arrangement, the export proceeds are received only as and when the goods are sold abroad and not at the time of shipment.

## Packing Credit/Pre-shipment Credit and Its Formalities

"Packing Credit" is the term used for the pre-shipment short-term finance obtained by an exporter through his bankers. A loan is granted to him by the bankers with the view to financing his manufacturing activity exclusively in relation to specific export order/contracts.

Application to the Bank: In order to avail himself of packing credit, an exporter has to make a formal application to his bank either in a specified format or make an ad hoc application, depending on the requirement imposed by the bank. To support his application, he should enclose:

(i) Firm contract with the buyer or export order;

(ii) Letter of credit received against the contract.

When the letter of credit has not been received by the exporter, he may avail himself of the packaging credit by furnishing the contract, and a letter confirming the order. The letter of credit and/or the contract in such cases should be presented to the bank which would endorse on it that packing credit has been availed of by the exporter on that particular contract.

When a confirmed letter is placed on an export house and a letter of credit opened accordingly, but the products for export are manufactured by, say, a small-scale industry, the manufacturer is eligible for packing credit from the bank. For this purpose, he should submit, along with his application for packing credit:

(i) A no-objection certificate from the export house, declaring that, against the specific contract, they have in turn placed their order on the small-scale unit and they have no objection if the manufacturer avails himself of packing credit to facilitate production.

(ii) A letter from the export house which has received the order stating that they would not avail of the packing credit against that portion of the order.

Amount of Loan: The amount of packing credit loan depends on the f.o.b. value of goods and the incentives thereof, and generally conforms to the norms set up by the ECGC under its Export Production Finance Guarantee Schemes. The limits laid down for this purpose by the ECGC are 50% over and above the f.o.b. value of the goods, subject to a maximum of 100% of the domestic cost of the export product. The ECGC covers the financial risk of the bank while such packing credit loans are extended.

Period for which Packing Credit Loans are Available: Packing credit loans are usually made available for 180 days. The period of credit may further be extended beyond 180 days, up to 270 days, with the prior approval of the Reserve Bank of India.

Interest Charges: These change periodically, and banks should be referred to know the prevailing rates. However the rates as of 16th August 2008 were as follows:

Export credit for 180 days:

With turnover less than 200 crores : 11%

With turnover more than 200 crores : 10.5%

Beyond 180 days up to 270 days :15%

Beyond 270 days up to 360 days :17%

**Post-Shipment Finance – Short-term**

Once goods are exported as per the terms of the contract, the exporter negotiates the documents through a bank with a view to realising the proceeds according to the payment terms agreed upon. If the payment terms are by a confirmed, irrevocable documentary credit, and if the exporter complies with all the conditions of the L/C, the exporter realises the full value of the goods exported against the presentation of documents to the negotiating bank in India. The bank purchases the bills.

If the goods exported attract export benefits, say, duty drawback, the exporter has to make a separate application to the concerned authorities, together with a proof of export or such other documents as are necessary to recover these receivables as well. Owing to the procedural formalities involved these incentives – such as drawback of duty – is received only after a lapse of some time after the exports.

In cases where the payment terms are other than through an L/C, say CAD (cash against documents), or D.A. (documents against acceptance), the exporter is normally paid only after the payment is received by his bank from the buyer.

Sometimes, an exporter offers payment facilities of 30 days, 60 days or 90 days from the date of the bill to his foreign buyer. Payment in such cases will be received only after the due dates of the bills.

Where the exporter has agreed to give credit, as mentioned above, to a foreign buyer, a "Usance Bill" is drawn, which is a draft for payment on a specified date later than the date of presentation. The usance bill or draft must bear a stamp duty before it becomes legally acceptable. This usance draft is accepted by the importer before he receives the custody of documents to take possession of the goods.

A definite period elapses before an exporter realises full payment for the goods exported.

As a measure of export promotion and to help the exporter to continue his export endeavors, the Reserve Bank of India has spelt out a scheme of post shipment finance. As per this scheme, a loan or credit is provided by a commercial bank to an exporter for the period between the date of actual shipment and the date of realisation of payment.

In the case of post-shipment credit, usance bills are normally drawn, and the interest rate applicable to them are as follows, as on 16th August 2008:

For transit period : 11%

as specified by FEDAI

For transit plus 30 days : 14.5%

For transit plus 180 days : 16.5%

Beyond six months : 17%

Credit is extended to the exporter against the bill of exchange drawn by him on the foreign buyer by discounting the bill or by giving an advance against the bill.

In extending this post-shipment credit; the following points should be borne in mind.

Terms of Payment: The various methods of payment terms for export transactions have been mentioned elsewhere in this chapter. Their relevance in the discounting of bills of exchange is discussed here.

If the payment is against a documentary letter of credit, which is confirmed and irrevocable, bills of exchange drawn on a foreign buyer against the letter of credit are accepted by a bank for discounting without any hesitation. Banks, however, thoroughly examine whether all the conditions stipulated in the letter of credit have been satisfied while drawing the bill of exchange. Once they are satisfied, the bill of exchange would be automatically discounted by them or an advance given against the bill of exchange.

If the bills of exchange on the buyer are on CAD basis or, for that matter, on DA basis, they are called collection bills. Banks may decide to advance money to an exporter against these bills. Before doing so, however, banks may usually obtain a credit report on the buyer on whom the bill is drawn through their correspondents in the foreign country. A good credit report is essential for the banks to allow discounting facilities to the exporter.

The same criterion is also adopted by banks while discounting bills drawn for fixed sums payable at 30, 60 and 90 days, as the case may be, after the date of the bill.

Credit Limit of an Exporter: Before accepting bills for discounting, banks normally ascertain the credit worthiness of an exporter and fix a limit for the credit offered to him. The bills of exchange are discounted against this limit. The limit is usually revolving in nature.

Rate of Negotiations: The rate at which negotiation is done depends on:

(a) The currency of the bill of exchange;

(b) The standing of the export organization – drawee;

(c) The payment terms – whether it is a bill against documentary credit, D/A, etc; and

(d) Period of maturity.

When bills are drawn for payment after 30, 60 and 90 days, a flat percentage rate is charged after taking into consideration the prevailing interest rate, the period of maturity of bill, and service charges for the collection of the bill, as also a certain amount of contingency allowance for the delay in banking channels.

It would help the exporter in obtaining the post-shipment as well as pre-shipment finance facilities if he carries a suitable ECGC policy for his export transactions. Normally, where the advances are huge, banks insist on the exporter taking a specific shipment or contract risk policy of the

ECGC before advancing loans to him. The details of various ECGC policies and their bearing on export finance are discussed later in this chapter.

## Post shipment Finance - Medium and Long-Term

Credits extended beyond 180 days are classified under medium and long-term credit. Those offered for a period of six months to five years are generally classified under medium-term credit and those beyond five years, under long-term credits.

When does the need arise for an exporter to approach the bank for post-shipment credit of medium and long-term loans? Often, an exporter is faced with a situation where he has to offer long-term payment terms to his customer. Especially in promoting the export of sophisticated engineering goods and turnkey jobs, payment terms extending over a few years are an essential pre-requisite. Such payments are usually called **deferred payments.**

Before we discuss financing under deferred payment terms, let us understand what deferred payment means to an exporter.

**Deferred Payment Terms:** Our exchange control regulations stipulate that payments for exports should be received in India within six months from the date of exports. In the case of Afghanistan and Pakistan, payment should be received within three months.

Where payments for exports are to be received after the six-month limit stipulated by the Exchange Control Department, a specific permission for such payment has to be obtained from that department.

Under a typical deferred payment contract, an exporter agrees to dispatch the goods to the buyer on (a) payment of initial sum of 20% of the contract value, (b) the balance amount of the contract value to be paid over a period of, say five years, in equal amounts or semi-annual installments, and (c) the interest charges at a fixed rate to be paid on the same installment basis on reducing balances.

A student of export marketing should understand the following salient features of the deferred payment terms for exports:

Normally in India, as stated earlier, payment within 180 days from the date of shipment is referred to as short-term credit. The credit extended between 180 days and 5 years is referred to as medium-term and anything beyond 5 years is known as long-term.

These kinds of medium and long-term credits are required for the export of capital goods and equipment, turnkey projects, etc.

For the guidance of the exporter, the Reserve Bank of India has provided an indicative list of items in respect of which facilities may be granted for export on deferred payment terms (See Annexure III).

**Period of Credit:** For capital and producer goods (Part A of the list), credit periods extending between 2 and 10 years may be offered, depending on the value of the contract, and normal business practice.

For consumer and other engineering goods (Part B of the list), credit is for a shorter period. Under no circumstance, however, should the credit offered exceed the life of the product. Refer Annexure II for products under Group A and Group B.

Credit for turnkey jobs and projects involving civil constructions, erection, etc., would be dealt with on the merits of the case.

**Advance Payment/Down Payment:** An advance payment equivalent to at least the foreign exchange outgo of the contract should be obtained. This foreign exchange outgo is computed on the basis of import inputs in the manufacture of a product, foreign commission payable, freight charges, etc. The advance payment in such cases usually works out at 20% to 25% of the contract value, provided that the import inputs are not of a high order.

**Deferred Installments:** The balance amount of the contract value for which deferred credit is offered is to be normally paid in equal half yearly installments over the agreed period. For the deferred installments, the exporter should obtain an irrevocable letter of credit confirmed by a foreign bank or a bank guarantee from an acceptable bank abroad to cover the deferred receivable and interest there on. A repayment guarantee from the Central Bank of the country guaranteeing the release of the foreign exchange at the appropriate time for the repayments of the deferred installments, together with the guarantee of the finance ministry will be acceptable where credits have been extended to government organisations in lieu of foreign bank guarantees.

It is advisable to check with the Exim Bank of India for the interest on these deferred payment transactions.

**Insurance on Deferred Receivables:** It is essential to take an insurance cover for all deferred payment contracts, against payment risks. Hence, the actual cost of credit to an exporter will consist of the bank interest and the ECGC charges.

## Foreign Exchange Cover

The foreign exchange market is unpredictable. The parity of Indian rupees with American Dollar changes everyday, and is capable of fluctuation. Over and above this, there is always a possibility of devaluation of a currency by the Government which changes the position overnight.

In order to protect the exporter against these fluctuations, and ensure he gets his payment in rupees in the way he had planned, the banks provide an exchange risk cover. This simply means that the exporter sells forward the currency to his bank under its Purchase Forward Exchange Contract. To put it in simpler terms, the exporter, once he exports, gets into a forward cover scheme with the bank, according to which he would receive a predetermined amount in Indian currency, irrespective of the fluctuation of American Dollar to the Indian rupee between the date of shipment and the date of receipt of the remittance from abroad. He has to pay a premium to the bank.

Where a contract is concluded in foreign currency and deferred installments are to be received in foreign currency, a forward exchange cover is to be taken out by an exporter with ECGC. The forward exchange cover guarantees a minimum exchange realisation for the foreign currency and covers the risk against devaluation of foreign currency. Annexure IV gives details of the scheme.

**Pre-shipment Finance:** The procedures adopted for pre-shipment credit against a deferred contract are the same as those applicable to short-term contracts. Pre-shipment credit is allowed by banks against a contract/letter of credit.

**Post-shipment Finance:** When an exporter enters into a deferred payment contract, the entire contract value, excluding the advance payment received by him, is realised by him over an extended period of, say, up to 5 years. This imposes a severe burden on his finances. To relieve him of this burden, as also to give incentives to exporters, the Reserve Bank of India has authorised commercial banks to extend to the exporters a "Term Export Credit" as post-shipment credit.

Depending on the nature of the deferred payment contract, post-shipment credit is given either directly by a commercial bank or in collaboration with Exim Bank.

## EXIM BANK OF INDIA

The Export-Import Bank of India (EXIM Bank) is a public sector financial institution, established on January 1, 1982. It has taken over the various export financing functions of the Industrial Development Bank of India. It was established by an Act of Parliament for the purpose of financing, facilitating and promoting foreign trade of India. It is the principal financial institution for co-ordinating the working of institutions engaged in financing export and import. The EXIM Bank Act also empowers the bank to finance export of consultancy and related services, finance export-oriented industries and provide international merchant banking services.

Lending Programmes: The main focus of EXIM Bank operation is on export credits for medium-term and long-term exports. Whenever a buyer of exported goods services from India, is allowed to defer payment, an export credit arises. Deferred export credit is available for the sale of Indian machinery, manufactured equipment and related services. Capital goods eligible for export credit have been identified.

It is divided into group A which is eligible for term credit beyond 12 years, and group B which is eligible for credit upto a maximum of 2 years (Details in Annexure II).

Such credit given may be in the form of supplier's credit or buyer's credit. Supplier's credit arises when an Indian exporter extends credit to the overseas buyer and finances himself through EXIM Bank. The bank extends credit directly to the buyer.

EXIM Bank operates three broad programmes of financing. These are – Loans, Re-discounting and Guarantees.

The Lending and Rediscounting programmes are divided into nine categories as indicated below:

**(a) Provide financial assistance to exporters** – This enables the Indian exporter to extend term credit to an importer overseas for the purchase of Indian capital goods. The exports include equipment, machinery and related services, projects exports, turnkey projects, construction projects etc. Export of this nature arises when an Indian company contracts supply agreements for the supply of equipments and services or a project export agreement involving the setting up of a textile mill, sugar plant, etc. The details are given in Annexure III.

**(b) Technology and consultancy services** – Indian companies borrow funds from EXIM bank and provide deferred credit to overseas buyers of

Indian technology or consultancy services. The details of this are given in Annexure IV.

**(c) Overseas investment financing** – The bank provides financing where an Indian company establishes a joint venture overseas, and requires funds towards equity participation.

**(d) Pre-shipment credit** – This loan of credit is available for companies that have won an export contract for capital goods and are seeking finance to produce the goods which entails a production period exceeding six months.

**(e) Overseas buyer's credit** – This is offered directly to foreign importers for the import of Indian capital goods and relative services with repayment terms spread over a period of years.

**(f) Lines of credit to foreign governments** – Lines of credit are offered to foreign government and foreign financial institutions. Such lines provide long-term finance for import of Indian capital goods, and related services. Annexure II gives details of such schemes.

**(g) Re-lending facility to banks overseas** – This facility to overseas banks is made available to enable them to provide term finance to importers for import of Indian capital goods. The overseas bank will facilitate the foreign buyer, they EXIM Bank, and supplier to avail of these facilities.

**(h) Export bills re-discounting** – This lending programme is available to commercial banks in India who are authorised to deal in foreign exchange. Such banks can re-discount their short-term usance export bills with the EXIM Bank. Exim Bank provides funds under this programme for a period of 90 days.

**(i) Refinance of export credit** – Under this programme, the commercial banks in India, who are authorised to deal in foreign exchange, can obtain from EXIM Bank 100% refinance of term loans extended for export of Indian capital goods. This credit is limited up to Rs.1 crore. For contract above Rs.1 crore, commercial banks can obtain financing participation under EXIM Bank's other programmes.

## Guarantees

The guarantee programme is available in the case of construction and turnkey contracts. Construction contract involves erection, civil works and commissioning. In a turnkey contract, say for setting up of a textile mill, supply of equipment accounts for the major value of the contract. In such contracts an Indian exporter usually requires bid bond, advance payment guarantee, performance guarantee, guarantee for retention money and guarantee for borrowings abroad. EXIM Bank participates with commercial banks in India in the issue of guarantees.

## Advisory Services

Through its International Merchant Banking Division, Exim Bank offers the following advisory services:

*(a)* Advise small-scale manufacturers on export markets and product areas;

*(b)* Work closely with Indian companies in designing financing packages for joint ventures in third countries;

*(c)* Advise Indian companies executing contract abroad on sources of favourable overseas financing;

*(d)* Provide access to Euro-financing sources and global credit sources to Indian companies engaged in exports;

*(e)* Advise on exchange control practices globally;

*(i)* Advise on design of packages for export-oriented industries in India.

## Forfaiting

This is a familiar mode of export transaction abroad, but has recently been introduced in India by Export-Import Bank of India.

The word 'forfait' is derived from the French word 'as forfait' which means the surrender of rights.

Simply put, forfaiting is the non-recourse discounting of export receivables. In a forfaiting transaction, the exporter surrenders, without recourse to him, his rights to claim for payment on goods delivered to an importer, in return for immediate cash payment from a forfaiter. As a result, an exporter in India can convert a credit sale into a cash sale, with no recourse to the exporter or his banker.

The full details of the forfaiting operations as envisaged by Exim Bank can be obtained from them.

## SMALL SCALE INDUSTRIES DEVELOPMENT BANK

SIDBI has been established by an act of parliament for promotion, financing and development of industries in the small-scale sector. It came into being in 1990. It is a wholly owned subsidiary of the Industrial Development bank of India (IDBI).

It provides refinance facilities to either scheduled banks or state financial corporations which lend to small scale sector in areas such as equipment purchase, term finance for operation etc. In terms of exports made by the small scale sector, it can get packing credit and post-shipment credit through their own branches, and SIDBI would refinance these loans given by the banks. Even after the export, the small scale unit can seek the help of the bank for discounting the bills, and SIDBI in turn will rediscount the bills that were earlier discounted by the scheduled bank.

## RESERVE BANK OF INDIA IN EXPORT FINANCING

RBI, the central bank of our country initiates policies such as interest rates for the export sector. As a matter of fact, the packing credit rate of interest as well as post-shipment credit rate of interest are advised by the RBI to the scheduled banks.

RBI always provides refinance facilities to scheduled banks who provide the necessary pre-shipment and post-shipment credit to export organizations.

In view of the fact that the rate of interest for exports is always lower than the regular market interest rate, a subsidy of 1.5% was also provided by the RBI to scheduled banks. But in these times of falling interest rates the subsidy may not be in place.

There used to be inordinate delays in the exporters getting the duty drawback. Hence a new scheme was introduced where the exporters, after exporting their goods, will have their shipping bills duly endorsed by customs, and can approach the scheduled banks for 90 day interest-free advances against their shipping bills. Such advances given by the scheduled banks were refinanced by the RBI for the same 90-day interest-free advances.

## ECGC–EXPORT CREDIT AND GUARANTEE CORPORATION

Export transactions by their method and operations involved, carry substantial risks which are both commercial and political in nature. This is especially so in regard to the financing of export transactions. Even the scheduled banks, which are authorised to extend easy financial terms for export endeavors are not equipped to take care of these risks. Nor are the exporters in a position to bear the risks attending export transactions. The need thus definitely exists for a specialized agency, which would take upon itself the responsibility of insulating both the exporter and the financial institutions from these risks. To provide these specialised services, the Government of India has established the ECGC, which is under administrative control of the Ministry of Commerce. By issuing suitable policies, it insures exporters against the attendant risks of export operations. Besides, it also provides financial guarantees to banks and exporters for exports against deferred credit payment terms.

We have given below some of the important policies of ECGC to give you an idea of the extent and scope of the coverage given in export insurance. But practicing exporters are advised get in touch with the corporation at the time of their exports to get the exact details of the coverage and cost.

The covers issued by ECGC could be divided broadly into four groups;

*(a)* Standard Policies issued to exporters to protect them against payment risks involved in exports on short-term credit;

*(b)* Specific Policies designed to protect Indian firms against payment risk involved in (i) exports on deferred terms of payment, (ii) services rendered to foreign parties, and (iii) construction works and turnkey projects undertaken abroad;

*(c)* Financial guarantees issued to banks in India to protect them from risks of loss involved in their extending financial support to exporters at the post-shipment as well as pre-shipment stages.

*(d)* Special schemes, *viz.,* Transfer Guarantee meant to protect banks which add confirmation to Letters of Credit opened by foreign banks, Insurance cover for Buyers Credit, Lines of Credit, Overseas Investment Insurance and Exchange Fluctuation Risk Insurance.

## (A) Standard Policies

ECGC has designed four types of standard policies to provide cover for shipments made on short-term credit.

*(i)* Shipments (Comprehensive Risks) Policy – to cover both commercial and political risks from the date of shipment.

*(ii)* Shipments (Political Risks) Policy – to cover only political risks from the date of shipment.

*(iii)* Contracts (Comprehensive Risks) Policy – to cover both commercial and political risks from the date of contract.

*(iv)* Contracts (Political Risks) Policy – to cover only political risks from the date of contract.

The Shipments (Comprehensive Risks) Policy is the one ideally suited to cover risks in respect of goods exported on short-term credit. This policy covers both political and commercial risks from the date of shipment. Risk of pre-shipment losses due to frustration of export contracts is nil or very low since goods exported on short-term credit are raw materials, primary goods, consumer goods or consumer durables which can be resold easily. Contract policies, which cover risks from the date of contract, are issued only in special cases when goods to be exported are manufactured to the non-standard specifications of a buyer.

Shipments to associate or to agents and those against letters of credit can be covered for only political risks by suitable endorsements to the Shipments Comprehensive Risks Policy. Premium is charged on such shipments at lover rates.

**1. Risks covered:**

The risks covered under the Standard Policies are:

(i) Commercial Risks

(a) Insolvency of the buyer;

(b) Buyer's protracted default to pay for goods accepted by him.

(c) Buyer's failure to accept goods subject to certain conditions.

( ii) Political Risks

(a) Imposition of restrictions on remittances by the government in the buyer's country or any government action which may block or delay payment to the exporter.

(b) War, revolution or civil disturbances in the buyer's country.

(c) New import licensing restrictions or cancellation of a valid import license in the buyer's country.

(d) Cancellation of export license or imposition of new export licensing restrictions in India (under contracts policy).

(e) Payment of additional handling, transport or insurance charges occasioned by interruption or diversion of voyage which cannot be recovered from the buyer.

(f) Any other cause of loss occurring outside India, not normally insured by commercial insurers, and beyond the control of the exporter and/or the buyer.

**2. Risks not covered:**

The Standard policies do not cover losses due to the following risks:

(a) Commercial disputes raised by the buyer, unless the exporter obtains a decree from a competent court of law in the buyer's country in his favour.

(b) Causes inherent in the nature of the goods.

(c) Buyer's failure to obtain necessary import or exchange authorisation from authorities in his country.

(d) Insolvency or default of any agent of the exporter or the collecting bank.

(e) Loss or damage to goods which can be covered by commercial insurers.

(f) Exchange fluctuation.

## (B) Specific Policies

The Standard Policy is a whole turnover policy designed to provide a continuing insurance for the regular flow of an exporter's shipments of raw materials, consumer goods and consumer durables for which the credit period does not exceed 180 days. Contracts for export of capital goods or turn-key projects or construction works or rendering services abroad are not of a repetitive nature. Such transactions are therefore, insured by ECGC on a case-to-case basis under specific policies.

All contracts for export on deferred payment terms exceeding Rs.1 crore in value and all contracts for turnkey projects and construction works abroad require prior clearance of the Working Group consisting of representatives from Reserve Bank of India, EXIM Bank and ECGC. Applications for this purpose are to be sent to EXIM Bank through the exporter's bank. An 'in principle' clearance by the working group enables the exporters to get necessary facilities from the institutions concerned.

## (C) Specific Policy for Supply Contracts

Specific Policy for supply contracts may take any of the following four forms:

*(i)* Specific Shipments (Comprehensive Risks) Policy to cover both commercial and political risks at the post-shipment stage;

*(ii)* Specific Shipments (Political Risks) Policy to cover only political risks at the post-shipment stage in cases where the buyer is an overseas Government, or payments are guaranteed by a Government or by banks, or are made to associates;

*(iii)* Specific Contracts (Comprehensive Risks) Policy;

*(iv)* Specific Contracts (Political Risks) Policy.

Contracts Policy provides cover from the date of contract. Losses that may be sustained by an exporter at the pre-shipment stage due to frustration of contract are covered under this policy in addition to the cover provided by the Shipments Policy.

## (D) ECGC's Special Policies

Besides the risks covered under standard policies, an exporter sometimes needs coverage of risks of other types connected with various export transactions. To suit the various needs of the exporters, the ECGC has devised the following Special Policies:

**(a) Construction Works Policy:** A contract for construction work comprises not only the supply of the material required but also the provision of services as well as the execution of civil engineering works connected with the completion of the contract. The ECGC's construction works policy provides cover for all payments that fall due to the contractor under this contract.

The ECGC wants the exporter to ensure that the contracts are well drafted to provide clarity of obligations of both the parties and for the resolution of disputes which may arise in the course of the execution of the contract.

The policy is issued to cover the specific contract and it takes effect from the date of the contract. The risk coverage is usually comprehensive in nature. Cover can also be provided for the contractor's equipment – such as cranes, bulldozers and trucks used for construction – against risk like confiscation, by a suitable endorsement on the policy.

**(b) Policy for Consignment Exports:** The ECGC also covers exports made on consignment basis. A Special endorsement for the purpose may have to be obtained by the exporter on the standard specific shipment policy. The cover obtained would provide for political risks from the date of shipment and commercial risks from the date of sale of overseas stock to the buyer, subject to the terms and conditions of policy.

**(c) Services Policy:** A services policy of the ECGC is designed to protect Indian exporters against the risk of non-payment for services rendered to foreign parties. Under this policy, technical and professional services are covered. The services policies are availed of for the coverage of both political and commercial risks.

## Financial Guarantees

In view of the peculiar nature of, and the risks connected with export financing, the ECGC has designed a number of financial guarantees which help scheduled banks to extend credit to exporters. Some of the important guarantees offered by the ECGC are:

*(a)* Packing credit guarantee;

*(b)* Post-shipment export credit guarantee;

*(c)* Export finance guarantee;

*(d)* Export production finance guarantee;

*(e)* Export performance guarantee; and

*(f)* Transfer guarantee.

**(a) Packing Credit Guarantee:** An exporter requires finance to undertake the procurement of raw materials and the manufacture and packaging of the goods meant for export. Packing credit for this purpose is extended by commercial banks to exporters. The packing credit guarantee covers the advance by a bank to an exporter and protects it against the risk of loss due to insolvency or protracted default on the part of the exporter to whom advances have been extended. Specifically, it protects the financing bank against *(i)* Non-delivery of shipping documents to the bank; *(ii)* Non-payment of the debt if shipments cannot be made.

The ECGC indemnifies the financing bank to the extent of 75% of the loss. The premium charges vary between 7 paise and 10 paise per Rs.100/- per month.

In the case of a small-scale merchant exporter whose turn-over does not exceed Rs. 2 lakhs, the ECGC indemnifies the bank upto 90% of the loss.

**(b) Post-shipment Export Credit Guarantee:** Commercial banks extend post-shipment credit to exporters through purchase negotiations and discount of their export bills. Against this credit, the bank is eligible to obtain a cover from the ECGC which protects it against defaults or insolvency on the part of the exporter. No doubt the standard policies and specific policies of the ECGC cover the exporter against the financial risks involved in these transactions, and the exporter should have taken this policy. They do not, however, protect him against non-payment for reasons beyond his control. To cover these risks and secure the advances made to an exporter the bank approaches the ECGC for a post-shipment credit guarantee. Normally, the bank is covered to the extent of 75% of the loss. A premium of 7 paise per Rs.100 per month is charged to the bank on such a credit guarantee executed by the ECGC.

**(c) Export Finance Guarantee:** This guarantee covers post shipment advances granted by banks to exporters against export receivables under duty drawback and incentives if any. The premium rate for this type of guarantee is 7 paise per 100 rupees per month and the cover is to the extent of 75%.

**(d) Export Performance Guarantee:** An exporter negotiating exports on certain types of contracts may need to arrange for bank guarantees for the following purposes:

(i) **Bid Bond:** The foreign buyer may require this when an exporter wants to quote for a tender. This is a guarantee certifying the genuineness of the offer submitted by the buyer.

(ii) **Advance Payment Guarantee:** After the exporter secures the bid, the buyer may pay the exporter a percentage of the value of the contract as an advance against the bank guarantee.

(iii) **Bank Guarantee for Performance of the Contract by the Exporter:** This guarantee will be required by the buyer when the contract is awarded to the exporter.

(iv) **Bank Guarantee for payment of Retention Money:** In order to ensure the performance, the buyer may retain a percentage of the contract value as retention money and agree to release it to the exporter against a bank guarantee.

(v) **Bank Guarantee for Loans of Foreign Exchange:** It may, in some cases, be necessary for an exporter to raise funds in foreign currency to finance his operations in connection with an export project. In these cases, the financing institutions abroad may need a bank guarantee to be furnished by the exporter.

The exporter approaches the bank for these guarantees. To cover the risks involved in such transactions, the bank obtains a counter-guarantee from the EGCG under the latter's performance Guarantee Scheme

The proposals for these guarantees may be made by the bank to the ECGC, on the basis of which, ECGC counter guarantee will be made available.

The ECGC indemnifies the bank upto 75% of the loss in the case of guarantees required by the exporter.

**(e) Transfer Guarantee:** An exporter always prefers to obtain a letter of credit confirmed by a reputed bank. Sometimes, he may ask his own bank in India to confirm a foreign letter of credit. When this letter of credit is confirmed, the bank binds itself to honor the drafts drawn by the beneficiary if they are in accordance with the letter of credit. The confirming bank may run the risk of the foreign bank not reimbursing the Indian bank, especially in the event of certain political situations such as war, civil war, transfer delays, moratorium, etc. To protect these banks against these risks that might delay or prevent the transfer of funds to the banks in India, the ECGC has devised the Transfer Guarantee Scheme, which safeguards the banks in India. In other words, the Indian bank, which confirms the letter of credit, will not suffer any serious loss even if the foreign bank fails to reimburse it, since the ECGC guarantee protects it. The usual coverage is 75% for commercial risks.

ECGC has, in the last few years, brought forward many progressive schemes and policies to encourage exports, and cover the risks of the exporters and the financial institutions. It is up to the exporters to make full use of these facilities. However, they should not forget the cardinal principle of making their own comprehensive commercial evaluation of the buyer, his previous record and antecedents before they embark on credit or insurance cover.

# ANNEXURE I

## Uniform Customs and Practice for Documentary Credits

## A. GENERAL PROVISIONS AND DEFINITIONS

### Article 1

These articles apply to all documentary credits, including, to the extent to which they may be applicable, standby letters of credit, and are binding on all parties thereto unless otherwise expressly agreed. They shall be incorporated into each documentary credit by wording in the credit indicating that such credit is issued subject to Uniform Customs and Practice for Documentary Credits, 1983 revision, ICC Publication No.400.

### Article 2

For the purpose of these articles, the expressions "documentary credit(s)" and "standby letter(s) of credit" used herein (hereinafter referred to as "credit(s)", mean any arrangement, however named or described, whereby a bank (the issuing bank), acting at the request and on the instruction of a customer (the applicant for the credit),

(i) is to make a payment to or to the order of a third party (the beneficiary), drawn by the beneficiary, or

(ii) authorizes another bank to effect such payment or to pay, accept or negotiate such bills of exchange (drafts), against stipulated documents, provided that the terms and conditions of the credits are complied with.

### Article 3

Credits, by their nature, are separate transactions from the sales or other contract(s) on which they may be based and banks are in no way concerned with or bound by such contract(s), even if any reference whatsoever to such contract(s) is included in the credit.

### Article 4

In credit operations, all parties concerned, deal in documents, and not in goods, services and/or other performances to which the documents may relate.

### Article 5

Instructions for the issuance for credits, the credits themselves, instructions for any amendments thereto and the amendments themselves, must be complete and precise.

In order to guard against confusion and misunderstanding, banks should discourage any attempt to include excessive detail in the credit or in any amendment thereto.

**Article 6**

A beneficiary can in no case avail himself of the contractual relationships existing between the banks or between the applicant for the credit and the issuing bank.

## B. FORM AND NOTIFICATION OF CREDITS

**Article 7**

(a) Credits may be either

(i) revocable, or

(ii) irrevocable

(b) All credits, therefore, should clearly indicate whether they are revocable or irrevocable.

(c) In the absence of such indication, the credit shall be deemed to be revocable.

**Article 8**

A credit may be advised to a beneficiary through another bank (the advising bank) without engagement on the part of the advising bank, but that bank shall take reasonable care to check the apparent authenticity of the credit which it advises.

**Article 9**

(a) A revocable credit may be amended or cancelled by the issuing Bank at any movement and without prior notice to the beneficiary. However, the issuing bank is bound to:

(i) reimburse a branch or bank with which a revocable credit has been made available for sight payment, acceptance or negotiation made by such branch or bank prior to receipt by it of notice of amendment or cancellation, against documents which appear on the face to be in accordance with the terms and conditions of the credit.

(ii) reimburse a branch or bank with which a revocable credit has been made available for deferred payment, if such branch or bank has, prior to receipt by it of notice of amendment or cancellation, taken up documents which appear on their face to be in accordance with terms and conditions of the credit.

**Article 10**

An irrevocable credit constitutes a definite undertaking of the issuing bank, provided that the stipulated documents are presented and that the terms and conditions of the credits are complied with:

(i) if the credit provides for sight payment – to pay, or that payment will be made;

(ii) if the credit provides for deferred payment – to pay, or that payment will be made, on the date(s) determinable in accordance with the stipulations of the credit.

(iii) if the credit provides for acceptance – to accept drawn by the beneficiary if the credit stipulates that they are to be drawn on the issuing bank, or to be responsible for their acceptance and payment at maturity if the credit stipulates that they are to be drawn on the applicant for the credit or any another drawee stipulated in the credit;

(iv) if the credit provides for negotiation – to pay without recourse - to drawers and/or bonafide holders, draft(s) drawn by the beneficiary, at sight or at a tenor, on the applicant for the credit or on any other drawee stipulated in the credit other than the issuing bank itself, or to provide for negotiation by another bank and to pay as above, if such negotiation is not affected.

(b) When an issuing bank authorizes or requests another bank to confirm its irrevocable credit and the latter has added its confirmation, such confirmation constitutes a definite undertaking of such bank (the confirming bank), in addition to that of the issuing bank, provided that the stipulated documents are presented and that the terms and conditions of the credit are complied with:

(i) if the credit provides for sight payment – to pay, or that payment will be made;

(ii) if the credit provides for deferred payment – to pay, or that payment will be made, on the date(s) determinable in accordance with the stipulations of the credit;

(iii) if the credit provides for acceptance – to accept drafts drawn by the beneficiary if the credit stipulates that they are to be drawn on the confirmation bank, or to be responsible for their acceptance and payment at maturity if the credit stipulates that they are to be drawn on the applicant for the credit or any other drawee stipulated in the credit;

(iv) if the credit provides for negotiation – to negotiate without recourse to drawers and/or bonafide holders, draft(s) drawn by the beneficiary, at sight or at a tenor, on the issuing bank or on the applicant for the credit or on any other drawee stipulated in the credit other than the confirming bank itself, or to provide for negotiation by another bank and to pay as above, if such negotiation is not effected.

(b) When an issuing bank authorizes or requests another bank to confirm its irrevocable credit and the latter has added its confirmation, such confirmation constitutes a definite undertaking of such bank (the confirming bank), in addition to that of the issuing bank, provided that the stipulated documents are presented and that the terms and conditions of the credit are complied with:

(i) if the credit provides for sight payment – to pay, or that payment will be made;

(ii) if the credit provides for deferred payment – to pay, or that payment will be made, on the date(s) determinable in accordance with the stipulations of the credit;

(iii) if the credit provides for acceptance – to accept drafts drawn by the beneficiary if the credit stipulates that they are to be drawn on the confirmation bank, or to be responsible for their acceptance and payment at maturity if the credit stipulates that they are to be drawn on the applicant for the credit or any other drawee stipulated in the credit;

(iv) if the credit provides for negotiation – to negotiate without recourse to drawers and/or bonafide holders, draft(s) drawn by he beneficiary, at sight or at a tenor, on the issuing bank or on the applicant for the credit or on any other drawee stipulated in the credit;

(c) If a bank is authorized or requested by the issuing bank to add its confirmation to a credit but is not prepared to do so, it must so inform the issuing bank without delay. Unless the issuing bank specifies otherwise in its confirmation authorization or request, the advising bank will advise the credit to the beneficiary without addition its confirmation.

(d) Such undertakings can neither be amended nor cancelled without the agreement of the issuing bank, the confirming bank (if any), and the beneficiary. Partial acceptance of amendments contained in one and the same advice of amendment is not effective without agreement of all the above named parties.

**Article 11**

(a) All credits must clearly indicate whether they are available by sight payment, by deferred payment, by acceptance or by negotiation.

(b) All credits must nominate the bank (nominated bank) which is authorized to pay (paying bank), or to accept drafts (accepting bank, or to negotiating bank), unless the credit allows negotiation by any bank (negotiating bank).

(c) unless the nominated bank is the issuing bank or the confirming bank, its nomination by the issuing bank does not constitute any undertaking by the nominated bank to pay, to accept, or to negotiate.

(d) By nominating a bank other than itself, or by allowing for negotiation by any bank, or by authorizing or requesting a bank to add its confirmation, the issuing bank authorizes such bank to pay, accept or negotiate, as the case may be, against documents which appear on their face to be in accordance with the terms and conditions of the credit, and undertakes to reimburse such bank in accordance with the provisions of these articles.

**Article 12**

(a) When an issuing bank instructs a bank (advising bank) by any tele transmission to advise a credit or an amendment to a credit, and intends the mail confirmation to be the operative credit instrument, or the operative amendment, the tele transmission must state "full details to follow" (or words of similar effect), or states that the mail confirmation is to be operative credit instrument or the operative amendment. The issuing bank must forward the operative credit instrument or the operative amendment to such advising bank without delay.

(b) The tele transmission will be deemed to be the operative credit instrument or the operative amendment, and no main confirmation should be sent, unless the tele transmission states "full details to follow" (or words of similar effect), or states that the mail confirmation is to be operative credit instrument or the operative amendment.

(c) A tele transmission intended by the issuing bank to be the operative credit instrument should clearly indicate that the credit is issued subject to Uniform Customs and Practice for Documentary Credits, 1983 revision, ICC Publication no. 400.

(d) If a bank uses the services of another bank or banks (the advising bank) to have the credit advised to the beneficiary, it must also use the services of the same bank(s) for advising any amendments.

(e) Banks shall be responsible for any consequences arising from their failure to follow the procedure – set out in the preceding paragraphs.

**Article 13**

When a bank is instructed to issue, confirm or advise a credit similar in terms to one previously issued, confirmed or advised (similar credit and the previous credit has been the subject of amendment(s), it shall be understood that the similar credit will not include any such amendment(s) unless the instructions specify clearly the amendment(s) which is/are to apply to their similar credit. Banks should discourage instructions to issue, confirm or advise a credit in this manner.

**Article 14**

If incomplete or unclear instructions are received to issue, confirm, advise or amend a credit, the bank requested to act on such instructions may give preliminary notification to the beneficiary for information only and without responsibility. The credit will be issued, confirmed advised or amended only when the necessary information has been received and if the bank is then prepared to act on the instructions. Banks should provide the necessary information without delay.

## C. LIABILITIES AND RESPONSIBILITIES

**Article 15**

Banks must examine all documents with reasonable care to ascertain that they appear on their face to be in accordance with the terms and conditions of the credit. Documents which appear on their face to be inconsistent with one another will be considered as not appearing on their face to be in accordance with the terms and conditions of the credit.

**Article 16**

(a) If a bank so authorized effects payment, or incurs a deferred payment undertaking, or accepts, or negotiates against documents which appear on their face to be in accordance with the terms and conditions for a credit, the party giving such authority shall be bound to reimburse the bank which has effected payment, or incurred a deferred payment undertaking or has accepted or negotiated, and to take up the documents.

(b) If, upon receipt of the documents, the issuing bank considers that they appear on their face not to be in accordance with the terms and conditions of the credit, it must determine, on the basis of the documents alone, whether to take up such documents, or to refuse them and claim that they appear on their face not to be in accordance with the terms and conditions of the credit.

(c) The issuing bank shall have a reasonable time in which to examine the documents and to determine as above whether to take up or to refuse the documents.

(d) If the issuing bank decides to refuse the documents, it must give notice to that effect without delay by telecommunication or, if that it not possible, by other expeditious means, to the bank from which it received the documents (the remitting bank), or to the beneficiary, if it received the documents directly from him. Such notice must state the discrepancies in respect of which the issuing bank refuses the documents and must also state whether it is holding the documents at the disposal of, or is returning them to the present or (remitting bank or the beneficiary, as the case may be). The issuing bank shall then be entitled to claim from the remitting bank refund of any reimbursement which may have been made to that bank.

(e) If the issuing bank fails to act in accordance with the provisions of paragraphs (c) and (d) of this article and/or fails to hold the documents at the disposal of, or to return them to, the presenter, the issuing banks shall be precluded from claiming that the documents are not in accordance with the terms and conditions of the credit.

(f) If the remitting bank draws the attention of the issuing bank to any discrepancies in the documents or advises the issuing bank that it has paid, incurred a deferred payment undertaking, accepted or negotiated under reserve or against an indemnity in respect of such discrepancies, the issuing bank shall not be thereby relieved from any of its obligations under any provision of this article. Such reserve or indemnity concerns only the relations between the remitting bank and the party towards whom the reserve was made, or from whom, or on whose behalf, the indemnity was obtained.

**Article 17**

Banks assume no liability or responsibility for the form, sufficiency, accuracy, genuineness, falsification or legal effect of any documents, or for the general and/or particular conditions stipulated in the documents or super imposed thereon; nor do they assume any liability or responsibility for the description, quantity, weight, quality, condition, packing, delivery, value or existence of the goods represented by any documents, or for the good faith or acts and/or omissions, solvency, performance or standing of the consignor, the carriers, or the insurers of the goods, or any other person whomsoever.

**Article 18**

Banks assume no liability or responsibility for the consequences arising out of delay and/or loss in transit of any messages, letters or documents, or for delay, mutilation or other errors arising in the transmission of any telecommunication. Banks assume no liability or responsibility for errors in translation or interpretation of technical terms, and reserve the right to translation or interpretation of technical terms, and reserve the right to transmit credit terms without translating them.

**Article 19**

Banks assume no liability or responsibility for consequences arising out of the interruption of their business by Acts of Gods, riots, civil commotions, insurrections, wars or any other causes beyond their control, or by any strikes or lockouts. Unless specifically authorized, banks will not, upon resumption of their lockouts. Unless specifically authorized, banks will not, upon resumption of their business, incur a deferred payment undertaking, or effect payment, acceptance or negotiation under credits which expired during such interruption of their business.

**Article 20**

Banks utilising the services of another bank or other banks for the purpose of giving effect to the instructions of the applicant for the credit do so for the account and at the risk of such applicant.

Banks assume no liability or responsibility should the instructions transmit not be carried out, even if they have themselves taken initiative in the choice of such other bank(s).

The applicant for the credit shall be bound by and liable to indemnify the banks against all obligations and responsibilities imposed by foreign laws and usages.

**Article 21**

(a) If an issuing banks intends that the reimbursement to which a paying, accepting or negotiating bank is entitled shall be obtained by such bank claiming on branch or office of the issuing bank or on a third bank (all hereinafter referred to as the reimbursing bank) it shall provide, such reimbursing bank in good time with the proper instructions or authorization to honour such reimbursement claims and without making it a condition that the bank entitled to claim reimbursement must certify compliance with the terms and conditions of the credit to the reimbursing bank.

(b) An issuing bank will not be relieved from any of its obligations to provide reimbursement itself if an when reimbursement is not effected by the reimbursing bank.

(c) The issuing bank will be responsible to the paying, accepting or negotiating bank for any loss of interest if reimbursement is not provided on first demand made to the reimbursing bank, or as otherwise specified in the credit, or mutually agreed, as the case may be.

**D. DOCUMENTS**

**Article 22**

(a) All instructions for the issuance of credits and the credits themselves and, where applicable, all instructions for amendments thereto and the amendments themselves, must state precisely the document(s) against which payment, acceptance or negotiation is to be made.

(b) Terms such as "first class", "well-known", "qualified", "independent", "official", and the like shall not be used to describe the issuers of any documents to be presented under a credit, if such terms are incorporated in the credit terms, banks will accept the relative documents as presented, provided that they appear on their face to be in accordance with the other terms and conditions of the credit.

(c) Unless otherwise stipulated in the credit, banks will accept as originals documents produced or appearing to have been produced:

(i) by reprographic systems;

(ii) by, or as the result of, automated or computerized systems;

(iii) if marked as originals, always provided that, where necessary such documents appear to have been authenticated.

**Article 23**

When documents other than transport documents, insurance documents and commercial invoices are called for, the credit should stipulate by whom such documents are to be issued and their working or data convent. If the credit does not so as stipulate, banks will accept such documents as presented, provided that their data content makes it possible to relate the goods and/or services referred to therein to those referred to, in the commercial invoice(s) presented, or to those referred to in the credit if the credit does not stipulate presentation of a commercial invoice presented, or to those referred to in the credit if the credit does not stipulate presentation of a commercial invoice.

**Article 24**

Unless otherwise stipulated in the credit banks will accept a document bearing a date of issuance prior to that of the credit, subject to such document being presented within the time limit set out in the credit and in these articles.

## D1. TRANSPORT DOCUMENTS: (documents indicating loading on board or despatch or taking in charge)

**Article 25**

Unless a credit calling for a transport document stipulates as such document a marine bill of lading (ocean bill of lading covering by sea), or a post receipt or certificate of posting:

(a) Banks will, unless otherwise stipulated in the credit, accept a transport document which:

(i) appears on its face to have been issued by a named carrier, or his agent, and

(ii) indicates despatch or taking charge of the goods, or loading on board, as the case may be, and

(iii) consists of the full set of original issued to the consignor if issued in more than one original, and

(iv) meets all other stipulations of the credit.

(b) Subject to the above, and unless otherwise stipulated in the credit, banks will not reject a transport document which:

(i) bears a title such as "Combined transport bill of lading", "Combined transport document", "Combined transport bill of lading or port-to-port bill of lading", or a little or a combination of titles of similar intent and effect, and/or

(ii) indicates some or all of the conditions of carriage by reference to a source or document other than the transport document itself (short from/blank back transport document), and /or

(iii) indicates a place of taking in charge different from the port of loading and/or a place of final destination different from the port of discharge, and/or

(iv) relates to cargoes such as those in Containers or on pallets, and the like, and/or

(v) contains the indication "intended", or similar qualification, in relation to the vessel or other means of transport, and/or the port of loading and/or the port of discharge.

(c) Unless otherwise stipulated in the credit in the case of carriage by sea or by more than one mode of transport but including carriage by sea, banks will reject a transport document which:

(i) indicates that it is subject to a charter part, and/or

(ii) indicates that the carrying vessel is propelled by sail only.

Unless otherwise stipulated in the credit, banks will reject a transport document issued by a freight forwarder unless it is the FIATA Combined Transport Bill of Lading approved by the International Chamber of Commerce or otherwise indicates that it is issued by a freight forwarder acting as a carrier or agent of a named carrier.

**Article 26**

If a credit calling for a transport document stipulates as such document a marine bill of lading:

Banks will, unless otherwise stipulated in the credit, accept a document which:

(i) appears on its face to have been issued by a named carrier, or his agent, and

(ii) indicates that the goods have been loaded on board or shipped on a named vessel, and

(iii) consists of the full set of originals issued to the consignor if issued in more than one original, and

(iv) meets all other stipulations of the credit.

Subject to the above, and unless otherwise stipulated in the credit, banks will not reject a document which:

(i) bears a title such as "Combined transport bill of lading", "Combined transport document", "combined transport bill of lading or port-to-port bill of lading", or a title or a combination of titles of similar intent and effect, and/or

(ii) indicates some or all the conditions of carriage by reference to a source or document other than the transport document itself short from/blank back transport document, and/or

(iii) indicates a place of taking in charge different from the port of loading and/or a place of final destination different from the port of discharge, and/or

(iv) relates to cargoes such as those in Containers or on pallets, and the like.

Unless otherwise stipulated in the credit, banks will reject a document which:

(i) indicates that it is subject to a charter party, and/or

(ii) indicates that the carrying vessel is propelled by sail only, and/or

(iii) contains the indication "intended", or similar qualification in relation to the vessel and/or the port of loading – unless such document bears an on board notation in accordance with article 27(b) and also indicates the actual port of loading, and/or the port of discharge – unless the place of final destination indicates on the document is other than the port of discharge, and/or

(iv) is issued by a freight forwarder, unless it indicates that it is issued by such freight forwarder acting as a carrier, or as the agent of a named carrier.

**Article 27**

(a) Unless a credit specifically calls for an on board transport document, or unless inconsistent with other stipulation(s) in the credit, or with article 26, banks will accept a transport document which indicates that the goods have been taken in charge or received for shipment.

(b) Loading on board or shipment on a vessel may be evidenced either by a transport document bearing wording indicating loading on board a named vessel, or shipment on a named vessel, or, in the case of transport document stating "received for shipment", by means of a notation of loading on board on the transport document signed or installed and dated by the carrier or his agent, and the date of this notation shall be regarded as the date of loading on board the named vessel or shipment on the named vessel.

**Article 28**

(a) In the case of carriage by sea or by more than one mode of transport, but including carriage by sea, bank will refuse a transport document stating that the goods are or will be loaded on deck, unless specifically authorised in the credit.

(b) Banks will not refuse a transport document which contains a provision that the goods may be carried on deck, provided it does not specifically state that they are or will be loaded on deck.

**Article 29**

(a) For the purpose of this article, transhipment means a transfer and reloading during the course of carriage from the port of loading or place of despatch or taking in charge to the port of discharge or place of destination either from one conveyance or vessel to another conveyance or vessel within the same mode of transport or from one mode of transport to another mode of transport.

(b) Unless transhipment is prohibited by the terms of the credit, banks will accept transport documents which indicate that the goods will be transhipped, provided the entire carriage is covered by one and the same transport document.

(c) Even if transhipment is prohibited by the terms of the credit, banks will accept transport document which:

(i) incorporate printed clauses stating that the carrier has the right to tranship, or

(ii) state or indicate that transhipment will or may take place, when the credit stipulates a combined transport document, or indicates carriage from a place of taking in charge to a place of final destination by different modes of transport including a carriage by sea, provided that the entire carriage is covered by one and the same transport document, or

(iii) state or indicate that the goods are in a Container(s), trailer(s), "LASH" barge(s), and the like and will be carried from the place of taking in charge to the place of final destination in the same Container(s), trailer(s), "LASH" barges, and the like under one and the same transport document, or

(iv) state or indicate the place of receipt and/or of final destination as "C.F.S.", (container freight station) or "C.Y". (container yard) at, or associated with, the port of loading and/or the port of destination.

**Article 30**

If the credit stipulates despatch of goods by post and calls for a post receipt or certificate of posting, banks will accept such post receipt or certificate of posting if is appears to have been stamped or otherwise authenticated and dated in the place from which the credit stipulates the goods are to be despatched.

**Article 31**

(a) Unless otherwise stipulated in the credit, or inconsistent with any of the documents presented under the credit, banks will accept transport documents stating that freight or transportation charges (hereinafter referred to as "freight") have still to be paid.

(b) If a credit stipulates that the transport document has to indicate that freight has been paid or prepaid, banks will accept a transport document on which words clearly indicating payment or prepayment of fright appear by stamp or otherwise, or in which payment of freight is indicated by other means.

(c) The words "freight pre-payable" or "freight to be prepaid" or words of similar effect, if appearing on transport documents, will not be accepted as constituting evidence of the payment of freight.

(d) Banks will accept transport documents bearing reference by stamp or otherwise to costs additional to the freight charges, such as costs of, or disbursements incurred connection with loading, unloading or similar operations, unless the conditions of the credit specifically prohibit such reference.

**Article 32**

Unless otherwise stipulated in the credit, banks will accept transport documents which bear a clause on the face thereof such as "shippers load and count" or "said by shipper to contain" or words of similar effect.

**Article 33**

Unless otherwise stipulated in the credit, banks will accept transport documents indicating as the consignor of the goods a party other than the beneficiary of the credit.

**Article 34**

A clean transport document is one which bears no superimposed clause or notation which expressly declares a defective condition of the goods and/or the packaging.

Banks will refuse transport documents bearing such clauses or notations unless the credit expressly stipulates the clauses or notations which may be accepted.

Banks will regard a requirement in a credit for a transport document to bear the clause "clean on board" as complied with if such transport document meets the requirements of the article 27(b).

## D2. INSURANCE DOCUMENTS

### Article 35

Insurance documents must be as stipulated in the credit, and must be issued and/or signed by insurance companies or underwriters, or their agents.

Cover notes issued by brokers will not be accepted, unless specifically authorised by the credit.

### Article 36

Unless otherwise stipulated in the credit, or unless it appears from the insurance document(s) that the cover is effective at the latest from the date of loading on board or dispatch or taking in charge of goods, banks will refuse insurance documents presented which bear a date later than the date of loading on board or dispatch or taking in charge of the goods as indicated by the transport document(s).

### Article 37

(a) Unless otherwise stipulated in the credit, the insurance document must be expressed in the same currency as the credit.

(b) Unless otherwise stipulated in the credit, the minimum amount for which the insurance document must indicate the insurance cover to have been effected is the CIF (cost, insurance and freight... "named port of destination") or CIP (freight/carriage and insurance paid to "named point of destination") value of the goods, as the case may be, plus 10%. However, if banks cannot determine the CIF or CIP value, as the case may be, from the documents on their face, they will accept as such minimum amount, the amount for which payment, acceptance or negotiation is requested under the credit, or the amount of the commercial invoice, whichever is the greater.

### Article 38

(a) Credits should stipulate the type of insurance required and, if any, the additional risks which are to be covered. Imprecise terms such as "usual risks" or "customary risks" should not be used; if they are used, banks will accept insurance documents as presented, without responsibility for any risk(s) not being covered.

(b) Failing specific stipulations in the credit, banks will accept insurance documents as presented, without responsibility for any risks not being covered.

**Article 39**

Where a credit stipulates "insurance against all risk", banks will accept an insurance document which contains any "all risks" notation or clause, whether or not bearing the heading "all risks", even if indicating that certain risks are excluded, without responsibility for any risk(s) not being covered.

**Article 40**

Banks will accept an insurance document which indicates that the cover is subject to a franchise or an excess (deductible), unless it is specifically stipulated in the credit that the insurance must be issued irrespective of percentage.

## D3. COMMERCIAL INVOICE

**Article 41**

(a) Unless otherwise stipulated in the credit, commercial invoices must be made out in the name of the applicant for the credit.

(b) Unless otherwise stipulated in the credit, banks may refuse commercial invoices issued for amounts in excess of the amount permitted by the credit. Nevertheless, if a bank authorised to pay, incur a deferred payment undertaking accept, or negotiate under a credit accepts such invoices, its decision will be binding upon all parties, provided such bank has not paid, incurred a deferred payment undertaking, accepted or effected negotiation for an amount in excess of that permitted by the credit.

(c) The description of the goods in the commercial invoice must correspond with the description in the credit. In all other documents, the goods may be described in general terms not consistent with the description of the goods in the credit.

## D4. OTHER DOCUMENTS

**Article 42**

If a credit calls for an attestation or certification of weight in the case of transport other than by sea, banks will accept a weight stamp or declaration of weight which appears to have been superimposed on the transport document by the carrier or his agent unless the credit specifically stipulates that the attestation or certification of weight must be by means of a separate document.

## E. MISCELLANEOUS PROVISIONS

### Quantity and amount

**Article 43**

(a) The words "about", "circa" or similar expressions used in connection with the amount of the credit or the quantity or the unit price stated in the credit are to be construed as allowing a difference not to exceed 10% more or 10% less than the amount or the quantity or the unit price to which they refer.

(b) Unless a credit stipulates that the quantity of goods specified must be exceeded or reduced, a tolerance of 5% more or 5% less, will be permissible, even if partial shipments are not permitted, always provided that the amount of the drawings does not exceed the amount of the credit. This tolerance does not apply when the credit stipulates the quantity in terms of a stated number of packing units of individuals items.

**Partial drawings and/or shipments**

**Article 44**

(a) Partial drawing and/or shipments are allowed, unless the credit stipulates otherwise.

(b) Shipments by sea, or by more than one mode of transport but including carriage by sea, made on the same vessel and for the same voyage, will not be regarded as partial shipments, even if the transport documents indicating loading on board bear different dates of issuance and/or indicate different ports of loading on board.

(c) Shipments made by post will not be regarded as partial shipments if the post receipts or certificates of posting appear to have been stamped or otherwise authenticated in the place from which the credit stipulates the goods are to be dispatched, and on the same date.

(d) Shipments made by modest of transport, other than those referred to in paragraphs (b) and (c) of this article will not be regarded as partial shipments provided the transport documents are issued by one and the same carrier on his agent indicate the same date of issuance, the same place of dispatch or taking in charge of the goods, and the same destination.

**Article 45**

If drawings and/or shipments by instalments within given periods are stipulated in the credit and any instalments is not drawn and/or shipped within the period allowed for that instalment, the credit ceases to be available for that and any subsequent instalments, unless otherwise stipulated in the credit.

## Expiry date and presentation

### Article 46

(a) All credits must stipulate an expiry date for presentation of documents for payment, acceptance or negotiation.

(b) Except as provided in Article 48 (a), documents must be presented on or before such expiry date.

(c) If an issuing bank states that the credit to be available "for one month", "for six months" or the like, but does not specify the date from which the time is to run, the date of issuance of the credit by the issuing bank will be deemed to be the first day from which such time is to run. Banks should discourage indication of the expiry date of the credit in this manner.

### Article 47

(a) In addition to stipulating an expiry date for presentation of documents, every credit which calls for a transport document(s) should also stipulate a specified period of time after the date of issuance of the transport documents during which presentation of documents for payment, acceptance or negotiation must be made. If no such period of time is stipulated, banks will refuse documents. In every case, however, documents must be presented not later than the expiry date of the credit.

(b) For the purpose of these articles, the date of issuance of a transport document(s) will be deemed to be:

(i) in the case of a transport document evidencing dispatch, or taking in charge, or receipt of goods for shipment by a mode of transport other than by air - the date of issuance indicated on the transport document or the date of the reception stamp thereon whichever is the later.

(ii) in the case of a transport document evidencing carriage by air-the-date of issuance indicated on the transport document, or, if the credit stipulates that the transport document shall indicate an actual flight date, the actual fight date as indicated on the transport document.

(iii) in the case of a transport document evidencing loading on board a named vessel – the date of issuance of the transport document or, in the case of an board notation in accordance with Article 27(b), the date of such notation.

(iv) in cases to which Article 44(b) applies, the date determined as above of the latest transport document issued.

**Article 48**

(a) If the expiry date of the credit and/or the last day of the period of time after the date of issuance of transport document(s) for presentation of documents stipulated by the credit or applicable by virtue of Article 47 falls on a day on which the bank to which presentation has to be made is closed for reasons other than those referred to in Article 19 the stipulated expiry date and/or the last day of the period of time after the date of issuance of the transport document(s) for presentation of documents, as the case may be, shall be extended to the first following business day on which such bank is open.

(b) The latest date for loading on board, or dispatch, or taking in charges shall not be extended by reason of the extension of the expiry date and/or the period of time after the date of issuance of the transport document(s) for presentation of document(s) in accordance with thereto, banks will reject transport documents indicating a date of issuance later than the expiry date stipulated in the credit or amendments thereto.

(c) The bank to which presentation is made on such first following business day must add to the documents its certificate that the documents were presented within the time limits extended in accordance with Article 48(a) of the Uniform Customs and Practice for Documentary Credits, 1983 revision, ICC Publication No. 400.

**Article 49**

Banks are under no obligation to accept presentation of documents outside their banking hours.

## LOADING ON BOARD, DISPATCH AND TAKING IN CHARGE (SHIPMENT)

**Article 50**

(a) Unless otherwise stipulated in the credit, the expression "shipment" used in stipulating an earliest and/or a latest shipment date will be understood to include the expressions "loading on board", "dispatch" and "taking in charge".

(b) The date of issuance of the transport document determined in accordance with Article 47(b) will be taken to be the date of shipment.

(c) Expressions such as "prompt", "immediately", "as soon as possible", and the like should not be used. If they are used, banks will interpret them as a stipulation that shipment is to be made within thirty days from the date of issuance of the credit by the issuing bank.

(d) If the expression "on or about" and similar expressions are used, banks will interpret them as a stipulation that shipment is to be made during the period from five days before to five days after the specified date, both end days included.

## DATE TERMS

**Article 51**

The words "to", "until", "till", "from", and words of similar import applying to any date term in the credit will be understood to include the date mentioned. The word "after" will be understood to exclude the date mentioned.

**Article 52**

The terms "first half", "second half" of a month shall be construed respectively as from the 1st to the 15th, and the 16th to the last day of each month, inclusive.

**Article 53**

The terms "beginning", "middle", or "end" of a month shall be construed respectively as from the 1st to the 10th, the 11th to the 20th, and the 21st to the last day of each month, inclusive.

## F. TRANSFER

**Article 54**

(a) A transferable credit is a credit under which the beneficiary has the right to request the bank called upon to effect payment or acceptance or any bank entitled to the effect negotiation to make the credit available in whole or in part to one or more other parties (second beneficiaries).

(b) A credit can be transferred only if it is expressly designated as "transferable" by the issuing bank. Terms such as "divisible", "fractionable", and "transmissible" add nothing to the meaning of the term "transferable" and shall not be used.

(c) The bank requested to effect the transfer (transferring bank), whether it has confirmed the credit or not, shall be under no obligation to effect such transfer except to the extent and in the manner expressly consented to by such bank.

(d) Bank charges in respect of transfers are payable by the first beneficiary unless otherwise specified. The transferring bank shall be under no obligation to effect the transfer until such charges are paid.

(e) A transferable credit can be transferred once only. Fractions of a transferable credit (not exceeding in the aggregate amount of the credit) can be transferred separately provided partial shipments are not prohibited, and the aggregate of such transfers will be considered as constituting only one transfer of the credit. The credit can be transferred only on the terms and conditions specified in the original credit, with the exception of the amount of the credit, of any unit prices stated therein, of the period of validity, of the last date for presentation of documents in accordance with Article 47 and the period for shipment, any or all of which may be reduced or curtailed, or the percentage for which insurance cover must be effected, which may be increased in such a way as to provide the amount of cover stipulated in the original credit, or these articles. Additionally, the name of the first beneficiary can be substituted for that of the applicant for the credit but if the name of the applicant for the credit is specifically required by the original credit to appear in any document other than the invoice, such requirement must be fulfilled.

(f) The first beneficiary has the right to substitute his own invoices (and drafts if the credit stipulates that drafts are to be drawn on the applicant for the credit) in exchange for those of the second beneficiary, for amounts not in excess of the original amount stipulated in the credit and for the original unit prices if stipulated in the credit, and upon such substitution of invoices (and drafts) the first beneficiary can draw under the credit for the difference, if any, between his invoices and the second beneficiary's invoices. When a credit has been transferred and the first beneficiary is to supply his own invoices (and drafts) in exchange for the second beneficiary's invoices (and drafts) but fails to do so on first demand, the paying, accepting or negotiating bank has the right to deliver to the issuing bank the documents received under the credit, including the second beneficiary's invoices (and drafts) without further responsibility to the first beneficiary.

(g) Unless otherwise stipulated in the credit, the first beneficiary of a transferable credit may request that the credit be transferred to a second beneficiary in the same country, or in another country. Further, unless otherwise stipulated in the credit, the first beneficiary shall have the right to request that payment or negotiation be effected to the second beneficiary at the place to which the credit has been transferred, up to and including the expiry date of the original credit, and without prejudice to the first beneficiary's right subsequently to substitute his own invoices and drafts (if any) for those of the second beneficiary and to claim any difference due to him.

**Assignment of proceeds**

**Article 55**

The fact that a credit is not stated to be transferable shall not affect the beneficiary's right to assign any proceeds to which he may be, or may become, entitled under such credit, in accordance with the provisions of the applicable law.

The Uniform Customs and Practice for Documentary Credits were proposed by the ICC Commission on Banking Technique and Practice.

This Commission brings together bankers from throughout the world with the object of:

_ defining, simplifying and hormonizing the practices and terminology used in international banking;

_ expressing the views of bankers before relevant international organizations, in particular the United Nations Commission on International Trade Law (UNCITRAL);

_ Serving as a forum for bankers to discuss common problems.

Each ICC National Committee may appoint members of the Banking Commission, and of the twenty other ICC Commissions covering most subject areas of interest to international business.

Seminars and conferences on practical aspects of the application of the UCP are also held every year in numerous countries; details on application from National Committees.

## Annexure II

## EXIM BANK ROLE & POLICIES

Exim Bank plays a four-pronged role with regard to India's foreign trade: those of a coordinator, a source of finance, consultant and promoter.

## CO-ORDINATION ROLE

Exim Bank is the Coordinator of the Working Group Mechanism for clearance of Project & Services Exports and Deferred Payment Exports (for amounts above a certain value – currently Rs. 200 crores). The Working Group comprises Exim Bank, Government of India representatives (Ministries of Finance, Commerce), Reserve Bank of India, Export Credit Guarantee Corporation of India Ltd. and commercial banks who are authorised foreign exchange dealers. This inter-institutional Working Group accords clearance to contracts (at the post-award stage) sponsored by commercial banks and Exim Bank, and operates as a one-window mechanism for clearance of term export proposals. On its own, Exim Bank can now accord clearance to project export proposals upto Rs. 200 crores in value.

## FINANCING SERVICES

Exim Bank offers a diverse range of financing services for the Indian exporter, including a variety of Export Credit facilities, and Finance for Export Oriented Companies.

### Export Credits

Exim Bank offers the following Export Credit facilities, which can be availed of by Indian companies, commercial banks and overseas entities.

### For Indian Companies executing contracts overseas

### Pre-shipment credit

Where the manufacturing cycle of the export contract exceeds six months, Exim Bank's Pre-shipment Credit facility provides access to finance at the manufacturing stage – enabling exporters to purchase raw materials and other inputs.

Exporters can also avail of our Foreign Currency Pre-shipment credit facility to import raw materials and other inputs required for export production.

### Supplier's Credit

At the post-shipment stage, this facility enables Indian exporters to extend term credit to importers (overseas) of eligible goods.

## For Project Exporters

Indian project exporters incur Rupee expenditure while executing overseas project export contracts. Exim Bank's facility helps them meet these expenses. These would generally include costs of mobilisation/acquisition of materials, personnel and equipment, payments to be made in India to staff, sub-contractors and consultants, and project-related overheads in Indian Rupees.

## For Exporters of Consultancy and Technological Services

Exim Bank offers a special credit facility to Indian exporters of consultancy and technology services, so that they can, in turn, extend term credit to overseas importers. The services covered include providing personnel for rendering technical services, transfer of technology/know-how, preparation of project feasibility reports, maintenance and management contracts, etc.

## Guarantee Facilities

Indian companies can avail of these to furnish requisite guarantees to facilitate execution of export contracts and import transactions.

## Forfaiting

Forfaiting is a financing mechanism that enables a company to convert credit sale to cash sale, on 'without recourse' basis. Exim Bank acts as a facilitator for the Indian exporter, enabling him to access the services of an overseas forfaiting agency.

## For Commercial Banks

Exim Bank offers Rediscounting facility to commercial banks, enabling them to rediscount export bills of their SSI customers, with usance not exceeding 90 days.

We also offer Refinance of Supplier's Credit, enabling commercial banks to offer credit of Indian exporters of eligible goods, who in turn extend term credit over 180 days to importers overseas.

## Other Facilities for Indian Companies

Indian companies executing contracts within India, but which are financed by multilateral funding agencies, can avail of credit under our Finance for Deemed Exports facility, aimed at helping them meet cash flow deficits.

## For Overseas Entities

Overseas buyers can avail of Buyer's Credit from Exim Bank, for import of eligible goods from India on deferred payment terms.

Besides, Exim Bank extends Lines of Credit to overseas financial institutions, foreign governments and their agencies, enabling them to lend term loans to finance import of eligible goods from India.

## Finance for Export Oriented Units (EOUs)

For the purpose of our financing, an Export Oriented Company is defined as any company with a minimum export orientation of 10% of net sales, or annual export sales of Rs.5 crores, whichever is lower.

### Project finance

For Setting up EOUs Exim Bank offers term loans for setting up new projects, and for acquisition of assets for modernisation/ upgradation/ expansion of existing units. The Bank also extends 100% refinance to commercial banks, for term loans sanctioned by the lending bank to an EOU.

### For Textile and Jute Industries

The Bank also extends finance to eligible units in textile and jute industries under the Technology Upgradation Fund Scheme, to enable them to upgrade their manufacturing facilities.

### For Software Industry

The Bank offers a comprehensive financing/services package for the software industry. These include project/equipment finance, working capital finance, overseas investment finance, besides support for obtaining product/ process certification, export marketing, and export product development.

To address the perceived constraint in the availability of trained software professionals, Exim Bank extends term loans to software exporters for establishment/expansion of software training institutes. Further, the Bank also facilitates setting up of software technology parks (STPs).

### For Indian Companies involved in Port Development and related activities

Exim Bank extends term loans to Indian companies involved in construction of ports/jetties, and for acquisition of fixed assets for stevedoring, cargo handling, storage and related activities like dry docks and ship breaking.

### Equipment Finance

### Finance for Production Equipment

To cater to the non-project related capital expenditure of EOUs, Exim Bank offers a line of credit for acquisition of imported/indigenous equipment, including equipment for packaging, pollution control, etc.

### For Vendors of EOUs

Under the Export Vendor Development finance facility, Exim Bank offers term loans to vendors of EOUs, to enable them to acquire plant and machinery and other assets required for increasing export capability.

### Working Capital Finance

Exim Bank provides term loans (of 1 year, 1-2 years, and upto 5 years tenor) to eligible EOUs, to help them meet their working capital (loan component) requirements.

## OTHER FACILITIES

### Finance for R & D and Export Product Development

Exim Bank offers term loans to EOUs for development of new technology to satisfy domestic and international environment and standards, and to help them develop and/or commercialise new product/process applications.

### Underwriting

Exim Bank extends underwriting commitment to Indian exporters, to help them raise finance from capital markets through public/rights issues of equity shares/debentures.

### Export Marketing Finance

Exim Bank offers term loans to Indian companies, to aid them in their efforts to penetrate and retain their presence in overseas markets, particularly in developed countries.

### Import Loans

Exim Bank finances bulk imports of consumable inputs and canalised items undertaken by manufacturing companies.

### Guarantee Facility

Exim Bank issues different kinds of guarantees for EOUs. These include: (a) export obligation guarantees; (b) deferred payment guarantees; and (c) guarantees in favour of commercial banks/lending institutions abroad on behalf of Indian exporters.

### For JVs between Indian and East Asian companies

Under the Asian Countries Investment Partners Programme, Exim Bank provides finance at various stages of a join venture project cycle viz., sector study, project identification, feasibility study, prototype development and technical, managerial assistance.

### Finance for Ventures Overseas

Exim Bank offers term loans to Indian companies, both for equity investment in their ventures overseas as well as for on lending purposes.

Besides, Exim Bank also undertakes Direct Equity Stake in Indian Ventures Abroad, to enable Indian companies to supplement their equity with Exim Bank's equity contribution.

**Export Services**

Exim Bank offers a diverse range of information, advisory and support services, which enable exporters to evaluate international risks, exploit export opportunities and improve competitiveness.

For Multilateral Agencies Funded Projects Overseas (MFPO) Exim Bank offers value-added information and support services to Indian Companies seeking business in projects funded by multilateral agencies such as the World Bank, Asian Development Bank, African Development Bank, European bank for Reconstruction & Development, and other official Development Agencies like the Overseas Economic Cooperation Fund of Japan. Services offered include:

* Identification of business opportunities in funded projects.

* Details on specific projects of interest.

* Information on procurement guidelines, policies and practices of multilateral agencies.

* Assistance for registration with multilateral agencies & advice on preparation of Expression of interest, Capability Profile, etc.

* Advice on bids, with regard to bid evaluation, review of bid documents, etc.

Apart from these, we also offer support services, such as liaising with Indian missions, monitoring bid performance, aids in pre qualification, etc.

**Commercial Services**

Exim Bank undertakes customised research on behalf of interested companies, in areas such as establishing market potential, defining marketing arrangements and specifying distribution channels. We also assist companies in developing export market entry plans, obtaining quality certifications and display of their products in our overseas offices.

**Country Profiles**

Exim Bank also undertakes country profiles, which assess the economic, political, currency and credit risks involved, along with the export opportunities in the country concerned.

**Financial Counselling**

Exim Bank offers advice on how to access foreign currency finance from multilateral institutions and import lines of credit, trade finance alternatives, collection/payment systems, as well as on the creditworthiness of business entities and banks.

**Internationalisation Support**

Exim Bank helps in identifying technology suppliers, partners, and in consummation of domestic and overseas joint ventures, through its network of alliances and its overseas offices. We also advise companies on regulatory clearances, and facilitate tying-up finance for equity and working capital.

**Information Access**

Exim Bank issues business opportunities alerts, which communicate business leads, acquisition opportunities, industry trends, as well as collaboration opportunities from the European commission's network, Bureau de Rapprochement des Enterprises, of which Exim Bank is a partner institution.

**Building Export Capability**

Eximius Learning Centres in Bangalore and Ahmedabad organises training programmes, workshops and seminars for exporters. These programmes, often on sector-specific issues, are conducted by international experts from trade promotion organizations and multinational companies.

The Bank also carries out research on issues related to international trade, economics, and sector/product/country studies, which it publishes in the form of Occasional Papers.

The Bank disseminates information on export opportunities and highlights developments that have a bearing on Indian exports, through its quarterly bulletin, Eximium: Export Advantage. Besides, this publication also carries a regular feature, Country Scan, which gives updates on the trade/ investment climate in various countries.

The Bank has in place and exporters' club, called the Eximius Club, which offers the Club members preferential access to a range of services, such as tracking of upcoming projects, advance and timely information on available opportunities and follow-up on bids submitted by them.

**International Merchant Banking Services**

Exim Bank provides advisory services to Indian exporters to enable them to offer competitive financial packages when they bid for exports.

❖ ❖ ❖

# 10

# EXPORT PROCEDURES

## COMMENCEMENT

It is essential for an exporter to register himself with the specified authorities. These are

**(a) Regional Licensing Authority** – The Joint Director General of Foreign Trade for the respective area is the authority under which an exporter has to register himself, and obtain an IEC number. The customs authorities will not allow one to export or import from the country unless he has obtained the IEC number. It should also be remembered that if an organization , after obtaining the number does not export or import any goods in a year, the authorities may strike off the IEC No from the list.

**(b) Registration with the export promotion council** – This is done on a prescribed form given by the council. This registration also helps the exporter to get any benefit/concession given under the export/import policy. If the product/service to be exported does not have any specific council or authority to which it is attached, the organization can register with FIEO (Federation of Indian Exporters' Organisation).

The procedural aspects of our export operations are quite formidable, and a student, or for that matter even an experienced exporter, is overwhelmed by the magnitude of procedural requirements at every stage of export execution – right from the time an export order is obtained until the realisation of export proceeds and the benefits thereof.

## PROCEDURES IN THE VARIOUS PHASES OF EXPORT

In this chapter, the treatment of procedures, right from the receipt of a confirmed order until the realisation of export proceeds and export benefits is based on the personal and practical experience of an exporter. Discussion of the relevant procedures involved in an export operation has been dealt with, with reference to various phases of export. These phases are:

I. Offer and receipt of confirmed orders;

II. Production and clearance of the products for exports;

III. Shipment;

IV. Negotiation of documents and realisation of export proceeds; and

V. Obtaining various export incentives.

### I. Offer and receipt of confirmed orders

The proposal submitted by an exporter (be it in the form of a letter or quotation) is referred to as the 'OFFER'. The offer, when accepted by the foreign buyer, becomes an order.

The offer made by the exporter is usually in the form of a 'proforma invoice'. Technically, this is just a document indicating the exporter's intention to sell, and is usually addressed to the prospective buyer. The proforma invoice would include the following:

**(1) The Consignee or the Buyer:** The complete name and address of the buyer should be clearly indicated. The consignee can be an individual, a limited company, a corporation or a government department.

In the case of a government department, it is essential to address the communication, as is the practice in many countries, by the designation of the official concerned, such as the Permanent Secretary, Public Works Department, Ministry of Public Works and Road Maintenance.

**(2) Description of Goods:** The proforma invoice should carry a brief description of the goods, indicating important technical specifications and physical features which make the identification of the product easy. Where detailed technical specifications are called for, a separate sheet giving these should be appended as a part of the proforma invoice.

**(3) Price:** The proforma invoice should indicate the unit and total prices of the product in internationally accepted or mutually agreed currency. It should indicate the total quantity of the products offered. There are certain products for which quantity discounts are given, and the invoice should clearly indicate the quantum of discount for a specific volume. Hence, the maximum quantity to which the invoice is applicable should also be made clear.

The basis of price indicated in the proforma should be f.o.b., c&f. or c.i.f. or any other internationally accepted term, as detailed in INCONTERMS in the Chapter on Export Pricing. The basis should be acceptable to the buyer. Oftentimes, the proforma invoice is submitted in response to a tender enquiry or other enquiries where the basis acceptable is clearly mentioned.

Export offers are normally submitted in currencies such as US dollars, Deutsch marks, pound sterling, etc. In arriving at these values, the exporter converts his Rupee prices into the respective currencies at the rate applicable on the day of the offer. Since the fluctuations in currency values occur very often, it is advisable to add an exchange variation clause. This clause clearly specifies the exchange rate at which the Indian Rupee has been converted into the foreign currency and mentions that, in the event of any changes in currency values, the exporter should realise the Indian Rupee equivalent, calculated on the basis of the prevailing rate.

In the case of large export contracts spreading over a long period of, say 5 to 10 years on deferred payments, a forward exchange contract is taken by the exporter with the ECGC, the actual cost thereof being included in the price quoted.

**(4) Conditions of Sale:** The proforma invoice submitted entails legal obligations on the part of the exporter to supply the product to the buyer, in the event of the invoice being accepted by him. Hence, it is necessary that the conditions of sale and other factors qualifying it should be clearly spelt out. Some of the important conditions are:

**(i) Validity:** The proforma invoice submitted should indicate the period for which it is valid for acceptance. The buyer has the right to accept the proforma invoice anytime within the validity period, and the exporter has to fulfill his obligations.

In view of this, the exporter should evaluate the various problems which may arise, such as increase in the price of his product, internal transport, shipping charges, freight and such other variables, and be reasonably confident that he will be able to fulfil his obligations.

In case of tenders, the validity period is stipulated by the buyer. In other cases, a period, which is consistent with the product concerned and with the international practice, has to be given.

**(ii) Escalation Clause:** This is normally included when the delivery is to be effected over a prolonged period, or in cases where certain elements of cost are known to be variable. In the former case, the escalation in prices asked for, is given in the form of the increase in the cost of raw materials or wages; or by means of a flat increase in the percentage value of f.o.b. on supplies made after a particular period (say, an increase of 2 1/2% of the f.o.b. value of the price indicated on supplies made six months after the date of the proforma invoice, and an increase of 5% of f.o.b. value on all supplies made 12 months after the date of the invoice). In the latter case, it is stated that certain elements of cost would be charged on an actual basis. A typical example would be the increase in shipping freight which cannot be determined earlier. Hence, it is normally included in the proforma, as given below:

"The f.o.b. prices quoted are firm during the validity period for acceptance. However, the sea freight and insurance charges indicated are based on the rate applicable as on the date, and would be recovered at actual charges paid at the time of shipment".

**(iii) Delivery Schedule:** The delivery period given in the proforma invoice should be realistic. In cases where c.i.f. quotations are given, the legal obligation is on the part of the exporter to make the goods available at the port of destination as per the delivery schedule indicated. In view of the vagaries in shipping, many of the exporters take the precaution of indicating clearly in the proforma invoice the clause, "subject to the availability of shipping space."

**(iv) Inspection:** Where inspection of goods is required, it is necessary to specify in the proforma invoice the authority which would conduct the inspection, as also the nature of inspection. Normally, export goods are offered for inspection before shipment, and hence the terms of reference for inspection should be made clear in the offer itself.

**(v) Force Mejeure Clause:** This is a detailed commercial clause in a proforma invoice which comes to the rescue of the exporter when he is prevented from fulfilling his contracts because of developments such as war, riots and other causes which are beyond his control.

**(vi) Payment Terms:** The mode of payment, such as Letter of Credit and the various clauses therein required by the exporter, have to be clearly stated.

**(5) Other Obligations:** Apart from the above, in the export of nontraditional goods, certain other obligations are agreed to by the exporter in the proforma invoice. These are:

(i) The assistance that would be rendered to the buyer in the form of after-sales service by the exporter or his agent.

(ii) Agreeing to making available spare parts for sale for the equipment supplied for a certain period of time, especially in cases where the products can go out of production due to the introduction of new/improved products.

(iii) Warranty for the equipment supplied, taking full responsibility for any manufacturing defect of equipment or part thereof, and free replacement during the specified warranty period.

**Confirmed Order:** When the proforma invoice is accepted by the buyer, it becomes a confirmed order. Normally, the duplicate copy of the proforma invoice is duly signed by the buyer, accepting the conditions therein and returning it to the exporter, who insists on the establishment of the documentary letter of credit, so that the buyer's commitment is complete. Experienced exporters treat an export order as confirmed only when the letter of credit is established.

It may also be possible in some cases for the buyer to accept the proforma invoice and confirm the order by a letter. However, orders of high value, as well as orders from public sector and government organisations, are in the form of a contract which clearly specifies the obligations of both the parties.

The proforma invoice and confirmed order are very important and basic documents in the execution of an export order/contract and hence they have been dealt with in detail in the preceding paragraphs.

## II. Producing the Goods

The next phase in the processing of an export order is to make arrangements for the items to be produced at the factory of the exporter or to be obtained form a supplier. All the operations from the time an indent for production is placed, till it reaches the export warehouse, are normally covered by this phase.

An exporter may be the export department of a manufacturing concern, or one, who has different sources of supplies developed with supporting manufacturers.

In the case of an exporter who is a department of a manufacturing concern, an internal indent is raised on the producing division, which indicates the quantity, the complete specifications of the item to be produced as well as the delivery dates by which the goods should be ready at the factory/warehouse of the exporter.

An exporter with no production facilities of his own, raises a formal purchase order on a supporting manufacturer. The purchase order would indicate the quantity and description of the times, delivery date, the payment terms and the other obligations of the supplier in connection with the purchase order.

In the case of purchase from such suppliers for domestic sales, the purchases will attract sales tax. However, in the case of export, Government has clarified that the transaction will be exempt from sales tax, provided that suitable evidence of export is produced against such purchases.

In the state of Maharashtra, a provision is available for non-payment of sales tax if the exporter/shipper produces what is known as "Form 14". The essence of declaration made by the exporter in this form indicates that whatever he has purchased for export has been exported, as a whole, in the same state in which he has purchased it. This provision is of great help to the exporting community, for it is very clear and encourages more exports from this State by established exporters.

**Excise Duty Rebate:** Excise duty is a levy imposed by the Government of India on all excisable items as specified by it and is usually collected at source, i.e., at the manufacturing stage. The manufactured products, as soon as they are ready for dispatch from the factory attract the levy. Only after the excise is paid can the products be removed from the factory premises.

Products meant for export are exempted from the imposition of excise duty. A simple procedure is adopted for this purpose. Excisable goods are exported either under a claim of rebate of duty paid or under a bond without payment of duty. The rebate is made under Rule 19 of the

Central Excise Rules, 1944, according to which, rebate of duty can be granted on excisable goods as notified from time to time.

For the purpose or claiming rebate when an excise duty is paid, an exporter submits to the Superintendent of Central Excise of the locality the following documents;

*(i)* Gate Pass - GP-1;

*(ii)* ARE-1 form.

Three copies of GP-1, together with five copies of ARE-1, are forwarded to Central Excise authorities. The GP-1 and ARE-1, merely give the description of a product and indicate its quantity as well as the value and the excise duty payable on it. On the basis of GP-1 and ARE-1 form, an official of the Central Excise visits the factory and inspects the packed goods to find out whether they are according to the details mentioned in the ARE-1 form. Once he is satisfied, he certifies the GP-1 and ARE-1 form, returns to the manufacturer the original of GP-1 and also the original and duplicate of the ARE-1 form. The third copy of the ARE-1 form is sent to the Maritime Collector of Central Excise in charge of the port specified in the ARE-1 form. (The Fourth copy is retained by the Central Excise, and the fifth copy by the exporter).

At the time of export, the exporter gets a suitable endorsement on the original and duplicate copy of the

ARE-1 form from an Officer of the Customs Department at the port. An application in the Specified form, attaching the endorsed copy of the ARE-1 form and bill of lading, is made to the Government for the necessary refund.

As opposed to the above procedure, finished products meant for export can also be cleared from the factory under an excise bond without payment of any excise duty whatsoever. For this purpose, the exporter has to execute a bond with the Excise Authorities. The bond is usually backed by a bank guarantee from the company for a specified amount. As this amounts to a "running bond account", the bond is arranged for a suitably large value with the approval of the excise authorities so that a number of export consignments may be exported under the bond without interruption.

**Sales Tax Exemption:** The government allows exemption from paying sales tax for export products. For this, the exporter should register with the Sales Tax Authorities. Sales Tax exemption is for the last two stages of transaction in a product before export.

In case the exporter does not produce the product himself but obtains it from a manufacturer for export, he has to avail of the facility by a filling form known as 'Form H' after the export of the product, and pass the benefit to the manufacturer.

**Pre-shipment Inspection of Export Cargo:** The Government of India has introduced a compulsory pre-shipment inspection for selected items of export to ensure that the products to be exported conform to high quality standards. The pre-shipment inspection scheme is administered by the Export Inspection Council (EIC). Under this scheme, the emphasis is on quality control rather than on inspection for export.

In case the export of the product is subject to export Inspection by the Agency, the exporter makes an application in the prescribed form to the Export Inspection Agency, enclosing the following documents with his application.

(i) Copy of the commercial invoice;

(ii) A crossed cheque or demand draft for the necessary fee in favour of the EIA or the Bank Passbook showing the necessary deposit in favour of the EIA;

(iii) A copy of the export contract; and

(iv) A declaration of the importer's technical specifications of quality and/or a sample approved by the importer in support of the declaration of specifications.

The application must be submitted well in advance of the expected date of shipment. After processing the application, the EIA fixes the date of inspection and an Inspector of the Agency visits the factory for the purpose of inspection of the consignment. This inspection is carried out on a sampling basis. Facilities for conducting a test may be provided to the Inspector if he makes a request for them. Where such facilities are not available, tests are conducted at independent laboratories and the results evaluated. If the Inspector is satisfied with the result, the samples are repacked and the entire consignment is marked and sealed in the presence of the Inspector. The inspector makes a report to the Deputy Director who, in turn, issues an Inspection Certificate in triplicate to the exporter. The consignment is now ready to be moved to the exporter's warehouse or to the port area for shipment.

A simple procedure is available in the case of a manufacturer exporter or a manufacturer whose products are regularly exported. The Export-

Inspection Council recognises the manufacturing unit as an "export-worthy unit". Once a manufacturing unit is declared to be export-worthy, the question of issuing an inspection certificate by the concerned Export Inspection Agency is reduced to a mere submission of an application on the part of exporter. Many exporters are beginning to follow this system of obtaining recognition of export-worthiness from the EIC for their manufacturing units.

The procedure adopted by the EIC for the grant of recognition as an export-worthy unit involves periodical and rigorous checks of the process of manufacturing during the various stages of production, as also a check of the process control and quality control system adopted by the unit itself. This check ensures that the unit is adequately supported with facilities for the enforcement of the quality control standards required by the EIC. The inspection checks in respect of this, are conducted by a panel of experts. Once the Council is satisfied with the findings of the inspection checks, the export-worthy status is granted to the unit. The working of the unit is, however, periodically monitored to ensure that quality standards do not go down.

Quite a few years ago, a committee was appointed by the government, to review export inspection problems, which has since come up with a progressive recommendation that, where export units have the necessary quality control facilities, a "self-certificate" procedure may be adopted so that these export units are authorised to issue their own Inspection certificates and are held responsible for the same.

## III. Shipment:

Shipping is the more popular method of despatching goods to an export buyer than despatch by air. The freight charges for shipping a cargo are very much less than those of air freight. Moreover, the physical size of products, sometimes, constraints the exporter to despatch them by air, especially when these products are heavy machinery or engineering goods.

Under "Shipment" we shall cover all the procedural aspects-from the time the product meant for export leaves the export warehouse, till it is loaded on board the ship and the relevant documents for such loading are collected from the shipping company. Since the type of work involved is somewhat specialised, it is usually performed by the exporter's clearing and forwarding agents.

**The clearing and Forwarding Agents** are specialised personnel who arrange for the completion of all the formalities connected with the shipment of goods. As soon as the export goods reach the warehouse, the exporter arranges for a complete set of shipping documents, to be passed on to the forwarding agent. These comprise —

(1) ARE-1 form in original and duplicate;

(2) Proforma invoice (in duplicate) and packing list, where necessary;

(3) GR-1 form (duplicate);

(4) Letter of credit covering the export order, together with the export contract or order in original;

(5) Certificate of inspection where necessary;

(6) Form of declaration (duplicate); and

(7) Shipping bill (five copies).

The procedure for the removal of excisable export goods from the factory of the exporter has been discussed elsewhere. When the goods are despatched from the factory, the original copy of the gate pass, as well as the original and duplicate copy of the ARE-1 from, are sent to the exporter, who passes them on to the forwarding agent along with other shipping documents, so that the necessary endorsements on them may be obtained from the relevant authorities at the time of shipment to enable the exporter to obtain a rebate on duty or obtain credit in his running excise bond ac

The details of the proforma invoice have also been discussed earlier in this Chapter. Along with the invoice an exporter furnishes a packing slip listing the items packed in the consignment, together with the price of each consignment listed in the packing slip.

**GR-1 form:** GR-1 form is an exchange control document required by the RBI. As per the exchange control regulations, an exporter has to realise the proceeds of the goods he has exported within 180 days from the date of their shipment from India. In order to ensure this, the RBI has introduced the GR-1 procedure.

The GR-1 form is identified by the number in the left hand top corner and the date. It is to be submitted in duplicate along with other shipping documents, and should indicate the exact quantity and description of an item planned to be exported and the value thereof. The quantity and value corresponds with those mentioned in the confirmed order received from the importer. The other important details that should be furnished in the GR-1 form are the name of the exporter, the importer, the currency in which the payment is excepted to be received, the country of destination, and a declaration of the commission/discount payable.

The GR-1 form procedure applied to exports made to all countries outside India, excluding Nepal and Bhutan.

In all cases, the GR-1 form must be completed in duplicate, and submitted to the customs along with other shipping documents with a view to obtaining the necessary permission to ship the goods. The customs authorities, after scrutinising it, retain the original copy and forward it to RBI. The duplicate of GR-1 from is returned to the exporter, to enable him to submit the same to RBI through the negotiating bank, through which payment is to be received.

**Shipping Bill:** A shipping bill is the main document required by the customs authorities for the purpose of granting permission for shipment. When goods are manufactured in India on which drawback duty is allowed, the shipping bill used is called the drawback shipping bill. Non-drawback shipping bills are used when the exporter imports an item from abroad for re-export or when drawback is not applicable. For our study, we shall discuss only the drawback shipping bill.

**A drawback shipping bill** is prepared in five copies. It contains the name of the exporter or the shipper, his address, the Code No., the description and quantity of goods to be shipped, the value of goods, the number of packages and the markings on them, the amount of drawback claimed, the port of destination, the name of the ship together with the name of the agent, etc. The five copies include the customs and statistical copy, the port trust copy, the drawback copy and the export promotion copy. The port trust copy is utilised for the purpose of claiming incentives.

**Export Licence:** The Government of India regulations require that an export licence be obtained for certain categories of export products before shipment is made. The licence has to be obtained from the licencing authority who is usually the Joint Chief Controller of Imports and Exports. One complete set of shipping documents with the prescribed application form is submitted to the JCCI&E for the grant of an export licence. the JCCI&E scrutinises the application with reference to quantity, value and description of goods in all the document. In case of items with floor prices, the authorities check whether the price to be realised as indicated in the document, is in line with the minimum floor price fixed by the Government. Once they are satisfied, the JCCI&E grants the licence for the export of goods by a suitable endorsement on all the copies of the shipping bill.

In the last few years, the Government of India has delicensed a number of products. The need of approaching the licensing authorities does not therefore arise, except for a few products.

**Customs Clearance:** According to prevailing customs regulations, no cargo meant for export can be loaded on a ship unless the customs authorities at the port accord their formal approval. After obtaining the export licence, where necessary, a complete set of shipping documents, including five copies of the shipping bill "under claim of drawback," is submitted by the exporter to the customs house concerned. An officer of the Customs Department of the rank of an appraiser, scrutinises the complete set of documents with a view to determining:

— Whether the description, quantity and value indicated in the shipping bill for which permission is sought for export, correspond with those mentioned in the contract entered into with the buyer, and whether they are authenticated in the letter of credit received from the buyer;

— Whether the prices are correct;

— Whether the formalities pertaining to exchange control, quality control, inspection and licensing have been complied with, wherever applicable.

The customs also check the details in the GR-1 form, including its number and date and the entry thereof in the other document. The original copy of the GR-1 from is retained by the customs and later, after recording the same in their register, forward it to the RBI. The original copy of the shipping bill, together with a copy of the proforma invoice, is retained by the customs. After an examination of the documents and an appraisement of the value, the customs appraiser makes an endorsement on the duplicate copy of the shipping bill, giving directions to the dock appraiser about the extent of physical examination to be conducted at the docks. The entire set of shipping documents-except the original GR-1 form, the original shipping bill and a copy of the proforma invoice is returned to the exporter's forwarding agent for further process in. With the endorsement on the duplicate copy of the shipping bill by the export department of the customs house, customs clearance for the export of products mentioned in the shipping bill is deemed to have been obtained.

**Carting Order:** The export cargo lying in the warehouse of the exporter has now to be moved inside the port area and subsequently loaded on board the assigned ship. The forwarding agent, for this purpose, has to obtain permission from the Port Trust authorities to allow him to physically move the goods inside the port area. This permission, which is given by the Superintendent of the Port Trust in charge of the shed where loading has to be carried out is called the carting order. The Shed Superintendent issues this carting order after verifying the endorsement of the steamer agent on the port trust copy of the shipping bill, as also the endorsement of the customs house on its duplicate copy. With this permission, the export cargo mentioned in the shipping bill is physically moved into the appropriate shed of the Port.

**Customs Examination of Cargo at the Docks:** The remaining copies of the entire set of shipping documents-mainly consisting of the duplicate, triplicate and export promotion copies of the shipping bill, the proforma invoice with the packing list, the original and duplicate of AR-4 form and the inspection certificate-is present to the custom appraiser connected with the shed. The main purpose of the customs examination at the docks is to verify whether the goods packed and kept ready for shipment are the same as those mentioned in the shipping bill. The customs appraiser, if necessary, may physically examine the goods packed inside the cases and satisfy himself before making his endorsement on the shipping bill, thus certifying that the goods have been examined. Once this endorsement, which is made on the duplicate copy of the shipping bill has been obtained, the goods are deemed to be "out of charge" of the customs.

**Let Ship:** The Preventive Officer of the Customs Department supervises the loading of the cargo on board the vessel nominated for its export. Before the goods are loaded on to the ship, permission for loading has to be obtained by the exporter's forwarding agent from the Preventive Officer. This permission is called the "Let Ship Order". The let ship order is given as an endorsement on the duplicate copy of the shipping bill. The shipping bill with the let ship endorsement is then handed over to the agent of the shipping company who, on the basis of this, arranges for the loading of the cargo. The let ship order thus constitutes an authorisation by the customs to the shipping company to accept the cargo on board the vessel.

**Mate Receipt:** As soon as the goods are loaded on board the vessel, the Captain or Master of the ship furnishes a document called the "Mate Receipt" to the Port Superintendent in charge of the shed. It is a document certifying loading of the cargo on board the vessel and contains other details, such as a brief description of the cargo, the number of packages, the shipping marks, the name of the vessel, and the date of issue. The mate receipt also contains a comment by the Master of the vessel on the condition of the cargo at the time of its receipt on board the vessel. Usually, damages to packing or improper packing finds a place in the Mate Receipt, which is ultimately reflected in the bill of lading. Such remarks on the bill of lading may not be acceptable to the buyer. Every exporter therefore tries to obtain a clean Mate Receipt, i.e., one without any adverse comment on the condition of the cargo at the time of shipment, by ensuring that no damage occurs at the time to loading.

**Port Trust Dues:** An exporter has to obtain the **bill of lading** from the shipping agent which gives him a title to the goods shipped on the vessel. This is given by the shipping agent only after the mate receipt is presented to him by the exporter or his forwarding agent, who arranges to pay the port charges and collects the mate receipt surrendered to the port authorities by the Master of the vessel. The mate receipt, thus collected, is furnished to the Preventive Officer, who records the certificate of shipment on the duplicate and export promotion copies of the shipping bill, as also on the original and duplicate copies of AR-4 forms. The drawback copy and the export promotion copy of the shipping bill together with the duplicate copy of theAR-4 are given back to the exporter's forwarding agent.

The exporter's forwarding agent surrenders the mate receipt collected from the port trust office to the agent of the shipping company and collects copies of the bills of lading.

At the end of this process, the exporter's forwarding agent returns to the exporter the following documents:

(i) A copy of the invoice duly attested by the customs;

(ii) Drawback copy of the shipping bill;

(iii) Export promotion copy of the shipping bill;

(iv) A full set of "clean on board" bill of lading, together with non-negotiable copies, as required by the exporter;

(v) The original letter of credit and the customer's order or contract; and

(vi) A duplicate copy of the ARE-1 form.

## MARINE INSURANCE POLICY

In the case of a c.i.f. quotation given to the buyer, the marine Insurance Policy has to be obtained by the exporter Marine Insurance is covered by the Marine Insurance Act. It covers the loss or damage of the goods in transit. The exporter gets a Marine Insurance Policy from the insurance organization, after paying the premium required. The policy will contain all the details of the goods exported, name of the buyer, conditions of the policy, the sum assured etc. The exporter dispatches the original signed copy of the Insurance, it the other documents like Bill of lading etc to the negotiating bank.

In case the goods are lost or damaged, the buyer should immediately intimate the loss to the exporter and also lodge a complaint with the insurance company with a survey done by the appropriate surveyor. The buyer should also get a 'Landing Remarks' certificate from the port authorities. Thereafter, the exporter who would have insured will lodge a claim with the insurance co with the following details

(A) Marine Insurance Policy

(B) Copy of Bill of Lading

(C) Survey report/Landing Remarks certificate

(D) Copy of the invoice and any other documents required by the Insurance Company.

### V. Realisation of export proceeds

Once the goods have been physically loaded on board the ship, the exporter should arrange to obtain his payment for the exports made by submitting relevant documents. The submission of the relevant set of documents to the bank and the process of obtaining payment consequently is called "negotiating the documents" through the bank.

A complete set of documents normally submitted for the purpose of negotiation is called a negotiable set of documents, which will usually consist of the following:

(1) Commercial invoice together with the packing slip if needed, and the draft (Bill of Exchange)

(2) Certificate of origin

(3) GR-1 form — duplicate

(4) Marine Insurance Policy in duplicate

(5) Letter of Credit in original.

(6) Bills of Lading — three negotiable copies and as many non-negotiable copies, as required.

**Bill of Lading:** The bill of lading is one of the most important documents in the entire process of exporting. It is a negotiable document. It is important because it carries with it the legal title to the goods shipped on board the vessel indicated therein. Besides, it is receipt given by the shipping company for the goods loaded on a particular ship. a bill of loading would contain a broad description of the goods, the quantity of goods, the total number of packages, gross and net weight the port of shipment, the port of discharge, the name of the ship, and the amount of freight paid. The significant details of a bill of lading are the number, the date of the bill of lading and the freight paid. The date on the bill of lading is highly significant, for it is taken as the date of the shipment of goods, and should therefore be within the validity date given in the documentary letter of credit.

A clean bill of lading is one in which no adverse entry about the apparent condition of goods has been made. When an adverse comment does appear on it, the bill of lading is termed as a claused bill of lading. The remarks on the mate receipt issued by the Master of the vessel about the apparent condition of goods at the time they were received on board the vessel, usually find a place on the bill of lading as well, thus making it a claused bill of lading.

Claused bill of lading is normally not accepted by the foreign buyer. Unless the letter of credit specifically permits the acceptance of such a bill, the exporter should endeavour to negotiate documents with a clean bill of lading, for otherwise the buyer has the right to refuse acceptance of goods because they do not conform to the conditions of the letter of credit. A bill of lading is transferable when a suitable endorsement for this purpose is made on it. It is therefore essential that the exporter should take due care while preparing it. The three most widely used endorsements are:

*(i)* "To order and endorsed in blank." Since it is endorsed in blank, any individual who against possession of it can get delivery.

*(ii)* "Endorsed to the order of...." When it is endorsed to the order of a person, bank or a company, only the party indicated in the endorsement can get delivery of goods. The endorsee can

further re-endorse the bill of lading in favour of another party, who can then take delivery of goods. If the bill of lading is made out in the name of the buyer or the foreign bank opening the credit as a consignee, either the buyer or the foreign bank, as the case may be, can take delivery of the goods.

*(iii)* A bill of lading issued after the goods are loaded on the vessel is called an "on board bill of lading." Negotiating banks usually accept only an "on board" bill of lading for the purpose of negotiation. A buyer usually asks for a full set of "clean shipped" or "on board" bill of lading as part of the negotiable documents required by him. The letter of credit would specify what constitutes the full set of bill of lading.

**Commercial Invoice:** A commercial invoice is a document prepared by the exporter giving details of the goods shipped, their brief description, the shipping marks, the unit and total f.o.b. c&f or c.i.f. values as the case may be, depending on the (L.C.) contract, the number and date of the bill of lading as well as the name of the ship carrying the cargo. The description of the cargo mentioned in the invoice should be on the same lines as found in the letter of credit. It is essential that the invoice is made out in the name of buyer or the consignee mentioned in the letter of credit.

**Certificate of Origin:** Sometimes import regulations of a foreign country may require that all imports consignments should be accompanied by a certificate of origin which states the country in which products under export were originally produced/manufactured. This is advisable, for it is quite likely that the goods produced in a particular country attract preferential tariff rates in the foreign market at the time of importation. Or it may be that goods produced in a particular country are banned for import in the foreign market. The certificate of origin helps the buyer in adhering to the import regulations of the country. Some of the foreign markets may accept the certificate of origin issued by a Chamber of Commerce of an exporting country. Others, especially countries in the Middle East and the Gulf, require these certificates to be legalised by their own respective consultants. An exporter submits a copy of the commercial invoice to the Chamber of Commerce, together with the nominal fee prescribed by the Chamber. On the basis of this, the Chamber issues a certificate of origin. Where legalisation is required by the Consulate, the certificate of origin issued by the Chamber of Commerce is submitted to the Consulate of the concerned foreign country, which makes its endorsement on the certificate.

Special certificates of origin are applicable for availing of concessions under Generalised System of Preferences as well as under commonwealth preferences. Under Generalised System of Preferences, the certificate of origin in the specified from usually in triplicate, is obtained from any one of the following agencies.

(1) Export Inspection Council and its agencies;

(2) Chief Controller of Imports and Exports.

The Central Silk Board, The Coir Board, The All-India Handicrafts Board and the Textile Committee are also authorised to issue certificates of origin for the products under their purview.

For concessions under Commonwealth preferences, the certificates of origin have to be submitted in special forms obtainable from the High Commission of the country concerned. The form is also known as "combined certificate of origin and value."

Where the contract with the foreign buyer is on c.i. (cost and insurance) or c.i.f. (cost insurance and freight) basis, the responsibility for taking insurance cover against all risks of damage to or loss of goods during the sea voyage is that of the exporter. On an application received from him describing the goods and mentioning the name of the ship on which the goods are loaded as well as the value of the goods for which the insurance is required, the insurance company issues a policy in the name of the exporter and endorsed in blank. The insurance company issues a policy in the name of the exporter and endorsed in blank. The premium charged by the insurance company would depend on the total value for which the goods are insured, the type of ship as also it age, and the port of discharge of the cargo as evidenced in the bill of lading. The premium rate when goods are loaded on deck of the ship is higher than when they are loaded in the hold of the ship. This is understandable, for the risks involved and the chances of damage to the cargo are more when these are loaded on deck of the ship.

The insurance policy issued by the insurance company should carry the name of the vessel, and the description of goods, corresponding to those found in the bill of lading. It comes into effect only after the date of the bill of lading.

Marine Insurance is a specialised subject as it covers many types of risks. The insurance cover, too, differs from material to material and also depends upon the risks involved. Suffice it is to say that the exporter should consult the insurer before taking out a suitable policy.

## NEGOTIATION

A complete set of negotiable documents is presented to the negotiating bank through whom the documentary letter of credit has been advised. Where the exporter has complied with all the terms and conditions of the letter of credit while submitting his documents to the negotiating bank, the documents are deemed to be clean. The letter of credit opened by the buyer through his bank (the opening bank) authorises drawing a bill of exchange against which payment will be made by the opening bank on behalf of the buyer, provided the terms and conditions specified in the letter of credit are complied with. A bill of exchange is a draft drawn by the negotiating bank on the opening bank or the buyer as the case may be, and is an instrument of payment which is negotiable. The drafts drawn are of two types,

(1) Sight Draft (2) Usance Draft.

If the letter of credit stipulates payment at sight, the exporter draws a "sight draft" on the buyer or his bank. When sight drafts are drawn by the exporter, he expects the buyer to arrange for payment immediately on presentation of the draft. Until payment for the draft is made, shipping documents will not be handed over to the buyer to enable him to clear the goods.

When the exporter has offered credit terms for payment, a "usance draft" is usually drawn by the negotiating bank of the exporter. It is drawn for payment after a specified period. The buyer on whom the draft is drawn retires the draft after 30 days, 60 days or 90 days as agreed between him and the exporter at the time of concluding the contract. The letter of credit opened by the buyer will clearly specify the credit period which has been agreed upon and would mention that the draft should be drawn for 30, 60 or 90 days, as the case may be.

For a credit period beyond 180 days, the exporter has to obtain the prior permission of the exchange control authorities in India, as discussed in the Chapter on Export Finance.

The bill of exchange drawn should correspond to the conditions stipulated in the letter of credit.

The letter of credit would further specify the details of the despatch of documents. The negotiating bank of the exporter would accordingly mail the complete set of documents. Usually, a set of documents is transmitted to the banker of the buyer specified in the letter of credit by the first available air mail, followed by a second set by the next available air mail, so as to ensure that even if the first set is lost, the buyer or his bank may take possession of the goods on the basis of the second copy. The process of negotiation is completed with the despatch of documents by the exporter's banker.

Besides the negotiation of the documents, the banker has to perform other formalities. As part of the negotiable set of documents, the exporter has submitted the duplicate copy of the GR-1 form. After negotiations are complete, and payment is physically received by the bank, the duplicate copy of the GR-1 form is sent to the RBI after due checks.

The exporter requires a commercial invoice attested by the bank for his use in claiming incentives. The bank attests the extra copies of the commercial invoice supplied by the exporter and returns them to him.

To enable the exporter to claim incentives applicable for exports, a certificate known as Form I or "Bank Certificate" is required.

The Form I or Bank Certificate describes the product exported, its value, the details of the invoice, the bill of lading against which the export was made, the rate of conversion for the exchange used, etc. In the case of c.i.f. contracts, the bank certificate specifies the f.o.b. value, freight and insurance under separate headings as evidenced in the bill of lading, insurance policy and invoice. The bank certificate also indicates the GR-1 form number against which the export was made. The original copy of the bank certificate is furnished to the exporter and the duplicate copy is sent to the JCCI&E of the area. A third copy may be kept for its official records.

## Realisation of Export Incentives

The incentives (or concessions)the exporter will get in today's context, and the manner in which they can be obtained are as follows;

(1) **Duty Drawback:** This refers to a rate fixed by the government based on the customs duty and excise duty components which go into the production of an export product. This does not refer to the finished product excise duty, but to the excise and customs duty paid on all the raw materials and components which go into the production.

Every year the Department calls for the latest data on these through the Export Promotion Councils, determine the drawback rate and publish it for the exporters by June of the year. These are mostly industry rates which means that an entity such as bicycles or trucks will be given an industry rate whatever the model or size is exported.

However if the exporter feels that his product, due to very many new factors deserves a higher drawback rate, he can apply for a 'Brand Rate', and the department after verifying the data can give a brand rate.

When the shipping bill is submitted to the customs for the shipping of goods, it consists of a set of five copies. The duplicate copy is known as the 'Drawback copy', and this will contain all the details like description of the product, the port of destination, the total amount of drawback as per government notification etc. This copy is endorsed by customs and sent directly by them to the drawback cell in the customs department situated in the port from which goods were exported. The exporter can approach this cell for his drawback payment with any additional details they may ask for.

## Central Excise Rebate

As mentioned earlier in the book, this can be claimed from the Central Excise Department after submitting the proof of exports in the ARE-1 form. In case it is a Central Excise Bond against which export is done, the exporter should approach the Excise Department which holds the bank account with the proof of export so that the credit is given.

## Octroi and Sales Tax Refund

After the export of the goods, the exporter can approach the department with proof of export and claim the refund.

## Aligned Documentation System (ADS)

Export in India was always distinguished by massive documentation work. In order to eliminate this and bring it down to a manageable level, a committee was set up and its findings were accepted and implemented by the government.

With effect from 1.10.1991, the new standardised documents came into effect. This is referred to as The Aligned Documentation System based on the U.N. layout key. The documents are aligned in such a manner that the common items of information are given in the same relative slots. This system also helps to prepare one "Master Documents" embodying information common to all documents, and xerox all the aligned documents by suitable masking and reproduction techniques.

Accordingly the standardised documents for Indian exports are:

1. Invoice
2. Exchange Control Declaration (GR) Form
3. Shipping Bill (Dock challan/Duty Draw Back and Port Trust Copy)
4. Bill of Lading.

❖ ❖ ❖

# 11

# COUNTERTRADE

The global financial crisis which erupted in September 2008 has adversely affected the country and international trade has taken a serious hit due to recession and financial constraints for the importing countries. In these circumstances one will not be surprised, if 'countertrade' where products/commodities of equal monetary value are exchanged between countries, once again comes to the fore. Hence it is worthwhile to know its background in India.

Countertrade has grown over a period of time. It is estimated that countertrade was used by businesses and governments in 15 countries in 1979, and it grew to 100 countries by the nineties. Many of the East European countries before their liberation, and many of the third world countries were prominent players.

Another area where it flourished was in defence supplies, usually referred to as 'Offset on Defence related exports'.

The government of India has no declared policy on countertrade. However, global tenders usually include a clause stating 'that all other things being equal, preference will be given to companies willing to agree to countertrade'.

Crude oil prices are increasing relentlessly and touched $147 per barrel early this year, and food prices are also escalating as never before. These have a great impact on international trade and it will not be surprising if countertrade comes to the central stage, when many countries struggle to fulfill their needs in energy and food.

## THE TREND

Countertrade is all about exporting, and receiving a commodity of equivalent value in lieu of payment. Here, the exporter does not take physical delivery of the commodity. Instead the commodity is held in the country of its origin, and depending upon the fluctuations in price, a futures contract is taken, and sold by the exporter on a subsequent date at the best price, to the highest bidder. In some cases the payment is also by means of a new project to be executed in the exporter's country.

There is no clear estimate of the total value of the countertrade transacted in the world. One of the oft quoted estimates is that over 40% of all international trade is by countertrade. However India whose international trade (exports and imports) is around US $ 400 billion, transacts very little by way of countertrade, whereas the developing and underdeveloped countries of the world with severe foreign exchange crunch would like India to trade by way of countertrade.

India did not have any machinery to effectively enter into countertrade. However things have changed considerably after Indian Commodity Exchanges have come into being in the recent past. It is understood that the Indian Commerce Ministry is working on a strategy to establish linkages between a few of the Indian Commodity Exchanges, the global networks and exporters. The object is to provide a platform for Indian exporters to park future and active commodities earned in lieu of payment from the countries to which they have exported, on a countertrade basis.

The absence of a suitable Commodity Exchange in India, which can take charge of the commodities earned by the exporters in lieu of payment, has been the main obstacle which has prevented any active countertrade taking place in India. It is possible that some of the Commodity Exchanges which have come into being in India could be designated to handle countertrade. The National Commodity and Derivatives Exchange (NCDEx) which is shortly going to become active, may be the one which may be chosen for the job.

With e-trade getting established in the world, e-trade Exchanges offer a huge database of counter trade products and parties who offer price quotations of commodities. This enables the exporter to determine fairly accurately, the payment equivalent of the commodities offered to him by way of countertrade. It also helps him to keep track of the global prices, to enable him to sell the commodities at the right time and right price to get the export proceeds of his original export transaction. For example Tradex, a global network which is backed by international companies is one such famous organization, and if the Indian Commodity Exchanges tie up with such a global network to access international trading patterns, it will become very easy for Indian exporters to tackle countertrade offers.

Incidentally there will be a need to change some of the existing regulations, such as the mandated period of receipt of export proceeds, the provision to offer the necessary post-shipment credit facilities (at present there is no provision to offer such credit on countertrade), and such of those RBI regulations which may come into conflict with this type of trading. These have to be sorted out by the government in consultation with the Reserve Bank of India and simplify the procedures.

A student of International Trade should know this type of transaction, its variants, origin and growth.

It is easier to understand COUNTERTRADE by describing some of the familiar forms of this type of trade.

## BARTER

The simplest form is by means of barter. This amounts to exchange of goods or services of equivalent value between the seller in one country and the buyer in another. Even though the intention is to exchange goods of agreed value simultaneously between countries, it seldom happens. In such cases, suitable payment guarantees are obtained so as to complete these transactions over an agreed period. This can be described as the oldest form of international trade and as the origin of present day countertrade.

It should be remembered that in India private organisations are not allowed to enter into barter trade with other countries without the permission of the authorities.

## BUY BACK

The exporter from a developed country who exports manufactured products, agrees to buy back, to the extent of his export or more, the same product to be produced with his help from another developing country.

It operates in the following manner:

The exporter agrees to establish a factory in the country of the importer on a turnkey basis, for a specified amount. The exporter is responsible for providing the technology, the machinery and also ensuring that the production comes up to the agreed quality and output norms. He agrees to buy back the products produced out of this arrangement - it can be a portion or the entire output. This is usually resorted to, to ensure a reliable source for some of the exporting country's needs, and also in cases where it is phasing out certain types of production due to high cost of labour or pollution constraints.

## SWITCH TRAD

A third party is brought into the countertrade arrangement to accept the goods that the original foreign company is unable to use or market itself. This is also known as a three-way counter purchase deal.

This always happens when one of the countries in a bilateral agreement has to take goods which it cannot not consume, and involves a third party from another country, which purchases such goods at a discount of 20% to 50% and sells them for hard currency, to settle the trading account.

This was greatly prevalent during the days when India had bilateral rupee trade accounts with many countries. These countries, which were always in great need of hard currency used to indulge in switch deals. These deals sometime used to depress the free market prices of Indian products, and therefore government used to strongly discourage the deals.

## COMPENSATION TRADING

This is the kind of sale in which part payment is in cash and the balance paid through a list of goods offered by the buyer. The goods available will, in some cases, be those which cannot be sold for convertible currency in the western markets. One would need the services of a specialist Trading House to realise cash from these goods.

## COUNTER PURCHASE

This is also referred to as parallel trading. It usually occurs when the buyer imports some sought after item like computers etc., for hard currency, but ties down the exporter to buy some goods from the importing country, and the goods thus purchased will be for an agreed value of say 30% of the contract value.

## ESCROW ACCOUNT TRADING

In this case the exports are made only after sufficient funds are raised on behalf of the buyer. The amount raised is kept in a blocked escrow account in convertible currency abroad, usually involving a specialist countertrader. When sufficient funds are available in the escrow account, L/C is opened against the escrow account, and goods are imported thereafter, by the buyer.

## THE ORIGIN

Even though countertrade has been prevalent in different forms, it was not significant. But of late it has become an established feature of international trade, and the majority of countries have come to realise its importance. It is estimated that counter trade comprises 20% of East-West trade and 40% of the trade of developed countries.

Countertrade will always play a predominant role in international trade. Its origin can be traced to the conflict between developed and developing countries, which is usually referred to as "North-South conflicts". The genesis of this goes back to the early colonial era, when the western powers supplied manufactured goods to their colonies and took back primary goods from their colonies on trade terms beneficial to them. After independence was achieved, the erstwhile colonies which were independent, sought and obtained better trade and more equivalent terms for trading. Consequently in the sixties and early seventies International Trade increased rapidly.

Exports of manufactured goods from developing countries also increased - some developing countries moved very fast and obtained the status of NIC - Newly Industrialised Countries. However, after a period in the early seventies, the main contention and observation of the developing countries were that the increase in prices of primary commodities/minerals which were their main source of export earning, had not kept pace with the increase in the cost of their manufactured imports. Further, their efforts to export high value-added manufactured exports were hindered by the developed countries through non-tariff barriers and quota systems. It should be remembered that many developing countries depend on one export product (coffee, cocoa, copper, textile, etc.) for their export earnings. A majority of developing countries still depend upon commodities/minerals for over 50% of their exports. Price realisation of the commodity exports has not kept up with the increase in the cost of their manufactured imports. The developing countries have been representing these strongly in international forums like UNCTAD. Actually, in 1974, they even proposed for a New International Economic Order (NIEO), whose main feature was to stabilise and increase commodity prices and indexation of their export prices, to prices paid by developing countries for imports of the manufactures. This was not acceded to by developed countries.

Another important factor was the first escalation of petroleum prices in 1973 which hit many developing countries hard, as they had to utilise the major portion of their export earnings for the import of petroleum products. The developing countries suggested an integrated commodity programme, according to which, a vast majority of commodities exported by them would be brought under one organisation, which would enable the countries which produce them to come together giving them collective bargaining power, as against the present practice of comparatively weak and smaller groups working for a single commodity price increase. The developed countries which are the main consumer countries for these commodities did not agree to such a system.

Yet another factor which has played a very important part in bringing countertrade to the fore is the oil price increase and the formation of OPEC (Oil Producing & Exporting Countries). The members of OPEC were working to a plan. They increased the oil prices fourfold in 1973 and ensured a continuous increase in prices thereafter until recently, when differences among them in their production quota resulted in strong intense competition and reduction of oil prices. These increases of prices, enabled the OPEC countries to have a very high surplus liquid cash availability. It is estimated that between 1973 and 1982 they deposited in commercial banks $200 billion (approx. Rs.2,00,000 crores). This provided ample money for the commercial banks to give loans to developing countries.

Until then, the foreign aid which most developing countries obtained, were through Overseas Development Assistance (ODA) through the World Bank and its associates. This new channel of loan through Commercial Banks enabled many developing countries to get more substantial loans than what they could have obtained normally through ODA, and satisfactorily serviced by their economies. When this surplus liquidity in the banking system ended in 1981, the developing countries turned to official institutions. By this time the ODA had been so weakened that their resources fell far short of the needs. This led to many developing countries resorting to countertrade as an emergent measure as they could not get aid or borrow for their import needs. Thus OPEC was also a contributing factor in a significant way for the developing countries resorting to countertrade.

The saga of oil price increase in 1974 and 1979, put a tremendous amount of surplus money at the disposal of the Banking system; and thus it strengthened the private capital markets. These in turn extended huge loans to developing countries. These loans were not used to improve the infrastructure or productive fields of economy, and in the early eighties the sudden dearth of these loan finances, led many developing countries to accumulate a debt burden which crippled their economies. Their failure to service the debts, drastically cut their capacity to get the needed foreign exchange as aid or loans from financial institutions. This has been one of the important economic events of this century which has cast a shadow on international trade, and affected its growth.

One of the earliest groups of countries to do countertrade were the East European countries. It should be remembered that these were not developing countries in the usual sense of the term.

The East European countries and USSR form part of the CMEA (Council of Mutual Economic Assistance) — formerly referred to as COMECON. They did not consider that trade with Western countries was essential; rather they preferred to do trade within their own group.

However, some of the factors, such as (a) hard currency shortage, (b) need for acquiring new technology, and (c) penetrations of western markets for their exports, made them resort to countertrade.

One of their important problems was food. Severe weather conditions together with low agricultural productivity necessitated the import of large amounts of food, which led to countertrade or barter.

Having centralised economies, they were able to organise countertrade through their Central Foreign Trade Organisation (FTO), which has control over all productive sources; and were able to organise countertrade in an effective manner. Many of the developing countries fashioned their countertrade on the pattern of their FTOs as a model. But it should be remembered that this model can be successful only in a centralised economy and not in a mixed economy situation.

In fact the development of countertrade by the Eastern Bloc through Vienna and later through London, was the starting point and training ground for many of the countertrade exponents and pundits who sprang up elsewhere.

The rising external debt was not the motivating factor of countertrade in the East European bloc, as it was for the developing countries.

## CONSTRAINTS

The constraints on countertrade were imposed by IMF and GATT. The spread of countertrade practices and pressures through the world, particularly the governments' insistence on countertrade in countries like Indonesia, Colombia and Ecuador, generated strong disapproval from the international economic institutions like IMF and GATT. The IMF is one of the staunchest opponents of government supported countertrade. In view of the fact that IMF goes to the help of many developing countries by providing funds for what it calls its adjustment programmes, to help them tide over balance of payment problems and economic recovery, its views carry considerable weight with the governments. Yet ironically it is mainly because of the strong steps insisted upon by the IMF for rapid balance of payment improvements, that developing countries are forced to look at countertrade for many of the basic economic activities which require imports.

The IMF's position on countertrade has been stated in its 1983 annual report on Exchange Arrangements and Exchange Restrictions:

"The Fund is generally concerned with their (countertrade practices) proliferation because they may be seen as undermining the objective of the multilateral trading system, the promotion of which was the basic objective for the setting up of the Funds, and also because they share many of the micro-economic disadvantages that are common in bilateral payment arrangements".

## FINANCIAL STRUCTURE FOR COUNTERTRADE

### Cost Factor

Countertrade involves many inherent costs, which will have to be borne ultimately by the country which seeks countertrade. If for example, an Indian exporter wants to increase his exports by countertrade, and offers product X, he has to seek the help of an international countertrade house or a national trading house. For rendering the service, the charges of such trading houses would amount to the following:

(i) A share of the management time and overheads that the trading house spends on setting the deal.

(ii) The specific service charge to be paid to the national or international trading house for handling the transaction.

(iii) The implicit discount on the product price to be given so as to dispose of the product quickly or in a new market. All these costs as a rule have to be borne by the exporter offering product X for counter trade. The costs have to be paid by taking special permission of the authorities, in case it is a foreign trading house. Invariably these costs tend to depress the ultimate realisation of the proceeds by the exporter.

## Mechanism

The mechanism or the financial structure is extremely important in the case of countertrade, since the transactions are not in line with the established norms of international finance such as, Letter of Credit, guaranteed deferred payment, official lines of credit etc. Further, the flow of goods from one country to the other will not be simultaneous, and hence there is a need for flexibility in the financial structure to ensure that the parties in the countertrade do not face any shortfall in realisation. Some of these mechanisms are:

**(a) Escrow Account:** This is a bank account used specifically for the counter trade transaction. The bank account is opened in an International bank jointly by the exporter and the importer. As and when transactions take place, the purchaser pays the amount to this joint account. However, such amount paid by either of the parties will be kept in the escrow account, until the transactions are completed by both the parties in the agreed period. Therefore, the debiting and crediting in the account is confirmed to the satisfaction of the parties, the account neutralised, and the interest which might have accumulated in the meanwhile, is shared by the parties as agreed to originally.

**(b) Bank Guarantee:** The goods are delivered under bank guarantees of both the parties. If either of the parties fails to fulfill the delivery commitment, the bank guarantee is encashed.

**(c) Forfaiting:** "Forfait" became popular in the early sixties. The transaction amounts to buying the liability, or in other words, a means of non-recourse financing for the exporter. The party, which agrees to export a certain product as countertrade has the facility of forfaiting or transferring its liability on to a financial institution for a certain consideration. The financial institution takes the complete responsibility of realising the amount and does not have any recourse on the exporter.

The practice is widely prevalent in transactions with Eastern Europe, and is resorted to, when insurance is not available for the national debt transaction from the official credit agencies.

## COUNTERTRADE IN INDIA

The emphasis on countertrade in India arose out of an important development in the last decade.

It was that the trade between India and other developing countries which were well established, were not increasing as it should have been. This is because of the fact that our purchasing power went down due to debt burden, oil shocks, as well as the stagnation of prices in the primary commodities and minerals which were our main exports, compared to manufactured goods imported by us from developed countries. Countertrade appeared to be an alternative which would keep the trade alive, as the developed countries needed a lot of Indian manufactured products and equipment.

But our efforts at countertrade have not met with great success. It has been only sporadic. We have not been able to devise a national machinery which will draw the public and private sector into the mainstream and give institutional support, to maximise our countertrade efforts to match the tremendous export potential we have. Only recent efforts as outlined in the beginning of this chapter give us hope that we can look forward to tackling this problem.

## SOME TYPICAL EXAMPLES OF COUNTERTRADE

(1) One of the famous countertrade transactions was between Brazil and Russia conducted in 1986. This was for a total value of US $35 million in which USSR imported microprocessors and computers, food processing plants, services in the field of construction/engineering for hydroelectric plants, and also a joint venture in deep sea fishing. Russia exported to Brazil petroleum products and machinery.

Counter trade is also used while importing high-tech products and systems, as also defence purchases. Typical examples of these types of deals are:

(2) Malaysia entered into a counter trade transaction with the Republic of Korea, for the import of Naval Patrol Boats, against which it exported timber, rubber products, crude petroleum etc. This transaction was worth Malaysian $20 million and the period of delivery was kept sufficiently long to enable Malaysia to fulfil its commitment.

(3) Malaysia purchased a complete Microwave Transmission system from West Germany, against which it exported rubber products, cocoa, refined pine oil etc. for a total value of Malaysian dollar 56 million. In this case the counter purchase was to the extent of 80%.

Some examples of Indian counter trades are:

(4) Against the purchase of rock phosphates and fertilisers by India from Jordan, earthmoving equipment, and other engineering items of a value of $4 million were exported from India. A road construction project was also obtained by an Indian construction company.

(5) India bought asbestos from Zimbabwe against which specific engineering goods were sold to it. In this transaction asbestos was imported, and the payment by India was kept in an escrow account which Zimbabwe used, to buy tractors, sewing machines, copiers and three-wheelers from India.

(6) India imported cloves from Madagascar against which commercial vehicles and spares were bought by Madagascar. The transactions were made by means of two independent letters of credit each of which was conditional on the complete fulfilment of the contractual obligations of the parties concerned.

## NATURE OF COUNTERTRADE

Countertrade can be termed as a natural response to a difficult world trading environment. It is a means resorted to by countries, which have limited reserves of convertible currency for the purchase of goods.

There have been numerous and conflicting estimates of the total value of the countertrade in the international arena. The word 'countertrade' is used today for all trade which has goods related payment. GATT used to estimate it to be around 8% of the total World Trade. The Organisation for Economic Cooperation and Development (OECD) estimates countertrade to account for 20% of the World Trade. Yet one more estimate by Japan's JETRO is 30%. But independent observers estimate it to be 40%

Countertrade has arisen and become prominent because of:

(1) Acute shortage of Foreign Exchange in many of the developing countries as well as the Eastern Bloc Countries, which had no other option.

(2) It is ironical that the prices for raw materials and other manufactures of developing countries were stagnant for a long time, and hence they had to resort to all means of earning more foreign exchange.

(3) The protectionism of the developed countries affected the export earnings of the developing countries. One way to fight it was the resort to countertrade, where the developed countries were forced to import goods produced in developing countries, if they wanted to sell their capital goods.

(4) The fierce competition among the developed countries for their exports sometimes resulted in countertrade.

However, the World Bank and IMF always looked down upon countertrade, and discouraged the same.

The **criticism against Countertrade** is:

(1) Countertrade, it is claimed, lays more emphasis on the modalities of the countertrade itself, rather than price, quality and financing.

(2) It is felt that the countertrade prices are always high in view of a complicated financial structure which delays payment.

(3) As countertrade is not tied to supply and demand of the market place, it is not as efficient as the free market system.

(4) As many countries do not choose to participate in countertrade, the competition is reduced and the prices may reign high.

❖ ❖ ❖

# 12

# GLOBALISATION

The word 'Globalisation' is used in so many connotations in India that one may wonder what exactly it signifies. The more surprising is the fact that certain people put all the economic ills of India at the doorstep of 'Globalisation'.

What does the word Globalisation denote?

In this chapter we are looking at 'Globalisation' as practised in India. It is not full unfettered Globalisation as understood by the west. It is governed by calibrated and guided changes the economy needs at every stage of its evolution. For example in India, in the financial sector capital convertibility is not allowed and there are also restrictions on the extent of foreign investment in various sectors of the economy. Hence, when we use the word Globalisation we refer to our version of it.

In this chapter, we are looking into how international trade, as it progresses, helps the national economy to align with world economy, which helps to increase the exports and imports of all countries

Globalisation will neither solve all the problems of the world nor is it responsible for all of them.

This becomes apparent and imperative in the international trade that a country undertakes. In Merchandising Exports, unless you produce and market a product to international standards of quality, price and delivery, you are out of business. To do that, you have to take steps to produce and export a product as the rest of the world does (unless you have a product so unique, that no one else can produce it). Where you will score over your competitors is that in one component of the manufacturing or marketing you do much better than the others. Hence, the moment you are in international trade, you are in the process of globalisation.

This process of getting 'globalised' in export trade naturally extends to the domestic market also. In other words, the customer in the domestic market will demand that the product you supply to the domestic market is of the same high quality as that of the international market.

There are also other important forces which are driving all countries towards globalisation.

The first of these is technology. The fast pace of the growth of technology is transforming every product and service all over the world. For example the cost of computing and communication is falling so rapidly, that the natural barriers of time and space that separate international markets have been disappearing.

The second driving force has been the liberalisation of International Trade. As a result of many rounds of discussions under GATT, and now WTO, all countries have lowered barriers of international trade. This has resulted in practically each and every country tending to increase its international trade; and consequently the competition has increased manifold. Hence the pressures for globalisation in production and using the latest technology have increased.

The third factor is the scarcity of capital — the diminishing of the funds available to countries from multilateral agencies like World Bank, IMF, Asian Development Bank etc., at a time when many of the countries in the developing world need it badly to improve their infrastructure and development. The only way out is to invite foreign capital for direct investment. Here also there are many countries which compete with us in attracting foreign capital. Unless we globalise (the word here is used to mean that the rules, regulations and the environment in the country becomes as in other parts of the globe) we are not in this race at all.

Countries which do not provide basic levels of infrastructure and commonly accepted international regulations, are not in a position to attract foreign investment.

Hence, the trend towards globalisation in the present state of world economy is clear. But its extent is some times exaggerated. Even though globalisation is on the increase, it has not yet led to complete product integration or price convergence, or financial market integration. It has a long way to go. And in economies like India, which is bound to grow to be one of the top five economies in the world in this millennium, the country cannot be swamped away completely by this process, either to lose its individuality, or its economic growth hindered.

Let us take the growth of Services Export from India. The Services Export, five years back was around US $ 9 billion. By any standards the growth of Services Export from India has been phenomenal. In the year 2002, the export of all services was of the order of US $ 20.7 billion, as against the merchandise export of US $ 50 billion. In Services Export the increase of the export of computer software and allied services are the highest. They are increasing approximately by 30%-50% every year. This increase has come about mainly because we have integrated our developmental efforts closely with the rest of the world in this endeavour. We are always ahead in new developments, by virtue of the large number of companies in India and abroad in which Indians are playing a significant role. This is a classic case of 'globalisation', where India has and will continue to benefit enormously.

We should study the evolution of trade and industry in other countries with a view to knowing how globalisation has helped them, and adopt those changes which will benefit India in the long run. We should always bear in mind that we have to compete fiercely in international markets, where no quarter is given or taken. At the same time India is trying to make a quantum jump in exports and economic growth, and bring up the standard of living of all sections of society in our country. No dogmas or preconceived notions will help in this effort; only hard practical decisions.

The student should have clear knowledge of the evolution of industry and trade in India over the last few decades, and the swift changes in the world economic scene in recent times, which is affecting us.

## CHANGING WORLD

In the last decade, there have been such drastic and fundamental changes all over the world, that it has become almost impossible for a country to exist in isolation, without falling in line with this process of 'globalisation'. In the case of India, the process of globalisation started a little earlier, and the policies enunciated by the government have only hastened the process. This chapter aims to make one aware of the various facets of this Globalisation Process that is taking place right now, and also help to comprehend the economic and monetary developments in the world, and how these will affect India's economy and exports, in which all of us have a stake.

It does not need a prophet to say that the world is changing and changing fast. The old order is no longer valid. Over the last four decades we had built a system around us in the fields of economy, business and industry, and in the process, developed a whole set of beliefs and ideas. It is only human that we find it difficult to abandon it all, and embrace a changing world order.

The fact that governments can plan for a whole country and enact laws on every aspect of economic activity to the minutest detail, ultimately culminating in what a country can produce, or import, and what its people can produce or consume, the kind and quality of lives they can lead, etc. no longer holds true. As one can observe, even the most dedicated centrally controlled economy of the communist world, which ardently believed in this ideology, has fallen apart. New rules of the game that are coming into its place, and the degree to which their lives will be bettered, is in a process of evolution in all such countries.

A strong belief was nurtured in most of the countries long ago, that if a country is endowed with ample natural resources, it could chalk out its own economic well-being and development. They went further, and prevented any foreign intrusion, saying that any foreign company coming into a country will come in only for exploitation and depletion of their resources, and not for genuine economic development. This led to the slogan of "self-reliance" and practically in 'reinventing the wheel'. This is particularly true of developing countries and was partly a hangover of the colonial past. It is a sort of protectionism as well. It was forgotten that what was of paramount importance to a country, was 'value addition' as it is called; or the utilization of the resources in the most economical manner to add wealth, whether done by a domestic company or foreign company.

A classic example of this is Brazil, a country which has perhaps the largest amount of natural resources. You can compare its development and standard of living with Japan, a country whose natural resources are the lowest, but which has thrived on the concept of "value addition" and developed an outstanding economy to give a very high standard of living. It just shows that mere possession of abundant natural resources is not a passport to rapid economic development of a country.

If one analyses what increases a country's exports, and consequently its wealth and capacity to provide a good standard of living to its people, it is what is referred to as the capacity of the country to "add value". For example if we have iron ore, we convert it to high grade steel in the most economical manner, and market it to the world. Later, we manufacture products out of steel and export them, rather than steel itself. If we have tea to export, we process it and sell it as packaged tea which can go straight to the supermarkets, rather than bulk tea, and thus provide added value.

This route was not taken early enough by our country. This may perhaps be traced to circumstances, and attitudes prevailing then and lack of infrastructure; and more than anything the capital needed for such a huge transformation.

## EARLIER STRATEGIES

Initially most developing countries were encouraged to export commodities in the sixties and seventies. By reasonable increases in the volume of exports every year, and steady exchange rates, the export earnings were on the increase. This brought in dependence on developed countries and complacency. However, the first oil shock in 1973 changed the situation completely. The western countries went in for a massive effort to reduce their energy requirements and consequently their dependence on oil. This brought in certain changes in their import pattern, and consequently the demand for commodities and raw materials exported by the developing countries decreased and fluctuated. There was also a drop in their prices, which decreased the earnings of the developing countries.

There were efforts to form a union of commodity suppliers around the world to hold the prices, like the oil exporting countries. But the effort did not succeed.

That was the time, when we in India looked around desperately, and laid stress on the export of non-traditional goods, namely 'manufactures' such as engineering goods, gem and jewellery, readymade garments etc. We laid down export policies year after year, and improvised them in all sorts of manner. The whole thrust of these policies over two decades, was to provide a separate framework of regulations for the export of products for the exporting community. In the process, we created a separate 'well-nurtured island' for the exports to grow.

It took us a long time to realise that this effort can give only limited success. What was needed were changes in the basic economic polices which would help modernization, foreign investments together with obtaining the latest technologies, and an environment for them to grow in and help development and export efforts. Unless production techniques based on the latest technologies were introduced in a manufacturing plant, we could not have a high quality export product.

In other words, we maintained a regulated economy, and expected exports to grow. We could only grow by fits and starts; but the rapid changes in the world in the last few years, and the third oil shock due to high oil prices during the first Gulf war practically knocked us out, and brought us to the brink of disaster.

In the middle of the eighties, India realised that by prolonging the old policies, and shying away from allowing new foreign investment to come into India with the latest technologies, the country denied itself the fruits of latest technologies in many fields. This was directly reflected in the engineering exports becoming stagnant. The liberalisation of policies started then, and the conspicuous gainers were the electronic and computer industries. Still, we were taking very tentative steps and did not realise that we were falling behind many smaller countries.

Meanwhile, other far reaching changes started to take place all over the world. The foremost of them all was that the communist states abandoned their ideologies, and were vying with one another to become market oriented economies. Both East and West Germany united into a single large State, which was unthinkable a few years earlier. It also brought into focus the realisation all over the world, that centralised economies were unable to produce a whole range of products of quality at an economic cost. And it became almost a dogma that market economies alone could give an edge in industrial production of international quality products which were badly needed by the people, all over the world.

## NEW POLICIES

The real globalisation process in India started with the new trade policy, and the new industrial policy, announced by the Indian government, soon after it took over in June 1991. One should also add here, that the country had almost come to the brink by then, with foreign exchange resources hardly enough to meet our needs for a fortnight.

Considering all the policy changes announced, the most significant change has been the dismantling of what was called Permit Licence Raj. Today, exporters, and those who need imports for production, can obtain the necessary foreign exchange from the market rate exchange mechanism. Further, there is no licence needed to start most of the industries, nor or there any restrictions on the capital and equity base. This step is the most significant one in our efforts of globalisation.

## Investment

The other significant change in the industrial policy has been the step to allow foreign investment, which can take a majority share of equity in all high priority industries except certain defence related industries. Any entrepreneur who invests, wants to have control of his capital and industry to ensure that it is healthy and progresses well. Earlier, in the past decade, many investors from abroad have by-passed India, and gone to the countries in the Far East and established themselves, because they could not have majority equity in India.

The government's decision on disinvestment in Public Sector Industries has also added to the changed approach to investment.

The capacity of foreign investment cannot be underestimated. Since the early '80s, foreign production (the revenues of such offshore enterprises) has been a bigger factor in international trade than the exports and imports. From 1984 to 1989, global foreign direct investment grew at 29% a year. Experts estimate that the value of all such 'foreign production' throughout the free world amounts to $ 4000 billion. They further state that such foreign production will continue to grow faster than exports and imports.

This single step of foreign direct investment, though taken belatedly, will definitely enable considerable foreign investment to come to India, and many worthwhile international industries would like to have their production base in India.

We should remember that they are not coming to India out of love for the country, but for reasons that are beneficial to them. The writer has heard the reasons from foreign investors and companies who want to come to India and have a production base in India.

These reasons are:

(1) India is a vibrant democratic country. Whatever the feelings of Indians about their democracy, the mature foreign investor looks at it positively. India is the only country (which became free after the second world war), which even fifty years after independence, has a democratic election on the lines of western countries, and has changed its governments at will.

(2) Investors feel that in India there is an independent judiciary, and even if government enacts any new law which inhibits the growth of industry, they have a resort for appeal to a judicial process which is reliable.

(3) India is one country, where practically all those who deal in Industry, Exports and Banking can speak English. More than that, we transact all our business, letters, contracts, bank negotiations etc. in English. Even our legal system is basically British which is recognised the world over. The fact that we have kept English going all these years, is helping us. The investors are amazed that most of our workers, with a small exception, can learn English words easily and follow the engineering drawings to the last detail, and produce the parts as well as, if not better, than their own workers.

(4) Even though there is violence in some parts of the land off and on, investors feel confident that India has the maturity and wisdom to find ways and means to solve them, and move on to concentrate on economic betterment.

(5) They are all aware that the Indian domestic market is large. They have confidence that the standard of living in India is bound to increase, and they would have a large market available to them in due course.

But what they are worried about are the productivity norms and work ethics in India. They feel that our wages are low, giving us an advantage, but that unless we raise our productivity to international norms, the low wage will not have any appreciable significance. This is changing fast.

Foreign investment is coming in at present, and it is bound to increase. It went to countries like Singapore, Hong Kong and South Korea in the sixties and seventies. Later the investors went to Thailand, Indonesia and Malaysia, who gave them a lot of encouragement. Some of these countries are saturated, and their infrastructure cannot assimilate any further investment. The Western investors are also not happy with many of the political systems prevailing.

Hence, the options are India, Eastern Europe and South America. Our trained technical force and political stability and forward-looking policies can give us an edge.

Another important reason propelling us towards globalisation is that in the changing economic scene in the country, there are many industries, in diverse fields, where sales and production are slowing down. Their only hope is to export and have overseas operations. This is a natural process of development and evolution of an organisation. We have to become multinational. The world over, companies have extended their operations to countries other than the ones in which they started, not only in search of growth, but also in trying to increase profits for growth in their home base.

There are many industries in India, which can and should take this path. The recent liberalisation of policies of the government has made this possible, and those industries or manufacturers, who use this intelligently, would reap a rich harvest. To put it in rather simplistic terms, we have to go multinational, on our own or with other international companies wherever possible.

There is always an apprehension on the arrival of a wellknown multinational company into the country and establishing itself. What we have to look at is, whether the multinational establishing itself is giving us a world class product at reasonable prices or not. The second factor is whether in the long-term it will increase India's ability to export, and provide employment, and whether it has the latest technology.

An example would illustrate this. Britain had a large number of automobile manufacturing firms in the second half of the 20th century, which made it a premier automobile manufacturing and exporting country. By 1998, practically all the British manufacturing firms were taken over by foreign multinationals, the last one to be taken over being Rolls Royce and Rover. But in the process what has happened to the industry? Britain's exports of automotive products which were US$14.0 billion in 1990, showed a sizeable increase to US$26.1 billion in 1997. Thus Britain gained in the process.

## CURRENCY

There is another aspect of globalisation which India is getting into. This was held back by government polices all these days, but it is no longer possible. The rupee is getting linked to international currencies much more than ever before, and international developments in currency will have an impact on Indian currency and economy.

Today the monies that flow across countries (which in simple terms, are the amount of American Dollars or German Marks or Japanese Yen etc. that an individual corporation or a country can buy against its own currency in the free world) have a great bearing on the exchange rate and even the Balance of Trade of a country. This is because in the free world market of currency, the currency transactions are very high. In the London Market alone, where inter bank transactions are done in all convertible currencies, the currency transactions which take place everyday is 10 to 15 times the amount needed to finance all the goods and services traded in a single day all over the world. In other words, the money flows or currency transactions in London alone in a day is 10 to 15 times that of the World Trade in a day. The implication of this is that these flows will affect the economy. Today the foreign trade of India is only around 20% of GDP of the country. Hence these transactions will not affect the entire economy overnight, but only certain sections which are susceptible to foreign trade.

This brings us to the next important implication that it is not only the country's Central Bank, but every business, and in particular, every organisation involved in exports/imports, that will have to learn to manage its foreign exchange exposure. It is as great and important a function of an organisation, as protecting it from other risks. This will also bring its own dividends if done in an organised and knowledgeable manner.

We should take effective measures to train and encourage our personnel in this area, and bring in more professionalism. Our management institutions should concentrate on training such a cadre of people who will have an important role to play in business and national economy.

## NEW TRENDS

All this amounts to the fact that certain trends are emerging in the international market due to the globalisation process.

These are:

(1) No country can stand in isolation, defying the fast moving international developments in the economic field. It should try to move with the times, while at the same time protecting its national interests.

(2) International trade is undergoing a trans–formation. The time has come for us to forget our old theories and dogmas, and take a pragmatic approach. Many of the old economic theories are not valid any longer.

(3) The recent developments in the world have thrown the economy of a large number of countries into such serious disarray, that they are prepared to go to any length in accommodating foreign investors, as well as go for exports in a big way. We should ensure that our regulations will welcome foreign direct investment in India in products where quality production is established for domestic and export markets, and also in the service sectors where export will be the main criterion.

(4) International trade and exports are much more important to India now than ever before. The aid that India is getting from the Aid India Consortium and other international institutions, will reduce in the years to come, as we have serious competition from East Europe and Russian States whose demands are equally strong. So the best option open to us it to integrate into the Global Economy in such a manner, that the process helps our economy and exports to grow fast, to keep pace with the country's expectations and demands.

## GLOBAL OUTLOOK

Globalisation in trade and industry has already taken root in the world. When it started, it created conflicts among nations and partners who were distrustful of one another, and many strategic alliances faltered and failed. Since then the countries have had greater exposure to one another's culture, changing economic policies, business practices, and the radical changes in the world economic structure itself. This has led to change in the outlook which has resulted in cooperation between countries on firmer grounds.

The European Economic Community is in one sense, an example of globalisation among the countries of Europe. The changes taking place in industries and marketing set-ups among the various countries of Europe for a unified, tariffless market is a pointer to the future. Similarly, The North American Free Trade Agreement (NAFTA) covers USA, Canada, and Mexico and will be a bigger common market.

India, due to many reasons, has lost the opportunity to be an active partner of any group. Hence the next best, or perhaps the only alternative available to us is globalisation in the trade and industry sector, so that we have an active presence directly or indirectly in many of the markets abroad.

India, coming in rather late into these trade groups, should avoid some of the setbacks in globalisation which many organizations, countries and governments have experienced. We should also be quite clear of the various undercurrents in the industry, as well as in the national policies of the governments concerned. We should remember that it takes rather long to understand the ways of the world, and the exporting community needs great perseverance to succeed in international trade. We should also be mature enough to understand that the policies of some of the governments will be so self-centered, that it is patently unjust. This is because their only concern is what they perceive to be good for their country, and what would help them in their domestic constituencies and elections. This is perhaps the price one pays for modern democracy. But we should be able to wear out this problem over a period.

The ultimate answer to this is to become economically so strong, that the world will respect us, and come to a mutually agreeable solution. Globalisation should be used as a means to that end.

The **ingredients** of globalisation are very many. Some of them are:

(1) It is well known that protectionism in developed countries is a serious impediment to the growth of trade. Apart from taking it up bilaterally, and in international forums, we should also simultaneously take the steps that other global producers have taken, such as shifting key components of production and marketing to the importing countries.

(2) We should make a conscious effort to change the outlook of our professional managers in our organisations from the national to the global arena. This is not as easy as many people think. In every field of trade and industry, we should develop a global outlook and move towards the idea that the world is our marketplace. It can no longer be a situation of one set of standards and quality for domestic trade, and a different one for overseas trade.

(3) One of the obvious and easy interpretations of globalisation is to have a joint venture with selected overseas partners for production or marketing. We have to get away from our earlier outlook of joint venture, which was primarily aimed at import substitution in the three decades after independence. What we are referring to in the changed context is the confluence of mutual interests of two partners, both of whom are going to gain from this venture. The approach has to be quite different.

(4) In a joint-venture, people are obsessed with total control. Every partner tries to have 51% equity, and once he gets it, feels he has total

management control. This concept has undergone a change. It is realised that a global company cannot be managed through only this control. What one should look for are strategic alliances on a long term basis. In a fast changing world of new technologies and consumer tastes, there has to be cooperation based on trust, good faith and sincerity.

(5) When we try to reach foreign markets through joint ventures, we must remember that we are saving a lot of money and investment, which we would otherwise have spent upfront (initially) if we had decided to tackle these markets on our own; apart from the time it would have taken us. But it will not help us in the long run. Globalisation is the answer. It is necessary to give a longer time-frame for the effort of globalisation to mature, and not be impatient for quick results. It is well worth the wait, even in a financial sense.

(6) The process of globalisation also leads to the import of capital into the country as Foreign Direct Investment (FDI), as well as foreign loans to the country or individual organisations. The cardinal rule in such investment is that they should be used for productive ventures which will give a good return, and improve the country's capacity to produce world class goods or services.

In recent years there have been serious problems in some South East Asian countries. Their economies which were doing very well, suddenly got into serious problems because of their currencies getting devalued considerably and many financial institutions going bankrupt, and consequently a drastic reduction in their imports. Subsequently, their economic growth became negative. This development was wrongly assigned to 'globalisation' and full convertibility of their currency. But a deeper analysis revealed that these countries had borrowed heavily as short term loans in the international market. Further, the loans were mostly used in a speculative manner in real estate business or lent indiscriminately, and not on productive ventures which would give a good return. When the real estate boom disappeared it affected the economy badly, and there was also a run on their banks.

The medicine administered by the World Bank and IMF on these economies to bail them out, were rigorous steps such as steep increase in interest rates, reduction in imports and public spending etc. This made the recovery of these nations very difficult.

This clearly shows that unless the country takes the basic precautions in ensuring that the loans given, local or foreign, are for good productive ventures, and treat the foreign loans especially with care in investing on projects which are productive and make their money management transparent and principled, it certainly will have serious problems. On that score one cannot put the blame on 'globalisation'.

## THE EVOLUTION

Globalisation is not a new phenomenon. Before the advent of the first world war in 1914-18, there was large cross border flow of goods, capital and people. There was no restriction on the nature of trade, the movement of people and also money as such. It was driven mainly by the fact that there were very few barriers in trade between countries. It should also be stated that a large part of the world did not participate in the pre-1914 global economy.

This lasted till the First World War and ended abruptly thereafter. After this war, the world moved into a period of fierce trade protectionism and rigid restrictions on the movement of capital. During the early 1930s USA sharply increased the tariffs, and other countries retaliated. It made the 'great depression' even greater. The volume of world trade decreased sharply. Also the international capital flows between countries virtually ceased as governments all over the world imposed capital controls, mainly with a view to insulate their countries from the greater global slump. This continued almost till the Second World War of 1939-45.

After the Second World War, the victorious countries decided to keep their exchange rates fixed – known as the Bretton Woods System,- named after the American town in which they met and decided this course. There were other trade restrictions also. However it was found that for economic recovery, and the resumption and growth of world trade it was necessary to reduce the trade barriers.

Thus was born GATT (General Agreement on Tariff and Trade). This came into being in 1947 in Geneva with 23 countries as its founder members. India was one of them. GATT became an important set up and its membership increased to include most of the countries of the UN, except the communist countries and East European countries. GATT organized many rounds of multilateral negotiations among all the member countries and gradually reduced import tariffs and other restrictions.

GATT was replaced by the World Trade organization WTO in 1995. WTO is more comprehensive, and has powers to investigate complaints and give its considered decisions on trade disputes which are enforceable.

By 1970 the Bretton Woods agreement on fixed exchange rates collapsed and currencies of various countries were allowed to 'float' against one another and the 'market', and the supply and demand patterns set the exchange rates.

This also gave rise to the rebirth of the Global Capital Market. Both USA and Germany relaxed the restrictions on capital movement and UK followed in 1979, and Japan in 1980. France and Italy did it very much later.

Certain other factors also aided the process of globalisation of goods and services. Communication has become easy and fast due to electronic exchanges between markets, and has led to greater international trade.

Secondly, GATT and later WTO have succeeded in reducing the barriers to trade among all countries and world trade has increased gradually.

Thirdly, practically all the countries have come to realize that to improve their economy and increase the standard of living of the people, they certainly need foreign capital investments as they cannot generate sufficient capital in their own country or by loans. Foreign Trade Investment has a great role to play in the growth of the economy. It is estimated that over the period 1980-96, world trade had increased twice as fast as output, and foreign direct investment had increased three times as fast as output.

The trend towards globalisation is clear. It has affected each country in a different manner based upon the policies of the country, and the extent to which it has adhered to WTO guidelines, and the advances in the industrialization and economic climate of the country concerned.

We saw earlier that globalisation leads to the integration of the national economy and the global economy. It is inevitable that this happens if India wants to become an economic power and be counted among the countries of the world.

Apart from being a developing country that is growing fast, India also presents a unique paradox that in certain sectors of business and economy it has proved to be in the top league, whereas in certain other sectors it is as abysmal as a least developed country. Hence we have to understand that this process of globalisation affects different sections of society in different ways.

## INDIA'S BASIC PROBLEM AND SUGGESTIONS

Due to all these developments, the following were noticed in India:

(a) The industrialization of India, as we had witnessed for a few decades after independence, such as new factories, new jobs and expansion of existing factories with additional employment, has not taken place in the last decade. The new jobs that the industrialisation of India was supposed to create to fulfil the needs of employment were not forthcoming.

(b) Reducing the trade barriers such as high import duties have allowed products of other countries to enter into India in various fields and they compete with Indian made products, whereas India in some cases is not able to compete with them, and many small industries as well as big, are affected by this.

(c) The expected increase in the availability of suitable jobs for those who are already in the employment market as well as for fresh induction of new entrants every year, are not available. The backlog is increasing enormously, and the government has not come out with concrete plans to solve this, and consequently the social tensions connected with it are on the increase.

(d) Irrespective of the official figures for inflation, there is a perceptible increase in the cost of living, due to the increase in the cost of basic necessities, and the income of a large section of the population is not keeping pace with these increases.

As mentioned earlier, for the first three decades after attaining independence, the emphasis was on local production of many industrial items, with the least possible import inputs. It was referred to as 'import substitution', which was the order of the day. This was necessitated as the country's foreign exchange reserves were very limited and were hardly enough to import the essential needs of the country. This resulted in that most of the industries in India were producing goods of 'adequate quality' for domestic needs, but were not able to meet stringent export norms.

The liberalization of the policies of import, the dismantling of the import-licence-raj, as well as efforts undertaken to meet the WTO requirements of reduction in tariff barriers all came together, and found the Indian industries wanting. Many of them did not have the latest technologies. Their cost of production was high and the sudden loss of the import duty protection that they had enjoyed earlier, disappeared. Of course many of them have overcome these handicaps now but the experience has taken its own time and toll.

The transformation of many of these industries which have rightfully tackled the problems, through getting the latest technology from abroad, improving productivity and reducing the cost of production, and improving the quality to international standards, are very commendable indeed. The one important consequence of such modernisations the world over is the reduction in the labour employed. It should be mentioned that the labour employed by India in the industries in the earlier years were always on the higher side, because the wage bill in many industries was not of such a high ratio, and they could afford it. But with wages rising, and the international competition becoming very high, there was no choice but to reduce the labour to sustainable proportion. All these resulted in considerable downsizing of organizations, to make them lean and competitive. The infusion of latest technology also resulted in using lesser manpower.

The steps taken have helped many industries to become competitive. A classic example of this is in the field of automobiles, where Tata Motors, who make Indian designed Indica Cars, are exporting them to Europe; and Hyundai who have their manufacturing base in Chennai are exporting their cars worldwide. Another striking example is the automobile ancillaries manufacturers, who hardly had a few million dollars of export earlier, exported goods worth US$750 million in the year 2002-03.

Even though these developments are praiseworthy, it should be admitted that all these came in the category of 'jobless growth' or by reducing the staff through voluntary retirement schemes.

In short, the brunt of the criticism against globalisation in India is that it does not help to create the huge employment opportunities the country needs badly.

In the early decades after independence, it was felt that India, which was predominantly agricultural in its economy, would be industrialized in due course. It was fervently believed that the labour displaced by the agriculture sector, would be absorbed in the industrial sector where employment opportunities were expected to grow phenomenally. But what happened over the decades, and the present developments enumerated above, have led to a situation where employment opportunities are not commensurate with the needs of the society.

It is estimated that unemployment is in the region of 30 million people. And every year about one million are added to this figure. Here we are not even talking about another 11 million people on the live register of employment exchanges, who are not happy with their jobs and are seeking change.

Even though there have been increases in a few service sectors such as IT, BPO, finance and retail for the educated and qualified, it hardly amounts to a million jobs all over the country.

It is estimated that two thirds of the population in India is involved in agriculture. Even though modern technology keeps reducing the employment potential in agriculture as well, this workforce cannot be redeployed quickly into other sectors. One obvious solution is to increase our production and export agriculture products. This will be very difficult since agriculture in the developed countries is subsidized to a great extent, and the international prices of agriculture products have been falling over the last two decades. Between 1980 and 2001, the price of rice crashed from $570/ton to $179/ton, of wheat from $219/ton to $131/ton, sugar from 80 cents per kg. to 20 cents per kg. and so on. Farmers are a powerful vote bank all the world over and they force the governments to keep the subsidies as well as high import tariffs.

However, there is one great possibility which has not been exploited thoroughly and expeditiously by India. It is in the area of Agro industries, and food processing industries. The value addition to agriculture will open up the international and domestic markets in a very big way, and as these are labour intensive, they will lead to better employment potential.

Let us look at one aspect of the agri-business – horticulture. Almost all major horticultural crops are produced in India from temperate, to tropical and sub-tropical fruits and vegetables, apart from proven medicinal specialities, spices, plantation crops, mushrooms etc. India produces 40 million tons of fruits (about 8% of the world output) and nearly 70 million tons of vegetables. But the post harvest losses are as high as 30% of fresh fruits and vegetables due to lack of adequate post harvest handling and storage facilities. Loss of the produce due to bad handling and storage, pest infestation damages, loss in transit and transport, are very high. Lack of attention to all these factors hinders the growth of this industry. This is an area where the government should give its top priority attention. It is not enough in making some broad policy statements; the government should get fully involved with the help of a highly knowledgeable technical group and get these facilities established in a professional manner. The employment potential and export prospects are so high that it does not brook any delay at all.

The government should take positive steps towards this by the following actions:

*(a)* Provide cold storage chains wherever needed.

*(b)* Give all possible facilities to convert as much of the cultivable wasteland (it is estimated that we have 250 million hectares of

cultivable wasteland) to hi-tech horticultural farms with all the latest facilities.

*(c)* Encourage export oriented units, and foreign collaborations wherever needed with the necessary infrastructural support.

*(d)* This country has excellent agricultural universities and research set-ups, and they should be utilized to give the necessary inputs for supply chain management and packaging and transport, as also product development.

*(e)* Encourage organic farming as it has a growing and profitable niche in the world market.

It is not suggested that the government should take up all these efforts on their own to develop a public sector monolith. They should choose and help suitable entrepreneurs and institutions who will ultimately provide new centers of production and employment. The emphasis is placed on the government taking suitable initiatives mainly because many of the facilities required are infrastructural needs which only the government can provide efficiently. They should draw appropriate plans and make the bureaucracy execute them in a time-bound manner. The markets for fruits and vegetables are huge, both nationally and internationally and the employment potential, especially for the rural unemployed is very great indeed.

The other important area is in the 'Service Sector' where there is a good scope for improvement, and which we have dealt with separately. There is big potential in the tourism sector where both the state and central governments should take initiatives with the help of the private sector.

The reason that we have dealt elaborately on the developments in India over the last few decades and how globalisation is affecting it, is to show that the need of the hour is to take steps – government and private sector working together – on a national basis to get India moving forward and show the world that it can meet these challenges that will make India a developed country by the year 2020. In this endeavour India's export trade will play its rightful role.

The main attributes needed for international trade are pragmatism and open-mindedness. Nothing is sacrosanct and permanent. One should approach each and every issue without any pre-conceived notion or set of rules. Experience can only give some signals; it cannot give solutions for all problems. A great statesman of our country, Rajaji, said that consistency is never a virtue, be it in politics or economics. One can perhaps add 'international trade' also to it.

❖ ❖ ❖